A PRACTITIONER'S GUIDE TO THE FSA REGULATION OF INVESTMENT BANKING

A PRACTITIONER'S GUIDE TO THE FSA REGULATION OF INVESTMENT BANKING

Consultant Editors
Nigel Boardman
John Crosthwait
Slaughter and May

First Edition

City & Financial Publishing

City & Financial Publishing
8 Westminster Court, Hipley Street
Old Woking
Surrey GU22 9LG
United Kingdom
Tel: 00 44 (0)1483 720707 Fax: 00 44 (0)1483 727928
Web: www.cityandfinancial.com

This book has been compiled from the contributions of the named authors. The views expressed herein do not necessarily reflect the views of their respective firms. Further, since this book is intended as a general guide only, its application to specific situations will depend upon the particular circumstances involved and it should not be relied upon as a substitute for obtaining appropriate professional advice.

This law is stated as at 31 January 2002. Whilst all reasonable care has been taken in the preparation of this book, City & Financial Publishing and the authors do not accept responsibility for any errors it may contain or for any loss sustained by any person placing reliance on its contents.

ISBN 1 898830 55 X
© 2002 City & Financial Publishing and the named authors.

British Library Cataloguing-in-Publication Data. A catalogue record for this book is available from the British Library.

Typeset by Type Study, Scarborough and printed and bound in Great Britain by Biddles Limited, Guildford and King's Lynn.

Biographies

Nigel Boardman is currently head of corporate practice at Slaughter and May. His broad practice includes domestic and international corporate finance, including mergers and acquisitions, general corporate advice, joint ventures, flotations, demergers, private acquisitions and disposals, public takeovers, issues of compliance and corporate governance and insolvency and restructurings.

He has acted for the leading investment banks in London and a large number of English and overseas companies. He became a partner in 1982 after a period as a corporate financier with a leading merchant bank.

Nigel is the author of the chapter on the legal aspects in Tolley's *Private Acquisitions Handbook*, and the author of a chapter on stakebuilding in Takeover Bids in *A Practitioner's Guide to the City Code on Takeovers and Mergers* (City & Financial Publishing, 2001).

John Crosthwait is a senior lawyer in Slaughter and May's Financial Regulation group. He is a member of the Securities Institute's Regulation and Compliance Diploma exam panel.

Bridget Barker graduated from Southampton University with a First Class Honours degree in law. She joined Macfarlanes as an articled clerk in March 1981 and after a year's secondment to a major New York law firm she returned to London in mid-1987. She became a partner in the corporate department in January 1988.

Bridget concentrates on investment companies, investment funds and financial services. She advises clients on establishing both onshore and offshore funds for retail and institutional investors. Her practice also encompasses advising on a variety of investment related regulatory and compliance matters. She is a regular contributor to both investment fund and compliance publications as well as being an active participant in the Investment Companies and Mutual Funds Committee of the International Bar Association. She is vice-chairman of the IBA Specialised Investment Funds Committee.

Anita Webbon joined the legal department of Morgan Stanley International in 1995, becoming executive director in 1999. Previously she had been at Linklaters for six years. She moved to the legal department of Goldman Sachs International as a senior counsel in 2000 and continues to advise on a wide range of financial services, legal and regulatory issues.

John Bennett is head of Berwin Leighton Paisner's corporate department and specialises in mergers and acquisitions, corporate finance and private equity transactions. He is named as a leading corporate lawyer in *Chambers Guide to the Legal Profession.*

John has contributed the Chapter *The Statutory Framework* to *A Practitioner's Guide to the Alternative Investment Market Rules* (City & Financial Publishing, 2001).

Marwan Al-Turki is a partner in the London office of Baker & McKenzie, where he leads the firm's European financial services group. Marwan advises regulators, exchanges, banks, brokers and investment managers on all aspects of their business, in particular in relation to carrying on their business on a pan-European basis. Marwan is fluent in English, Arabic, French, Spanish and Italian and has a basic command of German. He obtained his BA and MA from Oxford University and was admitted as a solicitor in England in 1987.

Christopher Pearson is a partner at Norton Rose. He is a corporate finance specialist with a substantial track record in public company and stock exchange transactions – including public company takeovers, other mergers and acquisitions (domestic and cross-border), flotations, joint ventures, securities offerings, company reconstructions and institutional investments.

Christopher is a contributor to *A Practitioner's Guide to the City Code on Takeovers and Mergers* (City & Financial Publishing, 2001) and is a member of the City of London Solicitors Company and represents Norton Rose on the City of London Law Society Company Law Sub-Committee.

Guy Morton is head of Freshfields Bruckhaus Deringer's financial services group. He has been with the firm since 1980 and has been a partner since 1986. His practice covers a range of regulatory, banking, financial services and company law work and he is a regular contributor to seminars and publications in these areas.

Guy is chairman of the City of London Law Society's Regulatory Sub-Committee which reviewed and commented on the Financial Services and Markets Bill and which continues to review and comment on the associated regulatory reforms in the UK. In 1999 he gave evidence to the Joint Committee of the House of Lords and House of Commons on the Financial Services and Markets Bill.

Adrian Clark was made a partner at Ashurst Morris Crisp in 1990. He specialises in all aspects of corporate finance including flotations, secondary issues, acquisitions and disposals of private companies and corporate reorganisations. Public company takeovers are a particular speciality. Adrian was secretary to the Takeover Panel from 1988 to 1990.

Tim Gee is a partner in the corporate department at Baker & Mckenzie. He is global head of M&A specialising in domestic and cross-border public and private M&A and equity capital markets work.

Lucy Fergusson has been a partner in the corporate department at Linklaters since 1996. She specialises in corporate, securities and stock exchange law and regulation, and mergers and acquisitions.

Stuart Evans is a partner at Simmons & Simmons. He has extensive experience within the field of corporate transactions, spanning mergers and takeovers, corporate disposals, new issues, rights issues, reconstructions and other related activities.

James Perry is head of the financial services practice at Ashurst Morris Crisp. He specialises in corporate transactional and regulatory matters with particular emphasis on the financial services sector. He has been a partner at Ashurst Morris Crisp since 1998.

David Toube is a barrister at Ashurst Morris Crisp. He advises clients on a broad range of authorisation and compliance matters. He has particular expertise on issues arising from the provision of online financial services.

Adrian Knight, a partner in the M&A Group, joined the London office of Shearman & Sterling in June 1999 from a leading English law firm. He has extensive experience of UK public M&A and cross-border M&A transactions, IPOs and other cross-border corporate finance transactions.

Foreword

Peter Sutherland
Chairman
Goldman Sachs International

2001 has been a particularly challenging year for both the investment banking industry and its regulator, the Financial Services Authority (the "FSA"). With stock markets falling across the globe, the huge drop-off in M&A activity and the number of IPOs led to widespread contraction and restructuring within the industry.

While struggling with these testing market conditions, investment banks also had to get to grips with a new regulatory regime. As everyone recognised, consolidation of regulation brings certain benefits, but any new regulatory environment poses fresh challenges to the regulated. For investment bankers, these included the FSA's market abuse rules, the transfer of the UK Listing Authority to the FSA and the impact of the establishment of the FSA on the City Code on Takeovers and Mergers.

The regulator also faced a year of challenges. Fresh from its own merger integration, bringing together nine different regulatory organisations with their varying cultures, the FSA has been busy cranking out reams of consultation documents on the new regime, and industry has been kept busy responding and adjusting.

All of this effort on both sides is critically important. Appropriately balanced, cost effective regulation is fundamental to the preservation of market confidence. Successful delivery of this regulatory philosophy has long been a key factor in London's success as a financial centre. It is equally important that the rules and their interpretation are clearly understood to those who must observe them.

As the first publication to focus exclusively on the new FSA regime's impact on investment banking, *A Practitioner's Guide to the FSA Regulation of Investment Banking* is a welcome addition, providing bankers with a constructive, comprehensible view of the new regulatory environment. A team of leading experts cover the full range of corporate finance and advisory activities, providing guidance that should prove indispensable to industry professionals and help to prepare them for the challenges to come.

Table of Contents

Chapter 1

The FSMA Regime

Nigel Boardman
Partner

John Crosthwait
Solicitor
Slaughter and May

1.1 Introduction

The Financial Services and Markets Act ("FSMA") generally came into force on 1 December, 2001, some four and a half years after the newly elected Labour Government announced in 1997 that it intended a radical reform of the UK's financial services legislation, covering investment and commercial banks, insurance companies, stock brokers, building societies, friendly societies and other types of financial services providers. The centre piece of the reform was the designation of the Financial Services Authority (the "FSA") as the UK's single financial services regulator.

Despite the FSA becoming the sole statutory regulator, the non-statutory Takeover Panel has retained its important role in governing takeovers. There is overlap of jurisdiction, however, especially in relation to the market abuse regime (*see* Section 1.8 and Chapter 8). The FSA has endorsed the Takeover Code which means the Takeover Panel may request the FSA to take enforcement action against authorised persons and approved persons who contravene the Takeover Code (Section 143 FSMA).

1.2 The FSA's role

The FSMA confers a wide array of powers on the FSA. It is constrained in these powers by Section 2 FSMA, which provides that the FSA must act in a way, so far as reasonably possible, which is compatible with its regulatory objectives of:

- market confidence;
- public awareness;
- protection of consumers; and
- the reduction of financial crime.

The FSA also has a number of matters to which it must have regard, including, for example:

(a) the principle that any burden it imposes should be proportionate to the benefits, considered in general terms, which are expected to result from the imposition of that burden;

(b) the desirability of facilitating innovation in regulated activities;

(c) the international character of financial services and the desirability of maintaining the competitive position of the UK; and

(d) the desirability of facilitating competition between those who are subject to any form of regulation by the FSA.

The matters just quoted all point to the FSA continuing the tradition of "light touch" regulation of investment banking and the promotion of the City of London as a world centre for investment banks. However, there are inevitably some tensions inherent in the FSA's remit. Financial innovation must be tempered by the need to protect consumers, for example, from aggressive and perhaps ill-considered selling of disadvantageous products.

The FSA has enormous powers; those with such powers are sometimes tempted to overuse them. The balance is difficult to strike, and maintain, between legitimate use of powers to curb excesses, and restraint from over-regulation so as to allow financial markets and their participants to flourish.

Although the FSMA is an extremely lengthy piece of legislation, for the most part it provides a statutory framework for more detailed rules made either by the FSA, mainly in respect of financial institutions authorised by FSA, or contained in statutory instruments (e.g. in respect of financial promotion or regulated activities).

1.3   Regulation of financial institutions

Section 19 FSMA provides that no person may carry on regulated activities without being authorised under the FSMA or exempt from authorisation ("exempt person"). This is known as the "general prohibition".

Breach of the general prohibition is a criminal offence and contracts entered into as a result of such a breach may be unenforceable.

Authorisation may be gained in three ways:

(a) by obtaining a permission to carry on one or more regulated activities from the FSA;
(b) by a firm from elsewhere in the EEA exercising passport rights under the single market directives; or
(c) by EEA firms exercising other rights to provide cross-border services conferred by the Treaty of Rome.

Where a European firm seeks to carry on a regulated activity not covered by its passport or other EU rights, it must seek top up permissions from the FSA.

Exemptions from authorisation are granted in Treasury Orders. Most of these exemptions are for governmental and public authorities or for international organisations. However, there are also specific exemptions for business enterprise schemes, charities and certain activities in respect of the gas industry and wholesale electricity trading arrangements.

1.3.1 Regulated Activities

In general, the scope of activities regulated under the FSMA is the same as under the predecessor legislation with the addition of some new matters such as the Lloyd's insurance market and the provision of residential mortgages.

Section 22 states that an activity is a regulated activity if it is: (i) carried on by way of business and (ii) is specified in an Order made by the Treasury. Schedule 2 contains an indicative list of activities and investments which essentially outlines the extent of the Treasury's power to include activities or investments within this Order. The Financial Services and Markets Act 2000 (Regulated Activities) Order 2001, SI 2001/No 544 (the "RAO") specifies all of the activities which are currently regulated under the FSMA.

The business test contained in Section 22 is, in yet another example of a detail of the FSMA regime being found in regulations, set out in the Financial Services and Markets Act 2000 (Carrying on Regulated Activities by Way of Business) Order 2001. This Order preserves to some extent the different tests applying to different kinds of activities under the previous regimes. So far as investment business is concerned, a person is not to be regarded as carrying on by way of business the investment activities specified in the RAO unless he "carries on the business of engaging in one or more such activities". This preserves the definition of "investment business" in the Financial Services Act 1986.

There are changes, however, to the territorial scope of regulation. By Section 418, a firm which has a UK head or registered office will be deemed to be carrying on regulated activities in the UK (irrespective of where the customers and the personnel dealing with those customers are located) if, amongst other things, the day-to-day management of the activity is the responsibility of the head office or another establishment maintained by the firm in the UK. The government has indicated that it would not generally regard a head office which is responsible for the central management and overall strategy of a group as necessarily meeting this test; the section is concerned with daily decision making functions, such as whether or not a firm should carry out a particular transaction. Nonetheless, this provision could have unexpected consequences. For example, it may mean that an issuer of commercial paper (which could amount to accepting deposits), has to be careful to ensure that even its issues in overseas markets comply with the conditions necessary for the issue to be excepted under the RAO.

The RAO broadly covers the same scope of regulation in respect of investment business as did the Financial Services Act.

With certain adjustments, the kinds of securities covered are the same: equity and debt securities, warrants, depository receipts and derivatives, including commodity derivatives.

Again, the activities regulated broadly follow the activities in predecessor legislation. So far as investment business is concerned, they include the following:

(a) *dealing as principal*: this covers market making, other short-term dealing for profit where the person concerned holds himself out as such a dealer, and underwriting (again where the person concerned holds himself out as an underwriter). In addition, "regular solicitation" of the public with a view to entering into principal transactions is a regulated activity. There is an exception, designed with takeover offerors in mind, where the person concerned is bidding for 20 per cent or more of the voting shares in a body corporate. However, regular solicitation with a view to taking stakes of less than 20 per cent could mean that the person concerned requires authorisation for his principal dealings. An example might be a venture capitalist who is a regular purchaser of minority stakes in companies;

(b) *dealing as agent*;

(c) *arranging deals in investments*: this covers both arrangements which "bring about" transactions and ongoing arrangements in which persons participate with a view to entering into transactions;

(d) *managing investments*: this covers managing "involving the exercise of discretion". Management of non-investment assets could be caught, if the arrangements for management envisage that the assets may consist of, or include investments;

(e) *safeguarding and administering investments*: this is the activity of custody;

(f) *sending dematerialised instructions*: this covers sending instructions in connection with securities held in a system for the dematerialised registration of securities and settlement of transactions such as CREST;

(g) *establishing etc a collective investment scheme*: this covers setting up, operating or winding up of collective investment scheme, acting as trustee of an unauthorised unit trust, or acting as the depository or sole director of an open-ended investment company;

(h) *establishing etc a stakeholder pension scheme*;

(i) *advising on investments*: this covers advice on the merits of investment activity in respect of a particular investment, or on the exercise of rights conferred by such an investment, given to a person in his capacity as an investor or in his capacity as an agent for an investor. It does not cover generic advice or advice given in newspapers, subject to certain conditions;

(j) *agreeing to carry on* any of the above activities.

There are numerous exclusions. But in assessing whether any particular exclusion applies, consideration must be given to the scope of the Investment Services Directive (the "ISD"). If a firm is a "investment firm" within the meaning of the ISD, then certain exclusions provided for in the RAO are not available to it.

The following exclusions are of particular relevance to investment banking:

(a) *companies issuing own shares or debentures*: a company is not regarded as engaging in a regulated activity by virtue of issuing its own shares or debentures or arranging for their issue;

(b) *intra-group activities:* a company dealing with or for another in the same group, or arranging for it to enter into a transaction, is not carrying on regulated activities except in certain narrow circumstances. Intra-group advice and discretionary management are also excluded;

(c) *activities in connection with joint ventures:* there is an exception, similar to the intra-group exception, for activities carried on in connection with commercial joint ventures;

(d) *sale of a body corporate:* this is a very important exception for sales of businesses effected by transfers of shares. It applies in two circumstances:

   (i) 50 per cent of the voting shares are being acquired (or a smaller stake which brings the acquirer's holding to that percentage level) and the vendor and the purchaser are both a body corporate, a partnership, a single individual or a single group of management/family members; or

   (ii) in other cases, the object of the transaction may reasonably be regarded as being the acquisition of day-to-day control of the affairs of the body corporate.

This exclusion is designed to take business sales outside the scope of regulation. However, the exception could apply to a public takeover where it is the intention of the offeror to take close control of the conduct of the target's business.

(e) *overseas persons*: a person without a permanent place of business in the UK may engage in transactions with or for persons in the UK, or give advice to persons in the UK provided that the persons in the UK are either authorised or exempt persons or the transaction or advice results from an approach or solicitation which does not contravene the restrictions on financial promotion (*see* Section 1.6 below).

1.3.2 Authorisation and permission

Parts III and IV FSMA provide for the authorisation of persons granted permission to carry on regulated activities. If a person receives permission from the FSA to carry on one or more regulated activities (e.g. deposit taking or giving investment advice), then that person becomes authorised as a result of obtaining the permission.

Incoming European firms exercising passport or Treaty rights to establish themselves, or to provide services in the UK will be automatically granted the relevant permissions to carry on the passported or Treaty business. However, if such a firm wishes to carry on a regulated activity not covered by passport or Treaty rights, then it will have to apply for a permission in the normal way.

Before granting permission for a person to carry out one or more regulated activities, the FSA must except for incoming European firms be satisfied that the applicant will meet, and will continue to meet, the "threshold conditions" set out in Schedule 6 to the FSMA.

The threshold conditions are broadly specified and designed to ensure that authorised persons are fit and proper to carry on regulated activities. The conditions also reflect the UK's obligations under the single market directives and the post-BCCI directive (European Parliament and Council Directive 95/26/EC of 29 June 1995). They include requirements that UK firms must have their head offices here, that a firm has adequate resources and does not have "close links" which would prevent the FSA supervising the firm effectively.

Permissions may be granted subject to requirements, either to take or to refrain from taking specified action (Section 43 FSMA). A permission may be varied or cancelled, either at the request of the firm or on the FSA's own initiative (Sections 44 and 45 FSMA).

A firm which is authorised but carries on a regulated activity not covered by its permission is liable to disciplinary sanction at the hands of the FSA. However, the firm would not be committing a criminal offence and its contracts would not be unenforceable (Section 20 FSMA). This is a major change from the position previously, where the traditional boundaries between differently regulated businesses had become blurred but transgression brought criminal liability and the possibility that contracts would be unenforceable. However, it is still the case under the FSMA that a contravention of the general prohibition by a person who is not authorised is a criminal offence and contracts may be unenforceable.

1.3.3 Powers of the FSA over authorised persons

The FSA's rule-making powers are generally confined to the ability to make rules applying to authorised persons only. However, these rules can apply to an authorised person's regulated and non-regulated activities alike, and capital resources rules can take into account the financial exposures of unauthorised group companies.

The basic approach taken in the FSMA has been to give the FSA the power to make rules in order to protect consumers (its so called "general rule-making power") and then to supplement that power in certain areas where the general rule-making power might not go far enough.

The FSA's general rule-making power allows it to make rules concerning the way in which authorised persons carry on regulated activities. Rules may only be made if they are in the interests of consumers. "Consumers" for these purposes is not confined to the retail concept of the term, and will include market counterparties, potential consumers and indirect consumers. The FSA's ability to make rules concerning an authorised person's non-regulated activities is exercisable only in order to protect the customers of that person's regulated business.

Examples of other rule making powers include the power to make stabilisation rules (which are also relevant to the conduct of persons who are not authorised) and the power to endorse provisions of the Takeover Code and Substantial Acquisition Rules: effectively so that the FSA can, at the request of the Takeover Panel, discipline an authorised person for breach of the Code. The FSMA provides for so called "evidential" rules to be made. An evidential rule can be used to determine whether another specified rule has been complied with or contravened. In essence, they are a form of guidance. They are designed to assist the FSA in formulating and issuing codes of practice.

The FSA also has the power to issue rules formulated at a high level of generality. These are the "Principles" for business and for individuals occupying positions of importance in authorised firms.

The FSA has power to issue codes. Some, such as the Code of Market Conduct concerning market abuse (which is also relevant to the conduct of non-authorised persons) and the Approved Persons Code concerning individuals working for or directing authorised firms, are specifically provided for in the FSMA.

The FSA's rules and Codes are collected together in its Handbook. Of most day-to-day relevance to authorised persons are the conduct of business rules and the Capital Adequacy rules. The Conduct of Business rules relevant to investment banking are discussed in Chapter 4.

1.3.4 *Control over individuals*

FSMA requires that individuals occupying key posts in, or in relation to, firms be formally approved by the FSA. This is known as the "approved persons" regime. This does not apply to incoming European firms unless they maintain a branch presence in the UK.

Individuals requiring approval are those performing "controlled functions", which broadly fall into three categories: those who exercise significant influence over a firm (i.e. senior management and compliance and money laundering officers); those who deal with customers; and those who handle clients' assets or money.

The FSA must be satisfied that any individual proposed for a controlled function is a fit and proper person to perform it. The FSA may have regard to an individual's training, competence and qualifications.

Once approved, individuals become subject to the Statements of Principles for Approved Persons issued by the FSA. These cover: acting with integrity and due skill, care and diligence, observing proper standards of market conduct and dealing openly and co-operatively with the FSA and other regulators.

Individuals who fall short of the standards expected of them may be disciplined by the FSA and are subject to fines or, in serious cases, to being banned from performing any controlled function with any firm.

In addition to these requirements obligations are imposed on the most senior executives of a firm concerning its organisation and control. *See* further Chapter 2.

1.3.5 Controllers of authorised persons

Reflecting European requirements, the FSMA requires notification and prior approval of any step which a person proposes to take, which would result in him acquiring, increasing or reducing various types of control over a UK incorporated authorised person (or its parent).

The terms "control" and "controller" are widely drawn. The key shareholding thresholds at which notification requirements are triggered are: 10 per cent, 20 per cent, 33 per cent and 50 per cent. Holdings of other group companies and associates will also be relevant. Notification must also be made where a person is able to exercise "significant influence" over the management of an undertaking by virtue of a shareholding.

Failure to comply with the notification and approval provisions of Part XII will constitute a criminal offence. The FSMA also contains powers allowing the FSA to restrict a person's rights with regard to its share-holdings (or even to apply for the shares to be sold) if the person holds the shares in breach of a notice of objection or any condition set out in an FSA approval.

1.3.6 *Investigations and discipline*

The FSA has wide powers to investigate the affairs of authorised persons under Part XI FSMA. The FSA can require the person under investigation, or anyone connected with it, to provide information or documents and also to attend to give evidence. In certain circumstances, third parties can also be required to attend and give evidence. However compelled evidence cannot be used against a person in criminal proceedings or in proceedings in respect of market abuse. There are exemptions for information subject to a banker's duty of confidentiality and communications subject to legal and professional privilege.

Disciplinary action taken against a firm or individual by the FSA will be decided on by an Enforcement Committee set up by, but whose members act independently of, the FSA. The Enforcement Committee may impose unlimited fines or other sanctions related to a firm's authorisation or an individual's approval.

There is a right of appeal from a decision of the Enforcement Committee to the independent Financial Services and Markets Tribunal, which is, in effect, part of the UK's court system.

1.3.7 *Statutory civil liability*

A firm which contravenes an applicable rule of the FSA may be liable to a "private person" who suffers loss as a result of the contravention (Section 150 FSMA).

However, the FSA's rules themselves may except specified provisions of the rules from this general position.

"Private person" means an individual (but not one carrying on a regulated activity or one relying on the overseas persons exclusion (Section 1.3.1 above)) or a person not being an individual who is not carrying on business of any kind.

In certain cases, statutory liability is extended to losses suffered by persons who are not private persons. Examples include contraventions of rules which prohibit contractual terms excluding a duty or liability, or which prohibit insider dealing.

There is also a right of action for a "private person" where a firm allows an individual to perform a controlled function without the individual being approved by the FSA, as outlined in Section 1.3.4 above or a temporary person.

1.4   Collective investment schemes

Part XVII FSMA provides a regime for collective investment schemes. This regime is mainly concerned with the rules for authorised unit trust schemes and recognised European schemes falling under the relevant European directives; such schemes mostly fall outside the ambit of a book on investment banking.

A number of investment vehicles, such as limited partnerships, consti-tute unrecognised collective investment schemes. The FSMA provides for restrictions on the promotion of such schemes. Broadly, they cannot generally be marketed to retail investors.

The promotion restrictions apply to authorised persons. Unauthorised persons, such as overseas entities are not subject to these restrictions but remain subject to the general restrictions on financial promotion discussed in Chapter 7.

1.5   Exchanges and clearing houses

Part XVIII FSMA provides for recognition by the FSA of investment exchanges and clearing houses (UK or non-UK). Recognised bodies are exempt from the need for authorisation.

Recognised clearing houses can be independent of any recognised exchange, thus allowing for the recognition of OTC clearing organisations.

1.6   Financial promotion

Financial promotion is a very important topic and has its own Chapter in this book. At this point, it will only be noted that the basic prohibition on financial promotion, Section 21 FSMA, is extremely wide, extending to any communication made by way of business of an invitation or inducement to engage in investment activity. Any medium of communication, including by word of mouth, is caught.

The consequences of breach of the prohibition are grave: a criminal offence is committed and resulting contracts may be unenforceable.

Given the width of the prohibition and the severity of the consequences of contravention (and indeed the potential ease of contravention) much depends on the exemptions contained in the Financial Services and Markets Act 2000 (Financial Promotion) Order 2001. Unfortunately, the Order is complex and obscure and many judge its provisions to be inadequate to permit ordinary business dealings which should not, on any view, be prohibited. For further discussion of these problems *see* Chapter 7.

1.7   Official listing

Part VI FSMA provides the statutory framework for official listing in the UK. It provides for the FSA to be the "competent authority for the purposes of listing". In exercising this role, the FSA is performing a somewhat different function from that of industry regulator and, mainly in recognition of this, it uses the title "United Kingdom Listing Authority" (the "UKLA") for this role.

The UKLA may admit to the official list any securities which it sees fit (unless subject to a prohibition made by the Treasury). Admission to the Official List is subject to compliance with the listing rules, requiring among other things the publication of listing particulars or prospectuses.

The UKLA has power to impose financial penalties on issuers of listed securities, or applicants for listing, who contravene listing rules. Such powers also extend to directors who are "knowingly concerned" in any contravention.

The UKLA has issued a statement of policy both as to the imposition of penalties and the amount of penalties (Section 93).

The listing regime is discussed in more detail in Chapter 10.

1.8   Market abuse

One of the most novel features of the FSMA is Part VIII which provides for the FSA to impose penalties for market abuse.

Part VIII does not create criminal offences but its sanctions are nearer the criminal realm than traditional civil sanctions. This is especially relevant in the context of the Human Rights Act 1998, which requires that persons subject to criminal proceeding be granted certain minimum safeguards, such as the right to an independent trial and protection against self-incrimination. Accordingly, the FSMA contains provisions governing proceedings for market abuse which are designed to deliver the necessary protections.

Market abuse is discussed in Chapter 8. In broad terms, it is designed to penalise behaviour which threatens the integrity of financial markets, such behaviour falling under one of three headings: use of inside information, market manipulation or distortion and the creation of false market impressions.

The FSMA provides that the standard against which behaviour is to be judged is that of a "regular user of the market", who is a "reasonable person who regularly deals on that market in investments of the kind in question".

The Government and the FSA have indicated that in their view the regular user is a hypothetical person whose standards do not necessarily equate to the standards of actual users of the market in question, if the actual standards are unacceptably low.

Section 119 FSMA provides for the FSA to produce a Code of Market Conduct which describes in detail behaviour considered to be abusive, and behaviour which is not so considered. The Code contains descriptions of behaviour which constitute a safe harbour – that is behaviour so described is conclusively presumed not to be market abuse. Safe harbours have in particular been granted to behaviour which complies with certain provisions of rules made by recognised exchanges or by the Takeover Panel in the Takeover Code or Substantial Acquisition Rules.

Proceedings for market abuse are initiated by the FSA alone. Any decision by the FSA that a penalty should be imposed (or instead of a penalty that a person should be publicly declared to be a market abuser) may be appealed against to the Financial Services and Markets Tribunal.

1.9   Financial crime

Section 397 FSMA provides that it is a criminal offence to make misleading statements, promises or forecasts or dishonestly to conceal material facts if the purpose or effect is to induce persons to enter into, or to refrain from, entering into investment transactions, or to exercise, or refrain from exercising rights attaching to investments. The Section also criminalises conduct which creates false or misleading impression as to the marketing or the price or value of investments. These provisions are discussed further in Chapter 8.

There is a safe harbour for stabilisation rules, discussed further in Chapter 9.

Section 146 FSMA provides that the FSA may make rules in relation to the prevention and protection of money laundering in connection with carrying on regulated activities by authorised persons. These rules, which are discussed further in Chapter 9 are in addition to the arrangements which authorised persons must put in place pursuant to the Money Laundering Regulations 1993.

Chapter 2

Senior Management Responsibilities and the Approved Persons Regime

Bridget Barker

Partner
Macfarlanes

2.1 Introduction

The collapse of Barings in February 1995 highlighted what the UK regulators felt was their inability to discipline the bank's senior management who were ultimately responsible for the operation of the bank but not closely involved in its day to day activities. As a result of both Barings and the pensions mis-selling the regulators, when considering the structure of the new financial services regime, decided to focus on the role and accountability of senior managers, not least by making them personally culpable for regulatory failures.

Since 1 December 2001 when the new Financial Services and Markets Act 2000 (the "FSMA") was implemented there has been a far greater emphasis than previously on the importance of the role of senior management in a firm and the particular responsibilities undertaken by named individuals as the responsibility for meeting regulatory standards rests on persons within corporate finance firms. HM Treasury and the FSA have made it clear that the senior management of firms have a "crucial role to play in ensuring that effective governance structures, systems and controls are operated, and that, as senior managers, they should be accountable for their actions".

The FSA stated in Consultation Paper 35 (Senior Management, Systems and Controls – December 1999) that its proposals in this area would:

(a) clarify regulatory expectations in relation to the revised Principles for Business of the Authority;

(b)   contribute to the promotion of compliance among senior manage-
      ment; and
(c)   reduce the need for detailed rules elsewhere in the Authority's
      Handbook of Rules and Guidance.

It is to be expected that the second aim will be achieved, particularly in
view of the amount of N2 training of senior management which has been
undertaken in the City. However, whether the Authority will succeed in
the other two aims, particularly the third one, when the printed version
of the new FSA Handbook is said to run to over five feet in height and
is full of cross references to senior management responsibilities, is a moot
point.

It is very clear that, in future, the FSA will be looking closely at the role
of senior managers. In explaining the FSA's new approach, shortly before
N2, Sir Howard Davies said:

> "When things go wrong, we shall look directly to senior manage-
> ment, whom we shall hold accountable. In the case of Barings or the
> pensions mis-selling debacle, senior management have not been
> held directly accountable. Now we have a system of personal regis-
> tration, where specified individuals at the top of the firm have
> clearly set out responsibilities for risk management and compliance,
> for which we hold them accountable."

2.1.1   Cautionary tales

The FSA's new approach has been given added emphasis by the outcome
of recent disciplinary proceedings brought against Refco Overseas, Capel
Cure Sharp and the Credit Suisse First Boston Group. All three cases were
concluded before 1 December 2001 the date on which the FSA assumed
its full powers and took over the duties of the Securities and Futures
Authority ("SFA").

*   Refco Overseas, a futures broker regulated by the SFA was fined
    £300,000 and £28,000 costs in relation to a fraudulent scam run by its
    Rome office which involved diverting profitable transactions to the
    account of one customer at the expense of other customers. The SEO
    of Refco responsible for overseeing compliance, was fined £15,000
    and required to pay £2,000 towards SFA's costs. The SFA found that
    the SEO had failed properly to oversee the compliance function,
    leading to consequent ignorance of the serious absence of internal
    controls and failure to allocate adequate resources to support the

compliance function and a failure properly to monitor the Rome branch.

- Capel Cure Sharp ("CCS"), a retail stockbroker regulated by the SFA was fined £700,000 plus costs of £75,000 for failing to ensure dividend reconciliations were performed in time and for failures in its handling of the pensions mis-selling review. Several top CCS executives left their jobs by resigning or taking early retirement although no individual was disciplined by the SFA.
- Credit Suisse First Boston Group ("CSFB") was fined a total of £540,000 and costs of £40,600 in relation to two cases of failures in supervising traders.

In the first case, CSFB failed to detect and prevent misleading documentation being provided by a trader to two customers. CSFB cancelled the transactions after discovering the problem and dismissed the trader. However, the case against the individual trader has now been passed to the FSA and the FSA may bring disciplinary proceedings against the unnamed trader.

In the second case, CSFB failed to oversee a former head of the convertible bond-trading desk, when he was overstating his profits without detection. The individual has been suspended for a year and faces a £50,000 fine and £10,000 in costs. The fine could have been higher, but the SFA stated that they took into account the fact that the individual concerned did not profit financially nor did he try to conceal losses or cause harm to customers.

The CCS and CSFB cases represented the two biggest ever fines handed out by the SFA. In all three cases, the systems and procedures relating to the compliance function had failed and responsible individuals at each of the three firms had to take responsibility for the failures.

2.2 Dual approach

The new regime incorporates a dual approach – the first, covering senior management responsibilities, being applicable to authorised firms themselves and the second, the approved person regime, which imposes personal obligations on individuals who undertake certain specified roles within a corporate finance firm.

The senior management regime, which forms part of the FSA's new High Level Standards (and therefore has general application to all authorised firms), is intended to ensure that the most senior executive in a firm takes responsibility for the clear apportionment of responsibilities among senior management and for overseeing the obligation of the firm to operate appropriate systems and controls. This responsibility can, if there is more than one senior executive, be shared. Breach of such responsibility will result in disciplinary action against the firm itself.

The other side of the coin is the approved persons regime which has extended the responsibility of individuals and made them personally responsible for regulatory failures. Following N2, persons who are approved by the FSA need to comply with a new set of Statements of Principle applicable to individuals (as opposed to the FSA's new Principles for Business which only apply to regulated firms) and any breach of those Statements of Principle will constitute a regulatory breach potentially giving rise to an unlimited fine, public or private censure, the removal of approved person status or a prohibition from being able to undertake a "controlled function" in future.

The implementation of the new approach can be seen throughout the FSMA and at a number of levels in the FSA's new Handbook. For example:

(a) Section 2(3) FSMA provides that in discharging its general functions the FSA must have regard, among other things, to the responsibilities of those who manage the affairs of authorised persons. The FSMA itself provides that certain "controlled functions" can only be performed by persons who have been approved by the FSA. It also sets out a procedure for making application to the FSA to become an approved person (i.e. a person who will carry on a controlled function) as well as provisions governing the issue of the Statements of Principle and codes of conduct applicable to individuals. The framework for disciplinary procedures is also contained within the new statute.

(b) Principle 3 of the 11 new Principles of Business, with which all regulated firms must comply, states that a firm must "take reasonable care to organise and control its affairs responsibly and effectively, with adequate risk management systems".

(c) The Senior Management Arrangements, Systems and Controls Sourcebook ("SYSC") elaborates upon Principle 3 and places a requirement on a firm to take reasonable care to maintain a clear and appropriate apportionment of significant responsibilities among its directors and senior managers.

(d) Chapter 10 of the Supervisory Manual (SUP 10) requires individuals performing the 27 specific activities (known as the controlled functions) to be "approved persons" and, therefore, individually approved and regulated by the Authority. Only certain of those activities will be applicable to corporate finance houses.

(e)   The Statements of Principle and Code of Practice for Approved Persons ("APER") contained in the High Level Standards set out various principles (together with guidance on the meaning of such principles) which are directly binding on individuals who are "approved persons".

(f)   The Fit and Proper Test for Approved Persons ("FIT"), also contained in the High Level Standards, sets out and describes the criteria which the Authority will consider when assessing the fitness and propriety of a candidate for a controlled function and also for assessing the continuing fitness and propriety of an approved person.

(g)   The Training and Competence Sourcebook ("TC") requires firms to ensure that persons performing certain functions are assessed as "competent" before performing such functions. This assessment includes consideration of technical knowledge, skills and their application, market and legal developments and the requirement that the employee has passed the appropriate approved examinations specified in the TC. Firms are also expected to have ongoing procedures in place in respect of training and assessment of their staff.

2.3   The FSMA

The FSMA provides that certain specified activities, known as controlled functions, can only be carried out by persons who have been approved by the FSA to carry out that particular function. Sub-sections 59(1) and (2) FSMA provide that an authorised person must take reasonable care to ensure that no person performs a controlled function under an arrangement entered into by, or by a contractor of, the authorised person in relation to the carrying on by the authorised person of a regulated activity, unless the FSA approves the performance by that person of the controlled function to which the arrangement relates. These provisions therefore place a statutory duty on authorised firms to identify each individual who will be undertaking a controlled, function whether an employee or not and ensure that they are appropriately approved by the FSA.

Importantly, Section 59(8) provides an exemption so that to a person who has been approved by the authority of a member state to be fit and proper to carry on business under one of the passports contained in one of the single market directives will not be subject to approval by the FSA. As a result the position of the senior management of a UK branch of a European passported business will be somewhat different to that of the senior management of a regulated firm which is authorised by the FSA.

2.3.1 *Controlled functions*

Section 59(4) provides that the FSA may specify which activities will constitute "controlled functions". However, it can only do this if in relation to the carrying on of a regulated activity by a firm it is satisfied that one of three conditions is met. These three conditions are set out in Section 59(5), (6) and (7) FSMA and provide that the function:

(a) is likely to enable the person responsible for its performance to exercise a significant influence on the conduct of the firm's affairs, so far as relating to the regulated activity;

(b) will involve the person performing it in dealing with customers of the firm in a manner substantially connected with the carrying on of the regulated activity; or

(c) will involve the person performing it dealing with property of customers of the firm in a manner substantially connected with the carrying on of the regulated activity.

The term "customer" is defined in Section 59(11) as a person who, in relation to an authorised person, is using, or who is or may be contemplating using, any of the services provided by the authorised person. Consequently, it covers persons who are both actual and potential customers.

The FSMA also provides in Section 59(9) that the FSA, when determining whether the first condition is met, must take account of the likely consequences of the failure to discharge that function properly.

2.3.2 *Obtaining approval*

Applications for approval from the FSA must be made by a firm, in accordance with Section 60 FSMA, on behalf of the relevant individual on the prescribed application form. The FSA has power to "require the applicant to provide it with such further information as it reasonably considers necessary to enable it to determine the application" (Section 60(3)) and to require the applicant to present information in such form or to verify it in such a way as the FSA may direct (Section 60(4)). If an individual is to be moved within an organisation and will be performing a different controlled function, the firm will need to submit an application to transfer form. Approval will only be given by the FSA if it is satisfied that the candidate is a fit and proper person to perform the function to which the application relates (Section 61(1)). The FSA may consider, among other things, the qualification of a candidate, any training he has undergone and his level of competence.

When an executive is appointed to a senior management position in a financial services organisation, a press release is often issued. Interestingly, under the new regime since such a position is likely to involve a controlled function, there can be no certainty that the particular individual will be able to take up such position until he has been appropriately approved by the FSA. It is possible that a firm may be able to make use of the provisions available for emergency or temporary appointments of persons performing significant influence functions (*see* Section 2.6.1.5 below) but, in those circumstances, the firm will be running the risk that the permanent appointment will not be approved by the FSA.

In any event, the FSA has three months from the date on which it receives an application to determine whether to grant the application or to give a warning notice that it proposes to refuse the application under Section 62(2). If the FSA decides to impose a requirement that the applicant must provide it with further information, the period for consideration stops running on the day on which the requirement is imposed but starts running again either on the day on which the required information is received by the Authority or, if the information is not provided on a single day, on the last day of the days on which it is received by the FSA.

If the FSA decides to grant an application for approval it must give written notice of its decision to each of the interested parties. As mentioned above, if it proposes to refuse an application it must give a warning notice to each of the interested parties and if it subsequently decides to refuse an application it must give a decision notice to each of the interested parties. The interested parties in relation to an *application* (as opposed to in relation to an approval – *see* below) are the applicant (i.e. the authorised person), the individual in respect of whom the application is made and the person by whom that individual's services are to be retained, if not the authorised person itself. If the FSA decides to refuse an application, each of the interested parties may refer the matter to the Financial Services and Markets Tribunal (the "Tribunal").

The Tribunal will operate as a judicial tribunal and conduct a full hearing of a party's appeal against a refusal to grant an application.

2.3.3 Withdrawal of approval

The FSA has power under Section 63 FSMA to withdraw an approval which it has already given if it considers that the person in respect of whom it was given is not a fit and proper person to perform the function to which the approval relates. When considering whether to withdraw its approval, the FSA may take into account any matter which it could take into account if it were considering an application in respect of the performance of the function to which the approval relates. If the FSA proposes to withdraw its approval it must give each of the interested parties a warning notice or if it decides to withdraw its approval it must give each of the interested parties a decision notice. If the FSA's approval is withdrawn, each of the interested parties may refer the matter to the Tribunal. The interested parties in relation to an approval are stated to be the authorised person on whose application it was given, the individual in respect of whom it was given and the person by whom the individual's services are retained if that is not the authorised person who made the application (Section 63 (6)).

2.3.4 Fitness and propriety

When assessing the fitness and propriety of a person to perform a particular function, the FSA will take into account the following factors set out in the Fit and Proper Test for Approved Persons ("FIT"):

- honesty, integrity and reputation;
- competence and capability; and
- financial soundness.

In determining a person's competence and capability, the FSA will have regard to whether a person satisfies the relevant requirements of the TC. The contents of TC are outside the scope of this Chapter but, in essence, TC requires persons performing advisory activities to be assessed as "competent" and, subject to certain grandfathering provisions and exemptions, to pass certain specified examinations.

2.4 Senior management arrangements, systems and controls (SYSC)

The Senior Management Arrangements, Systems and Controls Source-book ("SYSC") is contained in the FSA Rule Book as part of the High Level Standards for firms and individuals. SYSC requires that a firm must appropriately allocate to one or more individuals, the functions of:

- dealing with the apportionment of responsibilities; and
- overseeing the establishment and maintenance of systems and controls.

The obligations under SYSC are imposed on the firm itself rather than the individual senior managers. Although there are only a limited number of actual rules in SYSC there is a considerable amount of formal guidance as to how those rules must be interpreted by regulated firms.

2.4.1 Apportionment of responsibilities

SYSC 2.1.1R states that:

> "A firm must take reasonable care to maintain a clear and appropriate apportionment of significant responsibilities among its directors and senior managers in such a way that:
>
> (i) it is clear who has which of those responsibilities; and
> (ii) the business and affairs of a firm can be adequately monitored and controlled by the directors, relevant senior managers and the governing body of the firm."

Firms are required to make a record of the apportionment of responsibilities and keep such records up-to-date. These records might include organisational charts and diagrams, project management documents, job descriptions, committee constitutions and terms of reference. The chief executive officer is a key figure in complying with SYSC 2.1.1R and, in any event, under the approved persons regime, will be responsible for the controlled function of apportionment and oversight (*see* Section 2.5 below).

Non-executive directors are unlikely to be delegated responsibilities under SYSC. The FSA has clearly stated that provided that a non-executive director has personally taken due care in his role, a non-executive director would not be held liable in disciplinary proceedings either for the failings of the firm or certain individuals within the firm.

2.4.2   Overseeing systems and controls

SYSC 3.1.1R states that:

> "A firm must take reasonable care to establish and maintain such systems and controls as are appropriate to its business."

The guidance to these rules provides that the nature and extent of the systems and controls which a firm will need to maintain will depend upon a number of factors including:

- the nature, scale and complexity of its business;
- the diversity of its operations, including geographical diversity;
- the volume and size of its transactions; and
- the degree of risk associated with each area of its operation.

Each regulated firm is required to carry out a regular review of its systems and controls in order to ensure that they are appropriate.

2.4.3   The areas required to be covered by systems and controls

SYSC sets out the principal issues which the FSA expects an authorised person to consider when establishing and monitoring the systems and controls appropriate to its business. Not all must be addressed – it will depend on the size and nature of the operation.

2.4.4   Organisation/reporting lines

The guidance in SYSC states that a firm's reporting lines should be clear and appropriate with regard to the nature, scale and complexity of its business. These reporting lines, together with clear management responsibilities should be communicated as appropriate within the firm. Where the firm's governing body delegates functions, appropriate safeguards should be put in place in order to ensure that the recipient of the instructions is able to carry out the delegated function or task and that the extent and limits of any delegation is made clear to those concerned. Any delegatee must be suitable to carry out the delegated function or tasks taking into account the degree of responsibility involved. Consequently firms should ensure that all employees are fully aware of the nature and extent of their responsibilities. Any delegation must be appropriately supervised and monitored. Delegation to a junior who cannot handle a particular task could create a regulatory breach. Any delegation to a third party who operates outside the firm (defined in SYSC as outsourcing) is also governed by the guidance which relates to internal delegation. SYSC clearly states that a firm cannot contract out of its regulatory obligations and, therefore, must take reasonable care to supervise the discharge of outsourced functions by a contractor.

2.4.5 Organisation/segregation of duties

There may be circumstances when a firm should segregate the duties of individuals and departments in such a way as to reduce the opportunities for financial crime as well as any contravention of requirements and standards under the regulatory system. For example, where an organisation contains both a corporate finance division and a broking division, appropriate "Chinese walls" should be in place to ensure that insider dealing does not occur. Front and back office staff should always be segregated to prevent a single individual from being able to control transactions.

2.4.6 Compliance

It is a rule under SYSC 3.2.6 R that firms must to take reasonable care to establish and maintain effective systems and controls to ensure compliance with applicable requirements and standards under the regulatory system and for countering the risk that the firm may be used to further financial crime. (Financial crime includes (according to Section 6) any offence involving fraud or dishonesty, misconduct in, or misuse of information relating to, a financial market or money laundering). The guidance indicates that in many cases it will be appropriate for a firm to have a separate compliance function, the organisation and responsibilities of which should be documented. The compliance function should be staffed by an appropriate number of competent staff who are "sufficiently independent to perform their duties objectively" and should be adequately resourced and have unrestricted access to the firm's relevant records as well as ultimate recourse to its governing body, which in most cases will be the board of directors.

SYSC 3.2.8R provides that a firm which carries on "designated investment business" (which would include a corporate finance firm since it covers giving advice and making arrangements in respect of investments such as shares, debentures and derivatives) must allocate to a director or senior manager the function of having responsibility for oversight of the firm's compliance and reporting to the governing body in respect of that responsibility. This is the "compliance oversight function" referred to in Section 2.5.2.3 below. The reference to compliance in this rule relates to the Conduct of Business Rules and, although less likely to be applicable to corporate finance houses, the Collective Investment Schemes Rules.

2.4.7 Risk assessment

In addition, depending on the particular circumstances of its business, it may be appropriate for a firm to have a separate risk assessment function responsible for assessing the risks that a firm faces and informing the board and senior managers about them. Again, the organisational responsibilities of the risk assessment function should be documented. The function should be adequately resourced and staffed by an appropriate number of competent staff who are sufficiently independent to perform their duties objectively.

2.4.8 Management information

A firm's arrangements should be such as to provide the board with the information it needs to perform its responsibilities in identifying, measuring, managing and controlling risks of regulatory concern. The FSA has highlighted three factors which must be considered in this respect namely: relevance, reliability and timeliness.

Risks relating to the fair treatment and protection of customers will be of regulatory concern as will risks which impact on confidence in the financial system and its use for financial crime. Consequently, each firm must, taking into account its own particular circumstances, decide what information is required as well as how often and to whom it should be supplied.

2.4.9 Personnel

The guidance suggests that a firm's systems and controls should enable the firm to satisfy itself of the suitability of anyone who acts for it. For example, at the point of recruitment, a firm should assess an individual's honesty and competence. This may well result in firms being more demanding in their reference requirements from others while trying hard to protect their own potential exposure. Any assessment of the suitability of an individual should take account of the level of responsibility which will be assumed by an individual with the firm.

2.4.10 Audit committee

It may be appropriate for larger firms conducting a complex business to form an audit committee, which would examine management processes and systems and controls, or delegate much of the task of monitoring the appropriateness and effectiveness of its systems and controls to an internal audit function. An audit committee may also examine the arrangements made to ensure compliance with regulatory requirements and standards.

2.4.11 Strategy and business plans

SYSC states that a firm should plan its business appropriately so that it is able to "identify, measure, manage and control risks of regulatory concern". In certain circumstances, depending on the nature, scale and complexity of a firm's business, it may be appropriate to have business plans or strategy plans documented and updated on a regular basis to take account of changes in the business environment.

2.4.12 Remuneration policies

SYSC also recognises that it is possible that a firm's remuneration policies will, from time to time, lead to tensions between the ability of the firm to meet requirements and standards under the regulatory system and the personal advantage of those who act for it. The FSA states that "where tensions exist, these should be appropriately managed".

2.4.13 Business continuity

In some circumstances (again, having regard to the individual circumstances of its business) a firm should ensure that it can continue to function and meet its regulatory obligations in the event of unforeseen interruptions. Obviously, recent terrorist events have thrown this issue into greater focus. These arrangements should be regularly updated and tested to ensure their effectiveness.

2.4.14 Records

A further rule (3.2.20) provides that firms must maintain adequate records which, if they undertake business carried on in the UK, are capable of being reproduced in English.

2.4.15 *Who is responsible?*

If a firm has an individual chief executive (or someone with equivalent responsibilities with another title, such as a managing director or managing partner), the apportionment and oversight function would normally be allocated to that individual. However, if the firm is a body corporate and a member of a group, the function may, rather than being allocated to the firm's chief executive, be allocated to a director or senior manager from the group responsible for the overall management of the group or of a relevant group division. This can, however, only be done if it is appropriate (i.e. compatible with ensuring that the firm effectively complies with the requirement that it takes reasonable care to organise and control its affairs responsibly and effectively as set out in Principle 3 above). In such circumstances, the director or senior manager must be of a seniority equivalent to, or greater than, the chief executive of the firm.

A firm may allocate the apportionment and oversight function to other individuals but this must be in addition to the allocation to the chief executive. If a firm does not have a chief executive, the apportionment and oversight function must be allocated to one or more individuals selected from the firm's executive directors and senior managers.

It is possible, although unusual, for firms to have more than one individual as its chief executive. In those circumstances, the apportionment and oversight function will be allocated to all the chief executives.

In respect of an overseas firm, the chief executive may be the person responsible for the conduct of the firm's business within the UK, such as the manager of the firm's UK branch, or it may be the chief executive of the firm as a whole, depending on the circumstances.

However, an incoming EEA firm or incoming treaty firm (which is regulated for prudential purposes in its home state) is not required to allocate the function dealing with apportionment. However, for those systems and controls relating to matters which the FSA, as host state regulator, is entitled to regulate (e.g. compliance with Conduct of Business Rules), the function of oversight in respect of those activities must be allocated. Consequently, in such circumstances the function will be split. Such a firm need not allocate the function of oversight to its chief executive and may allocate it to one or more directors and senior managers of the firm.

2.4.16 *Control over Authorised Persons*

Under Part XII FSMA, the FSA must be given prior notice of, and approve certain actions which would result in amending the existing control over authorised persons. The policy and practice is detailed in the Supervision sourcebook ("SUP") Chapter 11.

The Act applies these requirements more widely to all UK incorporated authorised firms (including, e.g. commodities firms which are not subject to regulation under EC directives). Authorised open-ended investment companies are not subject to these provisions.

Certain difficulties under the previous regimes do not appear to have been tackled by the Act. For example, fund managers and nominees may, on occasion, find themselves inadvertently in breach of the provisions on notification. The Act also applies the pre-notification requirements to intra-group reorganisations. A new issue is that the Act may have the effect that FSA pre-clearance is required in order to permit contracts for an acquisition to be exchanged, not merely to complete the acquisition, as was the case under the predecessor regimes.

Secondary legislation has provided exemptions from Part XII requirements for certain friendly societies and building societies.

The change of control notification provisions now apply to any "step" which a person proposes to take which would result in him acquiring, increasing or reducing various types of control over a UK incorporated authorised person or its parent.

The terms "control" and "controller" are widely drawn to include shareholdings in a company and more generally the ability to control that company in other ways. Holdings of other group companies and associates will also be relevant. The key shareholding thresholds at which notification requirements are triggered are: 10 per cent, 20 per cent, 33 per cent, and 50 per cent. Notification must also be made where a person is able to exercise "significant influence" over management if his shareholding is below 10 per cent.

It is arguable that the parent company of a proposed controller might not "take steps" to acquire control of a target (and hence that it need not make pre-notification). However, Part XII is drafted in such a way that those group companies which do take steps and which have to make detailed pre-notification are likely to be required to give details of their parent companies anyway. The Act also requires persons who acquire or increase control without taking steps to do so, to notify the FSA when they become aware of the increase or decrease.

The FSA must reach a decision on changes of controller within three months of a notice being served. If it proposes to withhold its approval, or if it proposes to impose conditions, the FSA must serve a warning notice entitling the person to make representations. If the FSA still minded objects to the change of control, or is minded to impose conditions, the FSA will then serve a decision notice following which the applicant can refer the matter to the Tribunal. The Act requires that the FSA consult overseas regulatory authorities before giving notices of objections in certain circumstances. The relevant regulations require consultation with home state regulators where an EEA bank or investment firm proposes to acquire control over a UK authorised bank or investment firm.

Failure to comply with the notification and approval provisions of Part XII is an offence, carrying a maximum of two years' imprisonment and a fine. The Act also contains powers allowing the FSA to restrict a person's rights with regard to shareholdings (or to apply for the shares to be sold) if a person acquires or holds the shares in breach of a notice of objection, or any conditions set out in an FSA approval.

The Treasury has powers to provide for exemptions from the notification requirements, to alter the circumstances and shareholding levels at which they apply and to change the definition of "controller" in the Act. These powers are intended to allow the Treasury to update the Act in accordance with any future changes to European law.

2.5   Approved persons (SUP 10)

Corporate financiers are well used to the requirement for registration of individuals since their previous regulator, the Securities and Futures Authority (the "SFA"), required that anybody who wished to undertake corporate finance business must be registered to undertake investment business and, in addition, had to meet a certain level of training and competence.

However, the position under the SFA Rules had a contractual basis rather than a statutory one as the obligation was imposed through the service contracts of individuals with a firm. Following N2, Part V FSMA imposes statutory obligations, including registration requirements, on individuals in their personal capacity.

The principal reason for this new approach is the regulator's desire to ensure that individuals meet higher standards of behaviour. In particular, the registration of individuals enables the Authority to set criteria which are intended to ensure that only fit and proper persons are engaged in controlled functions in the financial services industry.

The full list of controlled functions is as follows:

The "controlled functions"		
Type	**No.**	**Description of controlled function**
Governing functions*	1	Director function
	2	Non-executive director function
	3	Chief executive function
	4	Partner function
	5	Director of unincorporated association function
	6	Small friendly society function
	7	Sole trader function
Required functions*	8	Apportionment and oversight function
	9	European Economic Area investment business oversight function
	10	Compliance oversight function
	11	Money laundering reporting function
	12	Appointed actuary function
Systems and controls functions*	13	Finance function
	14	Risk assessment function
	15	Internal audit function

The "controlled functions"		
Type	**No.**	**Description of controlled function**
Significant management functions*	16	Significant management (designated investment business) function
	17	Significant management (other business operations) function
	18	Significant management (insurance underwriting) function
	19	Significant management (financial resources) function
	20	Significant management (settlements) function
Customer functions	21	Investment adviser function
	22	Investment adviser (trainee) function
	23	Corporate finance adviser function
	24	Pension transfer specialist function
	25	Adviser on syndicate participation at Lloyd's function
	26	Customer trading function
	27	Investment management function

*Significant influence functions

SUP 10 sets out the details of the "approved persons regime". An "approved person" is a person, who is approved for one or more of the 27 controlled functions which are listed in SUP 10.4.5 R. In almost all cases, an approved person will be an individual. However, a director can be a body corporate and may accordingly require approval as an approved person. Certain functions are described as "significant influence functions" and these will be assumed by the more senior managers in an organisation. Certain functions relate to customers and these equate with the former SFA registration requirements for corporate financiers. The following sets out a brief explanation of the various controlled functions relevant to corporate finance firms.

2.5.1 Governing functions

Persons responsible for directing a firm's affairs will be performing the "governing functions" and will be required to be approved persons.

2.5.1.1   Director function (CF1)

Acting in the capacity of the director (other than a non-executive director) of a firm which is a body corporate (other than a limited liability partnership) is a controlled function. This will include a person in accordance with whose directions and instructions the directors are accustomed to act, that is a "shadow" director.

2.5.1.2   Non-executive director function (CF2)

This relates to a director "who has no responsibility for implementing the decisions or the policies of the governing body of a firm".

2.5.1.3   Chief executive function (CF3)

A person who, alone or jointly with one or more others, is responsible under the immediate authority of the directors for the conduct of the whole of a firm's business will be required to assume this function. However, in relation to an undertaking whose principal place of business is outside the UK, this function will relate to the person who was responsible for the conduct of the firm's business within the UK. As stated above, the Chief Executive would normally also be responsible for the apportionment and oversight function (*see* CF8, Section 2.5.2.1 below).

2.5.1.4   Partner function (CF4)

In respect of a partnership which has its principal purpose the carrying on of one or more regulated activities, each partner will perform the partner function. However, if the principal purpose of the firm is other than to carry on regulated activities, a partner will perform the partner function only to the extent that he has responsibility for a regulated activity. A partner in a firm will be taken to have a responsibility for each regulated activity except where the partnership has apportioned responsibility to another partner or group of partners.

If a firm is a limited liability partnership, the partner function extends to the firm as if the firm were a partnership and each member of the firm was a partner.

2.5.1.5   *Sole trader function (CF7)*
If a firm is a sole trader, the sole trader function is the function of acting in the capacity of the sole trader. However, the sole trader function applies only to a sole trader who employs one or more approved persons.

2.5.2   **Required functions**

As referred to above, SYSC requires that a firm must appropriately allocate to one or more individuals certain functions in respect of the management of that firm.

2.5.2.1   *Apportionment and oversight function (CF8)*
This function of acting in the capacity of a director or senior manager responsible for either or both of the apportionment function and the oversight function. Theoretically, this function could be split but, in most cases, both these functions will be allocated to the chief executive officer.

The apportionment function requires an individual to take reasonable care to maintain a clear and appropriate apportionment of significant responsibilities among its directors and senior managers (*see* Section 2.4.1 above). The oversight function requires an individual to oversee the establishment and maintenance of such systems and controls as are appropriate to its business.

2.5.2.2   *EEA investment business oversight function (CF9)*
An individual who is responsible for overseeing the establishment and maintenance of systems and controls in relation to designated investment business carried on from a branch in the UK of an incoming EEA firm will perform this function.

2.5.2.3   *Compliance oversight function (CF10)*
This covers the function of acting in the capacity of a director or senior manager who is allocated the responsibility for oversight of a firm's compliance and reporting to the FSA in respect of that responsibility. This function only applies to firms which carry out designated investment business.

Some firms, particularly firms with complex structures or which are part of a wider group, may find it appropriate to seek approval for the group head of compliance or others involved in the group's compliance to perform the compliance oversight function.

Although some firms use external compliance consultants, the responsibility for the compliance oversight function must rest with one or more directors or senior managers of the firm itself.

2.5.2.4 *Money laundering reporting function (CF11)*

The rules contained in the Money Laundering Sourcebook ("ML") provide that a firm must have a Money Laundering Reporting Officer unless:

- it is a sole trader with no employees; or
- its regulated activities are certain insurance business only; or
- it is an incoming firm only providing services into the UK.

The Money Laundering Reporting Officer must have a "sufficient level of seniority" within the firm so that he can carry out his controlled function effectively. The FSA is known to be looking carefully at anti-money laundering procedures and will no doubt expect the Money Laundering Reporting Officer to be a fairly senior person, who has a degree of influence, within a firm.

2.5.3 **Systems and control functions**

2.5.3.1 *Finance function (CF13)*

This covers the function of acting in the capacity of a senior manager with a responsibility for reporting to the governing body of a firm in relation to its financial affairs (e.g. the financial controller, chief finance officer or finance officer). If an individual is a finance director, and he is a director of the firm, he should be approved to perform the director function and not the finance function.

2.5.3.2 *Risk assessment function (CF14)*

A senior manager with responsibility for reporting to the governing body of a firm in relation to setting and controlling its risk exposure will be required to take this function.

2.5.3.3 *Internal audit function (CF15)*

This covers a senior manager with a responsibility for reporting to the governing body, or the audit committee (or its equivalent), of a firm in relation to its adherence to internal systems and controls, procedures and policies.

2.5.3.4 *Significant management functions*

These functions will only apply to a firm which apportions a significant responsibility to a senior manager of a significant business unit. It is likely that there will only be a few firms needing to seek approval for an individual to perform a significant management function. In most firms, those approved for the governing functions, required functions and, where appropriate, the systems and control functions, are likely to exercise all the significant influences at senior management level.

However, where the scale, nature and complexity of a firm's business is such that a significant responsibility is apportioned to an individual who is not approved under any of the above functions, a firm should consider whether the functions of that individual fall within a significant management function.

2.5.3.5 *Significant management (designated investment business) function (CF16)*

This covers acting as a senior manager with significant responsibility for a significant business unit which carries on designated investment business.

2.5.3.6 *Significant management (other business operations) function (CF17)*

The function of acting as a senior manager with significant responsibility for a significant business unit which carries on an activity which is not designated investment business.

2.5.3.7 *Significant management (financial resources) function (CF19)*

A senior manager with a significant responsibility for the making of material decisions or commitments of a firm's financial resources, its financial commitments, its asset acquisitions, its liability management and its overall cash and capital planning must take up this function.

Controlled Functions 1 to 19 outlined above are collectively described as the "significant influence functions", that is, one which is likely to result in the person responsible for its performance "exercising a significant influence on the conduct of a firm's affairs, so far as relating to a regulated activity of the firm".

As with all controlled functions, the significant influence functions may only be performed following an application being submitted to the FSA and approval being granted. Under Section 60, the FSA has up to three months to determine an application for approval to perform a controlled function. Consequently, the FSA permits "temporary" or "emergency" appointments of persons to perform a function that would otherwise be a significant influence function if that appointment is for less than 12 weeks in a consecutive 12-month period. This means that it is not necessary to obtain a precautionary approval for a deputy in order to cover holidays and emergencies. However, as soon as it becomes apparent that a person will be performing a controlled function for more than 12 weeks, the firm should apply for approval.

2.5.4 Customer functions

These functions relate to a person dealing with customers or dealing with the property of customers in connection with the carrying on of a regulated activity of the firm.

2.5.4.1 Investment adviser function (CF21)
This covers advising on investments and performing functions within the customer trading function (*see* below) in connection with advising on investments.

2.5.4.2 Investment adviser (trainee) function (CF22)
The function of advising on investments where the individual performing the function has not yet been assessed as competent in accordance with the rules of the TC.

2.5.4.3 Corporate finance adviser function (CF23)
The function of giving advice to clients only in connection with corporate finance business.

2.5.4.4 Investment management function (CF27)
The function of managing investments and, where ancillary to that function, functions within the customer trading function and the investment adviser function.

2.6 Statements of Principle and Code of Practice for approved persons (APER)

Section 64 (1) FSMA provides that the FSA "may issue statements of principle with respect to the conduct expected of approved persons". The section also provides that if the FSA issues such a statement of principle it must also issue a code of practice "for the purpose of helping to determine whether or not a person's conduct complies with the statement of principle". The "Statements of Principle and Code of

Practice for Approved Persons" are set out in a sourcebook ("APER") contained within the High Level Standards of the FSA Handbook. These apply to individuals rather than to the regulated firm itself.

The Statements of Principle are divided into two parts. Statements of Principle 1–4 apply to all approved persons whereas Statements of Principle 5–7 only apply to those persons performing a significant influence function, that is controlled functions 1 to 19.

Set out below are the seven Statements of Principle which apply to approved persons together with the significant provisions of the Code of Practice which apply to each principle in relation to corporate finance business.

2.6.1 The APER principles

2.6.1.1 Principle 1: "An approved person must act with integrity in carrying out his controlled function".
A person would not be in compliance with Principle 1 in the following circumstances:

(a) deliberately misleading (or attempting to mislead) by act or omission a client, his firm (or his auditors or appointed actuary) or the FSA. This behaviour might include:
  (i) falsifying documents;
  (ii) misleading a client about the risks of an investment;
  (iii) misleading others within the firm about the credit-worthiness of a borrower;
  (iv) providing false or inaccurate documentation or information, including details of training, qualifications, past employment record or experience;
  (v) destroying, or causing the destruction of documents (including false documentation), or tapes or their contents, relevant to misleading (or attempting to mislead) a client, the firm or the FSA;
  (vi) failing to disclose dealings where disclosure is required by the firm's personal account dealing rules;
  (vii) misleading others in the firm about the nature of risks being accepted;
(b) deliberately failing to inform, without reasonable cause, a customer, the firm or the FSA of the fact that their understanding of a material issue is incorrect, despite being aware of their misunderstanding.

This might include failing to disclose the existence of falsified documents;

(c)   deliberately preparing inaccurate or inappropriate records or returns in connection with a controlled function. This might include:

    (i)   preparing inaccurate training records or inaccurate details of qualifications, past employment record or experience; or

    (ii) preparing inaccurate records of transactions or holdings of securities;

(d)   deliberately misusing the assets or confidential information of a client or of its firm. This will include:

    (i)   misappropriating a client's assets;

    (ii) using a client's funds for purposes other than those for which they were provided;

    corporate finance firms will frequently be entrusted with confidential information and should have in place procedures, such as Chinese walls, to ensure that such information is not misused. In respect of such information, approved persons should also be aware of their responsibilities under Statement of Principle 3 in this respect.

(e)   deliberately designing transactions so as to disguise breaches of requirements and standards of the regulatory system;

(f)   deliberately failing to disclose the existence of a conflict of interest in connection with dealings with a client.

2.6.1.2 Principle 2: *"An approved person must act with due skill, care and diligence in carrying out his controlled functions".*

A person would not be in compliance with Principle 2 in the following circumstances:

(a)   failing to inform a customer or the firm (or its auditors) of material information in circumstances where he was aware, or ought to have been aware, of such information, and of the fact that he should provide it;

(b)   providing inaccurate or inadequate information to the firm or failing to disclose dealings where disclosure is required by the firm's personal account dealing rules;

(c)   undertaking, recommending or providing advice on transactions without a reasonable understanding of the risk exposure of the transaction to a customer. This might include recommending transactions in investments to a customer without a reasonable understanding of the liability (either potential or actual) of that transaction;

(d)   failing without good reason to disclose the existence of a conflict of interest in connection with dealings with a client;

(e)   failing to provide adequate control over a client's assets by, for example, failing to segregate a client's assets;

(f)   continuing to perform a controlled function despite having failed to meet the standards of knowledge and skill set out in the TC for that controlled function.

Principle 2 is very broad and is likely to be applicable where there is any significant failure within a firm. It can also be seen as part of an increased emphasis on training and competence issues for regulated firms.

2.6.1.3   *Principle 3: "An approved person must observe proper standards of market conduct in carrying out his controlled function".*

In many cases, the required standards under Principle 3 will be set out in the sourcebooks relating to Inter-professionals Conduct (MAR3) and the Code of Market Conduct (MAR1). Market codes and exchange rules will also be relevant. In particular, in the context of mergers, takeovers and the substantial acquisition of shares the Takeover Code and Substantial Acquisition Rules are explicitly endorsed by the FSA in MAR4 and any breach of these provisions by an approved person may be in breach of Principle 3.

Corporate finance firms need to be conscious of the new civil regime in relation to market abuse. In addition to the penalties the FSA may impose under Section 123 FSMA, a person conducting market abuse is likely to be in breach of Principle 3.

The Code of Market Conduct gives guidance for the purposes of determining whether or not behaviour amounts to market abuse in accordance with Section 119 FSMA.

The Inter-Professionals Conduct Sourcebook applies to firms which carry on regulated activities or regulated ancillary activities involving dealing, arranging or providing transaction-specific advice in respect of inter-professionals investment and the activity is undertaken with or for a market counterparty. As such, it replaces the old London Code of Conduct and is unlikely to be relevant for corporate finance firms.

2.6.1.4   Principle 4: *"An approved person must deal with the Authority and with other regulators in an open and cooperative way and must disclose appropriately any information of which the Authority would reasonably expect notice".*

A person would not be in compliance with Principle 4 in the following circumstances:

(a)   Failing to report promptly in accordance with his firm's internal procedures (or, if none exist, direct to the FSA), information which it would be reasonable to assume would be of material significance to the FSA, whether in response to questions or otherwise.

An approved person does not have a duty to report information directly to the FSA unless he is one of the approved persons responsible within the firm for reporting matters to the FSA. However, if an approved person takes steps to influence the decision so as not to report to the FSA or act in a way that is intended to obstruct the reporting of the information to the FSA, then the FSA will, in respect of that information, view him as being one of those within the firm who has taken on responsibility for deciding whether to report that matter to the FSA. Consequently, if an issue is brought to the board of a firm and the board decides not to report such issue to the FSA, all members of the board may be in breach of Principle 4 if the information is such that it would be "reasonable to assume would be of material significance" to the FSA.

The likely factors taken into account in these circumstances include:

(i)   the likely significance of the information to the FSA (in light of what it is reasonable for the individual to assume);

(ii)   whether the information related to the individual himself or to his firm; or

(iii)   whether any decision not to report the matter internally was taken after reasonable enquiry and analysis of the situation;

(b)   Where the approved person is, or is one of the approved persons who is, responsible within the firm for reporting matters to the FSA of, failing promptly to inform the FSA information of which he is aware and which it would be reasonable to assume would be of material significance to the FSA, whether in response to questions or otherwise. Again, relevant factors should be taken into account including:

(i)   the likely significance of the information to the FSA which was reasonable for the approved person to assume; and

(ii)   whether any decision not to inform the FSA was taken after reasonable enquiry and analysis of the situation;

(c) Failing without good reason to:
  (i) inform a regulator of information of which the approved person was aware in response to questions from that regulator;
  (ii) attend an interview, or answer questions put by a regulator, despite a request or demand having been made;
  (iii) supply a regulator with appropriate documents or information when requested or required to do so within the time limits attaching to that request or requirement.

2.6.1.5 *Principle 5: "An approved person performing a significant influence function must take reasonable steps to ensure that the business of the firm for which he is responsible in his controlled function is organised so that it can be controlled effectively".*

To some extent, Principle 5 imposes on senior managers the responsibilities imposed on the firm by SYSC. In both cases, it is necessary to establish clear reporting lines and job descriptions and ensure that employees of a regulated firm are adequately monitored and supervised.

A person would not be in compliance with Principle 5 in the following circumstances:

(a) failing to take reasonable steps to apportion responsibilities for all areas of the business under the approved person's control;
(b) failing to take reasonable steps to apportion responsibility clearly amongst those to whom responsibilities have been delegated. For example, a person would be in breach if he implemented confusing or uncertain reporting lines, authorisation levels or job descriptions and responsibilities;
(c) in the case of an approved person who is responsible for dealing with the apportionment of responsibilities (usually the chief executive), failing to take reasonable care to maintain a clear and appropriate apportionment of significant responsibilities among the firm's directors and senior managers. This might include:
  (i) failing to review regularly the significant responsibilities which the firm is required to apportion; or
  (ii) failing to act when that review shows that those significant responsibilities have not been clearly apportioned.
(d) failing to take reasonable steps to ensure that suitable individuals are responsible for those aspects of the business under the control of the individual performing a significant influence function. This might include:

(i)   failing to review the competence, knowledge, skills and performance of staff to assess their suitability to fulfil their duties, despite evidence that their performance is unacceptable;

(ii)   giving undue weight to financial performance when considering the suitability or continuing suitability of an individual for a particular role;

(iii)   allowing managerial vacancies which "put at risk compliance of the requirements and standards of the regulatory system" to remain, without arranging suitable cover for the responsibility.

The FSA has provided further guidance as to compliance with Principle 5. For example, it recommends that reporting lines should be made clear to staff and where staff have dual reporting lines, it states that there is a greater need to ensure that the responsibility and accountability of each individual line manager are clearly set out and understood. Where members of staff have particular levels of authorisation, these should be clearly set out and communicated to staff.

2.6.1.6   *Principle 6: "An approved person performing a significant influence function must exercise due skill, care and diligence in managing the business of the firm for which he is responsible in his controlled function".*

This is perhaps the broadest of the Statements of Principle which apply specifically to senior management. Principle 6 requires senior managers to have a full understanding of the nature of the business for which they are responsible. For example, in the context of corporate finance firms, a senior manager would be expected to understand the nature of any advice provided to clients and ensure that those persons providing services to clients are capable of performing those tasks at a satisfactory level.

A person would not be in compliance with Principle 6 in the following circumstances:

(a)   failing to take reasonable steps adequately to inform himself about the affairs of the business for which he is responsible. This might include:

(i)   permitting transactions without a sufficient understanding of the risks involved;

(ii)   permitting expansion of the business without reasonably assessing potential risks of that expansion;

(iii) inadequately monitoring highly profitable transactions or business practices or unusual transactions or business practices;

(iv) accepting implausible or unsatisfactory explanations from subordinates without testing the veracity of those explanations;

(v) failing to obtain independent, expert opinion where appropriate (a point worth underlining – failing to instruct your lawyers may be a breach of Principle 6!);

(b) failing to take reasonable steps to maintain an appropriate level of understanding about an issue or part of the business that he has delegated to an individual or individuals (whether in-house or outside contractors). This might include:

(i) disregarding an issue of part of the business once it has been delegated;

(ii) failing to require adequate reports once the resolution of an issue or management of part of the business has been delegated;

(iii) accepting implausible or unsatisfactory explanations from a delegate without testing their veracity;

(c) delegating the authority for dealing with an issue or a part of the business to an individual or (whether in-house or outside contractors) without reasonable grounds for believing that the delegate had the necessary capacity, competence, knowledge, seniority or skill to deal with the issue and also take authority for dealing with part of the business;

(d) failing to supervise and monitor adequately the individual (whether in-house or outside contractors) to whom responsibility for dealing with an issue or authority for dealing with a part of the business has been delegated. This might include:

(i) failing to take personal action or progress is unreasonably slow; or where implausible or unsatisfactory explanations are provided;

(ii) failing to review the performance of an outside contractor in connection with the delegated issue or business.

In assessing whether a person's conduct is in compliance with Principle 6, the FSA will take into account the competence, knowledge or seniority and past performance and record of the person to whom responsibility is delegated. The FSA gives an example of where a complex or unusual issue is delegated to a compliance department. In such circumstances, it would be unreasonable to delegate such a matter to the compliance department without ensuring it has sufficient capacity to deal with the matter adequately.

2.6.1.7   *Principle 7: "An approved person performing a significant influence function must take reasonable steps to ensure that the business of the firm for which he is responsible in his controlled function complies with the relevant requirements and standards of the regulatory system".*

Persons performing the compliance oversight function and the money laundering oversight function will have particular responsibilities under Principle 7. However, all senior managers will have responsibilities under this Principle to ensure that their specific areas of responsibility are conducted in accordance with the regulatory system. For example, if a director of a corporate finance firm is responsible for overseeing a specific transaction, that director will be responsible for ensuring that the firm complies with the FSA principles and rules when providing services in respect of that transaction.

A person would not be in compliance with Principle 7 in the following circumstances:

(a)   failing to take reasonable steps to implement (either personally or through a compliance or other department) adequate systems of control to comply with the relevant requirements of the regulatory system in respect of its regulated activities. In the case of an approved person who was responsible for overseeing systems and controls, failing to take reasonable care to oversee the establishment and maintenance of appropriate systems and controls;

(b)   failing to take reasonable steps to monitor (either personally or through a compliance or other department) compliance with the relevant requirements of the regulatory system in respect of its regulated activities;

(c)   failing to take reasonable steps adequately to inform himself about the reason why significant breaches (whether suspected or actual) of the relevant requirements and standards of the regulatory system in respect of its regulated activities may have arisen. This might include failing to investigate what systems may have failed, including, where appropriate, failing to obtain expert opinion on their adequacy;

(d)   failing to take reasonable steps to ensure that systems were controlled and reviewed and, if appropriate, improved, following the identification of significant breaches (whether suspected or actual) of the relevant requirements of the regulatory systems. This might include:

  (i)   unreasonably failing to implement recommendations for improvements in systems and procedures or to do so in a timely manner;

(e)   in the case of the Money Laundering Reporting Officer, failing to discharge the responsibilities imposed on him in accordance with the Money Laundering Sourcebook;

(f)   in the case of an approved person performing a significant influence function responsible for compliance, failing to take reasonable steps to ensure that appropriate compliance systems are in place.

2.6.2   Disciplinary powers

Section 66 FSMA enables the FSA to take disciplinary action against a person if that person is "guilty of misconduct". A person is guilty of misconduct if, while an approved person, he has failed to comply with one of the Statements of Principle. Any such proceedings must be brought by the FSA within two years of the FSA knowing of the misconduct.

Section 66(3) FSMA states that the sanctions available against approved persons are an unlimited penalty of such amount as the FSA considers appropriate or the FSA may publish a statement of his misconduct.

Although the FSMA does not specifically refer to other disciplinary sanctions applicable where there is a breach of the Statements of Principle, the likelihood is that any such breach may be relevant in determining whether an approved person is "fit and proper". Consequently, it is possible that a breach of a Statement of Principle may result in the FSMA withdrawing approval for an individual under Section 63 FSMA or prohibiting an individual from performing a specified controlled function under Section 56 FSMA.

2.7   Conclusion

The implementation of the FSMA has introduced a significant change of emphasis in the regulation of corporate finance and other investments firms. The FSA is now seeking to place greater responsibilities on senior management to ensure that firms are properly managed and maintain an appropriate "compliance culture". Matters such as reporting lines, job descriptions and regular assessments of staff must be central to the firm's approach to complying with the new regulatory system and, in particular, SYSC and the Statements of Principle.

Firms must also recognise that the FSA's requirements are extremely broad and somewhat vaguely defined. In the event of almost any failure within a regulated firm, management systems will need to be well developed and documented so that the FSA will not have the opportunity to assert that the problem has resulted from a failure in management systems or a breach of Statements of Principle 5 to 7. In this context, and since the FSA will have the considerable benefit of viewing events after the breach, all but the most diligent of senior managers may be vulnerable to the disciplinary powers of the FSA.

Chapter 3

Systems and Controls

Anita Webbon
Executive Director and Senior Counsel
Goldman Sachs International

3.1   Introduction

Before tackling the new FSA Senior Management Arrangements, Systems and Controls ("SYSC") requirements it is worth investing a few hours in reading one of the many accounts of the Nick Leeson/Barings saga. With this in mind, the rationale of the formalistic requirements of the new systems and controls framework can be more easily understood. Acceptance perhaps follows later, albeit from beneath the mountain of documentation – "capable of being reproduced in the English language on paper" (SYSC 3.2.20(2)R) – which will have been created to comply with the new requirements.

The author's remit is to discus the FSA's systems and controls regime, found in Block 1: High Level Standards of the FSA Handbook, in the module entitled "Senior Management Arrangements, Systems and Controls". As is apparent from the title of the module, the new regulations combine senior management arrangements with systems and controls requirements, making an account of one incomplete without consideration of the other. As explained in the FSA Handbook Development, Special Edition, June 2000, "Regulatory responsibilities of senior management: an overview": "the obligations of the firm can only be attended to by flesh and blood people ...". As is also clear from that document, the FSA perceives the Statements of Principle and Code of Practice for Approved Persons ("APER") in Block 1 of the FSA Handbook and the Approved Persons regime, to be found separately in the Supervision Manual ("SUP") – as providing the link between the requirements on each firm as an authorised person and its senior managers as significant influence controlled functions, to ensure that the "appropriate" systems and controls are in place.

Accordingly, reference will be made to both SYSC and APER (and separately, "the Principles" and "the Code") in seeking to identify the practical implications of the new systems and controls requirements.

3.2   The framework of SYSC

3.2.1   *High Level Standards*

The threefold purpose of SYSC, is set out in Chapter 1.2 of SYSC:

(a)   to increase certainty by amplifying Principle 3 of FSA's Principles for Businesses. (These also form part of the High Level Standards but should be distinguished from APER, containing the Principles and Code, which apply to Approved Persons);

(b)   to encourage firms' directors and senior executives to take appropriate practical responsibility for their firms' arrangements on matters likely to be of interest to the FSA, namely those which relate to:

    (i)   confidence in the financial system;

    (ii)   the fair treatment of firms' customers;

    (iii) the protection of consumers; and

    (iv) the use of the financial system in connection with financial crime;

(c)   to encourage firms to vest responsibility for effective and responsible organisation in specific directors and senior executives.

The concept of Principle 3 of the Principles for Businesses is not new. It reflects SIB Principle 9, which required a firm "to organise and control its internal affairs in a responsible manner, keeping proper records"; though it is written in the new language of the FSA. Thus, Principle 3 requires each firm to:

> "take reasonable care to organise and control its affairs responsibly and effectively, with adequate risk management systems."

However, the second and third purposes of SYSC articulate a new regulatory goal: that of achieving senior management responsibility and accountability in the management of firms. It is these aims, translated into SYSC and APER, which are likely to have a substantial practical impact on the organisation and management of firms.

As well as setting out standards for the framework of systems and controls, SYSC is intended to explain Principle 3 for Businesses and provide guidance and structure on APER, in particular by expanding on Principles 5–7 which apply only to significant influence controlled functions. Cross-referencing these different sets of provisions is complicated and made more so by references to the Combined Code of the Committee on Corporate Governance (the "Combined Code") and "Internal Control: Guidance for Directors on the the Combined Code", published by the Institute of Chartered Accountants in England and Wales ("the Turnbull report", after Nigel Turnbull who chaired the committee), on which more below. With so many provisions directed towards them, the new challenge of senior management responsibility and accountability may leave firms and significant influence functions feeling somewhat nervous about achieving compliance with the new regime.

There are, broadly, three key interlocking themes which emerge from the new SYSC regulatory framework, namely:

- management responsibility and accountability;
- corporate governance; and
- operational risk (although never specifically referred to in these terms in SYSC).

SYSC 3.2.20R which contains a general requirement to document "matters and dealings which are the subject of requirements and standards under the regulatory system", provides an overriding obligation of record keeping.

There are no relevant transitional provisions for any of these requirements, reflecting the regulatory view that SYSC is no more than a formalisation of existing requirements and standards presently observed in the industry.

3.2.2 Freedom to manage

The FSA's stated aim in creating SYSC, set out in the June 2000, Special Edition of FSA Handbook Development, is:

"To set standards which reflect the pivotal role of senior management in determining whether their firms live up to regulatory requirements;
but
To leave the senior management of each firm with the freedom they need to devise business structures and processes in accordance with their own commercial objectives."

The SYSC framework of systems and controls requirements is comprised almost entirely of guidance rather than rules, an approach that was reinforced after consultation on the proposals. Does this leave senior managers with the freedom to manage?

According to the FSA (SYSC 3.1.2G), the nature and extent of the systems and controls appropriate to a business will depend on a variety of factors including:

- the nature, scale and complexity of its business;
- the diversity of its operations, including geographical diversity;
- the volume and size of its transactions; and
- the degree of risk associated with each of its operations.

Chapter 3 of SYSC, which deals with systems and controls, contains only three rules about the framework:

(a) a firm must take reasonable care to establish "appropriate" systems and controls (SYSC 3.2.1R);
(b) systems and controls must address compliance with the requirements of the regulatory regime (SYSC 3.2.6R); and
(c) firms which carry on designated investment business must appoint a compliance officer (SYSC 3.2.8R).

The lack of rules means that SYSC guidance takes on significant practical importance in helping regulated firms to understand the meaning of the requirements. The SYSC guidance and the APER guidance (APER is of course all guidance/ evidential provisions, having been developed for the purpose of helping to determine whether or not a person's conduct complies with the Principles) suggest ways of addressing each of the themes. The guidance contains FSA's specific suggestions about what a firm is "expected" to consider in establishing appropriate systems and controls, under the following headings:

- organisation,
- compliance,
- risk assessment,
- management information,
- employees and agents,
- audit (committee and internal audit),
- business strategy,
- remuneration policies,
- business continuity and records.

These are considered in more detail below.

It is interesting to note that the Turnbull report asks about a broader range of risks including technological, legal, reputation and business probity issues which are directly relevant to financial services institutions. These broader risk issues factor into a more general discussion of operational risk. Although they are not mentioned in SYSC, they cannot be excluded from being part of "appropriate" systems and controls. Indeed, FSA does refer to operational risk in explaining its approach to supervision (SUP 1.3.4G).

It remains to be seen whether this regulatory suggestion of risk categories on "how to manage" will be imposed as the standard for regulated firms. The FSA have said that they will not use their guidance as a checklist when performing their supervisory role (June 2000, Special Edition of FSA Handbook Development and *see* further Section 3.4.4).

3.2.3 The requirements of SYSC

To comply with the SYSC regime, firms are required to satisfy three requirements:

(a) *Apportionment*: take reasonable care to establish and maintain a clear and appropriate apportionment of senior management responsibilities so that those responsibilities are clear and that the business and affairs of the firm can be adequately monitored and controlled by its senior managers and governing body (SYSC 2.1.1R);

(b) *Systems and controls*: take reasonable care to establish and maintain such systems and controls as are appropriate for their business (SYSC 3.1.1R);

(c) *Allocation*: allocate to one or more individuals the job of apportionment of senior management responsibilities and overseeing the

53

establishment and maintenance of the firm's system of internal controls. Where there is a chief executive, he must be one of the individuals with this responsibility (SYSC 2.1.3R). This is the bridge between the firm and the individual senior manager. The aim is to make individuals responsible to the regulator for decisions made in the business.

Compliance with each requirement must be documented.

As previous Chapters have dealt in detail with senior management apportionment and oversight responsibilities, the remainder of this Chapter addresses the requirement of "appropriate" systems and controls.

3.3 Appropriate systems and controls

3.3.1 Application of SYSC

The rules regarding the application of the requirements of SYSC 3 are complex. In general, the rules apply to regulated and ancillary activities of every regulated firm. There are a number of qualifications set out in summary below:

(a)   for EEA passported firms, the rules apply to a UK branch. There is a carve out for matters reserved to the home state regulator and Appendix 1 of SYSC attempts to define these. Note that Appendix 1, 1.1.6G advises that firms should seek legal advice on this interpretation, which is by no means straightforward;

(b)   for both UK incorporated firms and UK branches of non-EEA firms, the rules apply in a prudential context to activities (including unregulated activities – SYSC 1.1.5R) "wherever they are carried on" (SYSC 1.1.10R);

(c)   SYSC 1.1.5R(2) provides that SYSC 3 takes into account the activity of other members of a group of which the firm is a member. Guidance elaborates that the systems and controls which operate at group level will be relevant to determining the appropriateness of a firm's own systems and controls. This is an untested extension of FSA territorial scope.

Whilst there are certainly questions of application to be raised in defence of allegations of breach, in practice, it may be simplest for firms to assume that all of the requirements of SYSC3 apply when considering compliance with the new regime.

3.3.2 *Managing the firm in compliance with SYSC*

"A firm must take reasonable care to establish and maintain such systems and controls as are appropriate to its business." (SYSC 3.1.1R).

How should the senior management of a firm approach compliance with this requirement?

All or most of the firms subject to SYSC would, presumably, say that they are properly managed businesses. It is an unfortunate reality that the legacy of Barings and other control failures in the industry is that firms can no longer say "it works because it hasn't failed". For many firms, preparation for the implementation of SYSC has involved substantial review of the realities of how their business is managed.

SYSC in effect requires firms to prove that they are effectively managed – and gathering the proof in documentary format can present a significant practical challenge. Indeed, the quest for documentation, culminating in the holy grail of agendas and minutes of meetings may need to become the reality of SYSC compliant financial services management.

There is a corporate law framework prescribing minimum standards of corporate governance according to country of incorporation. Over the last several years, additional standards and guidance on corporate governance have been developed in the UK and these find some recognition in the new regulations. This is reflected in SYSC with the provision that, where a firm is following the Combined Code, FSA will give "due credit" (undefined) but not a safe harbour. According to the FSA High Level Standards Policy Statement in June 2000, this is on the basis that the requirements of the Combined Code do not apply to all those who are subject to SYSC and are not the same as those of SYSC. It seems that today it is the changing regulatory environment which is driving corporate governance decisions and the responsibilities of the boards of financial services institutions.

The Turnbull report echoes much of the language of FSA policy statements:

"A company's system of internal control has a key role in the management of risks that are significant to the fulfilment of its business objectives" (paragraph 10) and "should be embedded in the operations of the company and form part of its culture." (paragraph 22)

The Turnbull report expands the provision on internal controls into a generic, risk-based framework. The focus is on the responsibilities of the board rather than individual directors. The FSA has no power to make rules binding on boards as such and, in contrast to the Turnbull report, does not seek to rely on collective responsibility. This may be driven by the perception of "personal culpability" as a more meaningful hook. In determining whether there will be personal liability, the introduction to the Code emphasises that conduct must be deliberate or "below that which would be reasonable in all the circumstances". However, in determining whether there has been a breach of Principles 5–7, the opinion of the FSA about an individual's knowledge is also relevant. For the liability of corporate entities, as most of the relevant rules set the standard as one of reasonable care, only a failure to take reasonable care (or worse) should be a foundation for disciplinary action.

Against this background, the starting point for the regulated person keen to ensure compliance is to ask, how is the firm really managed? As SYSC deals with legal entities, not product lines, it is as well to start at the top with management by the "governing body". This is defined by FSA as "the board of directors, committee of management or other governing body of a firm . . ." Where the board of directors is the governing body, oversight management may be through the board meeting. These tend to be formally scheduled and documented through an agenda and minutes. If these meetings happen often enough and are actually attended by directors, they can provide the framework for management and oversight of a firm, albeit at a high level. The Turnbull report for example envisages board meetings where difficult questions are asked about the structure of a company's systems and controls. However, where board meetings are set piece occasions, with the challenge being to obtain a quorum of directors, this is unlikely to satisfy the requirements of the regulator about how the governing body of a regulated legal entity (and its individual directors) are satisfying their SYSC and other supervisory responsibilities.

As discussed in Chapter 2, the directors of a regulated legal entity fall squarely within the governing function significant influence category and as such are subject to the "significant influence" Principles (Principles 5–7), in addition to their common law duties and obligations as directors. Whilst not necessarily expected to have day-to-day management of the business themselves (APER 4.6.11G), directors are required to follow the same principles of delegation and supervision as other significant influence functions. This means that a director who disregards an issue once delegated or fails to take reasonable steps to maintain an appropriate level of understanding about an issue, may be in breach of the Principle 6 requirement to exercise due skill, care and diligence in managing the business of the firm (APER 4.6.7).

Moving down the chain of corporate governance, the next question might be whether there is a management committee which meets on a regular basis to monitor the operation of the business? Indeed, this management committee may be the "governing body" for regulatory purposes. In either case, it will be relevant to understand the relationship between the board and the management committee, including the delegation of powers from the board. The regulator would no doubt say that requisite documentation includes agendas and minutes of meetings. However, it may be that, as a practical matter, a fixed agenda and notes of follow up steps will be a more useful (and more easily attainable) set of documents to demonstrate appropriate systems and controls.

Next in the hierarchy is the Chief Executive function, defined by the FSA as the person who "alone or jointly with one or more others, under the immediate authority of the governing body, is responsible for the conduct of the whole of the business" (SUP 10.6.13G).

For each of the governing body, management committee and CEO, it is important to be sure that there is communication, including regular (scheduled) meetings with business and control function heads, to supervise the delegation of responsibilities to these individuals. It is important to address both business and non-business significant influence controlled functions. In each case there will be questions about the required level of formality and documentation of the content of these meetings. If meetings are not documented, the governing body and CEO must be able to prove by other (documented) means that they are supervising their delegation and monitoring and controlling the business with adequate systems and controls.

The so called "systems and controls" significant influence functions (Finance, Risk Assessment, Internal Audit) (SUP 10.8) are defined as reporting to the governing body on their areas of responsibility. Indeed, the significant influence controlled functions are divided between those that report to the governing body as part of the SUP definition (also including Compliance) and those which do not. The fact that not all controlled functions are perceived by the regulator (in the Approved Persons definitions) as having to report to the governing body/CEO does not discharge the responsibilities of the governing body/CEO in respect of delegation and supervision of functions, though it may allow additional flexibility in management.

Audit committees are suggested in the guidance (SYSC 3.2.15G) as a means of "examining management's process for ensuring the appropriateness of systems and controls". Such committees (often including "compliance" as part of the title and remit) can be a useful means of reporting on systems and controls and issues arising for non-business functions. For firms which have or are planning to create an audit committee to achieve or formalise SYSC compliance, forging the link back to each of the governing body, CEO and business head significant influence functions is key to demonstrating control and achieving maximum regulatory credit for effective controls.

Possibly the most difficult aspect of SYSC is achieving the balance between the additional documentation and formalisation of "management meetings" and the informal and "hands-on" management style to which many financial services firms would point as contributing to their success. It is also true to say that the "old boys network" or partnership mentality is under challenge from the determination of the regulator to translate management into organisational structures and documentation. The record keeping requirements of SYSC are discussed in Section 3.4.2.

3.3.3 Sharing and delegating responsibility

3.3.3.1 Sharing responsibility
Can more than one individual be "responsible" for a single significant influence controlled function? The FSA, in its frequently asked questions table (SYSC 2.1.6(3)G), suggests that the allocation function will likely be performed by one or two individuals only, compatible with delivering compliance with Principle 3, the apportionment requirement and the systems and controls requirement. It is worth remembering this when considering the allocation of individuals to other significant influence controlled functions. If the FSA believes that only one or two individuals should share the most senior role, it seems unlikely that they will welcome multiple individuals doing any of the other significant influence functions. By identifying more than two individuals for any role, a firm is imposing a further layer of "proof" on itself, namely to prove that responsibility is properly and completely allocated. Where functions are jointly performed the importance of effective communication between parties is paramount. If things "fall between the cracks", then each of the joint delegates and the person delegating responsibility are in danger of not having achieved effective controls.

3.3.3.2   Delegating responsibility:
Is this permitted? After what seems to have been a lengthy battle, delegation has become an acceptable management tool. The three important features of acceptable delegation are:

* clarity about what has been delegated;
* appropriateness both in terms of nature of delegation and choice of delegate; and
* effective supervision.

Delegation is discussed at length throughout the "significant influence" Principles. The significant influence function individuals are left in no doubt that delegation carries with it significant supervisory responsibilities and that responsibility cannot be disposed of by delegation. This applies both to internal and external delegation and at all levels including the governing body, who in practice generally delegate responsibilities to the significant influence controlled functions.

The guidance also reminds Approved Persons in connection with external delegation that, "a firm cannot contract out its regulatory obligations". In other words, as with all other delegation, outsourcing creates a continuing obligation of assessment of suitability and supervision. It is not enough to leave the external contractor to its own devices. Outsourcing also includes inter-company delegation, both within the UK and overseas. Given the backdrop of Barings, this is hardly surprising and means that the UK based CEO/significant influence functions must consider how overseas offices (which are often separate legal entities) are performing the tasks delegated to them by the regulated UK entity. The detailed outsourcing rules set out in FSA's Prudential Standards for Banks, which are relevant to this issue and provide the only detailed guidance on the regulatory approach to outsourcing, are beyond the scope of this Chapter.

3.3.4   FSA guidance on areas covered by systems and controls

The FSA's guidance suggests consideration of several specific areas as follows:

* organisation,
* compliance,
* risk assessment,
* management information,
* employees and agents,

- audit (committee and internal audit),
- business strategy,
- remuneration policies,
- business continuity and records.

Addressing each in turn:

3.3.4.1 Organisation:

This is key to SYSC with the emphasis being on clarity and communi-cation – in the view of FSA, clear reporting lines and job responsibilities are central to achieving effective controls. This is reinforced by APER (*see* e.g. APER 4.5).

Given the significance which has been placed on the importance of front and back office segregation and the consequences of failure to segregate (not only in the Barings collapse), it is perhaps surprising that segrega-tion appears only as a guidance note in SYSC and is suggested only "where it is made possible and appropriate by the nature, scale and complexity of the business". Having said this, the responsibilities placed on each significant influence controlled function to organise their respec-tive business areas to achieve effective controls encourages active management consideration of this area.

In discussing organisation, brief mention should be made of "issue esca-lation". This is not mentioned in its own right in SYSC, but is a theme of many provisions, including organisation (SYSC 3.2.3(5)G), Principle 6, suitability of individuals (APER 4.5.14G) and delegation (APER 4.6.13G). Part of effective organisation and control is an effective and well under-stood mechanism for identifying and resolving issues in a timely manner.

3.3.4.2 Compliance

A required function which must be allocated to a senior person with direct reporting to the governing body. The compliance officer is respons-ible for oversight of the firm's compliance with, at a minimum, the FSA's Conduct of Business and Collective Investment Scheme Rules. Together with the newly created apportionment and oversight responsibility, this position seems destined to be the focus of immediate regulatory attention when things go wrong. It should provide some comfort to compliance officers that each significant influence function will be subject to Principle 7, which requires each such individual to take reasonable steps to ensure that their business is compliant. Whilst taking steps through a compli-ance department will satisfy this requirement, this is only going to be so if it was reasonable to rely on (delegate to) the compliance function.

Resourcing the compliance department is an issue. There is express reference to ensuring that a delegate has the time to deal with the issue delegated. It will be important to demonstrate that senior managers are aware of and involved in the compliance effort as it relates to their business.

3.3.4.3   Risk assessment

Managing risk is mentioned but not elaborated in SYSC. "Risk assessment" is identified as a potential controlled function and defined in SUP as the function responsible for "setting and controlling risk exposure". This is expressly linked to credit and market risk in the accompanying guidance (SUP 10.8.5G). There is no broader concept of operational risk introduced into these provisions. This contrasts with the Turnbull report which approaches risk assessment as an integral part of internal controls. The appendix to the Turnbull report contains a set of questions for the board, entitled "Assessing the effectiveness of the company's risk and control processes". This provides a useful framework for a broader risk assessment exercise.

3.3.4.4   Management information

Management information is described as information the governing body needs to play its part in identifying, measuring, managing and controlling risks of regulatory concern. SYSC 3.2.11G, picking up on the language of the Turnbull report, says that management information should be "relevant, reliable and timely". There is no indication of the level of detail required to be contained in management information for the governing body/senior managers. However, it is envisaged that significant influence functions will have sufficient information to enable them to maintain an understanding about an issue or part of the business and that failure to do so will be regarded by the FSA as evidence of breach of Principle 6 (APER 4.6.6E). This is a clear indication that significant influence functions must keep themselves informed. The provisions provide the response to the senior manager who says "but I didn't know ...."; that "you should have". Personal culpability for the significant influence functions will be determined based on the knowledge that an individual had, or should have had, of regulatory concerns arising in the business under his control (APER 3.3.1(5)E).

Preparations for compliance with SYSC may well include reviewing available management information and considering with management whether they are seeing all that they need to see to enable them to effectively manage the business and satisfy this standard.

3.3.4.5   Employees and agents

Systems and controls are required to address the suitability and competence of employees. Although the human resources function ("HR") does not expressly feature in SYSC, this is one of the areas where HR most obviously has a part to play in SYSC compliance. The HR function should not be ignored when considering the wider HR risks of the very labour intensive financial services business. The training and competence regime, beyond the scope of this Chapter, reinforces this aspect.

Where there are employee performance issues, there are already tensions between regulatory and employment law issues. These may be magnified by the additional supervisory responsibility for the conduct of those whom a senior manager supervises, requiring the supervisor to assess individual performance and make decisions which may have personal consequences for the supervisor, about whether to allow individuals to remain in a position.

3.3.4.6   Internal audit function

The internal audit function is charged with the task of monitoring the appropriateness and effectiveness of systems and controls (SYSC 3.2.16G). There is important guidance at SUP 10.8.7G which notes that internal audit becoming a controlled function "does not require the person performing the function to have any special obligation towards FSA (such as reporting directly on matters to the FSA) nor will this cause FSA to call for internal audit reports as a matter of routine". It is helpful to have this in writing, although the reality for some time (and certainly post Barings) has been that when something goes wrong, there is an expectation that the FSA will ask for internal audit reports. If the internal audit function has highlighted issues which have not been followed up, then potentially both the internal audit function and other governing and management significant influence functions will be caught in the regulatory net.

3.3.4.7   Business strategy

In much the same away as for management information, an up-to-date business strategy is suggested (SYSC 3.2.17G) as a means of identifying, measuring and managing risks of regulatory concern. This is reinforced in APER 4.5.10G, where it is noted that strategy and plans will often dictate the risk which the business in prepared to take on. If the strategy of the business is to enter high risk areas, then, the guidance continues, the degree of control and strength of monitoring reasonably required will be high. Failing to exercise this degree of control may amount to conduct below that which would be "reasonable in all the circumstances" (APER 3.1.4G). The practical message is that, if a business strategy is high risk, then the infrastructure for controlling that risk needs to be developed at the outset.

3.3.4.8 Remuneration policies

Described in SYSC as the concern to manage the tension between complying with rules and the personal advantage of employees. This encompasses both the "star culture" issue of high earning individuals not being subject to rigorous scrutiny and the question of controlling employees remunerated directly according to volume of business done, where the regulatory fear is of motivation to do the business at any cost. All approved persons will be subject to Principles 1–4, which include the requirement to act with integrity and provide the regulator with a direct remedy against each individual for breach. In addition, significant influence functions are cautioned against giving undue weight to the financial performance of an individual or group when deciding, for example, whether to take disciplinary action against an individual (APER 4.5.14G). Regulated firms should be spreading the message that an individual's compliance attitude is a factor to be considered as part of personal performance. Remuneration committees have an important role to play in ensuring that this aspect is factored in to decisions about compensation. Indeed, these may be one of the significant committees whose meetings come under greater scrutiny under the new regime.

3.3.4.9 Business continuity

Can the firm continue to function and meet its regulatory obligations in the event of unforeseen interruption? As this Guide was going to print, the terrible events of 11 September 2001 were reverberating around the globe. It is a tribute to the determination and professionalism of the many thousands of financial services employees in the US and throughout the world that the financial services system remained intact. In making business continuity plans ("BCPs"), practitioners had previously thought that the Y2K effort would be our biggest challenge. It is immensely sad that this was not the case. In consequence, BCPs are now firmly back in the regulatory sights as firms review infrastructure and operations against further unforeseen events.

3.3.4.10 Records

Record keeping is one of the key areas of focus of SYSC and has potentially the most significant practical impact on the management of financial services institutions. The record keeping requirements of SYSC are considered in Section 3.4.2.

3.4   Practical implications of SYSC

3.4.1   *The language of regulation*

It is worth commenting on the language of SYSC – "adequate", "appropriate", "effective", "reasonable". These "high level" subjective indicators provide little guidance for firms and senior managers. The new lexicon of the regulator has yet to be translated into practice.

The way in which standards are developed from these words will set the tone of formality which the regulator is seeking from SYSC. At a time when risk assessment is being adopted by FSA as the means of regulating in the new millennium, it would be unfortunate if SYSC came to represent form over substance in regulation because firms did not match up to a formalistic concept of documented management controls envisaged by the regulator. We are assured by the FSA that this will not happen and it is true that the rules do leave open the option of pragmatic interpretation.

3.4.2   *Record keeping*

The obligations to keep records of the three requirements of SYSC are set out in SYSC 2.2.1R and SYSC 3.2.20R. These record keeping provisions were much discussed during the consultation stage (*see* e.g. the Policy Statement: High Level Standards: Issues arising from CP 35 and 26, June 2000, paragraphs 4.40, 4.41, 4.98 and 4.99. "It is not the FSA's intention to impose on firms a new obligation to document or record every decision.")

For apportionment and allocation requirements, guidance on what might amount to "appropriate" records suggests:

(a)   organisational charts and diagrams;
(b)   project management documents;
(c)   job descriptions; and
(d)   committee constitutions and terms of reference ("provided they show a clear description of the firms major functions").

These suggestions seem straightforward and indeed such documents will exist in many regulated firms. However, not every firm manages itself through formal document creation and there will be practical issues associated with the documentation requirements of SYSC.

A few observations on the above categories of documents:

3.4.2.1 Organisational charts and diagrams

These sound deceptively simple and, at a high level, can probably be readily created (if they do not currently exist) and provide a useful summary of management control. However, the financial services industry is a notoriously flighty one in terms of job mobility both within and between financial institutions. In practice, organisational charts can change with alarming regularity, especially in high mobility periods (post bonus or buoyant market conditions).

It may be practical in response to a heightened focus on documenting systems and controls, to institute a formal review or collection of organisational charts on a periodic, fixed basis, for example, at month end, by requiring that these be delivered to a central function. The task of keeping detailed organisational charts up to date should not be underestimated, particularly following the annual year-end promotion process.

Organisation charts also imply clear reporting lines and supervisory responsibilities both of which are an important part of demonstrating compliance with SYSC/APER. The "dotted line" or "communications line" needs to be understood and distinguished from the actual reporting line in order to achieve the effective controls required by Principle 5 (Implementing confusing or uncertain reporting lines does not, in the opinion of the FSA, comply with Principle 5). Dual reporting is not prohibited, but this creates a greater need to ensure that responsibility and accountability is clearly set out and understood (APER 4.5.12G) and *see* Section 3.3.3 on sharing responsibility.

3.4.2.2 Job descriptions

Who should have a written job description and how far into an individual's detailed job functions should or can a job description go? There are two aspects of regulatory job descriptions:

- senior management apportionment; and
- demonstrating effective controls at all levels.

Addressing the first aspect, SYSC suggests job descriptions as a means of documenting the clear and appropriate apportionment of significant responsibilities among senior managers. This suggests a 'regulatory job description', setting out for each significant influence function the area for which they have regulatory responsibilities. Note also that SUP

10.9.8R requires brief details of the job performed by each significant management function to be provided to the FSA on an annual basis. As regulation is by legal entity and each legal entity needs to formally approve its significant influence controlled functions, this may result in separate regulatory job descriptions for each individual by legal entity.

The second category is more difficult. Every approved person is subject to Principles 1–4. In addition, the Principles impose specific management responsibilities on significant influence functions in respect of the area of business of the firm for which they are responsible. This includes taking reasonable steps to ensure that the business is organised so it can be controlled effectively (Principle 5). The Code identifies implementing confusing or uncertain job descriptions as evidence of conduct not complying with Principle 5. To require a detailed, tailored job description for each individual Approved Person would not seem to add much in terms of control. By contrast, the task of creating a tailored job description for each individual would seem to impose an onerous administrative burden on firms. The FSA, have acknowledged the difficulty of imposing an absolute requirement to have job descriptions in their High Level Standards Policy Statement (June 2000) The guidance on job descriptions in the Code (APER 4.5.13G) says that "it may be appropriate for each member of staff to have a job description of which he is aware". This is an area of SYSC where regulatory interpretation will show whether there is an excess of form over substance. The regulator has been asking for job descriptions for many years. It will be interesting to see whether FSA now points to SYSC as requiring job descriptions and what will be the industry response. Will an industry practice develop of creating a regulatory job description for the significant influence functions or all functions; and if so, will these be uniform across the industry leading to a "best practice" standard not currently existing? Whatever the response, the industry needs to figure out generally how to demonstrate that individuals know what their job is. It is not immediately obvious that written job descriptions are the most practical response.

3.4.2.3 Project management documents

It is not clear what the FSA have in mind here. Possibly they envisage senior managers "monitoring and controlling" the firm by project planning; possibly this is a reference to implementing new initiatives. The former does not immediately suggest itself as a practical control mechanism; the latter is likely happening in a documented fashion already, at least for projects which require the commitment of firm resources. This may be an area where there is little or no change.

3.4.2.4 *Committee constitutions and terms of reference*

It is a useful exercise to build a picture of significant management committees. However, this is not always as straightforward an exercise as might initially be assumed. When is a committee a management committee? Who forms committees? Often groups begin to meet on an ad hoc basis and gradually take on an importance and decision making capacity not envisaged at the outset. Such groups may often be dynamic and valuable management vehicles. It would be unfortunate if these benefits were lost through over formalisation. It is equally the case that firms should be aware of where the decisions are being made and that power is properly delegated from the correct source. The meaning of the proviso that such documents should "show a clear description of the firm's major functions" is unclear.

3.4.2.5 *Procedures manuals and documented procedures*

These are a much discussed topic within the industry, raising the perennial question of how to record what is done in a useful way which is informative and clear without creating a rod for your own back. It is interesting that SYSC does not impose a requirement of written procedures, other than for the (required) compliance function (SYSC 3.2.6G) and the (suggested) risk assessment function (SYSC 3.2.10G). In both cases, SYSC provides that the "organisation and responsibilities" should be documented.

For the systems and controls provisions, the rules require "adequate" records of systems and controls (SYSC 3.2.20R). Ironically, fewer documents are listed here. Those specifically mentioned in Chapter 3.2 are management information and business plans, considered above in Section 3.3.4.

Finally on the subject of documents, a word on document retention policies. The rules provide that records made to satisfy the apportionment and allocation requirements must be retained for six years "from the date on which [*they*] were superseded by a more up to date record". Six years is the general civil liability limitation period in England.

SYSC 3.2.20R is more general. "Adequate" records must be made and retained of "matters and dealings which are the subject of requirements and standards under the regulatory system. Further, SYSC 3.2.21G suggests that, in general, records should be retained "for as long as is relevant for the purposes for which they are made". This is not helpful. Of course there are many specific document retention rules throughout the Handbook, but for the avoidance of doubt and dispute about what was a relevant period, firms would be well advised to review document retention policies and adopt a fixed document retention period.

3.4.3   Legal entity versus product line

SYSC places responsibility both on the legal entity and its significant influence individuals to organise the firm effectively on a legal entity basis. The rules do not talk of organising by business area. However, the FSA says that "the FSA's senior management regime is designed to be consistent with the operation of matrix management structures in international corporate groups" (FSA Handbook Development, Special Edition, June 2000). The example given there concerns the apportionment and oversight function and envisages an overseas head of group becoming the apportionment and oversight controlled function within the UK regulatory regime.

In examining the other controlled functions, the tensions between matrix and legal entity management and, in particular, management and reporting lines across these different structures, becomes more apparent. The prospect of registering a large number of overseas individuals as significant influence functions because they are the "global heads" of product or control functions is not an attractive one – for firms, individuals or regulators. In fact, the FSA envisages that only a few firms will register significant influence management functions on the basis that generally the governing, required and significant influence functions will exercise all significant influence at a senior level (SUP 10.9.2G). Where the firm is matrix managed on product lines, this would seem to lead to more rather than less registrations.

The FSA claims a certain amount of extraterritorial power, in particular concerning the registration of overseas personnel. Whilst it is not clear upon what legal basis the FSA will pursue overseas personnel, it does seem obvious that registering such individuals will give the FSA at least a starting point to assert jurisdiction. Perhaps recognising the inherent difficulties of this situation, the FSA has encouraged registration of senior managers within the UK wherever possible. In principle, it seems correct that somebody in the UK is responsible for the operation of the business operating within the UK. In order to accommodate this within group structures, the FSA have indicated that the senior manager (overseas) advising on strategy can be distinguished from the senior manager in the UK who has responsibility for day-to-day management. It is this latter individual who should be registered (SUP 10.7.4G, 10.7.7G, 10.9.5G).

Whilst this is not a bar to overseas reporting lines, the registered significant influence functions will wish to consider very carefully the scope of the businesses for which they are personally responsible. It is not difficult to envisage group or divisional policy decisions for example, a headcount freeze, impacting on the UK significant influence function ability to delegate or resolve issues, with potential consequences in terms of personal liability.

3.4.4 Is FSA approach to risk assessment compatible with SYSC?

The FSA's approach to supervision is set out in Chapter 1 of the Supervisory Manual. SUP 1.1.4G explains that the FSA aims to focus and reinforce the responsibility of the management of each firm to ensure that it takes reasonable care to organise and control the affairs of the firm responsibly and effectively and develops and maintains adequate risk management systems. The FSA have adopted a "risk-based" approach to supervision, in order to focus the FSA's resources on the mitigation of risks to the regulatory objectives, using a "standard risk assessment process" (SUP1.3.2G).

The FSA identifies several categories of risk, including: those which arise from the firm's strategy, business risk (including operational risk) and the internal systems and controls and the compliance culture of the firm. It seems likely that, in seeking to determine the adequacy of a firm's systems and controls, the FSA will be guided by the provisions of SYSC in determining what is an "appropriate" set of controls for each firm.

The FSA have assured the industry, for example in the June 2000 Handbook Development Special Edition, that they "will not second guess firms' choice of means as long as the chosen means can be expected to be reasonably efficacious". Provided that the new approach to supervision does not degenerate into a "box ticking" exercise, then there is scope for supervisory risk review to enhance the industry interpretation of SYSC in a way beneficial to both the regulator and the industry.

3.5 Conclusions

SYSC is seeking to impose more formality into the structure of financial services management. If implemented by regulators who are mindful of the real constraints on businesses and the importance of preserving flexibility and creativity at a management level, then SYSC brings with it the prospect of real improvements in the quality of management. There remains the danger of form over substance – a danger of which the regulator is both acutely aware and anxious to dispel concern. Ultimately, time will tell.

It is clear from what has been written in this and other Chapters that SYSC is focused on individual management responsibility and account-ability. The negative stance of the Code and its examples of what is not in compliance with the Principles contrasts with the positive framework of "questions for the board" contained in the appendix to the Turnbull report. The practical challenge in difficult markets is to adopt the positive stance and view these changes as an opportunity to enhance manage-ment, rather than a further cost of doing business. Senior management buy in to SYSC will be the key to its success.

Chapter 4

Rules Applicable to Corporate Finance Activities

John Bennett
Partner
Berwin Leighton Paisner

4.1 Introduction

The Financial Services and Markets Act 2000 (the "FSMA") prohibits a person from carrying on a regulated activity in the UK, or purporting to do so, unless authorised or exempt for the purposes of the FSMA (Section 19 FSMA). Any contravention of this general prohibition is a criminal offence (Section 23 FSMA) and resulting agreements are unenforceable (Section 26 FSMA) unless the court orders otherwise (Section 28 FSMA). The FSA can also obtain injunctions restraining breaches, ordering steps to be taken to remedy breaches and preventing disposals of assets (Section 380 FSMA).

An authorised person must comply to some degree, depending on the circumstances, with the rules and statements of principle set out in the FSA Handbook, including the Principles for Businesses and Conduct of Business Rules. In general, private persons (defined in the Financial Services and Markets Act 2000 (Rights of Action) Regulations 2001) who suffer loss because of a breach of a rule have a right of action for damages and the Treasury can specify particular rules which, if contravened, would be actionable by any person (Section 150 FSMA). Breach of an FSA rule is not in itself an offence and a breach does not itself make any transaction void or unenforceable (Section 151 FSMA).

Individuals who carry out specified controlled functions within authorised firms require prior approval from the FSA and are subject to the approved persons regime. This is dealt with in Chapter 2 of the book and is set out in the Handbook in the Statements of Principle and Code of Practice for Approved Persons and is backed by disciplinary sanctions.

The FSMA also contains a provision which prohibits any person, in the course of business, from communicating an invitation or inducement to engage in investment activity (known as a financial promotion) unless he is an authorised person or the content of the communication is approved by an authorised person (Section 21 FSMA). Breach of Section 21 FSMA, in addition to giving rise to civil liabilities, constitutes a criminal offence.

One of the most significant developments introduced by the FSMA is the creation of the market abuse regime (Section 118 FSMA). The new regime is designed to protect the UK's financial markets against market manipulators and insider dealers. It supplements, rather than replaces, the criminal offences of insider dealing, misleading statements and market manipulation. Although the market abuse provisions are not restricted to the regulated community, they are very relevant to those engaged in corporate finance activities (*See* Chapter 8 below).

4.2 Regulated activities

4.2.1 *General prohibition*

A person is prohibited from carrying on a regulated activity in the UK, or purporting to do so, unless authorised or exempt for the purposes of the FSMA (Section 19 FSMA). This is known as the "general prohibition".

4.2.2 *Territorial application of the general prohibition*

The FSMA has "inward application" to the carrying on of regulated activities in the UK from overseas. Overseas persons who carry on regulated activities in the UK therefore need to be authorised unless an exemption or exclusion applies. There is an exclusion for overseas persons contained in Article 72 Financial Services and Markets Act 2000 (Regulated Activities) Order 2001 (SI 2001/544) ("Regulated Activities Order"). This exclusion applies in two broad circumstances:

(a) the activities of dealing and arranging deals in investments are excluded so long as the business is conducted with or through an authorised person or a person with an appropriate exemption; and
(b) the activities of dealing and arranging deals in investments, managing investments or giving investment advice (among other things) are excluded where the overseas person has not solicited the business, or has solicited it in compliance with appropriate financial promotion rules.

Section 31 FSMA does provide for the automatic authorisation of:

(a)   firms "passporting" into the UK under a single market directive (e.g. the Investment Services Directive (Schedule 3 FSMA); and

(b)   firms exercising rights under the Treaty of Rome. Such firms are defined as persons whose head office is situated in an EEA state, other than the UK, who are recognised under the laws of that state as its national and who have been authorised under equivalent laws of their home state to carry on regulated activities (Schedule 4 FSMA),

provided that certain conditions are met and certain notifications are given to the FSA.

In certain respects, the FSMA has "outward application". Under Section 418 FSMA, a person who would not otherwise be regarded as carrying on a regulated activity in the UK will be so regarded if:

(a)   his registered office is in the UK, he is entitled to exercise passporting rights under a single market directive as a UK firm and he is carrying on a regulated activity to which that single market directive applies in another EEA state; or

(b)   his registered office is in the UK, he is the manager of a collective investment scheme which is the subject of particular Community rights and persons in another EEA state are invited to participate in the scheme; or

(c)   his registered office is in the UK and the day-to-day management of the relevant activity is the responsibility of his UK registered office or another establishment maintained by him in the UK; or

(d)   his head office is not in the UK but the activity is carried on from an establishment maintained by him in the UK.

4.2.3   Scope of regulation

An activity will be a "regulated activity" under the FSMA (Section 22) if:

(a)   it is an activity of a kind specified by the Treasury in secondary legislation; and

(b)   it is carried on by way of business; and

(c)   it relates to an investment of a specified kind.

The Treasury has specified the scope of regulated activities and investments in the Regulated Activities Order.

4.2.4   *The Regulated Activities Order*

Regulated Activities include

(a)   dealing in investments as principal or as agent;
(b)   arranging deals in investments;
(c)   managing investments;
(d)   safeguarding and administering investments;
(e)   sending de-materialised instructions;
(f)   establishing, operating or winding-up collective investment schemes;
(g)   advising on investments; and
(h)   agreeing to carry on any of these activities (except establishing, operating or winding-up collective investment schemes).

However, offering to carry out any of these activities is not a regulated activity. Instead, this is now caught by the restrictions on making financial promotions.

4.2.5   *Excluded activities*

Exclusions which may be relevant to corporate finance activities include:

(a)   *Dealing with or through an authorised person.* A person dealing as agent through an authorised person will not need to be authorised where the transaction is entered into on advice given to the principal by an authorised person or where the agent not been asked for, or has declined to give advice and has recommended that the principal seek advice from an authorised person. Furthermore, the agent must not receive any reward from a third party for which he has not accounted to the principal arising out of the transaction (Article 22 Regulated Activities Order). This exclusion may, for example, be of assistance in relation to the establishment of cheap dealing facilities for small shareholders;

(b)   *Absence of holding-out.* The exclusion which applies to dealing as principal provided there is no "holding-out" has been slightly narrowed so that anyone who underwrites investments and hold himself out as engaged in the business of underwriting investments will be carrying on a regulated activity (Article 15 Regulated Activities Order).

Other exclusions cover: trustees, nominees and personal representatives; activities carried on in the course of a profession or non-investment business; activities carried on in connection with the sale of goods or supply of services; groups and joint enterprises; activities carried on in connection with employee share schemes; and overseas persons.

Article 70 Regulated Activities Order contains a "corporate finance" exclusion for activities carried on in connection with the sale of a body corporate. The exclusion applies to dealings as principal and as agent and also to arranging deals and giving advice in connection with a transaction. The exclusion applies where either:

(a)   the shares being sold (or the shares held by the purchaser together with the shares being sold) comprise 50 per cent or more (previously 75 per cent) of the voting shares and the sale is between two parties each of whom is a body corporate, a partnership, a single individual or a group of connected individuals (as defined in Article 73); or

(b)   the object of the transaction may reasonably be regarded as being the acquisition of day-to-day control of the affairs of the body corporate. This is an alternative exclusion and may be relied on in circumstances where the conditions set out in (a) above are not met.

When an investment firm provides certain services (ie dealing in investments as principal or agent, arranging deals in investments and managing investments under Article 37) to third parties on a professional basis and in doing so would be treated as carrying on a regulated activity but for any of the exclusions dealing with absence of holding out, activities carried on in connection with the sale of goods or supply of services, groups and joint enterprises and activities carried on in connection with the sale of a body corporate, those exclusions are to be disregarded (and, accordingly, the investment firm is to be treated as carrying on the regulated activity in question). Subject to certain exceptions, an investment firm is defined for this purpose as a person whose regular business is the provision of core investment services to third parties on a professional basis.

4.2.6   Specified investments

Part III Regulated Activities Order specifies the investments which are relevant in determining whether a person is carrying on a regulated activity. These include, for example:

(a)   shares;

(b)   debentures, loans, bonds, certificates of deposit and other instruments creating or acknowledging indebtedness;

(c)   warrants and other instruments entitling the holders to subscribe for any of the foregoing investments;
(d)   certificates representing certain securities;
(e)   options to acquire or dispose of specified investments;
(f)   futures;
(g)   contracts for differences; and
(h)   any right to or interest in any of these investments.

4.2.7   By way of business test

An activity is only a regulated activity if it is carried on "by way of business" (Section 22 FSMA). The Treasury is given the power under Section 419 FSMA to specify the circumstances in which a person will be regarded as carrying on a regulated activity by way of business. Pursuant to this power they have issued the Financial Services and Markets Act 2000 (Carrying on Regulated Activities by way of Business) Order 2001 (SI 2001/1177) ("Business Order").

Article 3 of the Business Order is the principal provision and its effect is that a person is not to be regarded as carrying on by way of business an activity to which the Article applies unless he carries on the business of engaging in any one or more of such activities. The activities covered by Article 3 include: dealing in investments as principal or agent; arranging deals in investments; managing investments; safeguarding and administering investments; sending de-materialised instructions; advising on investments; and agreeing to do any of these activities. Isolated transactions, especially if not for commercial purposes, are unlikely to constitute carrying on the business of engaging in any such activity.

Whether or not an activity is carried on by way of business is ultimately a question of judgment that takes account of several factors none of which is likely to be conclusive. These include the degree of continuity, the existence of a commercial element, the scale of activity and the proportion the activity bears to the other activities carried on by the same person but which are not regulated.

4.3   Authorisation

A firm seeking to carry on regulated activities has to apply to the FSA to obtain permission for each of those regulated activities and any person who is granted such permission by the FSA is authorised. In addition to completing the required application forms, an applicant is required to satisfy the "threshold conditions" (these require the applicant to be fit and proper and to have adequate resources). The detail of how the FSA will exercise its authorisation functions are contained in the Handbook's Authorisation Manual.

Individuals who carry out specified controlled functions within authorised firms require prior approval from the FSA. The FSA's implementing rules divide the controlled functions into "governing functions", "required functions", "systems and controls functions", "significant management functions" and "customer functions". The detail of the approved persons regime is set out in Statements of Principle and the Code of Practice for Approved Persons. The FSA will be concerned to ensure that each of the relevant individuals is fit and proper to perform the relevant functions.

4.4   Corporate Finance

4.4.1   What is it?

There is no definition of corporate finance activities in the FSMA nor does the expression have a clear and unambiguous meaning to those involved in the financial services sector. Corporate finance activities may typically take one or more of the following forms:

(a) underwriting a public or private primary or secondary offering of investments or arranging underwriting/sub-underwriting;

(b) as agent, offering to buy or sell the entire share capital or a stake in the share capital of listed and unlisted companies including arranging management buy-outs and buy-ins;

(c) arranging for a company's securities to be offered to existing members/creditors or taken up through a private placement, arranging for another person to buy, sell or subscribe for a particular investment;

(d) advising a company or any other person in relation to a public or private primary or secondary offering of investments, the acquisition or disposal of the entire share capital or a stake in the share capital of listed and unlisted companies or an offer to buy or sell securities;

(e) arranging for a company's securities to be listed or dealt in on or off exchange;

(f) preparing and/or issuing listing particulars, a prospectus, public offer document, business plan or other document describing or relating to any person, its business and/or its securities (in the case of a body corporate) and issuing and approving any other financial promotion;

(g) appointing persons who are to provide professional services to a company in connection with the raising of finance (typically lawyers, accountants, stockbrokers or merchant bankers); and

(h) identifying, introducing and/or negotiating with potential purchasers or sources of funding.

4.4.2 *Regulation of corporate finance activities*

Clearly the FSMA's remit extends to a number of these activities either because they are regulated activities or covered by the financial promotions regime. The extent to which the activities of persons who carry on a corporate finance business constitute regulated activities will depend on their precise individual nature and scope. There is a possibility that they may amount to dealing or arranging deals in investments or giving investment advice. Although it may be possible to set up a business providing corporate finance services in such a way as to avoid the need for regulation, the activities of such a firm would be limited and the firm would have to implement a compliance programme in order to ensure that it did not at any time contravene the general prohibition. In practice, most firms carrying on "corporate finance activities" will seek authorisation even if this is on a precautionary basis.

Whether an activity constitutes a regulated activity is of relevance even for firms who are authorised. This is because the FSA may have given permission only to carry on certain regulated activities, and an activity outside the scope of such authorisation would contravene Section 20 FSMA which provides that a firm must not carry on regulated activities that fall outside its permission. A firm that does so has not committed a criminal offence and resulting transactions are not unenforceable, but the firm does risk disciplinary action. Contravention may also result in damages at the suit of any private person, or fiduciary acting for a private person, if they suffer loss as a result. Therefore, each authorised firm needs to review its current and anticipated regulated activities and ensure that these match the scope of its permission.

If an activity is not a regulated activity and if any financial promotion issued falls within an exemption from the financial promotion restriction, the practical effect for an authorised person is generally to disapply the rules set out in the Conduct of Business sourcebook in relation to such activities since these generally apply only to business which is investment business and certain related activities.

More detailed analysis of the extent to which corporate finance activities may be regulated is set out below:

4.4.2.1 *Dealing in investments*

A person is dealing in investments if he buys, sells, subscribes for or underwrites investments or agrees to do so, either as principal or as an agent. Typically, this includes a person who acts as a market-maker in a company's securities, who underwrites share offers or a person to whom shares are allotted with a view to that person making an offer for sale. Where persons are dealing in investments solely for their own account (rather than as an agent) it is possible that their activities will be excluded under Article 15 Regulated Activities Order unless they:

(a) act as a market-maker in those securities;
(b) hold themselves out as engaging in the business of buying securities of the kind to which the transaction relates with a view to selling them or of underwriting securities of that kind; or
(c) regularly solicit members of the public for the purposes of inducing them, as principals or agents, to buy, sell, subscribe for or underwrite securities.

4.4.2.2 *Arranging deals in investments*

Under Article 25 Regulated Activities Order, a person is arranging deals in investments if he agrees to make:

(a) arrangements with a view to another person buying, selling, subscribing for or underwriting a particular investment; or
(b) arrangements with a view to a person who participates in the arrangements buying, selling, subscribing for or underwriting investments.

Paragraph (a) above is concerned with arrangements made with respect to individual investment transactions. Paragraph (b) on the other hand, is concerned with arrangements of an ongoing nature. By way of example, the arrangements envisaged under an agreement made by a tied agent with an investment product provider pursuant to which the agent will, from time to time, procure business for the product provider will fall within the scope of paragraph (b). The agent will then, in the course of such arrangements, make arrangements falling within paragraph (a) each time he brings about a particular investment transaction for a customer with the product provider. Generally speaking, corporate finance business will be more concerned with paragraph (a) because corporate finance services will usually be concerned with the buying/selling of a particular investment such as the securities of a corporate client. Article 25 is subject to various Articles excluding certain activities from its scope. Those likely to be most relevant in the context of a corporate finance business are referred to in the following paragraphs.

Where a firm makes arrangements of any kind in relation to a particular investment it will be necessary to determine whether the firm's involvement brings about the transaction to which the arrangements relate. If they do not bring about the transaction, then the arrangements will not be regarded as regulated activities (Article 26 Regulated Activities Order). A firm is only likely to bring about an investment transaction if its involvement in the chain of events leading to the transaction is of sufficient importance that without that involvement, the transaction would not take place. This requires something more than the mere giving of advice (although such advice may amount to advising on investments regulated by Article 53 Regulated Activities Order – *see* below).

Whether or not a corporate finance firm is bringing about a particular investment transaction will depend upon the full extent of its involvement and the context in which the arrangements were made. It is possible to identify a few activities each of which, taken in isolation, may be regarded as unlikely to bring about a particular transaction although were any of these to be performed in accompaniment with other activities the total effect may be to bring about the transaction. These activities include:

(a)   appointing professional advisors;
(b)   preparing a prospectus/business plan; and
(c)   identifying potential purchasers or sources of funding.

Examples of arrangements which would be likely to bring about particular investment transactions (whether alone or in accompaniment with other activities) include:

(a)   assisting investors/subscribers to complete and submit application forms;
(b)   receiving application forms (whether or not along with cash payments) for processing/checking and/or onward transmission (e.g. to the company or its registrars, bankers or receiving agents);

(c)   negotiating terms for an investment (including an underwriting agreement) between the corporate client and a potential source of funding;

(d)   acting as an intermediary between a corporate client and a potential purchaser or source of funding to whom an introduction has been made; and

(e)   effecting a placement of securities with investors/institutions.

Paragraph (b) of Article 25 is much broader in scope than paragraph (a) and does not have the "bring-about" requirement. However, it is not likely to apply to ongoing arrangements made by a corporate finance firm where its corporate client is the only person participating in the arrangements and, in doing so, will be issuing securities. This is because the corporate client will not itself participate in the arrangements with a view to buying, selling, subscribing for or underwriting investments. In order for such a corporate finance firm to be arranging deals within the scope of paragraph (b), therefore, he must be making ongoing arrangements with its corporate client with a view to that client buying, selling (not issuing), subscribing for or underwriting investments. Alternatively, he must be making ongoing arrangements of some kind in which other parties take part with a view to their buying or selling or subscribing for or underwriting investments. This may arise, for example, where the corporate finance firm undertakes to other persons (i.e. it arranges) to provide them, from time to time, with details of prospective investment opportunities (by sending them new issue prospectuses or business plans). This is distinct from, for example, where a person merely maintains a list of potential recipients of prospectuses obtained from another source such as an association of venture capitalists or a purveyor of lists of potential investors because, in this case, there are no relevant arrangements. Where arrangements have been made, the corporate finance firm can be seen to be providing a service to the potential investors (keeping them informed of investment opportunities).

Article 28 Regulated Activities Order (Arranging transactions to which the arranger is a party) is designed to ensure that a person is not regarded as arranging deals in investments when he arranges a transaction to which he intends to be a party. However, on entering into such a transaction he may be dealing in investments as principal or agent. Where a corporate finance firm intends to subscribe for securities in a company and arranges to bring in other potential investors, this exclusion 28 will not apply to the arrangements if, as will usually be the case, the firm will not be a party to the transactions to be entered into between the other investors and the company.

There is an exclusion for a person who, for example, arranges for his corporate client to obtain bank financing which involves the bank acquiring a debenture over the company's assets.

Article 32 Regulated Activities Order (Provision of finance) excludes arrangements for the provision of finance to enable a person to buy, sell, subscribe for or underwrite investments. It applies only to ongoing arrangements of the type covered by paragraph (b) above. Where a person is arranging finance in relation to a particular investment transaction, it will be necessary to determine whether the arrangements he makes are such as to bring about the transaction. Furthermore, it is possible that firms whose ordinary business involves the provision of finance (such as a bank or other credit company) may be able to avail themselves of the exclusion contained in Article 67 for arrangements which are a necessary part of the provision of services in the course of any profession or business which does not otherwise consist of regulated activities.

The broad effect of Article 33 (Introducing) is to exclude arrangements which amount to introducing persons to an authorised or exempt person for the purpose providing independent advice or independent discretionary management services. It may therefore apply, to the extent that the arrangements might otherwise satisfy the terms of Article 25 (Arranging deals in investments), where a corporate finance firm introduces a corporate client to a stockbroker or merchant bank for advice in relation to the raising of finance. However, there must be arrangements of some kind in place pursuant to which introductions can take place. This exclusion will not be satisfied, for example, merely because the person who distributes a prospectus or business plan suggests that the recipient should seek independent financial advice before deciding whether to invest.

4.4.2.3   *Investment advice*
Investment advice is defined in Article 53 Regulated Activities Order as giving to persons in their capacity as investors, or as agents for investors, advice on the merits of their purchasing, selling, subscribing for or underwriting an investment or exercising any right conferred by an investment to acquire, dispose of, underwrite or convert an investment.

Therefore, for the provision of advice to constitute a regulated activity, it must:

(a)   be given to investors or their agents;
(b)   relate to the merits of their buying or selling etc; and
(c)   be in relation to a particular investment (as opposed to a class or type of investment).

Investment advice does not include general advice which does not apply to the provision of factual or technical information about companies or their securities where there is no actual or implied recommendation as to whether the securities should be bought, sold or held.

Advice corporate finance firms may provide to their client would not constitute investment advice if their clients received it in their capacity as issuers of securities (rather than as purchasers or sellers of investments) since they will not then be given the advice in the capacity of investor. However, were corporate finance firms, for example, to recommend investment in their corporate clients when effecting introductions to potential investors or sending out copies of their prospectuses, they are likely to be giving investment advice. Corporate finance firms may also be giving investment advice were they, for example, to give advice to the directors of a corporate client in their individual capacity on the merit of their subscribing for shares in their company.

4.4.2.4   *Mergers and acquisitions*
A corporate finance firm may assist its corporate client in connection with the sale or acquisition of a company or a substantial shareholding in another company. Whether or not this involvement will constitute a regulated activity will depend on similar considerations to those set out above, save that for the purposes of Article 53 Regulated Activities Order its corporate client will be acting as an investor (i.e. a purchaser or seller of investments) rather than as an issuer of securities. The firm may be able to rely on the exclusion in Article 70 for a person whose dealing, arranging or advising activities relate to a transaction which is intended to result in the change of control of a company from its existing proprietor to new proprietors. This is referred to in greater detail earlier in this chapter.

4.4.2.5   *Financial promotion*
A corporate finance firm may make contact with potential purchasers, vendors or sources of funding and may also from time to time be involved in issuing prospectuses, private placing documents, business plans and other communications aimed at securing a person's interest in an investment opportunity. Whether or not any such activities constitute regulated activities, the firm will need to bear in mind financial

promotion regime and will therefore need to be authorised or ensure that such communications are approved by an authorised person or that they are subject to an exemption.

There are numerous exemptions which may be relevant to corporate finance activities. These are set out in the Financial Services and Markets Act 2000 (Financial Promotions) Order 2001 (SI 2001/1335) ("Financial Promotions Order"). They cover, among other things, listing particulars and other documents permitted to be published by market rules and communications to certificated high net worth individuals, high net worth companies and certified sophisticated investors. There is also an exemption for communications relating to an offer of securities by a private company to persons with whom the company shares a common pre-existing interest and an exemption in respect of communications made in connection with the sale or purchase of a body corporate (which is similar to the equivalent exclusion from the regulated activities regime referred to above). Finally, there is an exemption for prospectuses and certain related advertisements issued in accordance with the Public Offers of Securities Regulations 1995.

4.4.3   Conduct of Business sourcebook

The Conduct of Business Sourcebook ("COBS") is part of the FSA Handbook of rules and guidance and sets out detailed conduct of business requirements for firms regulated by the FSA. COBS will apply, to some degree at least, to all firms carrying on regulated activities.

In general the COBS rules will apply to an authorised firm's provision of investment services to private and intermediate customers. The protections provided by the rules are not principally designed for business between market counterparties and will only apply to them where specified. All the COBS rules will apply to business with private customers. Many of the COBS rules will either not apply, or be limited in their application, to business with intermediate customers. Dealings between counterparties are governed by a new Code on inter-professional code.

Where the activity or service undertaken by a firm falls into the corporate finance business definition, the only provisions of COBS which will apply to those activities are those set out below.

4.4.4 Corporate finance business: applicable provisions of COBS

COBS reference	Subject
Chapter 1	Application and general provisions
2.1	Clear, fair and not misleading communication
2.2	Inducements and soft commission
2.3	Reliance on others
2.4	Chinese walls
2.5	Exclusion of liability
Chapter 3	Financial promotion, except COB 3.8.6G – COB 3.8.20G and COB 3.9
4.1	Client classification
5.3	Suitability
5.4	Customers' understanding of risk
7.1	Conflict of interest and material interest
7.12	Customer order and execution records
7.13	Personal account dealing
Chapter 9	Client assets

Importantly, there is no requirement for a client agreement and the know your customer, client suitability and best execution rules do not apply. Of the rules which do apply to corporate finance business the most important are those set out in Chapters 2 and 3 and Section 7.1.

The purpose of the rules in Chapter 2 is to set high level conduct of business requirements for all firms conducting designated investment business. The rules deal with the following matters:

(a) *fair and clear communication*. The rules are designed to give a customer the right to take action for a loss arising as a result of a firm breaching Principle 7 (Communications with clients) in the course of carrying on designated investment business; and

(b)   *inducements*. The rules are designed to ensure that a firm does not offer or accept an inducement to do business where this is likely significantly to conflict with the firm's duty, or the duty of the recipients of the inducement, to clients;

(c)   *reliance on others*. The rules clarify that a firm will be taken to be in compliance with the rules if it relies on others (e.g. in giving or receiving information through a client's agent) provided that it is acting reasonably in the circumstances.

Chapter 3 of COBS contains the rules for authorised persons on financial promotion. The rules apply to all authorised persons who communicate, or approve, a financial promotion. They do not apply to promotions made only to, or which may be reasonably regarded as directed at, market counterparties and intermediate customers. They are also disapplied for financial promotions in connection with a takeover subject to the Takeover Code or the requirements of another EEA state.

COBS makes various general rules on financial promotion which must be read in conjunction with more specific requirements. The general rules in COBS include the duty on the firm to arrange for an individual of "appropriate expertise" to approve any financial promotion and the firm must be able to show that it believes on reasonable grounds that the promotion is clear, fair and not misleading. "Appropriate expertise" will vary depending on the complexity of the financial promotion and the investment or service which it is promoting. After approving promotions, a firm must continue to monitor them to ensure that they continue to meet the requirements of the rules. The firm must ensure that a financial promotion is withdrawn if and as soon as it becomes aware that the promotion no longer meets the requirements of the rules.

The rules on conflicts of interest and material interest in Section 7.1 of COBS are designed to allow firms to manage situations where the interest of the firm may be in conflict with the interest of the client, or where the firm's clients have conflicting interests, so as to ensure the fair treatment of clients.

The rules provide that where a firm has a material interest or conflict of interest it must not knowingly advise or deal in relation to the relevant transaction unless it takes reasonable steps to ensure fair treatment for a client. The reasonable steps which a firm might take include:

- disclosure of an interest to the client;
- relying on a policy of independence;
- establishing internal arrangements (Chinese walls);
- declining to act for a client.

If a firm has a material interest or conflict of interest and is unable to rely on Chinese walls and it is not practical for the firm to rely on disclosure to the client, the firm may demonstrate that it has taken reasonable steps to ensure fair treatment for its clients by relying on a policy of independence. If a firm relies on a policy of independence, that policy should require an employee to disregard any material interest or conflict of interest when advising a client or when dealing with a client in the exercise of discretion. Such policy should also be recorded in writing at the firm and be made known to the relevant employee and it should be disclosed to a private client stating that the firm may have a material interest or conflict of interest relating to the transaction or service concerned.

What amounts to an acceptable policy of independence is not specified in the Rules. It is not clear how detailed the policy must be, whether specific interests must be referred to, or whether it will be enough merely to list broad categories of interest. It seems unlikely that the FSA would be prepared to accept a very widely drafted policy. Equally, it is unclear to what extent a standard letter can be despatched to all clients disclosing, for example, the existence of a market-making arm which might from time to time hold positions in particular investments.

4.5 Financial promotion

This subject is dealt with in detail in Chapter 7. The FSMA created a new concept of "financial promotion". This combined and simplified the old concepts of investment advertisements and cold calling. The new restrictions prohibit a person, in the course of business, from communicating an invitation or inducement to engage in investment activity unless he is an authorised person under the FSMA or the content of the communication is approved by an authorised person.

The new regime is relevant to both authorised and unauthorised entities. An authorised person proposing to issue or approve such a communication must also comply with the financial promotion rules issued by the FSA unless an exemption applies.

4.6 Market abuse

The FSMA created a civil regime relating to market abuse to supplement rather than replace the criminal regimes for insider dealing and market manipulation. By contrast with the position under many of the existing restrictions, under the market abuse regime, it will not be necessary for the FSA to demonstrate "beyond reasonable doubt" that there has been a breach. Further details of the new regime are set out in Chapter 8. In addition to the primary offence of market abuse, the FSMA creates a secondary offence of requiring or encouraging another person to engage in behaviour which would be market abuse if the encourager had carried out the behaviour.

Those who commit market abuse can be punished by an unlimited penalty or public censure, ordered to make restitution and restrained by injunction. The FSA has issued the Code of Market Conduct which gives appropriate guidance to market users as to whether or not behaviour amounts to market abuse. Although the new regime overlaps with existing regulations, successful enforcement of the new regime will be very much easier for the regulator.

The new regime, in particular the secondary offence of requiring or encouraging another person to commit market abuse, is likely to have a far-reaching effect on corporate finance business. Corporate finance activities clearly fall within the scope of the market abuse regime and firms carrying on corporate finance activities need to ensure that they do not act in a manner which falls below the standard reasonably expected by a regular user of the relevant market. Although this test is an objective one, the hypothetical regular user will take into account the position in relation to the market of the person carrying out the behaviour and higher standards may be expected of those involved in corporate finance business. Particular care needs to be taken by investment banks who help clients with or advise clients on the release of any information which may affect the market in the client's securities.

Chapter 5

Client Classification for Investment Banking Firms

Marwan Al-Turki
Partner
Baker & McKenzie

5.1   Introduction

Investment banking firms have long had to determine which regulatory regime (and regulator) applied (or did not apply) to the various investment banking and related activities which they undertake. The investment banking industry would have therefore welcomed at least one aspect of the enactment of the Financial Services and Markets Act 2000 ("FSMA"): on 1 December 2001, the Financial Services Authority (the "FSA") became the single regulator for, inter alia, the financial services, banking and insurance industries.

Having a single regulator means also having a single rulebook, rather than the various rulebooks or equivalent documents which may have applied up to N2. The FSA's Conduct of Business Sourcebook ("COB"), as its title suggests, provides the rules that authorised firms must comply with in the conduct of their business. As was the case before N2, COB rules that will apply in relation to an investment bank's clients will depend on how such clients are classified.

The client classification rules (the "Rules") are contained in Chapter 4 of COB and provide for three categories of client:

- private customers;
- intermediate customers; and
- market counterparties.

As with the previous regimes, firms must correctly categorise their clients, to ensure that the regulatory protections are greatest for those clients who need them most (i.e. private customers) and a firm's dealings with its clients are in compliance with the requirements applicable to the category of client concerned. The Rules are designed such that the regulatory requirements for firms are least onerous in relation to those clients who are most experienced with financial products and markets, that is, market counterparties. The Rules endeavour to retain a degree of flexibility, so that clients may be recharacterised (and thereby receive more or less protection, as the case may be), depending on their circumstances. This process is known as "opting down" or "opting up", depending on whether the client is receiving a higher or lower level of protection, respectively.

The FSA has attempted to draft the Rules so that they comply with the FSMA and, more particularly, with its regulatory objectives. The FSA is of the view that the Rules assist in furthering two such objectives: maintaining confidence in the financial system and securing the appropriate degree of protection for consumers.[1] The FSA considers that the Rules satisfy these objectives by tailoring the regulatory protections to suit the needs of individual customers.[2]

This Chapter examines how the Rules determine a client's classification and the consequences that flow from that classification. First, however, it provides a brief overview of the pre-N2 regime and the consultative process initiated by the FSA when considering these issues in setting the new regime.

5.2 COB

The Rules are contained in Chapter 4 of COB. The purpose of the Rules is to require an authorised firm to classify a person with whom it intends to carry on designated investment business or related ancillary activities.[3] Correct classification by an authorised firm of its client is essential so that it can apply the correct rules and ensure that the necessary regulatory protections are provided.[4]

---

[1] Sections 3 and 5 of FSMA, respectively.

[2] The Financial Services Authority, *Consultation Paper 43: Customer Classification*, February 2000, paragraph 1.4.

[3] Designated investment business is defined in the FSA Handbook Glossary by reference to an exhaustive list of investment activities that are specified in Part II FSMA 2000 (Regulated Activities Order) 2001– Specified Activities. An ancillary activity is defined as an activity which is not a regulated activity but is: (a) carried on in connection with a regulated activity; or (b) held out as being for the purposes of a regulated activity.

[4] COB 4.1.3G.

Before undertaking any designated investment business, a firm must take reasonable steps to find out which of the three categories (private customer, intermediate customer or market counterparty) apply to the client.

The Rules also contain provisions dealing with the position of agents. Where an authorised firm conducts designated investment business with a client who is acting as agent for another person (such other person being the "principal"), the agent, and not the principal, will be the firm's client if:

(a) the agent is another authorised firm or an overseas financial services institution;[5] or

(b) the agent is any other person, if the main purpose of the arrangement is not to avoid the duties that the firm would otherwise owe to the principal.[6]

There is an exception to this rule where the firm has agreed with the agent to treat the principal as its client.

It should be noted that the rule that the agent may be treated as the firm's client in the circumstances referred to above is narrow in its application, being primarily of relevance as to the application of COB or the Inter-Professional Chapter of the Code of Market Conduct, as the case may be. In particular:

(a) it does not relieve the firm of any the obligation to the principal under the FSA's Money Laundering Sourcebook (there is a different and wider definition of the term "client" in that Sourcebook);

(b) it is not relevant to the question of who is the firm's counterparty for the purposes of the Interim Prudential Sourcebook; and

(c) it does not relieve the firm from any obligation which it may owe the principal under the general law of agency.

5.3   Market counterparty

The FSA Handbook Glossary defines a market counterparty as:

---

[5] Defined in the FSA Handbook Glossary as an institution authorised to carry on any regulated activity or other financial service by an overseas regulator.

[6] COB 4.1.5R.

(1)   (except in COB 3(financial promotion)) a client who is:

    (a)   a properly constituted government (including a quasi-governmental body or a governmental agency) of any given country or territory;

    (b)   a central bank or other national monetary authority of any country or territory;

    (c)   a supranational whose members are either (*sic.*) countries or central banks or national monetary authorities;

    (d)   a State investment body, or a body charged with, or intervening in, the management of the public debt;

    (e)   another firm, or an overseas financial services institution, except in relation to designated investment business, and related ancillary activities, conducted with or for that firm or institution, when that firm or institution is an intermediate customer in accordance with COB 4.1.7R (Classification of another firm or an overseas financial services institution) (as described below);

    (f)   any associate of a firm (except an occupational pension scheme firm), or of an overseas financial services institution, if the firm or institution consents;

    (g)   a client when he is classified as a market counterparty in accordance with COB 4.1.12R (Large intermediate customer classified as a market counterparty) (as described below);

    but excluding:

    (A)   a collective investment scheme; and

    (B)   (except for the purposes of DISP) a client, who would otherwise be a market counterparty, when he is classified as a private customer in accordance with COB 4.1.14R (Client classified as private customer) (as described below).

(2)   (in COB 3(financial promotion)) a person in (1) and a person who would be such a person if he were a client.

5.3.1 Reclassification

Generally, where an authorised firm's client is another authorised firm or an overseas financial services institution, it is classified as market counterparty. However, the firm or overseas financial services institution (the "authorised client") may be reclassified as an intermediate customer if the activity carried on by the firm with the authorised client would be "inter-professional business"[7] and:

---

[7] The carrying on of regulated activities or ancillary activities where the regulated activities are specified in the definition of inter-professional business – *see* the FSA Handbook Glossary for the relevant criteria.

(a)   the authorised client is acting for an underlying customer;

(b)   the authorised client has decided that, for the interests of the underlying customer to be properly protected, the authorised client should benefit from the protections available to intermediate customers; and

(c)   the firm and the authorised client have agreed that the firm should classify the client as an intermediate customer when the authorised client is acting for the underlying customer.[8]

It should be noted that the above reclassification is not automatic – the authorised firm providing the relevant service must, within the parameters of the reclassification rule set out above, agree to the proposed reclassification. Where the firm does not agree, the client would need to find another firm willing to deal with it as an intermediate customer.[9]

An authorised client would also be classified as an intermediate customer where the activity would not be inter-professional business and the authorised client has not indicated that it is acting as principal or that it is a long-term insurer acting on behalf of its life fund.

It should also be noted that the classification of the authorised client as an intermediate customer only applies in the circumstances set out in COB 4.1.7R(2) (where the authorised client is acting for an underlying customer) or COB 4.1.7R(3) (where the activity would not be inter-professional business), as the case may be. The authorised client remains a market counterparty in its dealings with the authorised firm where the conditions specified in these rules are not met.

A regulated collective investment scheme ("CIS") is classified not in accordance with the above rules, but as a private customer. This rule has caused some discussion in the industry, since the types of authorised firms with institutional client bases which would include regulated CISs would not, prior to N2, have been authorised to conduct investment business with private customers. It may be said that, where the regulated CIS's ACD, as opposed to the CIS itself, may be regarded as the firm's customer, and this is supported by the facts and the underlying documentation, the ACD, which will itself be an authorised firm, will be classified in accordance with the rules referred to above for the classification of authorised clients.

---

[8] COB 4.1.7R(2).
[9] COB 4.1.8G(2).

Unregulated CISs are classified as intermediate customers. Again, the firm must determine whether it is the CIS itself or its manager or operator which is the firm's client and classify it accordingly.

As well as allowing a firm to "opt down" authorised clients from market counterparty to intermediate customer status, COB also allows the firm to "opt up" large intermediate customers from intermediate customer status so as to reclassify them as market counterparties (the authorised firm may of course initiate this change).[10] A "large intermediate customer" is a customer who would otherwise be an intermediate customer and who is one of the following:

(a) a body corporate (including a limited liability partnership) which has (or any of whose holding companies or subsidiaries has) called up share capital of at least £10 million (or its equivalent in any other currency at the relevant time); or

(b) a body corporate that meets (or any of whose holding companies or subsidiaries meets) two of the following three tests:
 (i) a balance sheet total of at least €12.5 million (or its equivalent in any other currency at the relevant time);
 (ii) a net turnover of at least €25 million (or its equivalent in any other currency at the relevant time); and
 (iii) an average number of employees during the year of 250;

(c) a local authority or public authority; or

(d) a partnership or unincorporated association which has net assets of at least £10 million (or its equivalent in any other currency at the relevant time) (and calculated, in the case of a limited partnership, without deducting loans owing to any of the partners); or

(e) a trustee of a trust (other than an occupational pension scheme, SSAS or stakeholder pension scheme) which has gross assets of cash and designated investments of at least £10 million (or its equivalent in any other currency); or

(f) a trustee of an occupational pension scheme, SSAS or stakeholder pension scheme where the trust has (or has had at any time during the previous two years):
 (i) at least 50 members; and
 (ii) assets under management of not less than £10 million (or its equivalent in any other currency at the relevant time).

---

[10] COB 4.1.12R.

5.3.2 Commencing business with a reclassified large intermediate customer

Before commencing business with the large intermediate customer as a reclassified market counterparty, the authorised firm must:

(a) advise the client in writing[11] that it will be classified as a market counterparty; and
(b) provide a written warning to the client that it will lose protections under the regulatory system.

The firm must have taken reasonable steps to ensure that the relevant written notices were delivered to a person authorised to take such a decision for the client. In addition, the firm must:

(a) for the categories of large intermediate customers which are large bodies corporate (including limited liability partnerships) referred to under (a) and (b) in the categories of large intermediate customers set out above, not have been notified by the client that it objects to being reclassified as a market counterparty; and
(b) for the categories of large intermediate customers other than large bodies corporate (including limited liability partnerships) referred to under (a) and (b) above, have obtained the client's written consent or be otherwise able to demonstrate that consent has been given.

The written warning provided by the firm should advise the client that it will lose all protections afforded to customers in COB, other than COB 9 (client assets) and Principles 6 (customers' interests), 8 (conflicts of interest) and 9 (customers: relationships of trust), as well as most of Principle 7 (communications with clients). In addition, the firm also needs to advise the client that, in respect of inter-professional business, MAR 3 (inter-professional conduct) applies.

5.4 Intermediate customer

The FSA Handbook Glossary defines an intermediate customer[12] as a client who is not a market counterparty and:

---

[11] Note that "in writing" communications may be provided electronically – COB 1.8.1G.
[12] The FSA resisted calls to change the name of this category. Some respondents felt that the name may cause confusion with terms such as "intermediary".

(1) (except in COB 3 (financial promotion)) a client who is not a market counterparty and who is:

    (a) a local authority or public authority;

    (b) a body corporate whose shares have been listed or admitted to trading on any EEA exchange;

    (c) a body corporate who shares have been listed or admitted to trading on the primary board of any IOSCO member country official exchange;

    (d) a body corporate (including a limited liability partnership) which has (or any of whose holding companies or subsidiaries has) (or has had at any time during the previous two years) called up share capital or net assets of at least £5 million (or its equivalent in any other currency at the relevant time);

    (e) a special purpose vehicle (being an SPV rated by a rating agency and used for issuing bonds or other designated investments (other than life policies) in a securitisation);

    (f) a partnership or unincorporated association which has (or has had at any time during the previous two years) net assets of at least £5 million (or its equivalent in any other currency at the relevant time) and calculated in the case of a limited partnership without deducting loans owing to any of the partners;

    (g) a trustee of a trust of a trust (other than an occupational pension scheme, SSAS or stakeholder pension scheme) which has (or has had at any time during the previous two years) gross assets of cash and designated investments of at least £10 million (or its equivalent in any other currency at the relevant time);

    (h) a trustee of an occupational pension scheme, SSAS or stakeholder pension scheme where the trust has (or has had at any time during the previous two years):

        (i) at least 50 members; and

        (ii) assets under management of not less than £10 million (or its equivalent in any other currency at the relevant time);

    (i) another firm, or an overseas financial services institution, when, in relation to designated investment business, or related ancillary activities, conducted with or for that firm or institution, that firm or institution is an intermediate customer in accordance with COB 4.1.7R (Classification of another firm or an overseas financial services institution) (as to which, please *see* above);

(j)   an unregulated collective investment scheme; or
(k)   an expert private customer reclassified as an intermediate customer (*see* below);

but excluding:

(i)   a regulated collective investment scheme (which, under COB 4.1.7R(4) is a private customer); and
(ii)   a client who would otherwise be an intermediate customer, but who has been:

(A)   opted up under COB 4.1.12R; or
(B)   (except for the purposes of DISP) opted down under COB 4.1.14R.

(2)   (in COB 3 (financial promotion)) a person in (1) or a person who would be such a person if he were a client.

As may be seen from the definition, it specifically excludes regulated CISs (as to which, please *see* above), intermediate customers whom the firm has opted up under COB 4.1.12R, as described above, and intermediate customers whom the firm has opted down to private customer status under COB 4.1.14R.

5.4.1   Criteria for classifying intermediate customers

As stated above, a firm may "opt up" large intermediate customers and reclassify them as market counterparties. In addition, in line with the pre-N2 regime, the Rules allow a firm to classify a client that would otherwise be a private customer as an intermediate customer if that private customer may be considered sufficiently "expert".[13] This classification may apply to the customer generally or may be limited to specific categories of designated investments or designated investment business.

In order to reclassify an expert private customer as an intermediate customer, the firm must take reasonable steps to determine that the client has sufficient experience and understanding of the relevant products and markets. The FSA has provided guidance as to the relevant criteria,[14] being:

(a)   the client's knowledge and understanding of the relevant designated investments and markets, and of the risks involved;

---

[13] COB 4.1.9R.
[14] COB 4.1.10G.

(b) how long the client has been active in these markets, the frequency of dealings and the extent to which he has relied on advice on investments of the firm;

(c) the size and nature of the transactions undertaken for the client in these markets; and

(d) the client's financial standing, which may include an assessment of his net worth or of the value of his portfolio.[15]

The guidance states that it is likely that a firm will need to have regard to more than one of these criteria, or to other criteria, before it can be satisfied that a client, who would otherwise be a private customer, is eligible to be classified as an intermediate customer.

The firm must warn the client in writing of the regulatory protections he will lose in relation to certain specified COB rules as a result of being reclassified as an intermediate customer, as well as explain any consequences of certain other specified COB rules being limited or modified in their application upon reclassification. The firm must also warn the client that he will lose the right of access to the Financial Ombudsman Service ("FOS"). Finally, the firm must warn the client that it may have regard to his expertise when complying with requirements under the regulatory system that communications must be clear, fair and not misleading.

The firm must obtain the client's written consent to the reclassification, or be otherwise able to demonstrate that informed consent has been given, after allowing the client sufficient time to consider the implications of losing the relevant regulatory protections.

5.5 Private customer

A private customer is defined by exclusion as a client who is not a market counterparty or an intermediate customer. As stated above, COB 4.1.14R allows an authorised firm to classify any client who would have otherwise been a market counterparty or an intermediate customer (other than a firm or overseas financial services institution) as a private customer. In classifying the client as a private customer, the firm must advise the client that it will not necessarily have rights under the FOS or the Compensation Scheme as a result of such reclassification.

---

[15] COB 4.1.10G. The rule contains the additional guidance that a firm will need to have regard to more than one of those criteria before it is satisfied that the client is eligible to be classified as an intermediate customer.

5.6 Classification review/record keeping

An authorised firm must conduct an annual review of its opt-up classifications where:

(a) an expert private customer has been reclassified as an intermediate customer; or

(b) a large intermediate customer has been reclassified as a market counterparty.[16]

The annual review should ensure that the reclassification remains appropriate to the designated investment business which the firm carries on with or for that client.

The authorised firm must make a record of its client's classification, together with sufficient information to support that classification. Such record must be retained for at least three years after the firm ceases to carry on business with or for that client. This period is extended to six years in relation to life policies or pension contracts and is indefinite in relation to pension transfers, pension opt-outs and FSAVCs.

5.7 Transitional provisions

The consultation process discussed above also considered what transitional treatment should be adopted by firms that were already authorised on N2 in relation to the classification of existing clients. Industry considered this issue to be one of the main areas where the new COB regime had the potential to impose unnecessary burdens on firms.[17]

The FSA made transitional rules that it considers will ensure continuity of classification in respect of a firm's clients, where those clients had been classified before N2.[18] These are highlighted below, beginning with those

---

[16] COB 4.1.15R.

[17] *Conduct of Business Sourcebook: Transitional Arrangements*, July 2001, paragraph 3.19.

[18] The transitional provisions are divided into those which apply indefinitely, generally labelled timeless (saving) provisions ("TSPs"), extra time provisions ("ETPs") which apply for a limited period (normally until 30 June 2002), and technical timing provisions ("TTPs") which give relief from certain periodic obligations to customers.

transitional rules that apply indefinitely to existing clients other than authorised firms or overseas financial services institutions:[19]

(a)   Where the existing client was classified as a market counterparty under the relevant SRO rules, it will retain that classification for COB purposes indefinitely.[20] However, where the client was classified as a market counterparty only in relation to a particular transaction or type of transaction, it must, from N2, be classified in accordance with COB 4.1.[21]

(b)   Where the existing client was classified as a non-private customer[22] under the relevant SRO rules, the firm may treat that client as an intermediate customer.[23] This does not preclude the firm from reclassifying a large intermediate customer as a market counterparty pursuant to COB 4.1.12R.[24] In addition, where the existing client had previously been classified as an "ordinary business investor", it may be treated as an intermediate customer.[25]

(c)   Existing clients classified as private customers under prior regimes may retain that classification for COB purposes without contravening any rule in the FSA Handbook.[26] This does not preclude a firm from reclassifying an "expert" private customer as an intermediate customer if the requirements of COB 4.1.9R are met.[27]

The transitional rules provide limited transitional relief where firms have existing clients classified as expert private customers. The transitional rules allow firms to treat those customers as either intermediate customers or private customers until 30 June 2002.[28] By that time, the

---

[19]   COB TR3 1.3G explains that there are no transitional rules regarding classification by a firm of a client which is another authorised firm or an overseas financial institution.

[20]   COB TR3 1.1R(2).

[21]   COB TR3 1.1R(3), which requires that such a client must be classified in accordance with COB 4.1.

[22]   Other than clients classified as expert private customers, to which COB TR1 1.6R applies (and other than authorised firms or overseas financial services institutions).

[23]   COB TR3 1.1R(4).

[24]   COB TR3 1.1R(5) permits such reclassification provided the firm complies with COB 4.1.12R(2).

[25]   COB TR3 1.1R(8).

[26]   COB TR3 1.1R(6).

[27]   COB TR3 1.1R(7).

[28]   COB TR1 1.6R.

firm should have undertaken the task of classifying the relevant client under the Rules.[29]

Similarly, the transitional rules allow firms previously exempted from authorisation under Section 43 FS Act to defer reclassifying their clients; firms may continue to treat their existing clients (except those clients which are other authorised firms) as market counterparties (in relation to their Section 43 business) until 12 months after N2.[30]

There are no transitional provisions relating to the classification of authorised firms or overseas financial institutions as clients. COB 4.1.7R will apply in those circumstances.[31]

5.8 Consequences of client classification

As stated above, the classification of clients determines the level of regulatory protection they will receive under COB. This Chapter does not deal in detail with each of the protections afforded to private customers pursuant to COB. To do so would, in effect, involve a consideration of the entire COB. Rather, we will assume that the reader is familiar with such protections and will highlight which of these regulatory protections are also provided to intermediate customers and market counterparties.

The final section of the Chapter considers briefly the consequences that may flow from an authorised firm incorrectly classifying a customer, in particular in relation to the rights of action provided for in the FSMA.

5.9 Regulatory protections

Where the client is classified as a market counterparty, only limited parts of COB will apply to any transactions between the authorised firm and such client. Instead, the transactions are framed by reference to the Principles for Businesses, as well as the Market Conduct Sourcebook

---

[29] COB TR1 1.7G notes that certain existing client protections are maintained during the transitional period. For example, COB TR1 1.7G notes that clients falling under COB TR1 1.6R retain their rights of access to the FOS until reclassification.

[30] COB TR1 1.8R.

[31] COB TR3 1.3G.

(Chapter 3) (MAR 3) where the transaction constitutes inter-professional business.[32]

As stated above, COB 4.1.11E specifies that the firm must warn an expert private customer that he will lose the protection of the relevant COB rules where he is reclassified as an intermediate customer. It states that the firm must warn the expert private customer that he will lose the protection afforded by the following rules, which apply exclusively to private customers:

- COB 3.9 (direct offer financial promotions). This Section includes provisions which apply to all direct offer financial promotions and other provisions which apply only to certain kinds of direct offer financial promotions.
- COB 3.12 (communication and approval of financial promotions of an overseas or an unauthorised person). Similar rules apply when a firm approves a financial promotion as they do when a firm communicates a financial promotion itself. A firm therefore has a similar responsibility for a financial promotion that it approves as for one that it communicates.
- COB 3.13 (additional requirements for financial promotions for an overseas long-term insurer). A firm must not communicate or approve a financial promotion to enter into a life policy with a person who is not an authorised or exempt person; or a company which has its head office, branch or agency in an EEA State other than the UK and which is entitled under the law of that State to carry on insurance business of the class to which the financial promotion relates; or a company authorised to carry on insurance business of the class to which the financial promotion relates in any country or territory which is listed in COB 3.13.1(2).
- COB 5.4 (customers' understanding of risk). Requiring that a firm takes reasonable steps to ensure that a private customer understands the nature of the risks inherent in certain transactions.
- COB 5.7 (disclosure of charges, remuneration and commission). Requiring that a firm ensures that a private customer is made aware of the costs to him, directly or indirectly, of financial services, so that he is better able to make informed choices.
- COB 6.1 (packaged product and ISA disclosure). Applies to a firm which sells, recommends or arranges for the sale of a packaged

---

[32] Annex 1G to the Inter-Professional Conduct rules provide further guidance as to the application of the Principles for Businesses, COB and MAR 3.

product to a private customer or (2) which manages, sells or recommends a cash deposit ISA for or to a private customer; or (3) which effects, recommends or arranges for a variation of a life policy for or to a private customer; or (4) which effects, personally recommends or arranges income withdrawals for or to a private customer.

- COB 7.9 (lending to private customers). This Section seeks to ensure that a firm lends money or grants credit to a private customer only in appropriate circumstances, and only if the customer has given prior consent in full knowledge of any resulting interest and fees.
- COB 7.10 (margin requirements). This Section applies to a firm which executes a transaction in a contingent liability investment with or for a private customer, in the course of, or in connection with, its designated investment business. It aims to ensure that a firm manages a private customer's exposure to contingent liabilities by diligently monitoring the firm's relevant provision of credit.
- COB 7.12 (non-exchange traded securities). This Section aims to ensure that a firm makes and retains records of customer orders and other transactions in the course of adhering to the customer order execution requirements in COB 7.4 (Customer order priority), COB 7.5 (Best execution) and COB 7.6 (Timely execution).

In addition, firms must explain the consequences to the client regarding the following rules that are either of limited application or otherwise modified for intermediate customers:

- COB 3 (financial promotion);
- COB 5.1 (polarisation and status disclosure). Requires a firm in relation only to advice on packaged products to act either independently for the private customer, or to act on a tied basis where advice is restricted to its own products, those of its marketing group and adopted packaged products. (Under review at the time of writing via *CP121: Reforming Polarisation: Making the market work for consumers*.)
- COB 8.1 (confirmation of transactions). Designed to ensure that customers are promptly advised of the essential details of a transaction. Firms are obliged to despatch these details, except in certain circumstances when they are supplied by someone else, or at a later date, or if the customer waives the right to receive the information.
- COB 8.2 (periodic statements). Applicable where a firm acts as an investment manager, or administers any other account or portfolio which includes designated investments, for a customer; or operates a customer's account containing uncovered open positions in a contingent liability investment.

The consequences of the client losing the protection of the following rules (which are capable of modification in their application to intermediate customers) must also be explained:

- COB 7.5 (best execution). This Section sets standards for firms when executing current customer orders in designated investments, particularly in the securities and derivatives markets, to obtain for customers the best price available to the firm, given the kind and size of such transactions.
- COB 9.1 (custody). A firm's obligations when it is safeguarding and administering investments.
- COB 9.3 (client money). A firm's obligations when it receives or holds money from, or on behalf of, a client in the course of, or in connection with, its designated investment business.

As stated above. the warning must note that an intermediate customer does not have right of access to the FOS. It must also note that the firm is entitled to take the person's expertise into account when complying with the requirement to provide communications that are clear, fair and not misleading.

The above does not purport to be an exhaustive list of the protections afforded to private, as opposed to intermediate, customers. Accordingly, a thorough examination of COB is recommended.

5.10   Consequences of incorrect classification

Where an authorised firm incorrectly classifies a client, transactions undertaken by the firm with the client are not voided or made unenforceable.[33] However, Section 150 FSMA does allow a "private person" who suffers loss as a result of the contravention of a rule to bring an action for damages against the authorised firm. A "private person" is defined as:

(a)   any individual, unless the loss is suffered in the course of carrying on a regulated activity (or in the course of carrying on any activity which would be a regulated activity apart from any exclusion made by Article 72 Regulated Activities Order (overseas persons)); and

---

[33] FSMA, Section 151(2). Section 151 also provides that it is not a criminal offence to contravene rules made by the FSA.

(b)   any person who is not an individual, unless he suffers the loss in question in the course of carrying on business of any kind.

Governments, local authorities and international organisations are excluded from the definition of "private person".[34]

5.11   Conclusion

Correct client classification by firms has always been an important initial (and, in certain circumstances, continuing) task. Firms cannot determine what regulatory protections apply to a client unless that client has been correctly classified. The COB client classification rules build on those previously made by the SROs. There is a greater flexibility now for clients to be "opted up" or "opted down" between the three categories. However, this flexibility merely reinforces the notion that greater protection should be available to the more vulnerable clients, where the service provider is significantly more experienced than the end user, while ensuring that transactions between market professionals, where the expertise of the provider and end user are more equal, are not subject to unnecessarily burdensome regulation.

---

[34] Financial Services and Markets Act 2000 (Rights of Action) Regulations 2001 (SI 2001 No 2256), Regulation 3.

Chapter 6

Conflicts and Confidential Information

Christopher Pearson

Partner
Norton Rose

6.1 Introduction

This Chapter is concerned with client confidentiality and the issues and difficulties faced by investment bankers in the mergers and acquisitions arena where conflicts of interest typically arise. This Chapter considers the law relating to a bank's duty of confidentiality to its clients, the regulatory framework in the UK within which a bank's duties and conflicts operate, and how banks manage conflicts of interest in practice. The Chapter also covers insider dealing, a subject which is intrinsically linked to the possession and use of clients' confidential information.

6.1.1 What is a "conflict of interest"?

In order to appreciate the analysis in this Chapter, it is important to define the concept of a "conflict of interest". The term is often used in a variety of different contexts and to mean a number of different things and, whilst the distinctions between the different types of conflicts may not necessarily be important (since a conflict is still a conflict), the circumstances in which they arise throw up different issues and different measures to address the conflict will be needed.

The first type of conflict is an *existing client conflict*. Here, the professional is acting for two clients at the same time and, consequently, he will owe fiduciary duties to both. In this scenario, there is an inherent conflict of interest since in principle a fiduciary cannot act at the same time both for and against the same client. It is important to note that the fiduciary obligations apply to the firm as a whole, not merely the individual person concerned. It follows, therefore, that a firm cannot, without the consent of both clients, act for both clients.

In contrast, in the context of a *former client conflict*, the fiduciary obligation no longer applies if there is no continuing retainer or client relationship. The issue here, however, is not one of a conflict of interest but of maintaining the obligations of confidentiality owed to the former client whilst at the same time acting in the best interests of the existing client.

One should also recognise that there are other types of conflicts. For example, there may be a *personal conflict* between the professional's own interest and that of his client (e.g. a bank which is paid a success fee or a percentage of the deal value has a personal financial interest in seeing the deal complete and to that extent there may be a conflict of interest with that of the client).

6.1.2 Background

Against the backdrop of a business environment that is getting smaller every day, industry sectors (not least the financial services sector) have witnessed relentless consolidation. In a corporate finance market where only a handful of "global" players have the reach and resources necessary to handle the largest deals, it is no wonder that potential client conflicts arise regularly. In the last few years, we have witnessed a massive move towards globalisation in the financial services sector. The intense competition, in particular in relation to commercial and investment banks, has continued apace resulting in rapid growth through consolidation as well as diversification in the nature and breadth of services offered through the combination of various financial functions offering various financial products. The list of recent banking mergers and acquisitions is lengthy – to name but a few: Royal Bank of Scotland/National Westminster Bank, Salomon Smith Barney/Schroders (investment banking), Credit Suisse First Boston/Donaldson Lufkin Jenrette, Bank of Scotland/Halifax, UBS/Paine Webber, Chase Manhattan Bank/J P Morgan (shortly after J P Morgan/Robert Fleming), Barclays Bank/Woolwich and Dresdner Kleinwort Benson/Wasserstein Parella. Consequently, the global market for financial services is shrinking.

The inevitable effects of consolidation and diversification of products and services are more complex conflicts. Moreover, the risk of conflicts has risen dramatically in recent years because of the success of the handful of global investment banks, based largely on the industry specialisation model. Sector specialists owe their success to the extensive range of client relationships throughout an entire sector. As these bankers restrict themselves to talking with a limited number of companies within a sector, the risk of unauthorised use or disclosure of confidential information inevitably increases.

Furthermore, the increasing number of law suits brought in connection with potential conflicts of interest demonstrates clearly that client confidentiality remains a real concern.

6.2 The duty of confidentiality and fiduciary obligations

6.2.1 The banker's duty of confidentiality

It is accepted that, under English law, a bank owes a duty of confidentiality to its customer. However, the scope of this duty is not precise since it is often difficult to say, with any degree of certainty, that a piece of information is or is not subject to an obligation of confidence. Furthermore, there are various exceptions to the obligation, both statutory and at common law, including where the disclosure is made with the express or implied consent of the customer and where disclosure is under compulsion of law. Whilst bankers should be familiar with the scope of the duty of confidentiality owed to their clients, it is not necessary, for the purposes of this Chapter, to consider the qualifications further since we are concerned here with the simple recognition of this duty and the maintenance of client confidentiality rather than the circumstances in which this fundamental duty may be disapplied legitimately.

6.2.2 The banker as a fiduciary

It is, therefore, clear that a bank owes an obligation of confidentiality to its customers at common law. At the same time, one should consider the nature of a bank's fiduciary relationship with its clients. Fundamentally, it is the fiduciary obligation of the loyalty owed by the banker (or indeed any professional) to his client which leads to the problems of conflicts. An opening observation about this area of law is that the rules relating to fiduciaries are long established, based on traditional equitable doctrines, but are simply out of date when applied in today's increasingly sophisticated market. Moreover, the established case law principally concerns solicitors and to a lesser extent accountants, not bankers.

So, what is a fiduciary? Millett LJ said in *Bristol & West Building Society* v *Mothew* [1998] Ch 1:

> "A fiduciary is someone who has undertaken to act for or on behalf
> of another in a particular matter in circumstances which give rise to
> a relationship of trust and confidence. The distinguishing obligation
> of a fiduciary is the *obligation of loyalty* (emphasis added). The
> principal is entitled to the single-minded loyalty of his fiduciaries."

Equity recognises certain categories of relationships in which one person
places trust and confidence in another as fiduciary relationships (so-
called "status"-based fiduciaries). English law recognises that the
categories of fiduciaries are not closed and that it is impossible to define
exactly when a fiduciary relationship comes into existence. However, in
practice, virtually all relationships between a professional and his client
will attract the label of fiduciary in view of the fact the professional will
receive information which is confidential or sensitive from the client.
Therefore, it is safe to say that bankers, as with solicitors and accountants, owe fiduciary duties to their clients.

As noted above, the special characteristic of a fiduciary is his obligation
of loyalty to the person for whom he acts. He has an obligation to defend
and advance the interests of the person to whom he owes the fiduciary
obligation. This fundamental duty consists of a number of facets, in
particular:

(a) an obligation to act in good faith;
(b) a duty not to make a profit out of this trust;
(c) a duty to ensure that he does not put himself in a position where
     his duty and interests may conflict; and
(d) a duty not to act for his own benefit or the benefit of a third person
     without the informed consent of his principal.

This relationship ends with the termination of the retainer between the
banker and his client; thereafter, he is not obliged to defend and advance
the interests of his former client. However, one particular fiduciary obligation survives the termination of the retainer, namely the obligation of
confidence.

6.2.3 What is confidential information?

In establishing that the obligation of confidentiality is ongoing, identifying what is confidential information in this context is clearly vital. Yet
there is no clear distinction as to what is and is not confidential information. In general, for there to be a breach of confidence:

(a) the relevant information must have the necessary quality of confidence;

(b) the relevant information must have been imparted in circumstances importing an obligation of confidence; and

(c) there must be an unauthorised use of that information to the detriment of the party communicating it.

As investment bankers should be regarded as fiduciaries, then like solicitors and other professionals it follows that communications between the banker and his client will in the normal course be presumed confidential. *Re Solicitors (A Firm)* [1997] Ch 1 is a useful authority in shedding some light on what constitutes confidential information for the purposes of conflicts. This case recognised that confidential information passing between a solicitor (in that case) and his client and otherwise acquired by him on behalf of his client may subsequently cease to be confidential. The judge went on to say that common sense requires recognition that not all confidential information acquired by a fiduciary will remain in the mind of the fiduciary or be susceptible of being triggered as a recollection after a lapse of a period of time. Therefore, for the purpose of the law imposing constraints upon fiduciaries acting against the interests of former clients, the law is concerned with the protection of information which:

- was originally communicated in confidence;
- at the date of the later proposed retainer, is still confidential; and
- is relevant to the subject matter of the new instructions.

6.3 Managing conflicts

Whilst it is clear that the banker should have regard to the strict equitable rules which govern client conflicts of interest, it is equally clear that the banker must look to means of anticipating and managing conflicts and of avoiding claims for breach of fiduciary duty. The most common means of achieving these objectives (often in combination) are:

- by express, informed consent of the client;
- by setting out the terms of the relationship with the client in an engagement letter; and
- by adopting Chinese walls.

111

6.3.1 Informed consent

The application of the "double employment" rule (i.e. a fiduciary cannot serve two masters) means that a banker may not act for two clients with potentially competing interests in a transaction unless they consent to him so acting. This was the conclusion reached by the Privy Council in *Clark Boyce* v *Mouat* [1994] 1 AC 428 where it was held that the solicitor in that case was permitted to act provided he had obtained the informed consent of both clients to his acting. Informed consent means:

> ". . . consent given in the knowledge that there is a conflict between the parties and that as a result the [solicitor] may be disabled from disclosing to each party the full knowledge which he possesses as to the transaction or may be disabled from giving advice to one party which conflicts with the interests of the other. If the parties are content to proceed upon this basis, the [solicitor] may properly act."

The most common method of obtaining client consent is by entering into a written engagement letter (*see* Section 6.3.2 below). Another question flowing from this is the extent to which the banker must disclose to the client(s) the nature of the conflict. Case law, which mostly deals with personal conflicts (i.e. between the professional and the client), suggests a strict approach in that the professional is responsible for making full disclosure of all material facts which might affect the client's decision whether to proceed or not. However it has been suggested that in light of *Clark Boyce*, the courts are unlikely to apply the same strictness to disclosure in the context of existing client conflicts.

6.3.2 The retainer

The retainer defines the obligations and terms of the relationship between the client and the professional and it is in this context that the courts determine whether and to what extent a conflict exists. It is, therefore, sensible and indeed common for banks to require that their clients sign engagement letters in advance of advising on any major transactions. Managing conflicts by resorting to such contractual techniques is beneficial for various reasons:

(a)   the fiduciary obligations may be limited by the terms of the engagement letter, for example, any conflicts which have been expressly or impliedly recognised by the client at the outset. This is the conclusion reached in the decisions of *Kelly* v *Cooper* [1993] AC 205, PC and *Clark Boyce* and a view endorsed by The Law

Commission ("Fiduciary Duties and Regulatory Rules", Law Com Report No. 236 (December 1995));

(b) the obligations will be limited by the retainer and therefore, the tasks undertaken by the banker will be clearly defined. (The services of the solicitor in *Clark Boyce* were sought in order to effect a conveyance, not to give advice as to the wisdom of the transactions);

(c) the client's consent/waiver of potential conflicts can be obtained when he signs the engagement letter, provided it is informed consent; and

(d) in the absence of express terms of the retainer, it is the professional's duty to advise his client in terms appropriate to the client's understanding and experience, the precise scope of which will depend in part upon the extent to which the client appears to need advice.

The retainer may contain exclusion clauses (which seek to exclude or limit liability for breach of duty), duty defining clauses and disclosure/conflicts waiver clauses. Such clauses must be construed in the context of the Unfair Contract Terms Act 1977 and the Unfair Terms In Consumer Contracts Regulations 1999 and the requirement of reasonableness. It follows, therefore, that a banker may wish to agree a narrowly defined retainer in order to avoid conflicts which could otherwise arise under a more broadly defined retainer. That said, this approach alone may be impractical and less straightforward in certain instances, for example:

(a) where the client is inexperienced, the courts are unlikely to permit the professional to limit himself to the retainer by giving significantly less advice than the client reasonably requires; or

(b) there will inevitably be instances in the course of a transaction when the client turns to his financial or other advisers for their advice or opinions – it is very difficult to operate within the confines of a very narrow retainer in those circumstances. Furthermore, the courts might treat the limited retainer as having been extended by conduct.

We now turn to consider the use of Chinese walls.

6.4 Chinese walls

6.4.1 Introduction

"Chinese wall" is the metaphor used to describe a set of rules, regulations, procedures and/or physical arrangements adopted by an organisation in creating an information barrier within the organisation which is intended to ensure that confidential information available to or known by certain members of that organisation is not made available to other members of the same organisation. A Chinese wall is usually set up in order to separate information-source departments (e.g. investment and commercial banking or specialist departments therein) from those which can convert the information into a financial benefit for the firm or its clients, such as the securities trading or the trust departments. Therein lie potential conflicts of interest between clients of the same bank. Therefore the so-called Chinese wall is seen as a practical solution to the problem of insider dealing (*see* Section 6.6 below).

Chinese walls have been a tried and tested method of keeping the affairs and interests of a client and a firm, or the client and another client, which may be adverse, separate so that the interests of the client or clients can be safeguarded. The setting up of Chinese walls is significant for two reasons: first, to rebut the presumption that knowledge of the confidential information is to pass to other members of the firm, and second, to show that there is no risk of disclosure. In as much as they operate as information barriers, Chinese walls are put in place to try to ensure that different departments within an organisation demonstrate independence in their decision-making (*see*, e.g. the Takeover Panel's approach in Section 6.5.2 below).

The legal position under English law appears to be that there is no rule of law that Chinese walls (or other similar information barriers) are insufficient to prevent disclosure. However, the crucial issue is the effectiveness of Chinese walls, which was questioned recently by the courts in *Prince Jefri Bolkiah* v *KPMG* [1999] 1 All ER 517, where the House of Lords examined in detail the use of Chinese walls, and subsequently in *Young* v *Robson Rhodes* [1999] 3 All ER 524. It is, therefore, necessary to analyse these cases.

6.4.2 The Prince Jefri *case*

6.4.2.1 *The facts*
Prince Jefri Bolkiah was the Minister of Finance of Brunei and the Chairman of the Brunei Investment Agency ("BIA"). The BIA was established in 1983 with the principal objective of managing the general reserve fund of Brunei and providing its government with money management services. KPMG acted as auditors of a substantial part of its investment portfolios (known as core funds). In addition to their audit work, KPMG also carried out associated advisory and consulting work

for BIA. In addition, between 1996 and 1998, KPMG were also instructed on behalf of Prince Jefri to undertake an investigation into his affairs in connection with major litigation involving the Manoukian Brothers. This investigation, code-named "Project Lucy", involved 168 staff including 12 partners and £4.6 million in fees.

The litigation settled in March 1998 and no further work was undertaken on Project Lucy. In June 1998 the Government of Brunei appointed a taskforce to investigate the activities of the BIA. KPMG performed certain further work described as "a natural extension of their audit function". They were then instructed to assist the taskforce in carrying out further investigations into the destination and present location of certain withdrawn funds. By this stage, KPMG no longer considered Prince Jefri to be their client and they accepted these instructions (code-named "Project Gemma") without contacting Prince Jefri. It was clear, however, that the work being undertaken by KPMG on Project Gemma was potentially adverse to Prince Jefri's interests and might well lead to civil or criminal proceedings against him.

KPMG recognised that the confidential information which they had obtained whilst working on Project Lucy might well be relevant to Project Gemma. On accepting instructions on Project Gemma, KPMG established a Chinese wall within the forensic accounting department to protect Prince Jefri's confidentiality. This involved ensuring that no one who possessed confidential information about Prince Jefri worked on Project Gemma and taking steps to ensure that such information was not disclosed to staff working on Project Gemma (of which there were about 50). In addition most of the work on Project Gemma took place in Brunei whilst the work in London was done in a separate building from the one housing the forensic accounting department. Prince Jefri sought an injunction restraining KPMG from continuing with work on Project Gemma.

6.4.2.2 *The decisions*
At first instance, Pumfrey J granted an injunction, holding that an accountant providing forensic services was in much the same position as a solicitor. He added that the court was satisfied that KPMG were in possession of confidential information from Prince Jefri and there was a high burden on KPMG to satisfy the court that there was not a real risk of its disclosure, inadvertent or otherwise, and held that he was not so satisfied on the facts.

115

The Court of Appeal (by a majority) reversed this decision. Lord Woolf MR, in giving the majority's leading judgment, favoured the "sensible and balanced approach" taken by the New Zealand Court of Appeal in *Russell McVeagh McKenzie Bartleet & Co.* v *Tower Corporation* [1998] NZLR 641, where three questions were considered:

(a)   Is there confidential information which, if disclosed, is likely to affect the former client's interests adversely?
(b)   Is there a real or appreciable risk that the confidential information will be disclosed? and
(c)   Does the nature and importance of the former fiduciary relationship mean that the confidential information should be protected by the court exercising its discretion and intervening?

The Court of Appeal in *Russell McVeagh* recognised that these factors would overlap and, therefore, one had to balance the different interests involved in order to determine whether relief should be granted in the particular case.

Lord Woolf MR noted some salient comments on the facts of *Prince Jefri*. For example, the short time span between the end of Project Lucy and the start of Project Gemma and KPMG's long-standing relationship with the BIA. In view of the fact that Price Jefri knew of KPMG's history with the BIA, he should have anticipated that if a conflict arose, then the BIA would wish to retain KPMG (given the inconvenience and expense involved in changing accountants). In these circumstances, KPMG's duty should be limited to making reasonable efforts to protecting the confidential information and Prince Jefri would not be entitled to an injunction unless he would suffer serious damage otherwise. On the balance of the evidence, the Court of Appeal was not satisfied that the claimant would suffer any "real prejudice" if the injunction were discharged. Lord Woolf MR opined that the continuation of the injunction would set an unrealistic standard for the protection of confidential information which would create impediments in the way large international firms conduct their practice which are not justified. (Waller LJ dissented.)

The House of Lords unanimously rejected the Court of Appeal's decision. Lord Millett, in giving the leading judgment, noted that as KPMG no longer acted for Prince Jefri, their fiduciary obligations to him ceased on termination of the retainer. The issue was thus one of confidential information. His Lordship was firmly of the view that the duty to preserve confidentiality is unqualified and, contrary to the Court of Appeal's view, it was insufficient to show that reasonable steps had been taken to protect it. A former client cannot be completely protected from accidental or inadvertent disclosure, but he is nonetheless entitled to prevent his former solicitor from exposing him to any avoidable risk. He went on to say that the court should intervene unless it is satisfied that there is no risk of disclosure. The risk must be a real one and not merely fanciful or theoretical, but it need not be substantial. Whilst Lord Millett recognises the role which Chinese walls can and do play in professional circles (e.g. his Lordship noted that the Financial Services Authority's Core Conduct of Business Rules endorse this mechanism), he circumscribed their use by emphasising quite emphatically that, insofar as Chinese walls are helpful to firms in eliminating the risk of leakage, they must operate as an "established part of the organisational structure of the firm". On the facts, the Lordships were not satisfied that the measures proposed and undertakings offered by KPMG to protect confidentiality were adequate and, therefore, granted the injunction.

6.4.3 The implications of **Prince Jefri**

The principles following *Prince Jefri* may be summarised as follows:

(a) where the professional is asked to act for two clients with conflicting interests at the same time, the fiduciary obligations of loyalty owed to each will clash and if he accepts instructions for both, he will then be in breach of fiduciary duty to one or both clients and unable to carry out his obligations to both. The problem is one of conflict, not merely confidential information. Therefore, the professional may not act for both without the informed consent of both clients. This merely reaffirms the principle enunciated in *Mothew* (the so-called "double employment" rule);

(b) where the conflict is between an existing client and a former client, there are no competing fiduciary duties of loyalty because there is no fiduciary obligation of loyalty to a former client, although there is an obligation to protect confidentiality;

(c) the professional who receives relevant confidential information from a former client may not act for a client whose interest conflicts with the former client unless the firm can show that there is no real risk of disclosure. In determining whether there is a risk, the former client must show the court that there is a real risk; however, this is not a balancing exercise; and

(d) a firm may be able to discharge this high burden by demonstrating that effective internal measures are put in place which will prevent disclosure. A Chinese wall is more likely to be "effective" if it is part

117

of an already existing institutional arrangement within the firm (as opposed to one organised on an ad hoc basis). Permanent Chinese walls are a common feature of most multi-service firms, notably investment banks where such barriers will be placed between the different departments (e.g. corporate finance, securities trading and equity research) which hold clients' confidential information.

6.4.4 *The* **Robson Rhodes** *case*

Soon after the House of Lords decision in *Price Jefri*, came *Young v Robson Rhodes*. *Prince Jefri* was considered by Laddie J in that case. Robson Rhodes, an accounting firm, were in the process of merging with Pannell Kerr Forster ("PKF"). Robson Rhodes were retained to provide forensic accounting services in an action bought by Lloyds' Names against the auditors of the Syndicate in question, who were PKF. Robson Rhodes told the Names they would have to cease acting because of the merger. Consequently, the Names sought an injunction to delay the merger until after the conclusion of the trial, on the basis that if the merger went ahead, the confidential information of the Names could not be protected. Laddie J refused to grant the injunction, holding that the Chinese wall offered by Robson Rhodes and various undertakings they required were adequate to protect the Names from disclosure of their confidential information.

It should be noted that the Chinese wall erected by Robson Rhodes was an ad hoc arrangement created specifically to protect the Names' confidential information following the merger of the two firms. Laddie J interpreted the *Prince Jefri* case, as meaning that the court must be satisfied that the Chinese wall which is put in place will be effective to prevent disclosure. He said:

> "The crucial question is 'will the barriers work?' If they do, it does not matter whether they were created before the problem arose or are erected afterwards. It seems to me that all Lord Millett was saying was that Chinese walls which become part of the fabric of the institution are more likely to work than those artificially put in place to meet a one-off problem."

In light of Laddie J's comments in *Robson Rhodes*, it would appear that the decision in *Prince Jefri* does not invalidate the creation of ad hoc Chinese wall arrangements in certain circumstances. To this extent, commentators and professionals alike have welcomed this clarification, since ad hoc (but effective) Chinese walls are an essential feature of the operation and competitiveness of the City of London and the professional firms and financial institutions within it.

In *Robson Rhodes*, in considering whether the Chinese wall proposed would be effective, the court distinguished *Prince Jefri* on its facts. In *Prince Jefri*, a very large number of staff in KPMG's forensic accounting department had worked on Project Lucy and membership of the team rotated over time. In contrast, the confidential information in *Robson Rhodes* was restricted to a few readily identifiable staff. In addition, all the documents and computer records relating to the Names' action had been removed from the firm. Nonetheless, Laddie J made it clear that although there were fewer potential disclosures than in *Prince Jefri*, it did not mean that the risk of disclosure in *Robson Rhodes* was merely fanciful. In the end, the court did not think it necessary to grant an injunction to prevent the merger in order to give adequate protection to the Names' interest. However, Laddie J ruled that the only way to ensure that the Names' confidential information was protected was to impose physical separation between such persons, that is to say, in practice, working in separate premises.

6.4.5 The current position

It is still too early to form any views on how the courts are applying *Prince Jefri* in practice. However, it does appear as if judges are shifting away from the strict line adopted by Lord Millett in *Prince Jefri*, in favour of the more flexible approach espoused by the Court of Appeal in that case.

6.4.6 Setting up a Chinese wall – practical considerations

Having analysed the legal position of Chinese walls, one should now consider the measures adopted in establishing and operating an effective Chinese wall. The most common features are as follows:

(a) the physical separation of the various departments and/or advisory teams, for example, separate buildings or at least with restricted access to different departments of the firm, and separate dining arrangements;

(b) storage of sensitive or confidential information in a physically separate location, or in the case of confidential information stored in electronic form, ring-fencing such sensitive information by means of passwords or other IT security measures;

(c)   an educational programme, normally recurring, to emphasise to staff members the importance of not improperly or inadvertently divulging confidential information, reinforced by issued written guidelines (thereby creating a coherent firm-wide policy);

(d)   strict and carefully defined procedures for dealing with a situation where it is felt that the Chinese wall is breached and the maintaining of proper records where this occurs; and

(e)   monitoring by compliance officers and disciplinary sanctions for breaches.

Another common practice in the City for monitoring the operation and effectiveness of Chinese walls and for avoiding liability under the insider dealing legislation is the adoption of "stop" or "watch" lists. Put simply, trading in a specified share is either prohibited until further notice (a "stop" list) or is closely monitored (a "watch" list). The latter is typically common in a firm's compliance programme with respect to employee trading. To avoid conflicts, a firm could decline to deal in the relevant security until the conflict ceases to exist, or cease to recommend the share if this would otherwise create a conflict between the firm's interest and those of its customers. Indeed such lists can be seen as a sign that Chinese walls are not solely being relied on – public perception remains skeptical that an organisation's different departments are acting independently and without benefit of information behind Chinese walls. The Law Commission's view is that there should be express consent to use such lists, otherwise firms risk breaching their duty to give best advice to discretionary customers.

6.5   The regulatory framework

Having considered the legal position of investment bankers as fiduciaries and the legal limitations of Chinese walls, we should now consider the operation of Chinese walls in the market. It has been noted that very little of the established case law relates directly to investment banks. Nonetheless, market regulation has developed to ensure that conflicts of interest and Chinese walls are dealt with properly by banks.

6.5.1   *The Financial Services Authority (the "FSA") and the Conduct of Business Rules*

The UK financial markets are presently facing a radical change to the way they are regulated. Financial services regulation will be overseen by the new unitary and statutory regulator, the FSA, which is empowered by the Financial Services and Markets Act 2000 (the "FSMA"). The Securities and Futures Authority (the "SFA") (whose members include banks) falls under the FSA's organisational umbrella. Consequently, the Rules of the SFA (which recommended procedures for the segregation of information and the avoidance of conflicts of interest) will cease to apply once the FSA becomes the single regulator of financial services on 30 November 2001 (so-called "N2" when the new regime and rules come into force). The SFA Rules are to be replaced by the FSA's Conduct of Business Sourcebook (the "COBS Rules").

Principle 8 requires a regulated firm to manage a conflict of interest fairly, both between itself and its customers and between one customer and another. The COBS Rules, as with the SFA Rules, recognise that a firm may manage conflicts of interest by establishing and maintaining internal arrangements restricting the movement of information within the firm, that is Chinese walls. The FSMA gives the FSA power to make Chinese walls rules under Section 147 FSMA, and these rules are reflected in COB 2.4.4R:

> "When a firm establishes and maintains arrangements that require information held by it in the course of carrying on one part of its business to be withheld from, or not to be used for, persons with or for whom it acts in the course of carrying on another part of its business, it may in those circumstances:
> (i)   withhold or not use that information; and
> (ii)   for that purpose, permit persons employed in the first part of its business to withhold information from those employed in that other part of the business,
> but only to the extent that the business of one of those parts involves the carrying on of designated investment business."

In this context, "maintains" includes taking reasonable steps to ensure that the Chinese walls remain effective and are adequately monitored. The same applies to an established arrangement maintained between different parts of the business (of any kind) in the same group (COB 2.4.4(2)R).

Unlike the SFA Rules, the new rules appear to provide greater comfort for banks and other regulated financial institutions in that conformity with COB 2.4.4R affords a defence against potential liability arising under the FSMA. The COBS Rules clearly state that conforming with the new rules on Chinese walls provides a defence against proceedings brought under Section 397(2) or (3) FSMA (which are largely akin to

121

Section 47 Financial Services Act 1986 relating to misleading statements and practices), nor would it amount to the new offence of "market abuse" under Section 118 FSMA (COB 2.4.5G).

The COBS Rules also stipulate rules and guidance for regulated firms in managing conflicts of interest fairly. COB 7.1.3R provides that:

> "If a firm has or may have:
> (i) a 'material interest' in the transaction to be entered into with or for a customer;
> (ii) a relationship that gives or may give rise to a conflict of interest in relation to a transaction in (i);
> (iii) an interest in a transaction that is, or may be, in conflict with the interests of any of the firm's customers; or
> (iv) customers, or customers and clients with conflicting interests in relation to a transaction,
> the firm must not knowingly advise, or deal in the exercise of discretion, in relation to that transaction unless it takes reasonable steps to ensure fair treatment for the customer."

The FSA also provides clear guidance (COB 7.1.4G) on how a firm could manage a conflict of interest, including disclosing the interest to a customer or relying on a policy of independence, or establishing a Chinese wall (COB 7.1.8G). COB 7.1.6G provides that in disclosing an interest to a customer, a firm should disclose to the customer (orally or in writing) any "material interest" or conflict of interest it has or may have (generally or in relation to a specific transaction) before advising the customer about the transaction or dealing on behalf of him in relation to the transaction. The firm at the same time should demonstrate reasonable grounds for believing that the customer does not object to the "material interest" or conflict. When it is not practical for a firm to act in accordance with COB 7.1.6G, it may demonstrate that it has taken reasonable steps to ensure fair treatment for its private customers by relying on a policy of independence.

Alternatively, if a firm decides it is unable to manage a conflict using one of the above methods, it could simply decline to act for the customer.

For the purposes of the COBS Rules, "material interest" means in relation to a transaction, any interest of a material nature other than (a) disclosable commission on the transaction; and (b) goods or services which can reasonably be expected to assist in carrying on designated investment business with or for clients and which are provided or to be provided under a soft commission agreement.

6.5.2 *The City Code on Takeovers and Mergers (the "City Code")*

The Rules of the City Code which governs the conduct of public takeovers in the UK, are underpinned by various General Principles, including the equal treatment of the offeree company's shareholders and the prevention of creating a false market in the securities of the offeror or offeree (General Principles 1 and 7). Consequently, investment banks must safeguard against potential conflicts which may arise in the course of a takeover and which may have a serious impact on the Rules of the City Code.

The Takeover Panel recognises that a financial adviser may have the opportunity to act for an offeror or the offeree company in circumstances where the adviser is in possession of material confidential information relating to the other party, for example, because it was a previous client or because of its involvement in an earlier transaction. In certain circumstances, it may be necessary for the financial adviser to decline to act because the information is such that a conflict of interest is likely to arise.

The City Code emphasises the importance of multi-service financial organisations familiarising themselves with the implications of conducting other businesses in addition to, for example, corporate finance or stockbroking. Such organisations must not only ensure total segregation of their operations but also conduct the operations without regard for the interests of other parts of the same organisation or of their clients (Appendix 3.2 City Code). The Takeover Panel has ruled that when a multi-service organisation is advising an offeror, then all principal dealings in relevant securities by any part of that organisation will be presumed to be in concert with the offeror, with one important exception in respect of dealings in a market-making capacity, provided the market-maker concerned is "exempt". In order to obtain exempt status, an application must be made to the Takeover Panel which in each case will need to be satisfied that the organisation has in place arrangements which ensure that market-making or fund management operations are operated independently of the other relevant parts of the business. The Takeover Panel has accepted that, in general, it is the intention of multi-service financial organisations to run the market-making operations independently and without regard to the interests of clients of the corporate finance arm of their organisation, thereby accepting in this respect the principle of Chinese walls.

In addition, consideration must be given to Rule 3 of the City Code which provides that the board of the offeree company must obtain competent independent advice on any offer. The Takeover Panel regards it as of paramount importance that the financial adviser should be sufficiently independent so that its advice should be objective beyond question. A financial adviser's independence may be queried if, for example, it had recently advised the offeror or has a very close advisory relationship with a major shareholder in the offeree company. Clearly, the independence of the financial adviser must be judged on a case by case basis, and where the independence of an adviser may be in doubt, it is strongly advisable that the Panel be consulted as early as possible.

A recent illustration of this issue was the role of Dresdner Kleinwort Benson ("DKB") in relation to the offer by Abbey National for Cater Allen in 1997. DKB's close and continuing advisory relationship with Abbey National meant that DKB was an inappropriate person to provide independent advice under Rule 3.1. The Panel however held that there was no reason why DKB should not continue to advise Cater Allen, alongside the Rule 3.1 adviser, should this be the wish of Cater Allen's board of directors.

6.6   Insider dealing

6.6.1   *Criminal Justice Act 1993*

Closely aligned to client confidentiality is the problem of insider dealing which may arise in circumstances where confidential or sensitive information is disclosed or discussed in the course of takeover transactions. The provisions relating to insider dealing are contained in Part V Criminal Justice Act 1993 ("CJA"), which came into force on 1 March 1994. Under Section 52 CJA, it is a criminal offence for an individual who has information as an insider to deal in price-affected securities, or to encourage another person (which, in this context, includes a company) to deal in such securities. It is also a criminal offence for such an individual to disclose the information to another person other than in the proper performance of his employment, office or profession. Persons convicted of insider dealing can be imprisoned for up to seven years and/or fined (Section 61 CJA).

An "insider" is an individual who knowingly has inside information from an inside source, that is if:

(a) he has the information through being a director, employee or share-holder of an issuer of securities (not necessarily of the same issuer to which the information relates); or

(b) he has it through having access to the information by virtue of his employment, office or profession; or

(c) the direct or indirect source of this information is a person falling within one of the above.

The provisions on dealing, encouraging dealing and disclosing information apply in respect of "price-affected" securities, which means that, if made public, the information would be likely to have a significant effect on the price or value of the securities concerned.

It is, however, common knowledge that few prosecutions are ever brought for insider dealing in the UK and given the high criminal standard of proof, even fewer convictions are made (only three between 1995 and 1999; contrast this with 162 civil cases won by the US Securities and Exchange Commission in the same period). This is one of the reasons why the UK Government has legislated a new regime of "market abuse" (*see* Section 6.6.3 below).

6.6.2   The Model Code

Whilst not strictly speaking involving client information, directors and other senior employees of listed banks should have regard to the Model Code whose purpose is to ensure that directors, certain employees and persons connected with them do not abuse and do not place themselves under suspicion of abusing price-sensitive information that they may have or be thought to have, especially in periods leading up to an announcement of results. The UK Listing Authority sees the Model Code (set out in the Appendix to Chapter 16 Listing Rules) as a minimum standard of good practice, rather than as a rigid set of rules, and directors should therefore err on the side of caution when uncertain as to whether a course of conduct will bring them into conflict with the Model Code. A breach of the Model Code will be regarded as a matter of utmost seriousness and could also lead to enquiries being made by the Department of Trade and Industry and by the London Stock Exchange.

6.6.3   Market abuse under the FSMA

As noted earlier, the system of regulation is currently being overhauled. The provisions of the new FSMA, which came into force on 1 December 2001, include a new statutory civil regime for the control of "market abuse" (*see* Part VIII FSMA). This regime is supplemental to rather than a replacement of the existing criminal regimes of insider dealing (described above) and market manipulation (Section 397 FSMA). The FSMA defines the concept of market abuse very widely thereby considerably extending the present law and enhancing the FSA's ability to tackle such abuse. Those who commit market abuse can be liable to an unlimited fine or public censure, ordered to make restitution and restrained by injunction. It will be interesting to see how this new concept will operate in the financial markets after N2 and also the extent to which the FSA will encroach on the Takeover Panel's jurisdiction over public takeovers in the UK.

The FSA has however made it clear in the COBS Rules that compliance with Chinese wall rules should provide conclusive evidence that dealing by a person within the same firm, but on the other side of a Chinese wall, was not "based on information" that could otherwise be regarded as a misuse of information (and, therefore, market abuse).

In the context of corporate finance transactions, investment bankers should note that the FSA has resisted granting, in its Code of Market Conduct, blanket "safe harbours" for market abuse in respect of compliance with the UK Listing Authority's Listing Rules or the City Code (the safe harbours only apply to specific rules thereof).

The new market abuse regime is covered in more detail in Chapter 8.

Chapter 7

Financial Promotion

Guy Morton
Partner
Freshfields Bruckhaus Deringer

7.1 Introduction

Financial promotion is one of the areas in which the Financial Services and Markets Act 2000[1] (the "FSMA") makes substantial changes to the previous regulatory regime. The separate provisions previously dealing with investment advertisements and unsolicited calls are replaced by a single new regime with its own new concepts and terminology. While the fundamental policy aims and regulatory structure have not changed, and while the exemptions under the new Act are in many cases intended to produce a result broadly comparable with the previous position, only experience will show how well this objective has been achieved. In any event, it will require a major effort for firms carrying on corporate finance activities to adapt their policies and procedures to the new rules and to work out their detailed application in practice.

In the overview document that accompanied the first draft of the Financial Services and Markets Bill[2] the Treasury stated that the existing regime dealing with the promotion of financial services needed to be brought up to date. It said that the aim of the Bill was to bring together the different regimes dealing with the regulation of advertisements and unsolicited calls into "a single, cohesive framework which takes full account of changing opportunities of technology". The new regime is intended to rationalise and modernise the existing legislation relating to investment promotions in the UK. For example, in the past it has been difficult to accommodate electronic media within the concepts of advertisements and unsolicited calls; these classifications have now been

---

[1] In this Chapter all references to sections, schedules or paragraphs of schedules are to the FSMA unless specifically stated otherwise.

[2] *See* HM Treasury consultation paper *Financial Services and Markets Bill: A Consultation Document – Part One: Overview of Financial Regulatory Reform* published in July 1998.

replaced with the more media neutral concept of an "invitation or inducement" to engage in investment activity.

The statutory basis for the new regime is Section 21 FSMA. This Section introduces a new, single "financial promotion" regime which will replaces the separate rules that previously governed investment advertisements, unsolicited calls (known also as "cold calls"), deposit advertisements and insurance advertisements. The effect of Section 21 is to prohibit unauthorised persons from issuing financial promotions unless the content of the promotion is approved by an authorised person or an exemption applies.[3]

7.2 Scope of the new regime

7.2.1 General

The financial promotion restriction in Section 21 FSMA replaces the investment advertisement and cold calling restrictions contained in Sections 56 and 57 Financial Services Act (the "FS Act"). Like the FS Act regime, the new financial promotion regime is relevant to both authorised and unauthorised entities. A person who is unauthorised may not generally make a communication to which the regime applies unless an authorised person approves the content of the communication or an exemption applies. An authorised person, when making or approving a communication which falls within the new financial promotion regime, will be required to comply with the FSA's Conduct of Business ("COB") rules relating to financial promotions,[4] subject to any applicable transitional provisions.[5]

However, the new regime is broader than those which it replaces. For example, Section 21 is media neutral and therefore applies to all "communications", a term which is significantly broader than advertisements and unsolicited calls and potentially brings solicited calls and other communications which do not amount to advertising (such as individualised communications) within the regulatory net. It also applies to communications relating to deposit-taking and insurance. The scope of the regime is, however, narrowed to some extent by the exemptions from

---

[3] *See* Section 21(1).
[4] These rules are contained in Chapter 3 of the FSA's *Conduct of Business Sourcebook*, June 2001.
[5] *See* further Section 7.6 below.

the basic prohibition which are contained in the Financial Services and Markets Act 2000 (Financial Promotion) Order 2001 (the "Financial Promotion Order").[6]

Most of the exemptions available under the FS Act regime[7] have been carried forward into the new regime. There are also a number of new exemptions, some of which have been introduced as a consequence of the broader scope of the prohibition and some of which are genuine new exemptions. These are discussed further in Section 7.4.6 below.

The FSA has recognised that the new regime is complex and in August 2001 it published draft consultative guidance on certain aspects of Section 21 and the Financial Promotion Order (the "FSA Guidance").[8] The draft guidance is designed to help companies and their advisers to understand the new arrangements and provides both a factual summary of the relevant provisions and the FSA's views on how the primary and secondary legislation could be interpreted where it believes that the provisions are unclear or open to misinterpretation.

7.2.2 Territorial scope

Under the FS Act regime, it was generally accepted that investment advertisements were caught if sent into the UK, but not if sent abroad from the UK. By contrast, cold calls were caught if made either into or out of the UK. The territorial scope of the new financial promotion regime in Section 21 is more widely drawn. It applies to communications originating both inside the UK (including those made only to people outside the UK) and to communications originating outside the UK, which are capable of having an effect in the UK. For example, a

---

[6] SI 2001 No. 1335, as amended by the Financial Services and Markets Act 2000 (Financial Promotion) (Amendment) Order 2001 (SI 2001 No. 2633), the Financial Services and Markets Act 2000 (Miscellaneous Provisions) Order 2001 (SI 2001 No 3650) ("Miscellaneous Order") and the Financial Services and Markets Act 2000 (Financial Promotion) (Amendment No 2) Order 2001 (SI 2001 No 3800) ("Amendment No 2 Order").

[7] As set out in the Financial Services Act 1986 (Investment Advertisement) (Exemptions) (No. 2) Order 1995 (the "1995 Order"), the Financial Services Act (Investment Advertisements) (Exemptions) Order 1996 (the "1996 Order") and the Common Unsolicited Calls Regulations 1991.

[8] *See* FSA consultation paper number 104 *The Authorisation Manual: Supplementary Consultation on Certifications, Financial Promotion and Related Activities, and Open-ended Investment Companies*, August 2001. This guidance will form an appendix to the FSA's Authorisation Manual.

communication which is posted on a website in Spain is caught (subject to any relevant exemptions) if UK investors can access it.

7.2.2.1   *Outward promotions*
The wide territorial scope of the regime was the subject of fierce debate and criticism, both during the passage of the Bill and in the consultation on the draft exemptions. The government was not persuaded to narrow the scope of Section 21 itself, since it wished to leave sufficient flexibility to move to a system of predominantly home country control of financial promotions if, and when, European legislation to that effect is introduced. However, it was at a late stage persuaded that it was not at present appropriate to apply the UK regime to outward promotions from the UK, other than unsolicited oral communications (which had also been regulated under the FS Act). Accordingly, Article 12 Financial Promotion Order generally exempts communications that are made to, or directed only at, persons outside the UK (*see* further Section 7.2.2.3 below).

7.2.2.2   *Inward promotions*
The new regime applies to communications originating outside the UK which are "capable of having an effect" in the UK.[9] Again Article 12 Financial Promotion Order limits the basic scope of Section 21 to permit inward communications which, although they originate outside the UK and are capable of having an effect in the UK, are not "directed at" persons in the UK. This is a welcome change from the position where under the FS Act regime, technically, any promotion available to persons in the UK was caught.[10]

7.2.2.3   *The Article 12 exemption*
As mentioned above, Article 12 Financial Promotion Order contains an exemption for communications that are made to, or directed only at, persons outside the UK (regardless of whether the communication originates inside or outside the UK). It therefore significantly restricts the scope of the Section 21 prohibition in relation to both outward and inward promotions. It also provides a safe harbour by indicating that a communication which satisfies certain conditions (these are set out in Article 12(4) and are reproduced below) will be conclusively regarded as being "directed only at" persons outside the UK.

---

[9] *See* Section 21(3).
[10] *See* Section 207(5) FS Act.

The Article 12 exemption covers non-real time and solicited real time communications[11] made from either inside or outside the UK. However, it is restricted in its application to unsolicited real time communications. It extends to such communications only if they are made from a place outside the UK and for the purposes of a business which is carried on outside the UK and is not carried on in the UK. The effect of this is that unsolicited real time communications which originate from the UK are subject to the financial promotion restriction, regardless of whether or not they are made to, or directed only at, persons outside the UK.[12]

Article 12(4) Financial Promotion Order sets out the conditions which are relevant in determining whether a communication is to be regarded as "directed only at" persons outside the UK. These are that:

(a)   the communication is accompanied by an indication that it is directed only at persons outside the UK;
(b)   the communication is accompanied by an indication that it must not be acted on by persons in the UK;
(c)   the communication is not referred to in, or directly accessible from, any other communication which is made to a person or directed at persons in the UK by or on behalf of the same person (a communicator would therefore need to be careful about, for instance, links on the communicator's general website to another site where the financial promotion is available);
(d)   there are proper systems and procedures in place to prevent recipients in the UK engaging in the investment activity to which the communication relates; and
(e)   the communication is included in a publication principally accessed in, or intended for, a market outside the UK or in a sound or television broadcast or teletext service transmitted principally for reception outside the UK.

In relation to outward promotions directed from inside the UK, if conditions (a), (b), (c) and (d) are satisfied, the communication will be regarded as directed only at persons outside the UK (i.e. it will fall within a safe harbour). In relation to inward promotions directed from outside the UK, the safe harbour will apply if only conditions (c) and (d) are satisfied. In other cases the conditions, though not conclusive, are of evidential value in determining whether or not the communication is

---

[11] *See* further Sections 7.4.2 and 7.4.3 below.
[12] This effectively preserves the territorial application of the prohibition on cold calls under Section 56 FS Act.

directed only at persons outside the UK (although a communication may be so regarded even if none of the conditions is satisfied).

With regard to condition (d), the FSA Guidance notes that there is no explanation in the Financial Promotion Order as to what constitutes "proper systems and procedures" in view of the different forms that systems and procedures may take. However, it is clear that persons seeking to rely on this exemption will need consciously to establish arrangements to prevent their dealing with recipients in the UK. The guidance indicates that such arrangements may include password-protected access to information or the programming of software to recognise and reject UK addresses (the most obvious example of this would seem to be a postcode check) or both. So long as the systems and procedures are "proper", the exemption will continue to apply even if on isolated occasions they fail to prevent dealings with a recipient in the UK.[13]

7.3 Key elements of Section 21

7.3.1 Promotional element

Section 21 provides that a person (A) must not, in the course of business, communicate an invitation or inducement to engage in investment activity, unless A is authorised under the Act or an authorised person approves the content of the communication or an exemption applies.

Section 21 was the subject of a great deal of debate during the passage of the Bill through Parliament. The main concern relates to its extremely wide scope, in particular the prospect of its catching communications which have no explicit promotional element. This concern centres on the use of the word "inducement", which could well be construed objectively so as to catch any communication likely to form the basis of an investment decision, whether or not it was issued with the intention of promoting any investment activity. Although the government indicated that it believes that the term involves a promotional element,[14] it decided not to include an express requirement for an intention to promote in the legislation.

---

[13] *See* Annex B, paragraph 1.12.6 FSA Guidance.
[14] The government stated that in its view the word "inducement" included "an element of incitement". This may be of some help in marginal cases, but does not remove the concern about a possible objective interpretation.

7.3.2 *Made in the course of business*

Section 21 applies only to communications made "in the course of business". Although the Treasury has been given the power to define this expression in secondary legislation,[15] it is not intending to exercise this power for the time being and the phrase is to be given its ordinary meaning.[16]

The purpose of including the words "in the course of business" was to exclude genuine non-business communications from the regime. The FSA considers that such communications include: friends talking in a pub, letters between family members and e-mails sent by individuals using an internet chat room or bulletin board for personal reasons.[17] Section 21 nevertheless catches a range of communications which, although made in the course of business, are essentially individual, private communications that did not fall within Section 57 FS Act. For example, if two commercial companies enter into correspondence about the possible acquisition by one of them of a subsidiary of the other, many items of the correspondence will in all probability constitute "communications" within Section 21. Under the FS Act regime, such correspondence would not generally have been regarded as covered by Section 57 FS Act because it would not have constituted a form of advertising. The practical importance of this point has however been greatly reduced by the Financial Promotion Order, which contains an exemption for "one-off communications" (*see* Section 7.4.6.2 below).

Although the FSA Guidance states that the phrase "in the course of business" requires a commercial interest on the part of the communicator,[18] it is important to note that the FSA has also said that the communication does not need to be made in the course of carrying on activities as a business in their own right.[19] For example, if a holding company wants to sell one of its subsidiaries, that sale will be "in the course of business", notwithstanding that the company is not in the business of

---

[15] *See* Section 21(4).

[16] *See* paragraph 4.6 of *Financial Services and Markets Bill: Financial Promotion – Second Consultation Document (A New Approach for the Information Age)* published by HM Treasury in October 1999.

[17] *See* Annex B, paragraph 1.5.3 FSA Guidance.

[18] *See* Annex B, paragraph 1.5.2 FSA Guidance.

[19] As is the test for carrying on regulated activities requiring authorisation – *see* Article 3 Financial Services and Markets Act 2000 (Carrying on Regulated Activities by Way of Business) Order 2001 (SI 2001 No. 1177).

selling subsidiaries. This illustrates the wide application of the regime in the context of corporate finance activities.

The FSA has also advised persons who carry on a business which is not a regulated activity to be careful in making communications that may amount to financial promotions.[20] For example, the guidance refers to a situation where a company makes communications to employees which could take the form of promotions concerning employees' share schemes and group-wide insurance arrangements, such as permanent health insurance and pension schemes. The FSA has commented that such communications may well be financial promotions made in the course of business, and as such, would need to be approved by an authorised person unless an appropriate exemption is available, such as that for employee share schemes.[21]

7.3.3   *Communicate or causing to communicate*

7.3.3.1   *"Communicate"*
The financial promotion restriction applies where there is a "communication" of an invitation or inducement to engage in investment activity. The word "communicate" appears to connote some degree of action on the part of the communicator and success in reaching the recipient. So long as a message is successfully delivered, it would not seem to matter that the recipient does not understand the content of the message.

It seems that a person may be involved in communicating even if he passively passes on information produced by someone else. This is the view of the FSA and it is arguably confirmed by the fact that an exemption has been granted to "mere conduits" such as the Post Office and other document distributors;[22] implying that such persons can be regarded as communicating financial promotions. Having said this, the wording of the financial promotions Order may not be a particularly strong indicator of Parliament's intended reading of "communicate", given that the order was made some time after the FSMA was passed.

The FSA Guidance also recognises that a wide range of persons may be involved in communicating a financial promotion, including:

---

[20] *See* Annex B, paragraph 1.5.5 FSA Guidance.
[21] *See* Article 69 Financial Promotion Order.
[22] *See* Article 18 Financial Promotion Order, and Annex B, paragraph 1.6.1 FSA Guidance.

(a)   the author of the financial promotion;
(b)   where different, the person who caused the financial promotion to be made; and
(c)   any persons who pass on the financial promotion.

The FSA considers that, although a person must take some active step to make a communication, a failure to take adequate safeguards to prevent a communication being made (or being reckless as to whether or not it is made) may nevertheless amount to making a communication.[23] However, the FSA has said that inadvertently leaving a document on a train will not amount to making a communication to someone who may pick it up, nor will a person be deemed to be communicating to someone who eavesdrops on a private conversation.[24]

7.3.3.2   *Causing a communication to be made*
In determining whether a person has caused a communication to be made it would seem that, in order for a person (A) to cause a communication to be made by another (B), A must have some degree of control or influence over B. This would be the case if B were acting on the actual authority, whether express or implied, of A. If A has no control over B, and B has a discretion as to whether or not to communicate information provided to it by A, it seems that A would not be regarded as having caused the making of any communication which B decides to make.[25]

For example, consider the following scenario: a person (A) passes a communication to a journalist (B). A intends and expects B to write articles based heavily on the information in the communication, but not to transmit the actual communication which is passed to him. In this scenario A would not be regarded as having caused the communication of any articles written by B because he has no control over B. In its guidance[26] the FSA has cited the following as examples of those who may be making or causing a communication to be made: anyone employed

---

[23] *See* Annex B, paragraph 1.6.2 FSA Guidance.
[24] *See* Annex B, paragraph 1.6.2 FSA Guidance.
[25] In *Attorney General of Hong Kong* v *Tse Hung Lit* [1986] 3 All ER 173 the Privy Council held that a person may only cause another to carry out a prohibited act if the act was done on the actual authority, whether express or implied, of the person said to have caused the act or in consequence of his exerting some influence on the acts of the other person. In reaching this conclusion the court referred to and adopted reasoning of the High Court of Australia in *O'Sullivan* v *Truth and Sportsman Ltd* [1957] 96 CLR 220.
[26] *See* Annex B, paragraph 1.6.2 FSA Guidance.

to distribute copies of the communication; placers of advertisements in publications or broadcasts; and also those publishers and broadcasters themselves.

7.3.4 *Invitation or inducement*

To constitute a financial promotion, the communication must be of "an invitation or inducement to engage in investment activity".

7.3.4.1 *Meaning of invitation*

An invitation to engage in investment activity is a communication which directly invites a person to enter, or offer to enter, into an investment agreement. Therefore, an invitation to treat, such as an advertisement that invites potential counterparties to contact a firm with a view to making it an offer to do business, will constitute a financial promotion. The FSA Guidance also refers to the following as examples of invitations: direct offer advertisements; prospectuses with application forms; and internet promotions where the response by the consumer will initiate the activity (such as "register now and begin dealing online").[27]

Whether a communication amounts to an invitation is to be objectively determined. The wording of the communication must be construed to determine whether, in substance, it amounts to an invitation. This means that actual intent on the part of the communicator (i.e. the intention to make an invitation) is not strictly necessary and that it is possible for there to be an invitation if the communication is reasonably understood as amounting to an invitation even though the maker did not intend this to be the case.

The presence in a communication of express wording to the effect that it is not intended to be an invitation, whether generally or to a particular category of persons (for instance, wording on a website to the effect that it is not addressed to persons within a particular jurisdiction), is likely to constitute strong evidence that it is not an invitation.[28] However, such a statement is not conclusive and a communication may still constitute

---

[27] *See* Annex B, paragraph 1.4.1 FSA Guidance.

[28] In *Alliance & Leicester Building Society* v *Babbs* [1993] CCLR 77, the Divisional Court held (on appeal from the magistrates court by way of case stated) that a brochure regarding personal loans which was sent to a nine year old boy did not constitute an invitation to a minor to borrow money contrary to the Consumer Credit Act 1974 because it contained a statement to the effect that loans were not available to applicants under 18 years of age.

an invitation, even though it is expressly stated not to be one. For example, this may be the case where the communicator's conduct is inconsistent with the express statement, for instance, where the communication states that it is not intended to be an invitation to a particular category of persons but an agreement is then entered into with a person in that category.

If a communication is to amount to an invitation, it will generally be necessary for there to be a specific controlled activity or controlled investment in contemplation.[29] Therefore, it is unlikely that general corporate advertising will constitute an invitation. This is also the FSA's view. Their guidance states that activities which are "purely profile raising and do not identify and promote particular investments or investment services" may not amount to an invitation (or indeed an inducement (*see* further below)).[30]

Finally, causation is not required in order for there to be an invitation. A communication can be an invitation even though it is unlikely that any investment decision will result from it and none does in fact result.

7.3.4.2   *Meaning of inducement*

There is no statutory definition of "inducement" and case law provides little guidance on its meaning. The word will therefore be given its ordinary meaning; the Oxford English Dictionary definition of "inducement" is "a thing that persuades or influences someone to do something". "Induce" is similarly defined as "succeed in persuading or influencing (someone) to do something". The word therefore connotes an element of causation between the communication and the investment decision. On this basis it would seem that the link between the communication and the investment decision must be close because:

(a)   the communication must be likely to cause some action; and
(b)   that action must be entering or offering to enter into an investment agreement or exercising rights in respect of an investment, not merely starting on a trail which may lead to one of those things.

So, for example, "image" advertising preparing the ground for an intended IPO before specific marketing commences, an invitation to a

---

[29] *See* further Section 7.3.5 below.
[30] *See* Annex B, paragraph 1.4.5 FSA Guidance. The FSA refers to companies sponsoring sporting events or placing their logo or name on goods as "purely profile raising".

presentation and a tombstone would not normally amount to inducements. Similarly, it is arguable that instructions or guidance as to the mechanics of engaging in investment activity should not amount to an inducement because there is no element of persuasion; communications of this sort only cause a person to engage in investment activity once he has made the decision to do so. Therefore, a Q&A session explaining how to accept a takeover or share offer, or answers by a call centre dealing only with the mechanics of accepting an offer may not be inducements.

However, the FSA Guidance provides only limited support for this view. Although it agrees that purely profile raising activities may be too far removed from any investment decision to be inducements, it also comments that an inducement is a form of communication which is "a step in a chain which leads . . . directly or indirectly, to a person engaging in investment activity".[31] It is unclear whether this represents a change in the official view of the point at which preparatory publicity (e.g. a "warm up" campaign for a securities issue) requires approval and becomes subject to the content requirements of the conduct of business rules.

An element of intention on the part of the communicator (intention being determined objectively from the facts) should be regarded as a necessary but not a sufficient condition of an inducement. If a communication is by its nature too remote to be an inducement, the mere presence of an intention to persuade will not make it one (the "image" advertising example). Having said this, if there is a clear intention to persuade, the remoteness test should in practice be applied cautiously. Conversely, even if a communication is objectively likely to persuade, it will still be necessary to consider whether the communicator would be regarded as having actively wished to persuade the recipient to engage in investment activity, rather than as being neutral as to whether or not the recipient did so.

The FSA Guidance indicates that the FSA shares the view both that an element of intention is necessary and that it must be determined objectively.[32] The guidance refers to various statements made by the Treasury in its consultation papers on financial promotion and to statements made in Parliament which also appear to support this view. So, for example, information available on the site of an internet service provider or a

---

[31] *See* Annex B, paragraph 1.4.3 FSA Guidance.
[32] *See* Annex B, paragraphs 1.4.2 and 1.4.3 FSA Guidance.

comparative table in a financial services portal which received no commission from participants may not be an inducement. Nevertheless, it may in practice be difficult to rely on a lack of intention to persuade in circumstances where a communication is shown to be likely to persuade the recipient to engage in investment activity (particularly where the communicator knows that the communication is likely to have this effect), except in cases where the role of the communicator is purely mechanical.

In determining whether a communication amounts to an inducement it will also be necessary to take account of the target audience. For instance, a communication which may amount to an inducement to A (an elderly lady in Brighton) will not necessarily amount to an inducement to B (an analyst in the City).

7.3.5 Engaging in investment activity

The phrase "engaging in investment activity" is defined in Section 21(8) as:

(a) entering or offering to enter into an agreement the making or performance of which by either party constitutes a controlled activity; or

(b) exercising any rights conferred by a controlled investment to acquire, dispose of, underwrite or convert a controlled investment.

The controlled activities and controlled investments are set out in Schedule 1 to the Financial Promotion Order. Broadly speaking, "controlled activities" and "controlled investments" are similar to the "regulated activities" and "specified investments" which are set out in the Financial Services and Markets Act 2000 (Regulated Activities) Order 2001[33] (the "Regulated Activities Order"). However, in respect of controlled activities, none of the exclusions set out in the Regulated Activities Order apply and there are a few differences between controlled activities and regulated activities, particularly in the areas of mortgages and funeral plans.

The meaning of "offer" in the context of the first limb of the definition of "engaging in investment activity" is narrower than, for example, the definition of "offer" found in the Public Offers of Securities Regulations 1995.[34] Regulation 5(b) POS Regulations defines "offer" so as to include

---

[33] SI 2001 No. 544.
[34] SI 1995 No. 1537.

an invitation to treat. There is no equivalent provision in the Financial Promotion Order.

7.4   The Financial Promotion Order

7.4.1   *Overview*

Section 21(5) FSMA allows the Treasury to specify, in secondary legislation, the circumstances in which the financial promotion restriction does not apply. Following the publication by the Treasury of three consultation documents on the new promotion regime and the Financial Promotion Order,[35] the final version of this key piece of secondary legislation, was finally made on 2 April 2001, with certain further changes being made on by the Financial Services and Markets Act 2000 (Financial Promotion) Amendment Order 2001[36] (the "Amendment Order") the Miscellaneous Order and the Amendment No 2 Order. The exemptions set out in the Financial Promotion Order, as amended, replace the exemptions in the 1995 Order, the 1996 Order, the Common Unsolicited Calls Regulations 1991 and the provisions on deposit advertisements and insurance advertisements in the Banking Act 1987 (Advertisements) Regulations 1988,[37] the Credit Institutions (Protection of Depositors) Regulations 1995[38] and the Insurance Companies Regulations 1994.[39] In general:

(a)   the scope of the existing regimes concerning deposits, insurance and investment services is preserved;

(b)   the existing exemptions are broadly retained;

(c)   similar exemptions from the existing investment advertisements and unsolicited calls regimes have been consolidated so far as appropriate;

(d)   the exemptions apply differently to individual unrecorded and interactive communications (referred to as "real time communications") which are unsolicited, thereby effectively preserving much of the existing unsolicited calls regime;

---

[35] These consultation documents were: *Financial Promotion – A Consultation Document*, March 1999; *Financial Promotion – Second Consultation Document (A New Approach for the Information Age)*, October 1999; and *Financial Promotion: Third Consultation Document*, October 2000 (the "Third Consultation Document").

[36] SI 2001 No. 2633.

[37] SI 1988 No. 645.

[38] SI 1995 No. 1442.

[39] SI 1994 No. 1516.

(e)   there has been a rationalisation and deletion of unused provisions under the existing regimes; and

(f)   new exemptions have been introduced for certain activities, including promotions made to high net worth individuals and sophisticated investors.

The exemptions in the Financial Promotion Order are split into three categories: exemptions applicable to all controlled activities (Part IV); exemptions applicable only to controlled activities concerning deposits and contracts of insurance, other than life policies (Part V); and exemptions applicable to any other types of controlled activity (Part VI).

The Financial Promotion Order makes a number of basic distinctions which play a key role in the application of the exemptions to different kinds of communication, and which make it possible for the regime to include differences in treatment which in some respects, though by no means all, correspond to differences between the treatment of investment advertisements and unsolicited calls under the FS Act. It is therefore important to understand the key definitions on which these distinctions are based.

7.4.2   Real time and non-real time communications

The first such distinction is that between real time communications and non-real time communications. Article 7(1) Financial Promotion Order defines a real time communication as any communication made in the course of a personal visit, telephone conversation or other interactive dialogue; any other communication is a non-real time communication.

Article 7(3) states that non-real time communications include communications made by letter or e-mail or contained in a publication.[40] There are also various factors[41] which will be treated as indications that a communication is non-real time, namely that:

(a)   the communication is made to, or directed at, more than one recipient in identical terms (save for details of the recipient's identity);

---

[40] "Publication" is defined in Article 2 Financial Promotion Order as: a newspaper, journal, magazine or other periodical; a website; any television or radio broadcast; and any teletext service.

[41] *See* Article 7(5) Financial Promotion Order.

(b)   the communication is made or directed by way of a system which in the normal course constitutes or creates a record of the communication which is available to the recipient to refer to at a later time; and

(c)   the communication is made or directed by way of a system which in the normal course does not enable or require the recipient to respond immediately to it.

The FSA Guidance suggests that a real time communication is, broadly speaking, one that enables interaction at the time it is made (e.g. communications at meetings and presentations). With regard to non-real time communications the FSA has said that it will generally not be possible to interrupt someone who is making such a communication and that a non-real time communication is one which may exist in enduring form.[42] The FSA considers that messages on internet chat-rooms will be non-real time, presumably on the basis that it is not possible to interrupt a person who places such a message and the message will exist in enduring form. It follows that mobile text messages will also be non-real time communications.[43]

However, notwithstanding the definitions included in the Financial Promotion Order and the FSA Guidance, the categorisation of communications may not always be straightforward. For example, a written communication handed over during the course of a personal visit would, on a literal reading of the definitions contained in Article 7 Financial Promotion Order, constitute a real time communication. Nevertheless, it is more appropriately regarded as a non-real time communication. The FSA agrees with this approach and its guidance states that any slides, handouts and other visual aides made available during a presentation will be non-real time communications.[44] A speech given at a meeting would probably be regarded as a non-real time communication on the basis that it is a one-way flow of dialogue which is not interactive.

In relation to real time communications, the Financial Promotion Order further distinguishes between solicited and unsolicited communications. Different exemptions apply depending on the classification of the communication and a larger number of exemptions apply to non-real time and solicited real time communications (which are treated similarly

---

[42] *See* Annex B, paragraphs 1.10.4 and 1.10.5 FSA Guidance.

[43] The FSA Guidance may be affected by the Amendment No. 2 Order, Article 3 which appears to contemplate that some written communications can be real time.

[44] *See* Annex B, paragraph 1.10.4 FSA Guidance.

by the Financial Promotion Order) than to unsolicited real time communications.[45]

7.4.3 Is the communication solicited or unsolicited (in the case of a real time communication)?

The second key distinction is that between solicited and unsolicited real time communications. This is set out in Article 8 Financial Promotion Order. A real time communication is solicited where the call, visit or dialogue either has been initiated by the recipient of the communication or takes place in response to an express request from the recipient. Any other call, visit or dialogue constitutes an unsolicited real time communication.

With regard to requested communications, it is important to note that it is the call, visit or dialogue which must be expressly requested by the recipient if the communication is to be regarded as solicited. Therefore, if a recipient is asked on an unsolicited call or during an unsolicited visit whether he wishes to receive information on a particular matter, that communication will be unsolicited. Conversely, if the call or visit itself was solicited, any communication made in the course of the call or visit will itself, prima facie, be regarded as solicited. However, Article 8(3) Financial Promotion Order provides that a communication is only to be treated as solicited if it is clear from all the circumstances surrounding the solicitation what investment activities or investments the solicited communication will relate to and the communication does in fact relate to those activities and investments. For example, if a person requests a visit from a representative of an investment product company with a view to receiving advice on an appropriate pension product, the representative would probably be making an unsolicited financial promotion if, during the visit, he raises the possibility of the person making an investment which would not be for the purposes of pension provision.[46] In light of the rules and guidance considered above, where it is intended to hold a general meeting to discuss investment opportunities it would be sensible to clarify the scope of the meeting in advance to ensure that it would be regarded as a solicited real time communication.

---

[45] This is on the basis that recipients will need more protection in relation to unsolicited communications. The exemptions applicable to unsolicited real time communications are based largely on the exemptions to the cold calling regime provided for in the Common Unsolicited Calls Regulations 1991.

[46] This example is taken from Annex B, paragraph 1.10.9 FSA Guidance.

Article 8 does not define what is meant by "express request", but does set out circumstances in which a person is not to be treated as expressly requesting a call, visit or dialogue. Such a request will not be regarded as having been made simply because a person:

(a) omits to indicate that he does not wish to receive any calls, visits or dialogue or any further visits or calls or to engage in any or any further dialogue; or

(b) agrees to standard terms which state that such visits, calls or dialogue will take place, unless he has signified clearly that, in addition to agreeing to the terms, he is willing for them to take place.

Limb (b) implies that a request which is phrased in generic terms can, if sufficiently clear, be regarded as "express".[47] There is no guidance in the Financial Promotion Order as to what a person must do in order to signify clearly that, in addition to agreeing to standard terms, he is willing to receive calls, visits or dialogue. In spite of the inconvenience that this may cause (arguably to both parties), cautious firms may seek two signatures to their customer documentation – one agreeing to the terms generally and another to a specific acknowledgment relating to such calls, visits or dialogue. On the other hand a clear and prominent provision appearing on the signature page would seem as a matter of ordinary language to amount to a "clear signification" for this purpose. It is unclear whether a person can be regarded as clearly signifying a willingness to receive calls, visits or dialogue merely by accepting standard terms by conduct; it seems unlikely that this is the case.

In some situations a person may make a financial promotion to someone who has expressly requested that it be made and also to other persons who have not requested it (for instance, where a person answers questions from an audience at a presentation). Article 8(4) Financial Promotion Order provides that this will represent an unsolicited financial promotion made to the persons other than the person who expressly requested the call, visit or dialogue in which the promotion was made *unless* those other persons are:

- close relatives of that person; or
- expected to engage in any investment activity jointly with that person.

---

[47] A view which corresponds to that generally held in relation to the corresponding test under Section 56 FS Act.

It is unclear whether the word "jointly" means that the relevant persons must be expected to act jointly in the strict legal sense, so that they are liable jointly for the whole of any commitments assumed and any property is held in joint names. If so, the scope of Article 8(4) would be quite narrow. The FSA suggests a rather less restrictive interpretation; in the context of one-off communications its guidance[48] suggests that persons will engage in investment activity jointly if there is some form of link or connection between them which makes it likely that they will take investment decisions jointly.[49]

7.4.4 *Required indicators*

Certain exemptions in the Financial Promotion Order require that a communication be accompanied by specified indications. Article 9 provides that, where this is the case, the indication must be presented to the recipient in a way that can be easily understood, and in a manner best calculated to bring the indication to the attention of the recipient and to allow him to consider it. This manner will be determined depending on the means by which the communication is made or directed.

7.4.5 *Communications made to/directed at certain recipients*

Some of the exemptions in the Financial Promotion Order distinguish between communications which are "made to" certain recipients and communications which are "directed at" certain recipients. Examples are Article 12 (communications to overseas recipients – *see* further Section 7.2.2.3 above), Article 19 (investment professionals), Article 41 (bearer instruments) and Article 49 (high net worth companies, unincorporated associations etc.).

A communication will be "made to" certain recipients if it is addressed to a particular person or persons (e.g. a telephone call or a letter). It will be "directed at" certain recipients if it is addressed to persons or groups of persons generally (for instance, an advertisement in a newspaper or on an internet website).[50] In the latter case, it does not matter if the financial promotion reaches persons other than those for whom it is intended, so long as it was not directed at them. Most of the exemptions which make the distinction between communications "made to" and

---

[48] *See* Annex B, paragraph 1.14.4 FSA Guidance.
[49] For example, a married couple, group of companies or members of an investment club.
[50] *See* Annex B, paragraph 1.10.11 FSA Guidance.

"directed at" certain recipients provide indications of when a communication will be regarded as directed at certain persons.[51] The exemptions
generally provide that compliance with all relevant indications will
conclusively establish that the communication is directed only at certain
persons and that compliance with one or more indications is of evidential value in establishing that this is the case. The long-standing practice
of including distribution restrictions and "rubrics" on documentation
relating to the sale and promotion of investments is likely to be reinforced
by these provisions; the terms of the restrictions will of course need to
be modified to reflect the Financial Promotion Order.

7.4.6   New exemptions

There are over 60 exemptions in the Financial Promotion Order and it is
not possible to examine all of them in detail in this Chapter. However,
some of the more important exemptions include the following.

7.4.6.1   *Investment professionals (Article 19)*
Article 19 provides that the financial promotion restriction does not
apply to any communication which is made only to recipients whom the
person making the communication believes on reasonable grounds to be
investment professionals, or which may reasonably be regarded as
directed only at such recipients.[52]

The categories of person who constitute "investment professionals" are
set out in Article 12(5) and are:

(a)   authorised persons;
(b)   exempt persons where the communication relates to a regulated
       activity in relation to which the person is exempt;[53]

---

[51] There are a few exceptions including Articles 41 and 46.

[52] This exemption broadly reflects Articles 8 to 10 of the 1995 Order (which exempted
investment advertisements directed at informing or influencing persons of a
particular kind) and Article 11(3)(a), (b) and (d) of the 1996 Order (advertisements
issued to persons sufficiently expert to understand the risks involved).

[53] "Exempt person" is defined in Section 417(1) FSMA and includes appointed representatives, recognised investment exchanges, recognised clearing houses and
those who are able to take advantage of the Financial Services and Markets Act
2000 (Exemption) Order 2001 (SI 2001 No. 1201).

(c)   any other persons whose ordinary activities involve them carrying on[54] the controlled activity to which the communication relates for the purposes of a business, or persons who it is reasonable to expect will carry on such activity for the purposes of a business;[55]

(d)   governments, local authorities or international organisations; or

(e)   persons who are directors, officers or employees of any person (X) falling within one of the above categories where the communication is made to that person in his capacity as director, officer or employee and where his responsibilities when acting in that capacity involve him in the carrying on of controlled activities by X.

Article 19(4) sets out the conditions which will be relevant in determining whether a communication is to be regarded as "directed at" the persons referred to above. The Article 19(4) conditions are that:

(a)   the communication is accompanied by an indication that it is directed at persons having professional expertise in matters relating to investments and that any investment or investment activity to which it relates is available only to such persons or will be engaged in only with such persons;

(b)   the communication is accompanied by an indication that persons who do not have professional experience in matters relating to investments should not rely on it;

(c)   there are in place proper systems and procedures to prevent recipients other than investment professionals engaging in the investment activity to which the communication relates with the

---

[54] This means that the application of the exemption between different kinds of controlled activity is somewhat uneven. In the case of the controlled activity of dealing in securities and contractually based investments (paragraph 3 of Schedule 1 to the Financial Promotion Order), quite a wide range of recipients of a communication may be expected to deal for the purposes of a business. With most of the other controlled activities, only a true professional provider of the relevant service is likely to be covered. The effect of this is particularly important in the case of deposit-taking and insurance, since relatively few exemptions apply to these controlled activities.

[55] Communications made directly to certain institutional investors, notably pension fund trustees, may therefore not fall within this exemption (though communications to their professional fund managers should do so). However, Article 49 expressly covers high value trusts, so this point is likely to be important only in relation to deposits and insurance products, to which Article 49 does not apply.

person directing the communication, a close relative of his or a member of the same group.[56]

If all of the conditions are met this will amount to a safe harbour and the communication will conclusively be regarded as directed only at investment professionals. Where only some are met, this will be of evidential weight in determining whether the communication can be regarded as directed only at investment professionals. However, a communication may still be regarded as directed at this audience even if none of the specified criteria are met. Provided the communication can reasonably be regarded as being directed at investment professionals, it does not matter if it is actually received by others. Therefore the effect of Article 19 may be to permit materials directed only at investment professionals to be put on an open access website (subject to the conditions set out above being satisfied).

7.4.6.2   *One off communications (Article 28)*

Article 28 Financial Promotion Order provides a new exemption for one off non-real time and solicited real time communications. This is extended by Article 28A[57] to one off unsolicited real time communications, subject to certain additional conditions being satisfied.

Article 28(3) specifies three conditions as relevant in determining whether a communication is to be regarded as "one off". As in the case of other articles, the article operates at three levels. If all three conditions are met, the communication is conclusively regarded as one off. If one or more, but not all, of the conditions are met, this fact is to be taken into account in determining whether the communication is one off. Finally, the article provides that a communication may still be regarded as one off even if none of the conditions are met (although, given the novelty of the "one off" test and the relatively narrow natural meaning of the phrase in ordinary language, it may be difficult to establish that a communication is "one off" in the absence of any of the conditions).

---

[56] Article 9 of the 1995 Order set out a similar non-exhaustive and non-conclusive list of indications to determine whether an advertisement was directed at informing or influencing persons of a particular kind. Article 10 set out indications that an advertisement is not so directed.

[57] Introduced by Article 2(a) Amendment Order.

The three conditions are as follows:

(a)   the communication is made only to one recipient or to one group who it is expected will engage in any investment activity jointly;

(b)   the identity of the product or service to which the communication relates has been determined having regard to the particular circumstances of the recipient; and

(c)   the communication is not part of an organised marketing campaign.

This last condition raises an issue as to the volume of communications necessary to constitute an "organised marketing campaign" and when a communication will be regarded as being "part of" such a campaign. A communication to 500 people would almost certainly be regarded as a marketing campaign but what about a communication sent to only 10 people? The FSA Guidance suggests[58] that where a person sends out a series of standard letters to a number of customers or potential customers this would be likely to be regarded as part of an organised marketing campaign. However, the guidance also suggests that if it can be demonstrated that a person has communicated details of a particular investment opportunity to several clients, having determined that it is suitable for each of them after considering their personal circumstances and objectives, the individual financial promotions to each client may be one off in nature. Accordingly, it would be prudent to assume that communications made even to a small number of recipients without any regard to their personal circumstances could be regarded as an organised marketing campaign. Such communications should therefore be avoided (absent the availability of another exemption), unless it is possible to demonstrate that the recipients were selected because the particular investment opportunity to which the communication relates was considered suitable for each of them.

As mentioned above, Article 28A extends the application of the exemption to one off unsolicited real time communications, provided that certain additional conditions are fulfilled, namely:

(a)   the communicator must believe on reasonable grounds that the recipient understands the risks associated with engaging in the investment activity to which the communication relates; and

(b)   at the time the communication is made, the communicator must believe on reasonable grounds that the recipient would expect to be contacted by him in relation to the investment activity to which the communication relates.

---

[58] *See* Annex B, paragraph 1.14.4 FSA Guidance.

It seems therefore that the exemption for unsolicited one-off communications is only likely to be of use in the case of communications to existing clients or where there is some pre-existing relationship between the communicator and the recipient. The condition relating to understanding of risk, in particular, will severely limit its usefulness in the context of corporate finance activities, since it will often preclude the application of the exemption to communications which a person wishes to make with someone who has been identified only as the holder of a particular kind of investment, with no other knowledge of his circumstances or expertise in investment matters.

The government has indicated that it considers that the exemption for one-off communications may be used more than once in respect of communications to the same recipient provided that the conditions of the exemption are met on each occasion.[59] The FSA Guidance indicates that the FSA shares this view.[60]

7.4.6.3 *Communications to certified high net worth individuals (Article 48)*
This is one of two new exemptions[61] permitting promotions to special categories of individual. It has been introduced as part of an attempt to facilitate capital raising from "business angels" and other sources of informal capital for start up and small companies.

Non-real time and solicited real time communications can be made to a person who has a current certificate of high net worth from an accountant or his employer which confirms that his annual income is not less than £100,000 or his net assets are not less than £250,000. In addition, he must have signed a statement (in the form prescribed in Article 48(2)(b)) within the previous 12 months confirming that he is a certified high net worth individual.

The Article also imposes conditions about the content of the communication. It must be accompanied by certain indications, namely:

(a)   that it is exempt from the general financial promotion restriction on the grounds that it is made to a certified high net worth individual;

(b)   of the requirements that must be met for a person to qualify as a certified high net worth individual;

---

[59] *See* paragraph 2.21 Third Consultation Document.
[60] *See* Annex B, paragraph 1.14.3 FSA Guidance.
[61] The other new exemption is considered in Section 7.4.6.4 below.

(c)   that the content of the communication has not been approved by an authorised person and that such approval is, absent the availability of an exemption, required by Section 21;

(d)   that reliance on the communication may expose the individual to certain risks (i.e. the risk of losing all monies invested); and

(e)   that expert financial advice should be taken if the recipient of the communication is in any doubt as to the investment to which the communication relates.

The communication can only be made to an identified individual and only if it relates to certain types of investments;[62] it cannot relate to investment activity involving the person who has given the certificate of high net worth.

It should also be noted that the exemption is not available where the communication is made to persons whom the communicator "reasonably believes" to be certified high net worth individuals. Therefore, in order safely to rely on the exemption, the communicator will need to have seen the certificate and the individual's statement before issuing the communication. In the FSA's view, a communication which is merely an enquiry seeking to establish whether a person holds a current certificate will not in itself amount to an invitation or inducement to engage in investment activity (and no exemption will therefore need to be found for the enquiry communication).[63]

---

[62] Broadly, these include shares and debt instruments of an unlisted company, warrants and certificates which relate to such shares and instruments, derivative products which relate to any of the former investments and units in a collective investment scheme which invests wholly or predominantly in shares and debt instruments of an unlisted company. The exemption is therefore available only in relation to "venture capital" type investments (i.e. shares and debt instruments in unlisted companies and instruments relating to them). This produces the rather odd result that the exemption is available for these comparatively risky categories of investment, but not for communications relating to more conventional investments such as listed shares. The distinction stems from the policy motivation for the exemption; whereas the scope of most exemptions is determined by considerations of investor protection, an important objective of this exemption was to benefit start up investments by giving them wider access to possible providers of capital.

[63] *See* Annex B, paragraph 1.14.13 FSA Guidance.

7.4.6.4 Communications to high net worth companies, partnerships etc. (Article 49)

This exemption applies to all communications including unsolicited real time communications. It permits communications to be made to high net worth companies, partnerships and certain other persons and provides that the financial promotion restriction does not apply to any communication which:

(a)   is made only to recipients whom the person making the communication believes on reasonable grounds to fall within the permitted categories of person; or

(b)   may reasonably be regarded as directed only at such persons.

The permitted categories of person to whom the communication may be made include:

(a)   any body corporate which has a called-up share capital or net assets of:

    (i)   not less than £500,000 (where the body corporate has more than 20 members or where it is a subsidiary undertaking of a parent undertaking which has more than 20 members); or

    (ii)   not less than £5 million (in the case of any other body corporate); and

(b)   any unincorporated association or partnership which has net assets of not less than £5 million.[64]

Article 49(4) sets out the conditions which are relevant when determining whether a communication will be regarded as directed at permitted categories of person. If all of the conditions set out in that paragraph are met, then the communication will fall within a safe harbour.[65] If one or more of the conditions is met, this will be of evidential weight in determining whether the communication can reasonably be regarded as directed at such persons. However, a communication may still be regarded as so directed even if none of the conditions are met. The conditions set out in paragraph (4) are as follows:

---

[64] This exemption therefore partially corresponds to that in Article 11 of the Financial Services Act 1996 (Investment Advertisements)(Exemption) Order 1996. Note, however, that it is no longer sufficient for the recipient of the communication to be a member of a group one or more of whose members satisfies the called-up share capital or net assets test; it must itself do so.

[65] Article 49(3).

(a) the communication includes an indication of the description of persons to whom it is directed and an indication of the fact that the controlled investment or controlled activity to which it relates is available only to such persons;

(b) the communication includes an indication that persons of any other description should not act upon it; and

(c) there are in place proper systems and procedures to prevent recipients (other than persons to whom the article applies) engaging in investment activity to which the communication relates with the person directing the communication, a close relative of his or a member of the same group.

7.4.6.5 *Communications to certified sophisticated investors (Article 50)*

This is the second new exemption that is designed to facilitate promotions to so-called "business angels", although (in contrast to Article 48) the scope of this exemption extends beyond investments in, or relating to, unlisted companies. The exemption potentially applies to any description of investment and to all types of communication (non-real time, solicited real time and unsolicited real time). It allows a communication to be made to a person who is a "certified sophisticated investor", that is an investor who has:

(a) a current certificate (signed by an authorised person)[66] stating that he is sufficiently knowledgeable to understand the risks associated with the particular investment; and

(b) signed a statement in the prescribed form[67] about his status.

Article 50(3) also requires the communication to be accompanied by certain indications which are broadly the same as those required in relation to communications to high net worth individuals under Article 48 (*see* Section 7.4.6.3 above). However, one difference is that a warning is required to the effect that the investor is at risk of losing all monies invested *or incurring additional liability* (the italicised words are not required by the Article 48 risk warning).[68]

---

[66] There does not, however, appear to be anything in Article 50 that would prevent an investor's certificate being signed by a company in the same group as the company with which the investor engages in investment activity.

[67] *See* Article 50(1)(b).

[68] The difference is presumably attributable to the wider application of the Article 50 exemption; unlike the Article 48 exemption, it extends to derivatives transactions which may give rise to liability beyond the amount invested.

If the above requirements are met the financial promotion restriction will not apply to any communication made to the certified investor provided that it does not invite or induce the recipient to engage in investment activity with the person who has signed the certificate and that it relates only to a "description of investment" in respect of which the investor is certified.

The FSA considers that a "description of investment" relates to a category of investment with similar characteristics.[69] It considers that the shares in one particular public limited company are the same description of investment as the shares in another public limited company, irrespective of the market sectors of those two companies. However, shares in a private company are not considered to be the same description of investment as the shares in a public limited company, as there are certain significant distinctions, notably in the ability to dispose of such investments.

The usefulness of this exemption in practice will also depend on the willingness of authorised persons to certify investors as sophisticated investors.

7.4.6.6   Sale of body corporate (Article 62)

This exemption is available in relation to any communication (real time or non-real time) which is made by a body corporate, partnership, single individual or group of connected individuals and which relates to a transaction to acquire or dispose of shares in a body corporate (other than an open-ended investment company) or to a transaction that is entered into for the purposes of such an acquisition or disposal provided that either:

(a)   certain conditions set out in Article 62(3) Financial Promotion Order are met (*see* further below); or

(b)   the object of the transaction may reasonably be regarded as being the acquisition of the day-to-day control of the affairs of the body corporate.[70]

---

[69] *See* Annex B, paragraph 1.14.16 FSA Guidance.

[70] This exemption consolidates the provisions of Article 5 of the 1995 Order and Article 7 of the Unsolicited Calls Regulations. However, the exemption has been liberalised in two respects. First, where one is relying on the first limb of the exemption (i.e. satisfaction of the conditions specified in Article 62(3)) the percentage of voting rights that must be acquired or disposed of has been reduced from 75 per cent to 50 per cent. Secondly, the exemption is now available even if the Article 62(3) conditions are not met if the object of the transaction may nevertheless be regarded as being the acquisition of the day-to-day control of the affairs of the body corporate.

The exemption is therefore available in relation to communications made by intending vendors and purchasers and, by an amendment to Article 62(1) (introduced by Article 2(c) Amendment Order), the exemption also covers communications made on behalf of such persons.[71] It would therefore be available where, for instance, a communication is made by a financial adviser on behalf of a potential purchaser.

The Article 62(3) conditions
The conditions which are set out in Article 62(3) are as follows:

(a)   the shares consist of, or include, 50 per cent or more of the voting shares in the body corporate; or

(b)   the shares, together with any already held by the person acquiring them, consist of or include at least that percentage of such shares; and

(c)   in either case, the acquisition or disposal is between parties each of whom is a body corporate, a partnership, a single individual or a group of connected individuals.

It seems that condition (c) above requires that the communication is made in connection with a bi-partite transaction with one (and only one) of a body corporate, partnership, single individual or group of connected individuals (not a group of connected companies) on each side of the transaction. Where the Article 62(3) conditions are relied on, a rubric to this effect may well be included in an information memorandum in relation to a company auction to allow the person issuing the memorandum to rely on the exemption. An alternative approach that may be used is to obtain written confirmations from the persons to whom the communication is made as to their status. For example, in the case of an information memorandum sent to a possible management buy-out team, the team might be asked to confirm that they:

•   are the promoters of the proposed buy-out vehicle;
•   are receiving the memorandum in their capacity as such; and
•   recognise that their bid should be made by a single body corporate.

Article 62(1) requires that the communication must "relate to" a transaction covered by the exemption. In relation to a transaction that meets the Article 62(3) conditions (i.e. a bi-partite transaction) the communication must therefore relate to a contemplated bi-partite sale or purchase.

---

[71] This reflects the position under Article 5 of the 1995 Order.

If this is the only type of agreement which the client will ultimately enter into, then the exemption should apply. However, the position is less clear where, having made the communication, the client subsequently changes its mind. Presumably the exemption cannot be retrospectively disapplied.

Object of transaction is the acquisition of day-to-day control of affairs of body corporate
A communication may also fall within the Article 62 exemption even if it does not satisfy the Article 62(3) conditions if "the object of the transaction may nevertheless reasonably be regarded as being the acquisition of the day-to-day control of the affairs of the company". It appears from a literal construction of this wording that, so long as the "object" test is satisfied in relation to the transaction, a person may rely on the exemption even if the transaction relates to less than 50 per cent of the shares in the relevant body corporate and/or in circumstances where the transaction is not bi-partite.

Although the alternative test is appropriate in circumstances where the acquisition or disposal is for less than 50 per cent of the voting shares in the relevant body corporate but effective control is nevertheless transferred, the rationale for dispensing with the requirement for a bi-partite transaction is is less clear and it is questionable if this result was intended. As drafted, the exemption would, for example, appear to be available to a single entity that makes a communication relating to a proposed acquisition of a controlling equity interest in a body corporate and then enters into an agreement with multiple entities to purchase the shares. Indeed, there appears to be no reason why the exemption could not be used in connection with a takeover bid.

7.4.6.7 *Follow-up communications (Article 14)*
Article 14 Financial Promotion Order allows a person to make a non-real time or solicited real time communication as a follow-up to a previous communication (the "first communication") provided that the first communication falls within one of the exemptions to the financial promotion restriction because, in compliance with the requirements of the relevant exemption, it is accompanied by certain indications or contains certain information.[72]

---

[72] The purpose of the Article 14 exemption is to avoid the need to repeat risk warnings each time a communication is made. Examples of communications to which this exemption may be relevant are communications to certified high net worth individuals (Article 48) and certified sophisticated investors (Article 50).

Although this exemption does not apply where the first communication was made under an exemption that did not require it to include any statements or information, the FSA Guidance indicates that, in such cases, it is likely that the exemption that applies to the earlier financial promotion would also apply to any follow up promotion.[73]

The requirements with which the follow-up communication must comply if it is to benefit from the Article 14 exemption are set out in Article 14(2) Financial Promotion Order. This paragraph provides that the communication must:

(a) be a non-real time communication or a solicited real time communication;
(b) be made by the same person who made the first communication;
(c) be made to a recipient of the first communication;
(d) relate to the same controlled activity and the same controlled investment as the first communication; and
(e) be made within 12 months of the recipient receiving the first communication.

Although the requirement set out in paragraph (d) above appears to be the most restrictive, it is not clear whether the communication needs to relate to the same category of investment as the first communication, for example to shares generally, or to the particular shares which are the subject of the first communication.

7.4.6.8 Participation in employee share schemes (Article 60)
Article 60 Financial Promotion Order contains the exemption relating to participation in employee share schemes. Notwithstanding the reference to "employee share schemes" in the heading to this article, it is not necessary for there to be a formally constituted scheme for the exemption to apply; it can be used in connection with communications relating to any issue of shares to employees.

The article exempts communications made by:

• a body corporate (C);
• a member of the same group as C; or
• a "relevant trustee" (as defined in Article 60(3)),

---

[73] *See* Annex B, paragraph 1.12.10 FSA Guidance.

but does not impose any restrictions on those to whom the communication may be made. However, the communication must be for the purpose of an "employee share scheme" and must relate to certain investments issued by C (*see* further below). "Employee share scheme" is defined in Article 60(2) as arrangements made, *or to be made,* by C or by a person in the same group as C to enable or facilitate:

(a) transactions in investments issued by C between or for the benefit of: (i) the bona fide employees or former employees of C or of another member of the same group as C; or (ii) their close relatives; or
(b) the holding of the investments in C by, or for the benefit of, such persons.

Accordingly, communications may be made even if no share scheme has been established at the time of the communication. However, the exemption will apply only if the communication relates to particular investments issued by C namely:

(a) investments falling within paragraph 14 (shares) or 15 (instruments creating or acknowledging indebtedness) of Schedule 1 to the Financial Promotion Order;
(b) investments falling with paragraph 17 or 18 of Schedule 1 (e.g. warrants and certificates representing securities), in as far as they relate to paragraph 14 or 15 investments; or
(c) investments falling within paragraph 27 of Schedule 1 (rights and interests in investments) so far as they relate to an investment referred to in paragraph (a) or (b) above.

7.4.6.9 *Others*

Articles 70 and 71 Financial Promotion Order deal with promotions in connection with listing applications and promotions included in listing particulars etc. They have broadly the same effect as Sections 58(1)(d)(i) and (ii) FS Act. Article 11 1995 Order dealt with advertisements required or permitted to be published by exchange or market rules. The corresponding provision in the Financial Promotion Order is Article 67, which has broadly the same effect as Article 11. However, it seems that the Article 67 exemption operates to exempt the communication rather than the contents of a communication. In other words, it seems that it is necessary for the rules of the relevant market to require the making of the particular communication in question in order to fall within the exemption. Article 11 exempted any advertisement which consisted in whole or in part of a document required or permitted to be published by the rules of a relevant market. This was significantly wider as it covered, for instance, a press advertisement consisting of extracts from accounts that were required to be published.

A similar and important exclusion is contained in Article 69, which exempts a range of non-real time and solicited real time communications. The exemption is available to body corporate (other than an open-ended investment company) ("A") which has relevant investments[74] issued by itself or by any parent undertaking that are listed on a relevant market. However, the communications must relate only to investments issued by A (or by another body corporate in the same group as A) and the following requirements must be satisfied:[75]

(a)   the communication must not invite or advise persons to under-write, subscribe for, or otherwise acquire or dispose of, a controlled investment (nor must it be accompanied by an invitation to do any of these activities);

(b)   the communication must not invite persons to effect any transaction with, or use services provided by, A (or any person named in the communication) in the course of an investment activity engaged in by A or the named person which falls within paragraphs 3 to 11 of Schedule 1 (nor must it be accompanied by an invitation to do any of these activities);

(c)   the communications must not contain, or be accompanied by, an inducement relating to a relevant investment other than one issued by A or by another body corporate in the same group; and

(d)   if the communication refers to or is accompanied by a reference to the price at which the investments have been bought or sold or the yield on such investments, it must be accompanied by an indication that past performance cannot be relied on as a guide to future performance.

Articles 67, 69 and 71 are all important in the context of corporate finance activity since they will often determine whether a communication by a listed entity needs to be approved by its broker or investment banking adviser.

---

[74] A "relevant investment" includes any investment specified in paragraphs 14 and 15 of Schedule 1 to the Financial Promotion Order (i.e. shares, debentures and other debt instruments) and paragraphs 17 and 18 (subscription warrants and certificates representing certain securities) to the extent that they relate to paragraph 14 and 15 investments. The investment must be permitted to be traded on, or dealt in, a "relevant market", which is defined in Article 69(1).

[75] *See* Article 69(3) to (6).

7.4.7 Combination of exemptions

Article 11 Financial Promotion Order permits all of the exemptions to be combined with any other exemptions that are available in relation to the particular controlled activity to which the communication relates. However, a few of the exemptions contain specific provisions expressly identifying exemptions with which they may be combined. It appears that the effect of these provisions is to restrict the possibility of their combination generally with other exemptions (thereby displacing Article 11). An example of such an exemption is Article 12 (communications to overseas recipients). By virtue of Article 12(5), the Article 12 exemption may be combined with the exemption for promotions to investment professionals (Article 19) and to high net worth persons (Article 49); the effect of this is that information on a website could be treated as exempt on the basis that it is directed at investment professionals and high net worth persons in the UK and otherwise only at persons outside the UK.

Article 49(2)(e) permits the Article 49 exemption to be combined with others. However, the approach adopted by Article 49 differs slightly from that used in Article 19. Article 19(6) provides that a communication may be treated as made only to or directed only at investment professionals even if it is also made to or directed at other persons to whom it may lawfully be communicated. The effect would appear to be broadly the same, although there does not appear to be any good reason for the difference in approach.

It should also be noted that there is no provision for combining the exemptions in Part V Financial Promotion Order (exempt communications: deposits and insurance) with those in Part VI (exempt communications: certain controlled activities).

7.5 Conduct of business rules

7.5.1 Application

The FSA's Conduct of Business Sourcebook (the "Sourcebook") was "made" by the FSA in June 2001. If a financial promotion is to be made by an authorised person or approved by him because there is no available exemption, that person will have to comply with the relevant conduct of business rules relating to financial promotion contained in Chapter 3 of the Sourcebook.

The rules apply generally in relation to all types of financial promotions. However, they are limited in their application to certain "exempt" promotions,[76] for example, certain promotions made to market counterparties and intermediate customers and to financial promotions which are subject to the Takeover Code or the requirements relating to takeovers or related operations of another EEA state (in order to prevent dual regulation) ("takeover exemption"). When a firm approves such a promotion, which is a non-real time financial promotion, it will have to comply with a limited number of COB rules, the most important of which requires it to be able to show that it has taken reasonable steps to ensure that the promotion is clear, fair and not misleading. This requirement does not, however, apply in the case of a financial promotion to which the takeover exemption applies.

In general it is worth noting that the exemptions under the COB rules are substantially narrower than under the conduct of business rules which applied under the FS Act regime. Those rules generally exempted from most of the detailed content requirements:

(a)   advertisements which would have been exempt from Section 57 FS Act if they had been issued by an unauthorised person; and

(b)   advertisements issued or approved by a firm in the course of corporate finance business.

With regard to territorial scope, the COB rules generally apply to all firms (as defined in the FSA's Handbook of Rules and Guidance):

(a)   communicating financial promotions to persons inside the UK;

(b)   communicating certain unsolicited real time financial promotions to persons outside the UK; and

(c)   approving non-real time financial promotions for communication to persons inside the UK.

Nationals of EEA states (other than the UK) must also comply with the rules in order to avail of the exemption in Article 36 Financial Promotion Order. Article 36 provides that the financial promotion restriction does not apply to non-real time or solicited real time communications communicated by an EEA national in the course of a controlled activity carried on by him in that state if he complies with the COB rules.

---

[76] *See* COB 3.2.5.

Different COB rules will apply depending on the type of financial promotion that is being approved or communicated (i.e. whether the promotion is real time, non-real time or, for example, the financial promotion is to be communicated and approved for an overseas or unauthorised person, or communicated using the internet or some other form of electronic media).

By virtue of Section 1.6.4 COB rules, the detailed contents requirements in Sections 3.8.6 to 3.8.20 and 3.9 of the rules do not apply to corporate finance business. Corporate finance business is defined in the glossary to the FSA's Handbook to include:

(a) Designated investment business with or for:
    (i)   issuers, holders or owners of designated investments relating to the offer, issue, underwriting, repurchase, exchange, redemption or variation of the terms of such investments;
    (ii)   market counterparties, intermediate customers, bodies corporate, partnership or supranational organisation relating to the financing, structuring, management and control of their business, activities or undertaking;
    (iii)   any person in connection with a takeover by or on behalf of that person or involving investments issued by that person, its holding company, subsidiary or associate;
    (iv)   any person in connection with a merger, demerger, reorganisation or reconstruction involving investments issued by that person, its holding company, subsidiary or associate;
    (v)   a shareholder (or prospective shareholder) of a body corporate established to effect a takeover or related operation where that business is in connection with the takeover or related operation;
    (vi)   persons acting as a principal in negotiations or decisions relating to the commercial, financial or strategic requirements of a business or any prospective business or (other than as an investor) assisting persons in transactions of the type described above; and
(b) own account business transacted in relation to the business described at (a) above not involving transactions with or advice to private customers.

As can be seen from the above, the definition of corporate finance business is essentially "transactional" based. Accordingly, certain types of activity which the corporate finance divisions of firms may perform for clients on an ongoing basis will be unlikely to fall within this definition, in particular, commenting and advising upon routine announcements not linked to particular transactions. This distinction is of particular significance in the context of approving financial promotions because outside the realm of corporate finance business the detailed content requirements in Sections 3.8.6 to 3.8.20 and 3.9 COB rules will apply.

7.5.2 COB rules applicable to non-real time promotions

Firms communicating or approving non-real time communications will be required to confirm that they have complied with the relevant COB rules before the promotion is communicated or approved. This confirmation exercise must be carried out by an individual (or individuals) with an appropriate level of expertise[77] and, after approving promotions, a firm must continue to monitor them to ensure that they continue to meet the requirements of the rules; if they do not, the firm must withdraw its approval.[78] This continuing requirement is new and potentially quite burdensome; it will present firms with some difficult questions about how to structure their procedures so as to minimise the risk of failure to comply. Firms must also keep records of any promotions which they have confirmed comply with the rules and such records must be "readily accessible" for inspection by the FSA.[79]

Firms must also ensure that the financial promotion complies with the particular form and content requirements set out in Section 3.8 COB rules. For example, the promotion must contain the name and address of the firm (or a contact within the firm from whom the firm's address can be obtained).

The basic substantive requirement defining the firm's responsibility in issuing or approving a promotion is that the firm must also be able to demonstrate that it has taken steps to ensure that the promotion is fair, clear and not misleading. This is the same as applied in many circumstances under the FS Act regime,[80] except that the previous wording did

---

[77] This will vary according to the complexity of the promotion and the investment or service to which it relates.

[78] *See* COB 3.6.3.

[79] The FSA has indicated that a record will comply with this requirement if it can be produced within 48 hours of a request.

[80] But note that under the applicable rule of the Securities and Future Authority (rules 5–9), a firm was not subject to this requirement when issuing (among others) an exempt advertisement (i.e., an advertisement which would have been exempt from Section 57 if issued by an unauthorised person) or a takeover advertisement, unless it also stated that it was regulated by the SFA.

not include the word "clear". Additional rules on form and content apply in relation to specific non-real time financial promotions (i.e. those which identify or promote a particular investment or service). For example, the COB rules require such promotions to include a description of the investment or service, the commitment required and the risks involved.[81] There are also detailed requirements to be complied with if the promotion contains information about the past performance of a specified investment, packaged product or the firm.

7.5.3   COB rules applicable to real time promotions

Firms communicating real time promotions will be required to take reasonable steps to ensure that any individual who is making a real time communication on behalf of the firm complies with specified requirements. These include ensuring that the individual does not make any untrue claims, that the communication is clear, fair and not misleading and that the individual does not contact the recipient at an unsocial hour or on an unlisted number unless the recipient has previously agreed to this.[82]

There are additional rules that apply in the case of real time financial promotions which are unsolicited and are not exempt. These rules prohibit the making of unsolicited real time financial promotions (which do not fall within any of the exemptions in the Financial Promotion Order), unless they are made to existing customers who would envisage receiving such promotions, or they relate to generally marketable packaged products provided that certain conditions are met (e.g. that the product is not a higher volatility fund), or they relate only to an activity carried on by an authorised or exempt person in relation to certain readily realisable securities or generally marketable packaged products.[83] Firms are not permitted to approve real time promotions made by others.[84] This reflects common sense (it is hard to see how one can approve the content of a conversation which is, by definition, unpredictable) and in effect preserves the previous position under which unsolicited calls were not permitted unless they fell within an exemption.

---

[81] *See* COB 3.8.8.
[82] *See* COB 3.8.22(6).
[83] *See* COB 3.10.3.
[84] *See* COB 3.12.2.

7.5.4   *Other promotions*

Certain other COB rules apply to particular types of financial promotions, for example, direct offer financial promotions,[85] and when communicating and approving financial promotions for an overseas or unauthorised person.

7.5.5   *Use of the Internet and other electronic media*

Internet promotions are expressly acknowledged in the COB rules. Although there are no internet-specific rules as such, there is guidance on the application of the general rules to internet communications (e.g. with regard to packaged products and the accessibility of key features and written contractual terms).

The FSA has also specifically considered such promotions in its guidance,[86] in recognition of the fact that the internet is a unique medium, providing easy access to a very wide audience while, at the same time, providing very little control over who is able to access the financial promotion. The FSA considers that the test for whether the contents of a particular website or page may or may not amount to a financial promotion is no different from that for any other medium. If a web page, operated or maintained in the course of business, invites or induces a person to engage in investment activity, then that page will be a financial promotion. The FSA takes the view that the person who caused the page to be created will be a communicator (and that, for example, any software engineers who may have been involved in establishing the website, provided they have no interest in it other than being paid for its design, will not be communicating it). An internet service provider may, however, be able to use the exemption for "mere conduits".[87]

---

[85] A direct offer financial promotion is a non-real time financial promotion which: (a) contains an offer by the firm or another person to enter into a controlled agreement (as defined in Section 30) with anyone who responds to the financial promotion, or an invitation to anyone who responds to the financial promotion to make an offer to the firm or another person to enter into a controlled agreement; and (b) specifies the manner of response or includes a form in which any response is to be made (e.g. by providing a tear-off slip).

[86] *See* Annex B, Section 1.20 FSA Guidance.

[87] Article 18 Financial Promotion Order.

There was some consideration during the consultation process about whether a hyperlink could constitute a financial promotion on the basis that the person creating it had either communicated or caused the communication of the website to which the link led.[88] The FSA has now provided detailed guidance on hypertext links. It has considered whether the link itself, the destination site reached via the link, the page that contains the link and websites representing a directory of website addresses or e-mail addresses, amount to financial promotions. In addition, the FSA has examined the position of website operators who host or create links to the websites of unauthorised persons.[89]

7.6   Transitional arrangements

Section 21 came into force on 1 December 2001 and firms need to have new rubrics, policies and procedures in place for dealing with financial promotions from that date. There are, however, certain limited transitional provisions relating to the new financial promotion regime. Article 74 Financial Promotion Order provides that where an authorised firm has approved a financial promotion pre-N2, the communication may be communicated by an unauthorised person for one month from N2.

There is also some transitional relief provided in relation to Chapter 3 of the FSA's Sourcebook. Extra time has been granted to firms to allow them to comply with the new rules. In summary:

(a)   with regard to "old" promotions: from N2 until 30 June 2002 a firm will be allowed to communicate non-real time financial promotions which complied with the content requirements of its previous regulator if the firm has approved them as complying with those rules pre-N2; and

(b)   with regard to new material and real time promotions: compliance with the rules of a previous regulator is generally a defence up until 30 June 2002.

---

[88] HM Treasury had in fact proposed in the first consultation document a specific exemption for hyperlinks. The government ultimately decided against such an exemption on the basis that the application of the financial promotion restriction only to invitations or inducements disposed of the need for a specific exemption for hyperlinks. It considered that if there was such an exemption this might actually prove counterproductive in that it may suggest that hyperlinks would (absent the exemption) breach the restriction.

[89] *See* Annex B, Section 1.20 FSA Guidance.

7.7 Breach of Section 21

Breach of the general restriction in Section 21 is a criminal offence which is subject to a maximum of two years imprisonment and an unlimited fine.[90] In addition, an agreement entered into with a customer in consequence of a communication made in breach of Section 21 (i.e. an unlawful communication) is unenforceable against the customer and the customer can recover money or property paid or transferred and compensation for any loss sustained as a result of having parted with it.[91] The agreement will be unenforceable even if the person who entered into the agreement with the customer did not make the unlawful communication. However, the court has a discretion to allow enforcement of the agreement or obligation and to allow any money or property transferred to be retained if it is satisfied that this would be just and equitable in the circumstances.[92]

---

[90] *See* Section 25. It is, however, a defence for a person to show that he took all reasonable precautions and exercised all due diligence to avoid committing the offence.

[91] *See* Section 30(2).

[92] *See* Section 30(4). In deciding whether this is the case, the court must have regard to whether the applicant reasonably believed that he was not making an unlawful communication (where the applicant made the communication). If the applicant did not make the communication, the court must have regard to whether he knew that the agreement was entered into in consequence of an unlawful communication.

Chapter 8

Market Abuse, Misleading Statements and Practices

Adrian Clark*

Partner
Ashurst Morris Crisp

8.1 Introduction

8.1.1 *Market abuse*

This Chapter is principally concerned with the new market abuse regime created by, and set out in, Part VIII Financial Services and Markets Act 2000 (the "FSMA"). The market abuse regime allows the Financial Services Authority (the "FSA") to impose civil sanctions for certain behaviour amounting to market abuse.[1]

Market abuse is behaviour which:

(a) misuses information which is not generally available,
(b) gives false or misleading impressions, or
(c) amounts to market distortion,

where such behaviour is in relation to a qualifying investment traded on a prescribed market and a regular user of that market would consider that behaviour to have failed to meet the standards of behaviour reasonably expected of a person in that position in relation to that market.

If a person has engaged in such behaviour (or has required or encouraged another to do so), the FSA may, subject to limited defences, impose a penalty. Alternatively it may publish a statement that the person has engaged in market abuse.

---

* The author would like to thank his colleague Vanessa Marrison, for her invaluable contribution to this Chapter.
[1] Section 123 FSMA.

8.1.2 The Code of Market Conduct

The provisions in Part VIII FSMA concerning market abuse[2] cover just six and a half pages. However, they are supplemented by the Code of Market Conduct ("COMC")[3] giving guidance on whether or not behaviour amounts to market abuse.

If a person behaves in a way which COMC describes as not amounting to market abuse, then that is conclusive.[4] Such instances are referred to in COMC as safe harbours and are marked in its margin by a "C". Otherwise COMC is simply an indication of whether behaviour may be taken to amount to market abuse, and such parts of COMC are marked with an "E".[5] COMC also contains another level of text – additional explanatory guidance, indicated in its margin by the letter "G". This is expressly stated not to form part of COMC, albeit that it is contained within it, but rather is guidance which the FSA is empowered to give.[6]

8.1.3 Misleading statements and practices

Towards the end of this Chapter that part[7] of the FSMA which deals with criminal offences relating to misleading statements and practices will also be looked at. Broadly, it provides for criminal offences in respect of the making of certain misleading statements and the creation of certain misleading impressions concerning investments. If a person has made such statements or created such impressions then, subject to limited defences, he or she may be imprisoned for up to seven years or fined or both.

The FSMA confers on the FSA (amongst others) power to institute prosecutions for these offences, so that, together with its powers to impose

---

[2] Sections 118–131 FSMA.

[3] Made pursuant to Section 119 FSMA, the Code of Market Conduct is to be found in the FSA's Handbook, at Chapter 1 of the Handbook's market conduct sourcebook ("MAR"). It is also published separately and will be available as a separate document to persons who are not authorised. The current version, at the time of writing, on which this chapter is based is Release 001, December 2001.

[4] Section 122(1) FSMA.

[5] Section 122(2) FSMA.

[6] Pursuant to Section 157 FSMA.

[7] Section 397 FSMA.

penalties under the new market abuse regime, the FSA now has a variety of powers at its disposal should it consider them appropriate.[8]

8.1.4   Legislative objectives

By way of background, it is useful to understand both the primary aim of the new market abuse regime and also why it was felt necessary to implement the new civil market abuse regime in addition to existing legislation with similar aims, such as the misleading statements and practices offences.

The primary objective of the new market abuse regime is the deterrence of abusive behaviour which could undermine confidence in, and ultimately the integrity of, UK financial markets. It is intended to complement and supplement existing legislation and regulation in this area.[9]

The UK already had a variety of legislation aimed at areas that, whilst not specifically labelled as market abuse, could be said to be essentially that. For example, the Criminal Justice Act 1993 (the "CJA 1993") deals with insider dealing criminal offences and the Financial Services Act 1986 (the "FS Act") had made certain misleading statements and practices criminal offences.

However, successful prosecutions for these criminal offences have been rare. As the FSA stated:

> "these criminal offences cover a relatively narrow range of very serious misconduct where there is a clear intention to abuse the market and other users. However, market confidence, integrity and efficiency can also be damaged by a broader range of misconduct and by the effect of that misconduct on markets. It is this broader range of misconduct that the new framework seeks to address."[10]

---

[8] Section 401 FSMA. Note that Section 402 of FSMA also confers on the FSA power to institute prosecutions for insider dealing offences under the Criminal Justice Act 1993. *See* parts 8.12 and 8.13 for more.

[9] *See* for example, Consultation Paper 10, June 1998, Market Abuse, Part 1: Consultation on a draft Code of Market Conduct, paragraph 2 and also Consultation Paper 59, July 2000 Market Abuse: A Draft Code of Market Conduct, paragraphs 1.1 and 1.2.

[10] *See* Consultation Paper 59, July 2000, Market Abuse: A Draft Code of Market Conduct, paragraph 2.10.

Accordingly, it was felt that a civil[11] regime was needed to deal more effectively with behaviour that affected confidence in the markets, even though it fell short of a criminal offence. Consequently, the new market abuse regime was devised.

8.1.5 Coverage of this Chapter

The new market abuse regime, as supplemented by COMC, is clearly intended to be important in helping the FSA to maintain confidence in the UK's markets. It will play a key role, as its place in this Guide suggests, in the FSA's regulation of investment banking and markets generally.

However, within the confines of only one Chapter, it is not possible to mention everything in COMC. COMC goes into considerably more detail than this Chapter has at its disposal. Readers of this Chapter should, therefore, bear in mind that it cannot, and does not, cover all points raised by COMC or all examples or guidance given in it.

Neither is it possible to canvass all the issues which were raised in the many consultation papers and other written materials published in the course of the preparation of both the statutory provisions and COMC. The FSA started consulting on market abuse and COMC back in June 1998.[12]

---

[11] In the course of the preparation and passage of the FSMA, there was much debate on several key areas, including whether the new market abuse regime was a civil regime or more criminal in nature. As a result of this debate including the tendency of many to give the regime a criminal categorisation, it was felt necessary, early on in the passage of the Financial Services and Markets Bill (the "Bill"), to set up a Joint Committee on Financial Services and Markets (the "Joint Committee") to consider a number of issues, including the question of possible infringement of the European Convention on Human Rights (the "ECHR"). The first report of the Joint Committee noted that a strongly supported view was that the market abuse statutory provisions, as they then stood, were criminal in nature for the purposes of the ECHR. The Government then took advice on this matter and a number of changes were made to the Bill to address this. The FSA believes that the current regime is civil for ECHR purposes.

[12] Consultation Paper 10, June 1998, Market Abuse, Part 1: Consultation on a draft Code of Market Conduct (to be referred to, hereafter, as Consultation Paper 10, Part 1, June 1998). Consultation Paper 10, June 1998, Market Abuse Part 2: Draft Code of Market Conduct (to be referred to, hereafter, as Consultation Paper 10, Part 2, June 1998).

A feedback statement on responses was issued in March 1999,[13] and this was followed by a further consultation paper in July 2000[14] with a revised draft of COMC. In November 2000 a third consultation paper with a supplement to the draft COMC was issued.[15] COMC, when issued in (as it then was) "final" form in April 2001, was accompanied by a policy statement which summarised the main responses in the consultation process, the main changes being made as a result of it and why, in certain areas, the FSA would not be making changes ("Policy Statement, April 2001").[16]

Throughout this consultation process, responses were received from many bodies, not least the Company Law Committee of the Law Society[17] which shed very useful light on the development of, and

---

[13] Feedback statement on responses to Consultation Paper 10, March 1999.

[14] Consultation Paper 59, July 2000, Market Abuse: A Draft Code of Market Conduct (to be referred to, hereafter, as Consultation Paper 59, July 2000).

[15] Consultation Paper 76, November 2000, supplement to the Draft Code of Market Conduct (to be referred to, hereafter, as Consultation Paper 76, November 2000). This concentrated particularly on (i) the prohibition on requiring or encouraging others to commit market abuse, (ii) interaction between the market abuse regime and the Listing Rules and (iii) the interaction between the City Code and SARs and the market abuse regime.

[16] The full title of the policy statement is Policy Statement, April 2001, Code of Market Conduct, Feedback on Consultation Paper 59 and Consultation Paper 76 (to be referred to, hereafter, as Policy Statement, April 2001). The version of the Code issued at this time was described as "final". Final meant near final, that is approved by the Board of the FSA but with some final cross-references to be added. It was to be "issued" when the FSA received the power to exercise its legislative function. However, note that later the FSA decided that there were actually some further changes that needed to be made to the Code in certain respects (*see Market Watch*, Markets & Exchanges Division's Newsletter on Market Conduct Issues, Pilot Issue July 2001) and accordingly the Code was re-approved by the Board of the FSA on 19 July 2001 and later reissued. The current version of the Code, at the time of writing, on which this chapter is based is Release 001, 01 December 2001.

[17] For example, *see* (i) Memorandum by the Company Law Committee – Financial Services and Markets Bill, November 1998, No 367; (ii) Memorandum by the Company Law Committee – Market Abuse, November 1998, No 368; (iii) Law Society Company Law Committee and City of London Law Society Regulatory Sub-Committee: Joint Memorandum To The Financial Services Authority on Consultation Paper 59 and (iv) Financial Services Working Party of the Law Society Company Law Committee and City of London Law Society Regulatory Sub-Committee: Joint Memorandum To The Financial Services Authority on Consultation Paper 76.

thinking behind, this new regime, which has changed considerably since its inception.[18]

However, in a single Chapter on the new regime, it is not possible to concentrate in any detail on prior drafts and responses to those drafts, except where such background information sheds particularly useful light on the current provisions, their meanings and intention. Accordingly, it is only in this respect that they will be mentioned, although this is not to underestimate their importance to an understanding of this new regime and its development.

8.2 Prescribed markets, qualifying investments and relevant products

8.2.1 Prescribed markets

Market abuse is only relevant to behaviour in relation to qualifying investments traded on prescribed markets. (This is actually wider than it seems since it includes behaviour occurring in relation to "relevant products" of those qualifying investments, for which *see* more below).[19]

The FSMA provides that the Treasury may prescribe the markets to which the market abuse provisions apply and the investments which are qualifying investments in relation to those markets.[20] Accordingly, the Financial Services and Markets Act 2000 (Prescribed Markets and Qualifying Investments) Order 2001 (the "Prescribed Markets and Qualifying Investments Order") was made.[21] This prescribed all markets established under the rules of UK recognised investment exchanges (the "RIEs"). These are investment exchanges recognised under Section 290(1)(a) FSMA, which at the date of writing are: COREDEAL Limited, The

---

[18] For example, the statutory provisions as originally set out in the draft Bill that accompanied the Treasury's document required that the three types of behaviour "would be likely to damage the confidence of informed participants that the market was 'true and fair'". Some respondents saw this as creating too much uncertainty and it was dropped. Also, the original statutory provisions lacked, not only any need for intent, but also any safe harbours for honest and careful persons. Following the recommendations of the Joint Committee (*see* footnote 10 above), safe harbours were added to the market abuse regime.

[19] Section 118(1)(a) and 118(6) FSMA.

[20] Section 118(3) FSMA.

[21] Financial Services and Markets Act 2000 (Prescribed Markets and Qualifying Investments) Order 2001, No. 996.

International Petroleum Exchange of London Limited (the "IPE"), Jiway Limited, The London International Financial Futures Exchange Administration and Management (the "LIFFE"), The London Metal Exchange, The London Stock Exchange plc (including AIM), OM London Exchange plc, Virt-x Exchange Limited and Virt-x plc. OFEX has also been designated as a prescribed market.

The qualifying investment in question must be "traded on" one of the prescribed markets. This includes investments that are currently trading subject to the rules of a prescribed market, and also investments which have not yet traded subject to the rules of a prescribed market from the point they start trading subject to the rules of a prescribed market (including the first trade). It also includes investments which have traded in the past and can currently be traded (i.e. the fact that an investment has not traded recently is irrelevant to the question of whether it is traded on a particular market). (COMC does, however, state that there will probably be no ongoing market in an investment if it has not traded for a long time, or only in insignificant volumes, and so behaviour in respect of that investment is unlikely to amount to market abuse).[22]

As to grey market or "when issued" trading (i.e. before the products trade on an exchange), the FSA, in an issue of frequently asked questions, has confirmed that for new issues by previously unlisted issuers, e.g. initial public offerings, the shares in question are not "traded on" a prescribed market ahead of the issue or commencement of the market's "when issued" trading. However, information which is disclosed about them, say, in a prospectus, could be covered by the market abuse regime if, say, a misleading impression based on that information persists until when they are actually trading. For secondary issues, where there is an existing listing, the behaviour in the further issue can be said to be in relation to a qualifying investment (i.e. the existing tranche which is already listed and traded on the prescribed market).

8.2.2 *Qualifying investments*

The Prescribed Markets and Qualifying Investments Order also prescribes what are qualifying investments for the purpose of the market abuse regime. These investments are all of the kind specified for the purposes of Section 22 FSMA and are broadly, similar to those that regulated under the FS Act, namely, deposits, shares, investments

---

[22] Paragraph 1.11.5G COMC.

creating indebtedness, instruments giving entitlements to investments, options, futures and contracts for differences. These, and others, if traded on prescribed markets, are therefore qualifying investments for the purpose of the market abuse regime.

8.2.3 Relevant products

As already stated, market abuse has to occur in relation to qualifying investments traded on a prescribed market. That said, Section 118(6) FSMA goes on to explain this requirement further and provides that, as well as the behaviour in question relating directly to those qualifying investments, such behaviour also includes:

(a)   behaviour occurring in relation to anything which is the subject matter, or whose price or value is expressed by reference to the price or value, of those qualifying investments; and

(b)   behaviour which occurs in relation to investments (whether qualifying or not) whose subject matter is those qualifying investments.

This extends the scope of the market abuse regime beyond behaviour directly relating to qualifying investments traded on prescribed markets. COMC explains this matter by stating that behaviour in relation to qualifying investments includes behaviour in relation to other investments, not themselves qualifying investments traded on prescribed markets, since such behaviour can have a damaging effect on confidence in prescribed markets and qualifying investments. These related investments are referred to in COMC as "relevant products".[23]

COMC then gives six categories of behaviour in the following relevant products which would be caught by Section 118(6). These categories are essentially just a splitting up of Section 118(6) into its constituent parts:

(a)   anything that is the subject matter of a qualifying investment;

(b)   anything whose price is expressed by reference to the price of a qualifying investment;

(c)   anything whose price is expressed by reference to the value of a qualifying investment;

---

[23] Paragraph 1.11.8E COMC.

(d)   anything whose value is expressed by reference to the price of a qualifying investment;

(e)   anything whose value is expressed by reference to the value of a qualifying investment; and

(f)   investments (whether qualifying or not) whose subject matter is a qualifying investment.[24]

For something to be the "subject matter" of an investment or qualifying investment, there needs to be a clear (e.g. contractual or documented) relationship between the two. Various examples are given, such as gilts which are deliverable under the terms of a gilt futures contract traded on LIFFE. The gilts are relevant products since they are the subject matter of a gilt futures contract (which is a qualifying investment). Also, the subject matter of an over-the-counter option on a basket of UK shares (which is an investment) traded on a prescribed market is a qualifying investment (i.e. the underlying shares are qualifying investments) and, therefore, the over-the-counter option itself is a relevant product. Accordingly, in these examples if the behaviour in question relates to the gilts or to the over-the-counter option and satisfies the requirements of market abuse, then that behaviour will fall within the market abuse regime.[25]

On the question of the price and/or value relationship between qualifying investments and relevant products, COMC again gives examples. These include spread bets in relation to a basket of UK shares traded on a prescribed market, where the value of the spread bet is expressed by reference to the price of the shares and so is a relevant product. Also, where the price of an over-the-counter contract in relation to Brent Crude is expressed by reference to the price of a Brent Crude futures contract which is traded on the IPE (which is a qualifying investment), the over-the-counter contract is, therefore, a relevant product.[26]

Section 118(6) is a key part of the statutory provisions relating to market abuse of which we need to be aware, since it extends the ambit of the regime beyond what we might, at first, expect. The scope of the market abuse regime is, and is intended to be, wide.

---

[24] Paragraph 1.11.9E COMC.

[25] Paragraph 1.11.10E COMC.

[26] Paragraph 1.11.10E COMC.

8.3 Behaviour

8.3.1 What behaviour?

Market abuse involves behaviour, which can be by one or more persons jointly or in concert.[27] Behaviour can include inaction as well as action.[28] COMC gives the example of someone who fails to make a particular disclosure where under a legal or regulatory requirement to do so. Such inaction could amount to market abuse.[29] This is highly relevant to, for example, listed companies and their directors.

The behaviour must "occur in relation to" a qualifying investment traded on a prescribed market which, as described above, can include a relevant product.

COMC lists seven types of behaviour which come within the scope of the market abuse regime, although this list is not exhaustive:

(a) dealing in qualifying investments;
(b) dealing in commodities or investments which are the subject matter of, or whose price or value is determined by reference to, a qualifying investment;
(c) arranging deals in respect of qualifying investments;
(d) causing or procuring or advising others to deal in qualifying investments;
(e) making statements or representations, or disseminating information, which is likely to be regarded by the regular user as relevant in deciding the terms on which transactions in qualifying investments should be effected;
(f) providing corporate finance advice and conducting corporate finance activities in qualifying investments; and
(g) managing qualifying investments belonging to another.[30]

8.3.2 Behaviour by whom?

The persons who may be covered by the new regime include not only authorised or regulated persons but also unauthorised persons. It covers all market users. As the FSA stated:

---

[27] Section 118(1) FSMA.
[28] Section 118(1) FSMA.
[29] Paragraph 1.3.2E COMC.
[30] Paragraph 1.3.1E COMC.

"The Government has said that the new market abuse framework extends the current regulatory regime in two important respects. First, its coverage extends to unauthorised persons as well as author-ised persons, so that in future all users of markets will be subject to the same requirements."[31]

8.3.3 Behaviour where?

The behaviour in question must occur in relation to qualifying invest-ments traded on prescribed markets, which are UK recognised invest-ment exchanges and OFEX. However, this does not mean it is only behaviour in the UK that is caught. The FSMA provides that behaviour is to be disregarded unless it occurs (a) in the UK or (b) in relation to qualifying investments traded on a market (to which the section applies) which is situated in the UK or accessible electronically in the UK.[32] This second limb is saying that the regime is not limited only to qualifying investments traded on those prescribed markets which are traditional markets which one can say are (physically) situated in the UK, but also covers any of those prescribed markets which may simply be accessible electronically from the UK even though not physically located in the UK.

8.4 The regular user test

8.4.1 Introduction

The FSA states:

"... in many aspects the regular user test is the cornerstone of the market abuse regime."[33]

Not only are each of the three conditions (relating to misuse of infor-mation, the giving of false or misleading impressions and market distortion) clearly referable to the regular user, but overall even if the provisions of one or more of the three behaviour-related conditions are met, market abuse only occurs if the regular user regards one or more of the types of behaviour detailed in the conditions as having failed to meet the standard of behaviour reasonably expected. As the FSMA provides – what is required is behaviour

---

[31] *See* Consultation Paper 59, July 2000, paragraph 1.3.
[32] Section 118(5) FSMA.
[33] Policy Statement, April 2001, *see* paragraph 5.1.

"which is likely to be regarded by a regular user of that market who is aware of the behaviour as a failure on the part of the person or persons concerned to observe the standard of behaviour reasonably expected of a person in his or their position in relation to the market."[34]

8.4.2 Who is the regular user?

The FSMA provides that the "regular user, in relation to a particular market, means a reasonable person who regularly deals on that market in investments of the kind in question".[35] That is all the FSMA itself says on the subject of the regular user. COMC devotes two and a half pages to what it calls the regular user test. It provides that in order to decide whether behaviour is market abuse it is necessary to consider objectively whether a "hypothetical reasonable person, familiar with the market in question, would regard the behaviour as acceptable in the light of all the relevant circumstances".[36]

The hypothetical regular user in COMC appears to be imbued with an altruistic characteristic of considering the greater good of the market and of investors which is not necessarily an aspect of the character of the average market user. For example, COMC mentions the need for behaviour which does not compromise the fair and efficient operation of the market as a whole or unfairly damage the interests of investors.[37]

In Policy Statement, April 2001 the FSA made it clear, in response to some comments that suggested the impression could be drawn that the FSA itself was the regular user, that this is not the case. Neither can the FSA require the regular user to act in a particular way or to take any particular factors into account. Hence, in COMC, when seeking to give guidance on behaviour which the regular user is "likely" to regard as amounting to market abuse, the FSA felt it could not be categorical and could only indicate what is "likely".[38]

---

[34] Section 118(1)(c) FSMA.
[35] Section 118(10) FSMA.
[36] Paragraph 1.2.2 COMC.
[37] Paragraph 1.2.3(5)E COMC.
[38] Policy Statement, April 2001, *see* paragraph 5.3.

8.4.3 What is the regular user likely to take into consideration?

COMC lists matters the regular user is likely to consider in determining whether the behaviour in question falls below the expected standards. This is likely to include:

(a) the characteristics of the market in question, the investments and the users of the market;

(b) the rules of the market in question (although compliance is not generally an absolute defence (*see* 8.4.4)), and if the person is based overseas, the extent to which the behaviour is in compliance with the standards prevailing in that overseas jurisdiction;

(c) prevailing market mechanisms, practices and codes of conduct although COMC notes that "there may be circumstances in which the actual standards prevailing in a market may not meet the standards expected by the regular user" (*see* 8.4.5);

(d) the actual person in question, as the standards in question are the standards reasonably to be expected of that person given his experience, level of skill and standard of knowledge. (Here COMC gives the example of different standards to be expected of a retail investor than of an industry professional); and

(e) the need for market users to act in a way that does not compromise the fair and efficient operation of the market as a whole, nor unfairly damage the interests of investors.[39]

8.4.4 Compliance with other rules

One of the points the regular user is thought likely to take account of is rules and regulations of the market in question and any applicable laws. COMC provides that it may often be appropriate to take into account the extent to which the behaviour is in compliance with other applicable rules, such as RIE rules, the City Code on Takeovers and Mergers (the "City Code") or FSA rules. Whilst not determinative (i.e. compliance with such rules alone will not always mean the behaviour does not amount to market abuse, unless the subject of a safe harbour (*see* Section 8.8 below)), weight is likely to be given to such compliance.[40]

---

[39] Paragraph 1.2.3E COMC.
[40] Paragraph 1.2.8G COMC.

8.4.5 Compliance with generally accepted standards and normal market practice

During the consultation process, there was extensive consideration of what was regarded as "normal market practice" and the question of whether the FSA could give comfort that such practices would not amount to market abuse.[41] This issue is now addressed in COMC, although full comfort is not given as the FSA disagreed with respondents on the issue.

The regular user is likely to consider it relevant that the behaviour in question conforms with standards that are generally accepted by the market's users. As the FSA stated:

> ". . . the regular user . . . will not operate in a vacuum, unaffected by the standards that do prevail in markets."[42]

However, in Policy Statement, April 2001, the FSA considered whether the way in which the regular user test works would mean that standards and practices prevailing in a market at any time would *always* equate to those expected by the regular user. Many respondents to the consultation on COMC felt this to be the case and argued against the FSA's view. Notwithstanding these responses, the FSA stated that it remained of the view that this was not so. It is quite clear on this point. It stated:

> "There may be circumstances in which the actual standards or practices prevailing in a market may not meet the standards expected by the regular user."[43]

It also stated:

> ". . . the FSA is not of the opinion that because a practice is accepted by some (or indeed many) users of the market it must automatically equate to the standard expected by the reasonable user . . . Accepted practices will need to be judged against the objective standards expected by the regular user."[44]

---

[41] *See*, for example, Consultation Paper 59, July 2000, paragraphs 6.6 and 6.7 and Policy Statement, April 2001, paragraph 5.5.

[42] Consultation Paper 59, July 2000, paragraph 6.7.

[43] Consultation Paper 59, July 2000, paragraph 6.6.

[44] Policy Statement, April 2001, paragraph 5.5.

Accordingly, it is possible that accepted practices may not be acceptable. This could leave market users in doubt as to whether particular behaviour does or does not fall below the standard expected by the hypothetical regular user. The question they may need to ask themselves is – do the standards and practices they propose to adhere to promote the fair and efficient operation of the market as a whole and not unfairly damage the interests of investors? This approach would follow the guidance in COMC.[45]

However, the FSA also states in COMC that it does not anticipate that divergences between generally accepted standards and the standards expected by the regular user will be frequent. Also, it would expect to deal with such situations by considering whether to issue guidance or amend COMC signalling its views concerning the unacceptable behaviour and thus enabling market participants to alter their conduct accordingly. Whilst it recognises that this approach will often be more appropriate, there may still be occasions where the FSA feels that enforcement action does need to be taken.[46]

8.4.6   The relevance of intent and purpose to the regular user

The FSA has said:

> "The focus of the market abuse regime remains firmly on the effects of behaviour, and not the intentions behind such behaviour."[47]

Also, as COMC states:

> "The statutory definition of market abuse does not require the person engaging in the behaviour to have intended to abuse the market."

This is, however, mitigated first by the defences that may be available (*see* Section 8.10 below). Also, in some circumstances when the regular user is deciding if behaviour falls short of the standards expected (e.g. market distortion), the purpose of the perpetrator is likely to be an additional relevant circumstance to be looked at. Thirdly, COMC states that a mistake which the person in question took all reasonable care to

---

[45] Paragraph 1.2.10G COMC.
[46] Paragraph 1.2.11G COMC.
[47] Consultation Paper 59, July 2000, paragraph 6.14.

prevent and detect, is unlikely to fall below the objective standards expected.[48]

8.4.7 Varying standards across national markets

Where behaviour occurs on an overseas market but has an impact on a prescribed market, the regular user is likely to consider the local conventions in the relevant market and whether the person is in the UK. However, compliance with such conventions will not conclusively prove the behaviour in question is not market abuse.[49]

8.4.8 Innovative transactions and the regular user

Policy Statement, April 2001 noted that a number of responses which it received expressed concern as to how market practitioners would be able to assess innovative transactions as against what the regular user is likely to think of them. In this regard, the FSA has made it clear that it wishes to encourage innovation, not stifle it and will be prepared to give individual guidance regarding proposed transactions from a market abuse perspective.[50]

The regular user test is difficult to apply to innovative transactions. COMC on this matter, therefore, makes it clear that it is not exhaustive in its descriptions of behaviour that do or do not amount to market abuse and that for proposed innovative transactions, it is open for a person to seek guidance both from the FSA and, for members of RIE, from the relevant exchange.[51] A person may request individual guidance orally or, if the issue is complex, in writing (but not on a no names basis). The FSA expects the person making the request to have taken reasonable steps to research the topic and to identify the rule or other matter on which its guidance is sought.

The FSA will endeavour to provide a quick and timely response. The extent to which a person can rely on guidance given will depend on many factors, such as the degree of formality of the original query and the guidance given. Essentially, written guidance is binding, whereas oral guidance (even if recorded) will not be binding unless the FSA confirms in writing that they will be bound by it. The FSA also makes it

---

[48] Paragraphs 1.2.5E and 1.2.6E COMC.
[49] Paragraph 1.2.9G COMC.
[50] Policy Statement, April 2001, paragraph 5.8.
[51] Paragraph 1.2.13G COMC.

clear that if circumstances change and the premises upon which the guidance was given no longer apply, the guidance will cease to be effective.[52]

The FSA issues a newsletter entitled – *Market Watch* Markets & Exchanges Division's Newsletter on Market Conduct Issues. This newsletter will include "frequently asked questions" ("FAQs") on the new regime, and will update market participants on topical issues.[53]

8.5   Misuse of information

8.5.1   Introduction and objectives

The principal conditions in the market abuse regime relate to three types of behaviour. First, behaviour based on misuse of information. Second, behaviour giving rise to false or misleading impressions. Lastly, behaviour which would, or would be likely to, amount to market distortion.[54]

The misuse of information condition is met if that behaviour is based on information:

(a)   not generally available to market users;
(b)   but which, if it were available, would, or would be likely to be regarded by a regular user of the market as relevant when deciding the terms on which transactions in investments of the kind in question should be effected.[55]

COMC notes that market users rely on the timely dissemination of relevant information which they reasonably expect to receive and that those possessing such information ahead of its general dissemination should refrain from basing their behaviour on that information or from encouraging or requiring others to engage in behaviour based on it until it is disseminated.[56]

---

[52] *See* Chapter 9, Individual Guidance, Supervision Module of FSA Handbook for more.
[53] Markets & Exchanges Division's Newsletter on Market Conduct Issues, Market Watch, Pilot Issue July 2001.
[54] Section 118(2) FSMA.
[55] Section 118(2)(a) FSMA.
[56] Paragraph 1.4.3E COMC.

COMC then gives some detail as to what behaviour will amount to market abuse under this condition. It requires four circumstances to be present:

(a) dealing in qualifying investments or relevant products based on information which the person possesses and which has a material influence on his decision to deal, that is, it must be one of the reasons for dealing but need not be the only reason;

(b) where the information is not generally available to those using the market;

(c) where such information is likely to be regarded by the regular user as relevant when deciding the terms on which transactions in the relevant investments should be effected ("relevant information"); and

(d) where the relevant information relates to matters which the regular user would reasonably expect to be disclosed to the particular market, whether at the time in question or in the future.[57]

8.5.2 *Information generally available*

Information will be regarded as generally available if one or more of the following is satisfied:

(a) the information can be obtained by research conducted by users of a market;[58] or

(b) the information has been disclosed to a prescribed market through an accepted information dissemination channel or otherwise under the rules of that market; or

(c) the information is contained in records open to public inspection; or

(d) the information has otherwise been made public, including through the internet or other publication or is derived from information which has been made public; or

(e) the information has been obtained by observation; or

(f) the information has been obtained by other legitimate means.

Legitimate means might include observation of a public event, which includes information which is discussed in a public area or can be observed by the public without infringing rights of privacy, property or confidentiality. If it is such information, it will be considered to be

---

[57] Paragraph 1.4.4E COMC.
[58] Section 118(7) FSMA.

generally available and the fact that other users of the market cannot themselves obtain that information because of limitations in their resources, expertise or competence does not alter that.[59]

COMC gives examples of information published overseas and information available on payment of a fee as information which might be obtainable by legitimate research and consequently be regarded as generally available. Also, a passenger on a train who sees a burning factory and tells his broker to sell shares in its owner will be acting on information generally available.[60]

8.5.3   Relevant information

What is "relevant information" will always depend on the circumstances of the case. The regular user is likely to consider the extent to which:

(a)   the information is specific and precise;
(b)   the information is material;
(c)   the information is current;
(d)   the information is reliable (which will include the proximity of the person providing it to the original source and the reliability of the original source);
(e)   there is other material information which is already generally available to inform users of the market; and
(f)   the information differs from information currently generally available, so that it can be said to be fresh information.[61]

COMC gives a few examples of relevant information. For example, where the qualifying investment in question is issued by a company, or is a derivative relating to a qualifying investment issued by a company, information concerning the business affairs or prospects of the company or a related company would be relevant information. So, listed companies now not only risk breaching the Listing Rules for failing to disclose information in accordance with the Listing Rules, but may also find themselves within the market abuse regime. Also, if the qualifying investment is a derivative relating to a commodity, information or events affecting the supply of the commodity, for example, as to the business operations of major suppliers of it, would be considered relevant information.[62]

---

[59] Paragraph 1.4.6E COMC.
[60] Paragraphs 1.4.7G and 1.4.8G COMC.
[61] Paragraph 1.4.9E COMC.
[62] Paragraph 1.4.11E (1) and (2) COMC.

COMC also looks at information which relates to possible future developments (which do not give rise to a current expectation of disclosure) and states that additional factors are to be taken into account in determining the relevance of that information, namely:

(a)   whether the information provides, with reasonable certainty, grounds for concluding that the possible future developments will occur; and

(b)   the significance those developments would assume for market users were they to occur.[63]

The FSA has stated that use of information which will become disclosable in the future (although it may not currently be disclosable) should be restricted in the same way as information which is currently disclosable. This means that simply because it is not *currently* disclosable does not render its use ahead of its future dissemination acceptable. As the FSA states:

> "the use of information may be restricted before it is formally required to be disclosed, or before the market would generally expect it to be available."[64]

8.5.4   Information reasonably expected to be disclosed

The fourth circumstance necessary for behaviour to be market abuse in this misuse of information condition is that the information relates to matters which the regular user would reasonably expect to be disclosed to other users of the particular market, whether at the time in question or later.[65]

---

[63] Paragraph 1.4.10 COMC.

[64] *See* Policy Statement, April 2001, paragraph 6.14 and CP 59, July 2000, paragraphs 6.34–6.36.

[65] In Consultation Paper 59, July 2000, paragraph 6.24, the FSA noted, in relation to this fourth element which requires the information to relate to matters which the regular user would reasonably expect to be disclosed to market users that, in applying the regular user test to misuse of information behaviour, it had identified this additional element which has the effect of narrowing the range of information potentially covered by the market abuse regime. This also reflected the view that there would always be times when certain market users have access to information that is not generally available to others and that the reality of markets is such that it is not possible for all information to be known to all participants and indeed the regular user has no expectation that this should be so.

COMC states that information will only fall within this circumstance if it is either:

(a)   information required to be disclosed in accordance with legal or regulatory requirements (referred to as "disclosable information"); or

(b)   information routinely the subject of public announcement even though not subject to a requirement to disclose (referred to as "announceable information").[66]

Disclosable information includes City Code required disclosures, Listing Rules required disclosures for officially listed securities and RIE required disclosures for prescribed markets.[67]

Announceable information includes information which is to be the subject of official announcement by governments, monetary, fiscal or regulatory authorities. It also includes changes to published credit ratings of companies whose securities are qualifying investments or relevant products and changes to the constituents of relevant securities indexes.[68]

COMC also mentions some information that would not be regarded as announceable which includes surveys based on information which is generally available, for example CBI surveys and MORI opinion polls.[69]

In respect of possible developments there is an additional factor to be taken into account when determining whether that information is disclosable or announceable. This is whether the information provides, with reasonable certainty, grounds to conclude that the possible developments will occur and therefore a disclosure or announcement will be made.[70]

The example which COMC gives to explain this is of a listed company which is required to announce any major new developments and, so, if it entered into a significant contract with a major supplier, it would be under an obligation to announce at the point it enters into the contract. Such information is both relevant information and disclosable at that

---

[66] Paragraph 1.4.12E COMC.
[67] Paragraph 1.4.14E COMC.
[68] Paragraph 1.4.15E COMC.
[69] Paragraph 1.4.16G COMC.
[70] Paragraph 1.4.13E COMC.

stage. But, if the test mentioned above is met, that is, the regular user concludes that, in relation to information on the possible future entry into the supply contract, that development will occur and a disclosure or announcement will be made, then the information would fall within the definition not only of relevant information, but also of disclosable/announceable information at an earlier stage, namely at the time when there are grounds to conclude, with reasonable certainty, that the contract will be entered into and disclosure relating to it will have to be made. So if the regular user feels there are grounds to conclude that the contract will be entered into and disclosure will have to be made, any dealing based on that information at the earlier stage (i.e. before it is made public) could fall within the market abuse regime.[71]

8.5.5 Differing markets, same information

Where information is required to be disclosed to Market A, arranging deals ahead of that disclosure in qualifying investments traded in Market A, or in their relevant products, will amount to market abuse. However, where that information is also relevant to Market B, arranging deals in relation to qualifying investments traded on Market B, or in their relevant products, based on that information ahead of its disclosure will only amount to market abuse if there are disclosure obligations in relation to Market B.[72]

The example given in Policy Statement, April 2001, assuming Market A is the equity market and Market B a commodity market is helpful:

(a) dealing or arranging deals in an equity, a derivative on that equity or a spread bet on that equity on the basis of relevant information not generally available would continue to be covered (because in the equity market there is a duty to disclose); yet

(b) dealing or arranging deals, on the basis of the same information, in a commodity derivative to which it was also relevant (where there was no disclosure obligation), would not be covered.

The FSA goes on to point out that even given this change, it is incumbent on all market participants to ensure they also comply with all other applicable regulation that may be relevant to them. For example, a listed commodity producer, faced with an unexpected drop in production

---

[71] Paragraph 1.4.18E COMC.
[72] Paragraph 1.4.17E COMC.

which requires a profit warning, will be required by the Listing Rules to disclose significant news without delay. Whilst hedging its position in the commodity derivatives market ahead of Listing Rules disclosure may not now amount to market abuse, it still needs to consider whether such hedging before disclosing is consistent with its Listing Rules obligations. The FSA has acknowledged that this is a complex area and has stated that it intends to explore further issues in this regard and take discussions forward.[73]

8.5.6 Safe harbours

There are several safe harbours provided in COMC for use of information:

(a) arranging deals in order to comply with a legal (including contractual) or regulatory obligation in circumstances where the obligation existed before the relevant information was in the person's possession;[74]
(b) arranging deals where the person's possession of the relevant, not generally available, information did not influence the decision to do the dealing.[75] (One of the several examples given is where the information was held behind an effective Chinese Wall and the person dealing or arranging was on the other side of it);[76]
(c) arranging deals where it is based on information as to that person's or another person's intentions to deal, or on information concerning transactions that have taken place.
    This intentions-related safe harbour comes under the sub-heading "Trading Information",[77] and was explained in the Consultation Paper 10, Part 2, June 1998 as a reflection of the fact that people will always have an advantage over others, namely that they know the trades they have done and also what they intend to do. They might be about to, for example, build a stake or position themselves ahead of an expected price move or take advantage of a pricing difference between exchanges.[78] This safe harbour reflects the fact that market users ought not to be restricted from trading due to such

---

[73] Policy Statement, April 2001, paragraphs 6.8–6.13 inclusive.
[74] Paragraph 1.4.20C COMC.
[75] Paragraph 1.4.21C COMC.
[76] Paragraphs 1.4.24C COMC.
[77] It was initially known as order-flow information.
[78] Consultation Paper 10, June 1998, paragraphs 93–96 inclusive on order-flow information.

information both as to their own intentions and those of others.[79] (Note that whilst there was discussion in Consultation Paper 59, July 2000 as to whether this safe harbour should be limited only to information as to one's own intentions, the FSA felt it should be left as is and noted the protections afforded to customers by the Conduct of Business Rules generally and especially those relating to confidentiality. Note also the carve-outs from this safe harbour described below).

An example given in Consultation Paper 59, July 2000 illustrates the intention here. Firm A learns that Firm B intends to execute a large trade on behalf of a fund manager. Firm A is able to position itself in the market to benefit from the impact of that trade when it happens. Firm A would be free to trade on the basis of that information, as it concerns another person's intention to trade.

The FSA has stated that, subject to the customers of authorised firms being properly protected as addressed by appropriate Conduct of Business Rules (including obligations of confidentiality owed to customers), it agrees that market users should be able to take advantage of their ability to understand, analyse and assess the implications of transaction flows through the market.

However, there are two carve-outs from this safe harbour, where the view is taken that a person's knowledge of their own or another's intentions or positions ought to restrict their ability to trade. These are dealing or arranging deals (i) based on information as to a possible takeover bid (subject to the limited safe harbour in (d) below) and (ii) based on information relating to new offers, issues, placements or other primary market activity.

A final point on this safe harbour is that all other rules must still be adhered to, such as conduct of business rules for authorised persons, which include, for example, rules as to dealing fairly and in due turn;[80]

(d) dealing or arranging deals for the facilitation of takeover bids and other market operations if engaged in by a person (or someone acting for him or by another person acting in concert with him) where (i) the dealing or arranging is in connection with the acquisition or disposal of an equity stake in a company; is engaged in solely for the purpose of that acquisition or disposal; or is engaged in by a concert party of a person making or potentially making an

---

[79] Paragraph 1.4.26C COMC.
[80] Paragraph 1.4.27G COMC.

acquisition or disposal for the sole benefit of that person and (ii) the information being used consists only of certain facts listed in COMC. Examples of such information include – information that investments of a particular kind are, or are not, to be acquired and information that has been legitimately obtained by the bidder in relation to the target.[81]

This safe harbour is intended to include (i) the seeking of irrevocable undertakings or expressions of support in a bid, (ii) making arrangements in connection with securities to be offered as consideration in a bid, or to fund a bid, including underwriting and placing arrangements and any associated hedging arrangements by underwriters or placees and (iii) making arrangements to offer cash as an alternative to securities consideration.[82]

Whilst explaining that a person should not be prevented from stake-building in a company with a view to pursuing a bid or engaging in other market operations simply because he knew that he would be making a bid and the information is relevant, COMC also makes it clear that this does not mean the bidder, or potential bidder, may undertake any other type of transaction in the target's shares or in other investments (e.g. in contracts for differences or in securities of other companies) in relation to which the information is relevant information. It states a bidder will be engaging in market abuse if he enters into transactions in qualifying investments that merely provide an economic exposure to movements in the price of the target company's shares. Also, anyone acting for a bidder will engage in market abuse if they deal for their own benefit in qualifying investments or relevant products in respect of which the information on the proposed bid is relevant; and[83]

(e)   agreeing to underwrite an issue of securities will not of itself amount to a misuse of information.

Some of these safe harbours are similar to, if not the same as, defences, or parts of defences, to the insider dealing offences in the CJA 1993. For example, the market information defence of the CJA 1993 is similar to its counterpart in the market abuse regime. Some respondents to the consultation process wanted all the CJA 1993 defences to be made available in COMC and to be replicated exactly. It was argued that the

---

81 Paragraph 1.4.28C(2) COMC.
82 Paragraph 1.4.29E COMC.
83 Paragraph 1.4.30E COMC.

relevant part of the CJA 1993 was derived from European legislation aimed at preventing market abuse.[84] In response to this the FSA said:

> "... we do not consider that the case is made for complete replication of CJA defences in COMC. The purposes of the criminal and financial penalties approach are different, as are the tests that need to be met."

It goes on to state that certain elements of the CJA 1993 defences can be found in COMC, although it notes, in particular, that the no expectation of profit defence is not included since it is irrelevant to the market abuse regime, where the mischief that is sought to be prevented is abuse of the market, not personal gain.[85]

As a result, while some analogies may be drawn with insider dealing defences, it needs to be remembered that the two regimes are separate, as are the defences/safe harbours, and must be considered as such.

8.6 False or misleading impressions

8.6.1 Introduction and objectives

The second of the three conditions which amounts to market abuse is concerned with behaviour which is likely to give a regular user of the market a false or misleading impression as to the supply of, or demand for, or as to the price or value of, investments of the kind in question (a "False Impression").[86]

Market users expect the price or value of investments and their trading volumes to reflect the proper operation of market forces. If there is improper conduct which leads to a False Impression market users will feel they can no longer rely on them and this in turn will undermine confidence in the integrity of the markets.[87]

---

[84] *See* Law Society Company Law Committee and City of London Law Society Regulatory Sub-Committee, Joint Memorandum To The Financial Services Authority on Consultation Paper 59, paragraph 6.2.

[85] Paragraph 6.55 of Consultation Paper 59, July 2000.

[86] Section 118(2)(b) FSMA.

[87] Paragraph 1.5.3E COMC.

8.6.2 *General factors to take into consideration*

The issue to be considered here is whether the behaviour in question would be likely to give rise to, or to give an impression of, a price or value or volume of trading which is materially false or misleading.

There must be a real likelihood (i.e. beyond a bare possibility) that the behaviour will create a False Impression, although the effect need not be "more likely than not".[88]

Factors to be taken into consideration are:

(a) the experience and knowledge of the market users in question;
(b) the structure of the market (including its reporting, notification and transparency arrangements);
(c) the legal and regulatory requirements of the market and accepted market practices;
(d) the identity and position of the person responsible for the behaviour in question (if known); and
(e) the extent and nature of the visibility or disclosure of the person's activity.[89]

COMC then sets out more particular descriptions of behaviour that will amount to market abuse under this condition. These relate to artificial transactions, disseminating information, disseminating information through an accepted channel and a course of conduct.

8.6.3 *Artificial transactions*

Behaviour will constitute market abuse where a person enters into a transaction in qualifying investments or relevant products where:

(a) the principal effect of the transaction will be likely to be, to inflate, maintain or depress the apparent supply of, demand for, or price or value of a qualifying investment or relevant product so that a false or misleading impression is likely to be given to the regular user; and
(b) the person in question knows, or could reasonably be expected to know, that the principal effect of the transaction would be such.

---

[88] Paragraph 1.5.4E(2) COMC.
[89] Paragraph 1.5.5E COMC.

This will be market abuse unless the regular user would regard:

(a)   the principal rationale for the transaction as a legitimate commercial rationale; and

(b)   the way in which the transaction is to be executed as proper.[90]

"Legitimate commercial rationale" is not defined. A transaction which creates a False Impression will not normally be considered to have a legitimate commercial rationale where the purpose was to induce others to trade in, or to position or to move the price of, a qualifying investment or relevant product. Neither will a transaction the purpose of which was to make a profit, or avoid a loss, automatically be considered to have a legitimate commercial rationale. If the transaction generally either opens a new position, so creating an exposure to market risk, or closes out a position, so removing market risk, that will tend to suggest the likelihood of a legitimate commercial rationale.[91]

Whether a transaction is executed in a proper way will depend on whether the regular user regards it as having been executed in a way which takes into account the need for the market as a whole to operate fairly and efficiently.[92]

COMC then lists factors to be taken into account when determining whether behaviour amounts to market abuse in terms of artificial transactions although their presence is not conclusive. These include, for example, whether the transaction coincides with a time around which the supply of, demand for, or price or value of the qualifying investment or relevant product is relevant to the calculation of for example, settlement prices (e.g. close of trading or end of quarter); whether those involved in the transaction are connected parties; and whether a person places a bid (or offer) which is higher (or lower) than the previous bid (or offer) only to remove it from the market before it is executed.[93]

A number of examples are also given, including fictitious transactions and arrangements for the sale or purchase of qualifying investments or relevant products (other than, amongst other things, on stock lending or borrowing terms) where there is no change in beneficial interest or market

---

[90] Paragraph 1.5.8E COMC.
[91] Paragraphs 1.5.9E and 1.5.12E COMC.
[92] Paragraph 1.5.10E COMC.
[93] Paragraph 1.5.11E COMC.

risk or if there is a transfer of beneficial ownership or market risk, it is only between persons acting in concert or colluding together.[94]

8.6.4 Disseminating information

This behaviour is concerned with disseminating information which is, or if it were true would be, relevant information where the person knows, or could reasonably be expected to know, that it is false or misleading and disseminates it in order to create such an impression. An example given is posting misleading statements on an internet bulletin board concerning a company's takeover where the person knows the information is misleading and intends to create such an impression.[95]

8.6.5 Disseminating information through an accepted channel

COMC provides that users of accepted channels of dissemination should be able to rely on the accuracy and integrity of their information. So, for example, a company, or its financial advisers or public relations advisers, need to take reasonable care to ensure that all announcements etc are not false or misleading.[96]

8.6.6 Course of conduct

Behaviour will amount to market abuse where a person engages in a course of conduct where the principal effect will be, or is likely to be, the giving of a False Impression to the regular user and the person could reasonably be expected to know that the principal effect of the conduct on the market will be such. Again, this is unless the regular user would regard:

(a) the principal rationale for the conduct as a legitimate commercial rationale; and
(b) the way in which the conduct is engaged in as proper.

The exact nature of conduct which may give a False or Misleading Impression will vary according to the characteristics of the market. Examples given are of the movement of physical commodity stocks, or of an empty cargo ship, which could create a False Impression in relation to a commodity or the deliverable into a commodity futures contract.[97]

---

94 Paragraph 1.5.14E COMC.
95 Paragraphs 1.5.15E and 1.5.17E COMC.
96 Paragraphs 1.5.18E and 1.5.20E COMC.
97 Paragraphs 1.5.21E and 1.5.22E COMC.

8.6.7 Safe harbours

There are a series of safe harbours for certain permitted transactions. These include stock or commodity lending or borrowing transactions so as to meet commercial demand.

There is also a safe harbour for disclosure expressly permitted by certain rules if done in the way specified. Examples given include disclosure pursuant to rule 9.10(j) of the Listing Rules (where the notification of a new issue is expressly permitted to be delayed where it is subject to an underwriting arrangement) and disclosure pursuant to Section 198 Companies Act 1985 (requiring disclosure of certain interests in shares).

There is also a safe harbour for effective Chinese Walls or similarly effective arrangements where there was nothing known, or which ought reasonably to have been known, to the disseminator of the information which should have led him to conclude it was false or misleading.[98]

8.7 Market distortion

8.7.1 Introduction and objectives

Policy Statement, April 2001 states that the distortion condition of the market abuse regime, the third of the three behaviour-related conditions which needs to be considered, "remains the most controversial of COMC".[99] Before looking at some of the reasons why, the basic condition will be considered.

A person must not engage in behaviour that gives rise to market distortion, that is, behaviour which interferes with the proper operation of market forces and with the interplay of proper demand and supply so having a distorting effect.[100]

COMC also notes, as is clearly apparent when comparing this condition with the previous condition relating to the creation of false or misleading impressions, that, in some circumstances, behaviour which falls within this market distortion condition may also fall within that prior condition.[101]

---

[98] Paragraphs 1.5.24C, 1.5.25C, 1.5.26G, 1.5.27C, 1.5.28C and 1.5.29E.
[99] Policy Statement, April 2001, paragraph 8.1.
[100] Paragraph 1.6.3E COMC.
[101] Paragraph 1.6.7E COMC.

As with the other two behaviour-related conditions of the market abuse regime, market abuse can occur by someone distorting the market in a relevant product as well as in a qualifying investment, because FSMA, as regards this condition, refers to "investments of the kind in question" and not simply to qualifying investments. However, that said if the distorting behaviour occurs in a relevant product, it will be necessary to show that this has an effect on the prescribed market, for example damaging confidence in that market, since that is the mischief which the FSMA is designed to address.[102]

8.7.2   Elements of the market distortion test

What is required here is that the regular user would, or would be likely to, regard the behaviour as such as would, or would be likely to, distort the market in the investments in question. "Likely" is to be interpreted as in the previous condition, as a real likelihood, although the effect need not be more likely than not.[103]

Behaviour will amount to market abuse if it interferes with the proper operation of market forces *with the purpose* (not necessarily the sole purpose, but an actuating purpose) of posting prices at a distorted level.[104]

One of the main concerns regarding this condition was its apparent potential to catch legitimate behaviour. COMC sets out two types of behaviour unlikely to amount to market abuse. It provides that it is unlikely that behaviour by market users when trading at times and in sizes most beneficial to them (whether for the long term, the short term or for risk management) and when seeking maximum profit from such dealings will, of itself, amount to distortion.[105] COMC also provides that it is unlikely that prices which are outside their normal range will necessarily be indicative of behaviour with the purpose of positioning prices at a distorted level and that high or low prices can be the result of the proper interplay of supply and demand.[106]

COMC then looks at two types of behaviour which will amount to market abuse under this condition, namely price positioning and abusive squeezes.

---

[102] Policy Statement, April 2001, paragraph 8.5.
[103] Paragraph 1.6.4E(2) COMC.
[104] Paragraph 1.6.4E(1) COMC.
[105] Paragraph 1.6.5E COMC.
[106] Paragraph 1.6.6E COMC.

8.7.3   Price positioning

Behaviour will constitute market abuse where a person enters into transactions with the purpose of positioning the price of a qualifying investment or relevant product at a distorted level.[107] Again, we see the need
for purpose here, as is also the case with abusive squeezes (*see* Section
8.7.4 below).

COMC states that the trading of significant volumes where there is a
legitimate purpose for the transaction (e.g. index tracking) and where the
transaction is executed in a proper way is not restricted by COMC. As to
what is the "proper way", whilst COMC mentions fairly concrete matters
such as the rules of prescribed markets which have requirements that
transactions be executed in the proper way, for example, rules as to
reporting and executing cross trades, and states that behaviour in accordance with these is unlikely to distort the market, it also mentions that
execution in a proper way is in "a way which takes into account the need
for the market as a whole to operate fairly and efficiently". This more
nebulous concept is less straightforward (and yet one more reason to
support the view that the regular user is an altruistic market user (*see*
Section 8.4.2 above)).[108]

Factors which will be taken into account when deciding if there has been
such price positioning include timing issues (e.g. whether the transaction
coincides with the time of calculation of reference or settlement prices or
valuations, such as at close of trading), whether the person has any direct
or indirect interest in the price or value of the investment in question,
volume issues (e.g. size of the transaction in relation to reasonable expectations of the market at the time) and several price related factors (e.g.
whether immediately after an increase or decrease, the price returned to
its previous level).[109]

Examples include a trader simultaneously buying and selling the same
investment (i.e. trading with himself) at a price outside its normal
trading range, where he does so while holding a position in an option
for which the price of the investment is relevant to the option's settlement value, where his purpose is the positioning of the price of the
investment at a distorted level, to make a profit or avoid a loss. Also, a
fund manager placing a large order to buy relatively illiquid shares to be

---

[107] Paragraph 1.6.9E COMC.
[108] Paragraph 1.6.10E COMC.
[109] Paragraph 1.6.11E COMC.

executed at, or just before, close, with the purpose of positioning those shares at a distorted level to improve quarterly performance figures.[110]

8.7.4 Abusive squeezes

Abusive squeezes occur where a person who has (a) a significant influence over the supply of, or demand for, or delivery mechanisms for, a qualifying investment or relevant product and (b) a position (directly or indirectly) in an investment under which quantities of the qualifying investment or relevant product are deliverable, engages in behaviour with the purpose of positioning at a distorted level the price at which others have to deliver, take delivery or defer delivery to satisfy their obligations.[111]

Not all squeezes, which can occur relatively frequently due to the proper interaction of supply and demand, are abusive and having a significant influence is not of itself abusive.[112]

Factors determining whether there has been an abusive squeeze include the extent of the willingness of a person to relax his control to help maintain an orderly market and the extent to which his activities risk causing settlement default, not just on a bilateral basis but on a multilateral basis.[113] These factors do not impose additional obligations on market users: for example, they do not impose an obligation to lend where one does not already exist, but behaviour is less likely to amount to an abusive squeeze if a person is willing to lend the investment in question.[114] Nonetheless, COMC states that the regular user would not expect market users to put themselves in positions where they have to rely on holders of long positions lending when they may not be inclined to and may be under no obligation to do so.[115]

8.7.5 Safe harbours

The only relevant safe harbour is behaviour which complies with London Metal Exchange rules governing the behaviour expected of long position holders.[116]

---

[110] Paragraph 1.6.12E (1) and (4) COMC.
[111] Paragraph 1.6.13E COMC.
[112] Paragraph 1.6.14E COMC.
[113] Paragraph 1.6.10E (1) and (2) COMC.
[114] Paragraph 1.6.16E COMC.
[115] Paragraph 1.6.17G COMC.
[116] Paragraph 1.6.19C COMC.

8.8 Safe harbours generally

8.8.1 Introduction[117]

Having looked at the three behaviour-related conditions for market abuse and having included reference, in each, to specific safe harbours, it will be useful to look at the issue of safe harbours generally in a little more detail.

The FSMA provides for two types of statutory exemption from the market abuse regime. First, it provides that behaviour does not amount to market abuse if it conforms with a rule which includes a provision to the effect that behaviour in accordance with such rule does not amount to market abuse.[118] Second, it provides that if a person behaves in a way described by COMC as behaviour which does not amount to market abuse, then it is indeed not market abuse.[119] COMC, where it refers to both of these types of statutory exception, refers to them as safe harbours.[120]

8.8.2 Safe harbours for rules

The first of the FSMA's safe harbours are those of the FSA's rules which specifically state that behaviour in accordance with them does not amount to market abuse.

The aim behind this provision of the FSMA is to deal with cases where there may be doubt or confusion as to whether the behaviour required, or expressly permitted, by the rule in question might otherwise be considered to amount to market abuse. Broadly, it would be unfair if behaviour expressly required or permitted by a rule led to a risk of sanction under the market abuse regime. Also where there are rules as to timings, methods of dissemination and contents of announcements

---

[117] It is outside the scope of this Chapter to look in any great detail at the thinking of the FSA when coming to decide what should be granted safe harbour status and why. A lengthy explanation of the FSA's rationale concerning its safe harbour policy can be found in Consultation Paper 76, November 2000, pp 12–14, together with its thinking on interaction of the draft Code of Market Abuse with the Listing Rules, pp. 15–26, and its thinking on interaction with the City Code, pp. 27–33, both of which areas merited consideration on the issue of appropriate safe harbours.

[118] Section 118(8) FSMA.

[119] Section 122(1) FSMA.

[120] Paragraph 1.7.1E COMC.

and standards of care to be observed, there is a need for certainty as regards those matters and the granting of safe harbours in respect of them disposes of arguments that the disclosure in question should have been in another way, at a different time, with a different content etc.[121]

Rules to be given safe harbour status are the FSA's price stabilisation rules, rules relating to Chinese Walls and certain rules in the FSA's Listing Rules. The particular paragraphs of the Listing Rules that merit safe harbour status are to be found in Annex 1G to COMC and also in the appendix to chapter 1 of the Listing Rules. They include, by way of example, paragraph 8.3 (circulation of draft (pathfinder) listing particulars) and paragraphs 9.4 and 9.5 (permitted selective disclosures concerning matters in the course of negotiation), as well as several others.[122]

Note also, for the sake of completeness that the FSA has stated that the RIE rulebooks do not permit or require behaviour which amounts to market abuse. Accordingly, there are no safe harbours.

8.8.3 Safe harbours provided in COMC

The second of the two types of safe harbour is where COMC itself specifies that certain behaviour will not amount to market abuse. This has been covered above in 8.5.6, 8.6.7 and 8.7.5.

8.8.4 City Code matters

The FSMA, as a result of a compromise at the last minute during the passage of the legislation, also makes specific mention of the City Code. It provides, at Section 120, that with the Treasury's approval, COMC may include provision to the effect that behaviour conforming with the City Code either does not amount to market abuse (at all), or does not amount to market abuse in specified circumstances, or does not amount to market abuse if engaged in by a specified description of person. Section 120 also provides that, if COMC is to contain such a provision, the FSA must keep itself informed of the way in which the Panel interprets and administers the relevant provisions in the City Code.

As time passes and the particular episodes which occasioned the last minute insertion of this part of the market abuse statutory provisions

---

[121] *See* CP 76, November 2000, paragraphs 3.2–3.9 for more.
[122] Paragraph 1.7.3 COMC.

fade in people's minds, readers of the provisions may wonder why the City Code merits its own section within the FSMA. They may also ask what particularly special treatment, if any, is to result. The answer to this is, prima facie, there is none. As the FSA stated:

> "Although Section 120 of the Act specifically covers the application of safe harbours to the City Code (but not to SARs), the same overall policy approach has been adopted for the City Code and SARs as it has for FSA and RIE rules."[123]

That policy was largely to consider, and consult on, what provisions of the City Code and SARs merit safe harbour status and to accord it to them. Those provisions are to be found listed in Annex 2G to COMC. As with the rationale taken when deciding which FSA rules merited safe harbour treatment, the aim is to cover those provisions of the City Code that deal with possible areas of market abuse and also those disclosure type rules which need the certainty of a safe harbour. They are:

(a) safe harbours for behaviour conforming with any rules of the City Code or SARs relating to timing, dissemination, availability, content and standards of care applicable to disclosures, announcements,[124] communications or releases of information, which are specified in Annex 2G; and

(b) a safe harbour for behaviour conforming with Rule 4.2 of the City Code (where restrictions on dealings by the offeror and concert parties in the offeree may be lifted in accordance with the provisions in that rule),[125]

so that in each of these cases behaviour does not of itself amount to market abuse in terms of false or misleading impressions or market distortion (but not in relation to behaviour based on the misuse of information condition), so far as the behaviour is expressly required or permitted by the rule in question (and so long as it does not breach a General Principle).

Absent a safe harbour, as is consistent with the FSA's approach on similar matters, whilst it considers that the regular user would regard compliance with the City Code or SARs as relevant to his assessment of whether a person's behaviour had fallen below the relevant standards, it also

---

[123] *See* Consultation Paper 76, November 2000, paragraph 5.2.
[124] Paragraph 1.7.7C COMC.
[125] Paragraph 1.7.8C COMC.

states in COMC that compliance of itself will not necessarily lead the regular user to consider that the behaviour does not amount to market abuse. The example it gives is of a person building a stake in compliance with the SARs but based on relevant information.

However, whilst it is right to point out that, despite Section 120 FSMA, the same overall policy as to safe harbours has been applied by the FSA as regards the City Code as, say, to the Listing Rules, Section 120 does also contain the provision that requires the FSA to keep itself informed of the way in which the Panel interprets and administers the City Code. Whilst the FSA must itself decide whether the City Code provisions given safe harbour status have been complied with (to do otherwise would be an unlawful delegation of its powers), it must also comply with the above-mentioned provision to bear in mind the way the Panel would interpret the particular matter. The FSA, in the regular user section of COMC, introduces a number of references to the City Code and the Panel and, also, specifically states that it will consult the Panel and will attach considerable weight to the Panel's views in applying the City Code and the SARs. On the subject of these additional references the FSA has said:

> "[they] . . . highlight the significance of the City Code and the views of the Panel for the market abuse regime."[126]

How any interaction between the FSA and the Panel works out in practice remains to be seen. However, there are now in existence "Operating Guidelines between the FSA and the Panel on Market Misconduct",[127] the aim of which is to assist the FSA and the Panel when considering cases of possible market misconduct which are, or could be, of mutual interest. These guidelines cover, inter alia:

(a)   co-operation and information sharing;
(b)   what to do when issues arise during current bids; and
(c)   investigations conducted other than during a bid (including indicators for deciding which party should exercise its powers and how to proceed if there are concurrent investigations).

---

[126] Paragraph 1.2.8G COMC.
[127] Operating Guidelines Between the Financial Services Authority and the Panel on Takeovers and Mergers on Market Misconduct, available at www.fsa.gov.uk/pubs/other/market_conduct.

8.9   Requiring or encouraging market abuse

8.9.1   Introduction

As well as penalties for, or statements concerning, the commission of market abuse, the FSMA also allows the FSA to impose penalties on, or publish a statement concerning, a person who requires or encourages another to commit market abuse. Specifically, this is where the FSA is satisfied that a person "A" has, by taking or refraining from taking any action, required or encouraged another person "B" to engage in behaviour which, if engaged in by A, would amount to market abuse.[128]

The requiring or encouraging regime in Section 123(1)(b) is completely separate from the primary market abuse regime covered in Section 118. Accordingly, there is no prima facie regular user test and it is simply for the FSA, rather than the hypothetical regular user, to decide whether a person has required or encouraged under the terms of the section (albeit that the regular user test does come into play in working out whether, if the behaviour required or encouraged had been engaged in by A, it would have amounted to market abuse). Nonetheless, it is for the FSA to decide if, by action or inaction, A has required or encouraged B.[129]

There is no need for the FSA to prove that A has benefited from the behaviour, if any, of B.

Strictly speaking COMC addresses the primary market abuse types of behaviour pursuant to Section 118 and so any guidance that it contains concerning the requiring or encouraging misdemeanour is not legally part of it. (This is why the parts of COMC on requiring or encouraging are all marked with a "G" rather than an "E".)

So, what is required here is (a) that the behaviour would have amounted to market abuse if carried out by A and (b) action or inaction by A which requires or encourages B to engage in the behaviour in question.

8.9.2   What will constitute requiring or encouraging?

There are many ways that a person, by taking or refraining from taking any action, may require or encourage another.[130] Whether action or

---

[128] Section 123(1)(b) FSMA.
[129] Section 123(1)(b). *See* also part 11.8 COMC.
[130] Paragraph 1.8.3G COMC.

inaction will amount to requiring or encouraging will depend on circumstances such as acceptable market practices, the experience, level of skill and standard of knowledge of the person concerned and the control or influence the person has in relation to the person who engages in the behaviour in question.[131]

Examples of action or inaction that would be considered as requiring or encouraging include a director in possession of relevant and disclosable information (other than trading information) which is not generally available to market users instructing an employee to deal in qualifying investments or relevant products to which such information is relevant.[132]

Also, early or selective disclosure of information which a regular user would expect market users to have will generally constitute requiring or encouraging. This is the case unless there is a legitimate purpose for the early or selective disclosure, such as that the Listing Rules allow it. Additionally, any such disclosure should be accompanied by a statement that the information is given in confidence and the recipient should not base any behaviour in relation to qualifying investments or relevant products on it until it is made generally available.[133] Such statement may be included in the express or implied terms of any contract governing the relationship between the persons making and receiving the disclosure.

8.9.3   *What will not constitute requiring or encouraging?*

Disclosure for a legitimate purpose (and consequently what will not be regarded as requiring or encouraging) includes:

(a)   disclosure by a person to professional advisers and/or the professional advisers of any persons who may be involved in a transaction for the purpose of obtaining advice, and

(b)   disclosure by a person to another with whom he is negotiating a transaction. The gathering of irrevocable undertakings is also covered as is advice to a client (who is considering the acquisition or disposal of a stake in a company) to acquire or dispose of a stake in the target company, if done in a certain way and for certain purposes.[134]

---

[131]   Paragraph 1.8.4G COMC.
[132]   Paragraph 1.8.3G(1) COMC.
[133]   Paragraph 1.8.5G COMC.
[134]   Paragraphs 1.8.6G and 1.8.7G COMC.

To address some of the concerns that were raised about risks to authorised intermediaries, particularly that they might be considered to have required or encouraged simply by executing transactions on behalf of clients which amounted to market abuse, COMC now makes it clear that where the originator of the transaction appears to have engaged in market abuse and acted through an intermediary, that intermediary's behaviour will not amount to requiring or encouraging market abuse unless he knew, or ought reasonably to have known, that the originator was engaging in market abuse.[135]

8.10 Defences

8.10.1 Introduction

The FSA may not impose a penalty if there are reasonable grounds for it to be satisfied that the person in question either (a) believed, on reasonable grounds, that his behaviour did not amount to market abuse or the requiring or encouraging of others to commit market abuse or (b) took all reasonable precautions and exercised all due diligence to avoid behaving in a way that amounted to market abuse or the requiring or encouraging of others.[136] Strictly speaking these are not defences: they are simply instances when the FSA may not impose a penalty. However, for ease of reference, they will be referred to as defences in this Chapter.

COMC does not include a section regarding these defences. However, the FSMA requires the FSA to prepare and issue a statement of its policy concerning the imposition, and amount, of its market abuse penalties which must also include an indication of when the defences would be available.[137] The FSA's statement as to sanctions for market abuse, including its indication of when the defences will be available, is to be found in chapter 14 of its Enforcement Manual (to be found in its Handbook) entitled *Sanctions for market abuse*.

What follows will only concentrate on what chapter 14 says on the subject of the defences, although it also contains other useful information

---

[135] Paragraph 1.8.8G COMC.
[136] Section 123(2) FSMA.
[137] Section 124(1) and (3) FSMA.

as to sanctions for market abuse and the FSA's general policy as regards its enforcement action in relation to market abuse.[138]

8.10.2 *Reasonable belief defence*

Factors relevant to the defence concerning whether the person in question reasonably believed that his or her behaviour did not amount to market abuse or the requiring or encouraging of others to commit market abuse are:

(a) the extent to which the person took reasonable precautions to avoid engaging in market abuse (or requiring or encouraging);
(b) the extent to which the behaviour in question was or was not similar to behaviour described in COMC as amounting to market abuse (or requiring or encouraging);
(c) if the FSA had issued guidance on the behaviour in question, to what extent the person sought to follow it;
(d) to what extent the behaviour complied with the rules of any relevant prescribed market or any other relevant market or any other regulatory requirement or code of conduct or best practice;
(e) the level of knowledge, skill and experience to be expected of the person; and
(f) to what extent the person can show that the behaviour engaged in was engaged in for a legitimate purpose and in a proper way.[139]

8.10.3 *Due diligence defence*

Factors relevant to the second defence, as to whether the person took all reasonable precautions and exercised all due diligence to avoid engaging in market abuse (or requiring or encouraging), are:

(a) to what extent the person followed internal consultation procedures; for example, did the person consult his or her internal legal or compliance department or line management;
(b) to what extent the person sought appropriate expert legal or other expert professional advice and followed it;

---

[138] For example, it contains sections on: factors relevant to determining whether to take action in market abuse cases; FSA's choice of powers: financial penalties/public statements; determining the level of a financial penalty in a market abuse case; the FSA's endorsement of the Takeover Code and SARs.

[139] At paragraph 14.5.1G(1) of Chapter 14.

(c) to what extent the person sought advice from market authorities or, where relevant, the Panel, and followed it;

(d) if the FSA had issued guidance on the behaviour, to what extent the person sought to follow it; and

(e) the extent to which the behaviour complied with the rules of any prescribed market, or any other relevant market or other regulatory requirements or codes of conduct or best practice.[140]

Whilst the FSA must prove market abuse, it is for the person in question to persuade the FSA that a defence is met.

8.11 Proceedings for market abuse

8.11.1 *Power to impose penalties or publish a statement*

The FSA decides whether to take action against any person for market abuse. If it does so, it must follow procedures laid down in the FSMA which include the issuing of warning notices, decision notices and final notices before imposing penalties or issuing a statement.[141] This Chapter will not consider these procedures further.

8.11.2 *Right of a person to appeal to the Tribunal*

If the FSA decides to take action against a person for market abuse, that person may refer it to the Financial Services and Markets Tribunal (the "Tribunal").[142]

A reference to the Tribunal must be made within 28 days from the date on which the decision notice is given (or such other period as may be specified in rules made under Section 132). The Tribunal may consider evidence, whether or not it was available to the FSA at the relevant time, and can decide what action the FSA should take and will remit the matter back to the FSA with such directions as it considers necessary to give effect to its decision. During the period within which a matter may be referred to the Tribunal and, if it is so referred, until any reference, or any appeal against the Tribunal's determination, has been completed, the FSA must not take the action specified in its decision notice. An order of

---

[140] At paragraph 14.5.1G(2) of Chapter 14.

[141] *See* Sections 126, 127, and Part XXVI of FSMA.

[142] Section 127(4) FSMA.

the Tribunal is like a county court order and the FSA must act in accordance with it.[143]

A party to a reference to the Tribunal may, with permission, appeal to the Court of Appeal (or in Scotland, the Court of Session) on a point of law. Permission may be given either by the Tribunal itself or those two courts. If either of those courts considers the decision of the Tribunal to have been wrong in law, it may remit the matter back to it for rehearing and determination or itself make a determination. An appeal from these two courts is only allowed with their permission or the leave of the House of Lords.[144]

8.11.3 Powers of the FSA to apply to the courts for injunctions and restitution orders

The FSA may apply to the courts for an injunction and in certain circumstances the court may impose an order restraining the market abuse,[145] or may make an order for remedial action to be taken,[146] or may make an order restraining the person concerned from disposing of his assets.[147]

The FSA may apply to the courts for a restitution order and the court may, where profits have accrued as a result of market abuse or where loss or other adverse effect has been suffered by other persons as a result, make a restitution order. Amounts paid to the FSA are to be paid to any qualifying persons as the court directs. The court is empowered to ask to be supplied with accounts and to have them verified. No such restitution order may, however, be made if the court is satisfied that the person concerned believed, on reasonable grounds, that his behaviour did not constitute market abuse or requiring or encouraging another to commit market abuse or where such person took all reasonable precautions and exercised all due diligence to avoid behaving in that way.[148]

The FSA may, when the court is considering whether to grant an injunction or restitution order, also apply to it to consider whether the circumstances are such that a penalty should be imposed and the court may

---

[143] Section 133 FSMA.
[144] Section 137 FSMA.
[145] Section 381(1) FSMA.
[146] Section 381(2) FSMA.
[147] Section 381(4) FSMA.
[148] Section 383 FSMA.

make an order that the person in question pay a penalty of such amount as it considers appropriate.

8.12 Relationship with criminal law and regulatory proceedings

8.12.1 What COMC says

COMC does not make lawful, or permit, any activity that contravenes the criminal law or applicable legal or regulatory requirements. In particular it does not modify the obligations of persons deriving from the rules of prescribed markets or other relevant rules or codes of conduct or good practice. Accordingly, it is still necessary to ensure that behaviour, even if it does not amount to market abuse, does not breach, for example, the insider dealing provisions of the CJA 1993 or Section 397 FSMA as to misleading statements and practices. Equally, that it does not breach applicable rules, for example, Principle 5 of the Principles for Businesses – the requirement for firms to observe proper standards of market conduct and, for example, The Code of Practice for Approved Persons, which, amongst other requirements, requires approved persons to observe proper standards of market conduct in carrying out their controlled function.[149]

8.12.2 Generally on enforcing the new regime vis-à-vis criminal offences

The FSA is empowered under the FSMA both to bring criminal prosecutions for the criminal offences of insider dealing, misleading statements and misleading practices, as well as to bring civil proceedings for market abuse.

In deciding whether to commence criminal proceedings for insider dealing or misleading statements and practices, the FSA will apply the basic principles in the Code for Crown Prosecutors. This will mean it will look at two tests:

(a)   whether there is sufficient evidence to provide a realistic prospect of conviction against each defendant on each criminal charge (the evidential test); and

---

[149] Paragraphs 1.9.1G, 1.9.2G and 1.9.3G COMC.

(b)   whether, having regard to the seriousness of the offence and all the circumstances, criminal prosecution is in the public interest (the "public interest test").[150]

Given that within the overall purpose of protecting confidence in, and the integrity of, UK markets, the new market abuse regime is specifically intended to plug a perceived regulatory gap so that more behaviour that amounts to market abuse can be caught and effectively dealt with, it is probable that, in applying the evidential test, if any great doubt of obtaining a criminal conviction exists, the FSA would instead choose to proceed under the market abuse regime.

Indeed, the above is arguably more likely to be the case given that the FSA has stated that its policy is that it will not seek to impose penalties for market abuse where a person is being prosecuted for, or has finally been convicted or acquitted of, a criminal offence arising from substantially the same allegation. Similarly, it is the FSA's policy not to commence a criminal prosecution for market misconduct where it is seeking to bring, market abuse proceedings arising from substantially the same allegations. (Note however, that the FSA may still bring other actions, such as seeking injunctions and restitution orders.)[151]

8.13   Misleading statements and practices

Section 397 FSMA is the replacement for Section 47 FS Act, although set out slightly differently. As before, there are two criminal offences, one relating to the making of statements or concealing of facts and the second relating to the engaging in of an action or course of conduct creating a false or misleading impression.

8.13.1   *The misleading statements offence*

The first offence (the misleading statements offence) applies to a person who:

(a)   makes a statement, promise or forecast which he knows to be misleading, false or deceptive in any material particular; or
(b)   dishonestly conceals any material facts whether in connection with a statement, promise or forecast made by him or otherwise; or

---

[150] Paragraph 15.7.1 of Chapter 15.
[151] Paragraphs 15.7.4G and 15.7.5G of Chapter 15.

(c)   recklessly makes (dishonestly or otherwise) a statement, promise or forecast which is misleading, false or deceptive in a material particular[152] and

he does so for the purpose of inducing, or is reckless as to whether it may induce, another to

(a)   enter or offer to enter into, or to refrain from entering or offering to enter into, a relevant agreement; or

(b)   (b) to exercise, or refrain from exercising, any rights conferred by a relevant investment.[153]

Whilst this offence in the FSMA is different from Section 47(1) FS Act in that it has now been split between two sub-sections instead of just the one, it is predominantly the same. The principal differences are (i) the addition of the words "in a material particular" and (ii) in relation to the concealing of material facts, the addition of the words "whether in connection with a statement, promise or forecast made by him or otherwise".

8.13.2   *The misleading practices offence*

The second offence (the misleading practices offence) applies where a person does any act or engages in any course of conduct which creates a misleading impression as to the market in, or price or value of, any relevant investments for the purpose of creating that impression and thereby induces another person to acquire, dispose of, subscribe for or underwrite those investments or refrain from doing so or to exercise, or refrain from exercising, any rights conferred by those investments.

This offence is exactly as it was set out in the FS Act, other than the reference to relevant[154] investments, instead of investments (*see* below).

8.13.3   *Relevant agreements and relevant investments*

Relevant agreement[155] means an agreement relating to an activity of a specified kind, or which falls within a specified class and which relates to a relevant investment. A relevant investment means an investment of

---

[152] Section 397(1) FSMA.
[153] Section 397(2) FSMA.
[154] Section 397(3) FSMA.
[155] Section 397(a) FSMA.

a specified kind or which falls within a specified class and includes any asset, right or interest.[156] The relevant schedule of FSMA[157] and order[158] that describe these activities and investments mention, amongst other things, in respect of activities – dealing in investments, arranging deals in investments, investment advice and using computer-based systems for giving investment instructions; and in respect of investments – securities, instruments giving entitlements to investments, options, futures and contracts for differences and rights in investments.

8.13.4 Defences

The defences for these two offences have been altered somewhat, although only in relation to limited aspects. This is first to provide that in relation to the first limb of the misleading statements offence, namely the making of a statement, promise or forecast, it is a defence to show that the statement, promise or forecast was made in conformity with either price stabilising rules or control of information rules.[159]

In relation to the misleading practices offence, the defences are that:

(a)   he reasonably believed that his act or conduct would not create an impression that was false or misleading as to the matters in question; or
(b)   he acted or engaged in the conduct (i) for the purpose of stabilising the price of investment and (ii) in conformity with price stabilising rules; or
(c)   he acted or engaged in the conduct in conformity with control of information rules.[160]

Control of information rules are rules which the FSA may make concerning the disclosure and use of information held by an authorised person. Such rules may, for example, (i) specify circumstances in which A may withhold information which he would otherwise have to disclose to B, or (ii) require A not to use for the benefit of B information A holds which A would otherwise have to use in that way.[161]

---

[156] Sections 397(10) and (13) FSMA.
[157] Schedule 2 less a few paragraphs.
[158] The Financial Services and Markets 2000 (Misleading Statements and Practices) Order 2001, SI 2001 No. 3645.
[159] Section 397(4) FSMA.
[160] Section 397(5) FSMA.
[161] *See* Section 147 FSMA for more.

8.13.5 Jurisdictional limitations

The misleading practices offence is not committed unless the act is done, or course of conduct is engaged in, in the UK or if the false or misleading impression is created in the UK.[162]

The misleading statements offence is not committed unless:

(a)   the statement, promise or forecast is made in or from, or the facts are concealed in or from, the UK or arrangements are made in or from the UK for the statement, promise or forecast to be made or the facts to be concealed; or

(b)   the person on whom the inducement is intended to or may have effect, is in the UK; or

(c)   the agreement is or would be entered into or the rights are or would be exercised in the UK.[163]

The words that have been added by the FSMA that were not in Section 47 FS Act are those (a) that relate to arrangements being made in or from the UK for the statement, promise or forecast to be made or the facts to be concealed.

8.13.6 Penalties

A person guilty of an offence under Section 397 is liable, on summary conviction, to imprisonment for up to six months or a fine of up to the statutory maximum and, on indictment, to imprisonment for up to seven years or a fine or both.[164]

8.14   Powers of the FSA to institute proceedings

The FSA has been given non-exclusive power to institute proceedings for criminal offences under the FSMA (such as in relation to the misleading statements and practices offences mentioned above) and, also, under the CJA 1993 as to insider dealing and, also, in relation to money laundering.[165] These powers, together with its power to impose penalties (or publish statements) for market abuse, represent an impressive range of powers which have been placed at the disposal of the UK's new super regulator.

---

[162] Section 397(7) FSMA.
[163] Section 397(6) FSMA.
[164] Section 397(8) FSMA.
[165] Section 402 FSMA.

Chapter 9

Stabilisation

Tim Gee
Partner
Baker & McKenzie

9.1 Introduction

Stabilisation is the term used to describe a market practice which is commonly employed in offers of equity securities and debt securities whereby the stabilising manager of the offer supports the price of the relevant securities for a limited period after the offer, primarily by means of purchases in the secondary market.

The traditional justification for permitting stabilisation is that it prevents artificial downward distortions in the price of securities with a view to keeping price volatility to a minimum and so ensuring an orderly market in the securities. It is believed that this encourages new issues and the raising of capital, thereby benefiting both potential issuers and the market generally. Issuers (particularly small and medium-sized companies) will be more likely to access the capital markets if they know that there is likely to be some initial support for the price of their securities. Stabilisation may also contribute to a lower cost of funding for the issuer. Investors may feel more confident about investing in an issue if there is an expectation that, at least for a limited period of time, the price of the issue is being actively supported.

On the other hand, stabilisation is clearly potentially manipulative in that it may support the price of a security above that which would otherwise prevail if the market were left to find its own level thereby placing some investors and market participants at a potential disadvantage. As a result, stabilisation must comply with a specific and detailed set of rules if it is to qualify for a "safe harbour" against the criminal offences of price (or market) manipulation and insider dealing and civil liability under the new market abuse regime. The price stabilising rules (referred to in this Chapter as the "Rules") have been made by the Financial Services Authority (the "FSA") pursuant to the power conferred upon it by Section 144 Financial Services and Markets Act 2000 (the "FSMA") and became effective on 1 December 2001. The Rules are contained in Chapter 2 of the Market Conduct Sourcebook in Book 2 of the FSA's Handbook of rules and guidance. They supersede the price stabilising rules which formed Part 10 of The Financial Services (Conduct of Business) Rules 1990 made by the FSA pursuant to Section 48 Financial Services Act 1986.

9.2   How stabilisation works

Stabilisation involves supporting the price of securities issued or sold in primary offers (such as initial public offers) and certain secondary offers. The stabilising manager undertakes this action by purchasing or agreeing to purchase the securities or certain related securities (including convertible and exchangeable securities, depository receipts and derivative securities) in the secondary market with a view to supporting the market price during the permitted stabilising period and otherwise in compliance with the Rules. Action to suppress the price of securities (or "downward stabilisation") is not permitted by the Rules. The stabilising manager will usually be the lead manager of the offer or another manager appointed by the lead manager, although the Rules now provide that the stabilising manager need not be one of the managers of the offer.

As an ancillary action to stabilisation, it is common practice for the stabilising manager to "over-allot" the offer (i.e. allot more securities than are actually being issued by the issuer or sold by a selling shareholder) so as to facilitate the subsequent purchase of securities by stabilising action. This leaves the stabilising manager with a net "short" position in the securities, having pre-sold more than 100 per cent of the offer. When the offer begins to trade in the after-market:

(a)   If the price falls below the offer price, stabilising purchases are made in the market to close out the short position. This will result in the stabilising manager realising a profit (being the difference between the offer price and the purchase price).

(b)   If, conversely, the price has risen above the offer price, closing out the short position by market purchases would involve the stabilising manager in losses. This risk is commonly eliminated through the grant to the lead manager on behalf of the managers of an over-allotment option (sometimes referred to as a "Green Shoe option") which enables it to purchase from the issuer or offeror at the offer price the additional securities required to close out the short position. It is also possible (although not usual) for the lead manager to be granted an over-allotment option the exercise of which is not linked to the closing out of a short position arising from over-allotment.

In an equity offer the stabilising manager may have the benefit of a stock loan from one or more existing shareholders of the issuer. The stock loan allows the stabilising manager to close out the short position created by the over-allotment on the closing date of the offer, thereby avoiding deferred settlement of the over-allotted securities. The stock loan itself creates a new short position for the stabilising manager which will be closed out during, or at the end of, the stabilising period by the redelivery to the stock lenders of securities purchased pursuant to either stabilising action or the over-allotment option.

Any profits or losses arising from stabilisation will be for the account of the stabilising manager (or the syndicate of managers) and not the issuer or offeror. There will typically be provisions in the agreement among managers to allocate the benefit and risk among the managers in pre-agreed proportions.

9.3 How stabilisation is documented

The terms on which stabilisation is undertaken have historically been contained in the principal transaction documents relating to the offering.

9.3.1 *The offering document*

Where stabilisation is undertaken, offering documents (prospectuses or listing particulars) have typically included disclosure on or near the cover page to the effect that:

(a) in connection with the relevant offering the lead manager (or the manager which has been appointed as stabilising manager by the lead manager) may over-allot or effect transactions which stabilise or maintain the market prices of the securities being offered at levels above those which might otherwise prevail in the open market;

(b) such transactions may be effected on the London Stock Exchange or other relevant stock exchange or otherwise; and

(c) such stabilising, if commenced, may be discontinued at any time.

Certain disclosure requirements with respect to prospectuses and listing particulars arise as a result of the provisions of the Rules (discussed in Section 9.5.3 below) and the Listing Rules of the UK Listing Authority (the "UKLA"). The Listing Rules require issuers seeking a listing for their securities to make certain disclosures in their prospectuses and listing particulars with respect to stabilisation and the over-allotment option. Listing Rules 6.B.5(b) (shares) and 6.I.5(b) (debt securities) provide that where an issuer or a selling security holder has granted an over-allotment option or it is otherwise proposed that price stabilising activities may be entered into in connection with an offering then the prospectus or listing particulars must contain:

(a)   a statement that price stabilising activities may be entered into;
(b)   a statement that any securities issued or sold under an over-allotment option are to be issued or sold on the same terms and conditions as the securities that are subject to the main offering; and
(c)   the number of securities subject to the over-allotment option, the option period, the option price, any other terms of the option and the purpose for which the option has been granted; for example, for the purpose of satisfying short positions entered into by a stabilising manager in connection with the over-allocation.

Even before the introduction of these Listing Rules it was common for issuers in securities offerings to provide similar disclosure in their offering documents. In particular, it is typical in the section of an equity offering document describing the plan of distribution or underwriting of the securities to disclose:

(a)   that the managers may over-allot the offering to create a short position which may be satisfied by making stabilising purchases in the market and/or by exercising any over-allotment option granted to the managers by an issuer or security holder;
(b)   the terms of any over-allotment option;
(c)   that the stabilising activities are to be carried out by a single entity or a single entity per jurisdiction;
(d)   that stabilisation may only be carried out for a limited period of time; namely, during the 30 day period following the closing date for the offering as permitted by the Rules; and
(e)   that the stabilising manager is not obliged to engage in stabilisation activities and may discontinue any of those activities at any time.

The offering document may also disclose the nature of the proposed stabilisation activities as they operate between members of the syndicate and between syndicates.

9.3.2 *The underwriting agreement*

The underwriting agreement, which governs the underwriting and related arrangements between the managers and the issuer and any selling security holder, will likely contain an acknowledgement that the stabilising manager appointed by the lead manager will have the power to carry out stabilisation in accordance with applicable law. Where an over-allotment option has been granted by the issuer and/or any selling security holder to the managers the underwriting agreement will also provide:

(a)   to whom the over-allotment option is granted;

(b)   by whom the over-allotment option is granted;

(c)   the maximum number of securities which may be sold pursuant to the over-allotment option. This is usually a number constituting no more than a maximum of 15 per cent of the number of the securities in the main offering. Where the securities are shares in a UK incorporated public company, the number of securities is sometimes expressed in terms of a formula for the reasons set out in Section 9.4.4;

(d)   whether the over-allotment option may be exercised in whole or in part;

(e)   whether the over-allotment option may be exercised on one occasion or on more than one occasion; and

(f)   the purpose for which the over-allotment option has been granted. The over-allotment option is usually expressed as being granted solely to cover over- allotments.

9.3.3 *Underwriting syndicate documentation*

The relationship between the managers in the underwriting syndicate will usually be governed by the invitation telex, the allotment telex, any agreement among managers and/or intersyndicate agreement.

The invitation telex invites prospective managers to join the lead manager in underwriting the proposed offering and sets out the principal terms of such offering. These will include a reference to the fact that stabilisation activities may be carried out in accordance with the Rules.

Similar language referring to the conduct of stabilisation may also be included in the allotment telex sent to members of the underwriting syndicate confirming the allotment of securities.

The agreement among managers will likely contain the most detailed provisions relating to the conduct of stabilisation. A typical agreement among managers would include provisions:

(a)　identifying the stabilising manager in each jurisdiction;

(b)　authorising the lead manager to over-allot and the stabilising manager to purchase and sell for long or short account and to liquidate any long position or cover any short position, in each case at such prices as it may determine;

(c)　specifying that all such purchases and sales (even if made before the execution of the underwriting agreement) including any related expenses (such as foreign exchange expenses) shall be for the account of each manager pro-rata to their underwriting commitment;

(d)　placing a limit on each manager's net commitment for long or short account resulting from stabilising purchases or sales (including over-allotments); and

(e)　for issues specific to a transaction, such as the relationship between the stabilisation activities being carried out in different jurisdictions.

An intersyndicate agreement will likely deal with similar matters, but will focus on stabilisation as it affects the relationship between underwriting syndicates.

9.3.4　*International Primary Market Association documentation and recommendations*

The International Primary Market Association ("IPMA"), the trade association for banks and investment banks in their capacity as underwriters and managers of international issues, provides Standard Form Agreements Among Managers for both fixed-price non-equity (Version 1) and equity related (Version 3) issues which include provisions relating to stabilisation. These Agreements may be adopted by including (1) a reference to the relevant IPMA version of the standard form agreement in the invitation telex, and (2) a statement that the execution of the subscription agreement will constitute acceptance of the relevant IPMA Agreement Among Managers.

IPMA also makes recommendations to IPMA members relating to the conduct of stabilisation and the sharing among the underwriting syndicate of profits and losses arising from stabilising activities.

9.4 The principal legal risks associated with stabilisation

9.4.1 *Misleading statements and practices (Section 397 FSMA)*

A person who knowingly or recklessly makes a statement, promise or forecast which is misleading, false or deceptive or who dishonestly conceals material facts is guilty of a criminal offence if such action is taken with the intention of inducing (or recklessly as to whether it will induce) others to deal or refrain from dealing in relevant investments. It is also a criminal offence for a person to do any act or engage in any course of conduct which creates a false or misleading impression as to the market in or the price or value of investments where that is done for the purpose of creating that impression and of thereby inducing another person to acquire or dispose of those investments or to refrain from doing so, unless he can show that he reasonably believed that his act or conduct would not create such an impression. Since the purpose and effect of stabilisation is to support the price of relevant securities at a higher level than might otherwise prevail, it could fall within the scope of these prohibitions.

9.4.2 *Insider dealing (Part V Criminal Justice Act 1993)*

It is a criminal offence for an individual who has "inside information", and has that information "as an insider", to deal in securities on a regulated market or through a professional intermediary. For an offence to be committed, the individual must know that the information is inside information and he must have knowingly acquired it from an inside source. There are also offences of "encouraging dealing" and "disclosure" by individuals who have inside information. For these purposes, inside information is, broadly speaking, specific or precise unpublished information relating to a particular issuer or particular securities which, if made public, would be likely to have a significant effect on the price of any securities. Since the persons carrying out stabilisation are likely to be in possession of inside information there is a risk that an offence could be committed.

9.4.3   Market abuse (Part VIII FSMA)

Essentially, market abuse is behaviour:

(a)   which occurs in relation to "qualifying investments" (e.g. shares or other securities) traded on a prescribed market (e.g. the London Stock Exchange);

(b)   which satisfies one of three conditions (involving either (i) the misuse of relevant information not generally available to other market users or (ii) the giving of false or misleading impressions or (iii) market distortion); and

(c)   which is likely to be regarded by a "regular user" of that market as a failure on the part of the person concerned to observe the standard of behaviour reasonably to be expected of a person in his position in relation to the market.

If it is satisfied that a person has either engaged in market abuse or required or encouraged another to do so, the FSA may impose on that person a penalty or publish a statement that he has engaged in market abuse. The FSA also has the power under the FSMA to apply to the courts for injunctions and restitution orders (and may itself impose a restitution order) against persons engaging in market abuse.

Stabilisation of the price of securities at a level higher than that which might otherwise prevail could constitute market abuse.

9.4.4   Disclosure of interests in shares (Part VI Companies Act 1985)

One further potential risk applies in connection with the rules regarding notification of interests in shares under Part VI Companies Act 1985. The taking of an over-allotment option and the making of stabilising purchases and sales potentially involve the acquisition and disposal of interests in shares which are disclosable to the market. Were such disclosures to be made, of course, they might undermine the whole purpose of the stabilising action. Accordingly, there has been a practice in certain circumstances of avoiding structuring the over-allotment option in a way to avoid the disclosure obligation arising. This has been achieved by expressing the number of shares which are to be the subject of the over-allotment option by reference to a formula which is designed to ensure that the overall disclosable interest in shares that the stabilising manager has remains at a constant level, so that individual stabilising purchases and sales do not need to be disclosed.

Although the Rules do not cover the point specifically, it is arguable that the use of the formula mechanism might constitute market abuse. However, the market's expectation is that the FSA will not seek to impugn the use of formula mechanisms under the market abuse regime.

9.4.5 Safe harbour

Stabilisation will, however, qualify for a "safe harbour" against both the criminal offences of price (or market) manipulation and insider dealing and civil liability for market abuse if it is conducted in conformity with the Rules. However, in the context of an offer of shares by a UK incorporated public company, there is no "safe harbour" from the disclosure obligations under Part VI Companies Act 1985.

9.5 The Price Stabilising Rules

The key features of the Rules are summarised below:

9.5.1 *Persons and transactions to which the Rules apply*

In principle, the Rules are available to any person (whether or not an authorised person under the FSMA) who wishes to avail himself of the relevant "safe harbour". However, the main beneficiaries are likely to be lead managers (and their appointed agents) when they are contemplating or carrying out an "offer for cash" of securities. "Offer for cash" is defined as an offer of certain types of securities (principally shares, bonds, Government securities, warrants and depository receipts) where:

(a)   the offer is made at a specified price;
(b)   the securities have been admitted to trading (or are the subject of an application for admission to trading) on an exchange specified in the Rules (e.g. a recognised investment exchange or recognised overseas investment exchange) or are, or may be, traded under the rules of the International Securities Markets Association;
(c)   the total cost of the securities subject to the offer at the offer price is not less than £15 million (or the foreign currency equivalent); and
(d)   the offer is public in character and is to be, is, or has been the subject of a public announcement.

Securities for which an offer for cash is made are referred to in the Rules as "relevant securities".

225

Included within the definition of "offer for cash" are both initial public offers ("IPOs") and public offers of additional securities to rank alongside securities already in issue (secondary offers). The relevant guidance note states that an offer is likely to be regarded as public in character where it is made in a prospectus: other offers which may be regarded as public are offers to a section of the public, placements that are not essentially private and distributions. However, the use of the word "offer" and the fact that there has to be a public announcement are considered to indicate that a sale (e.g. by means of a block trade) of securities already in issue is not within the definition.

The Rules, so far as they provide a defence to any person, have the same territorial application as the provision alleged to have been contravened.

A contravention of the rules in Chapter 2 of the Market Conduct Source-book does not give rise to a right of action for damages by a private person under Section 150 FSMA.

9.5.2 *Nature and extent of permitted stabilising action*

During the stabilising period the stabilising manager may:

(a) purchase or agree to purchase any of the relevant securities (or certain "associated securities", which include securities exchangeable for or convertible into relevant securities, depository receipts and derivative securities) with a view to supporting (but not suppressing) the market price of the relevant securities;

(b) take what is referred to in the Rules as "ancillary permitted stabilising action", including (among other things):

    (i) making allotments of a greater number of relevant securities than will be offered or selling or agreeing to sell relevant securities (or associated securities) so as to establish a short position in them (or achieving an equivalent result through the use of derivatives);

    (ii) buying or subscribing for (including pursuant to the exercise of an over-allotment option) relevant securities (or associated securities) in order to close out or liquidate any short position established as mentioned above (without regard, in such a case, to the general limits on pricing referred to in Section 9.5.4 below).

The stabilising period is the period beginning with the date on which the earliest public announcement of the offer which states the offer price is made and ending on the 30th day after the closing date (or, if earlier, the 60th day after the date of allotment) except that, in the case of bonds and Government securities, the period begins with the date on which the earliest public announcement of the offer is made (whether or not that announcement states the offer price).

9.5.3 *Restrictions on stabilising action (including disclosure requirements)*

Before stabilising action is taken, the Rules require the stabilising manager to take all reasonable steps to satisfy himself that:

(a) from the beginning of the introductory period adequate disclosure of the possibility of stabilising action is made;

(b) any requirement of the principal investment exchange on which the relevant securities (or associated securities) are or will be traded to inform it of possible stabilising action has been complied with;

(c) the stabilising manager has (if the requirement to do so is applicable to it) established the register required for recording stabilising action and other matters required to be recorded (*see* further Section 9.5.6 below); and

(d) where the offer relates to an issue of relevant securities, the issuer has been informed of the existence of the FSA's informational guidance (which is intended to help issuers identify the information that they might seek when appointing underwriters to manage their offers and the text of which is reproduced as an Annex to the Rules), either in relation to the offer in question or to a previous one.

What constitutes "adequate disclosure" for these purposes is determined by the nature of the communication issued by the issuer or the stabilising manager. For certain categories of communication (screen-based statements, public announcements and invitation telexes (or the equivalent)) it is sufficient to give some indication of the fact that the offer may be stabilised (e.g. by use of the term "Stabilisation/FSA"). In the case of the preliminary and final offering documents, it is necessary to include wording substantially similar to the following:

> "In connection with this [issue] [offer], [name of stabilising manager] [or any person acting for him] may over-allot or effect transactions with a view to supporting the market price of [description of relevant securities and any associated securities] at a level higher than that which might otherwise prevail for a limited period after the issue date. However, there may be no obligation on [name of

stabilising manager] [or any agent of his] to do this. Such stabilising, if commenced, may be discontinued at any time, and must be brought to an end after a limited period."

Where the offering document is aimed at private customers, the stabilising manager should consider drawing attention to the availability of an FSA consumer factsheet (available on the FSA's website) which explains to potential investors the significance of possible stabilisation. It is expected that managers will draw attention in the document to the factsheet.

Communications which are not issued to, or directed at, persons in the UK may omit, or include an adapted version of, the language required by the Rules.

For the purpose of these disclosure requirements, the "introductory period" runs from the time of the first public announcement from which it could reasonably be deduced that the offer was intended to take place to the start of the stabilising period. However, the disclosure requirements in respect of screen-based statements and public announcements apply from the start of the introductory period or, if later, the date that is 45 days before the day proposed for the issue of the relevant securities until the start of the stabilising period.

The rules of the London Stock Exchange (the "Exchange") require a member firm that is to act as a stabilising manager to inform the Exchange and to request that it publish a statement that stabilising transactions may be made by the member firm during the stabilising period. The member firm is also required to inform the Exchange on the day before the start of the stabilising period of the security to be stabilised, the stabilising manager and contact, the stabilising period, the time when the issue price will be determined (if applicable) and the actual issue price when it is finally determined, and any associated security being stabilised.

The stabilising manager is also prohibited from taking stabilising action in a number of other situations specified in the Rules:

(a) where, at the time when the offer price of the relevant securities was determined, the market price of those securities (or of any associated securities) was falsely higher than the price which would otherwise have prevailed (or, in the case of associated securities, the true market price) and the stabilising manager knew or ought reasonably to have known that this was attributable to an act or course of conduct in breach of Section 397(2) or (3) FSMA;

(b)   where the terms of conversion, subscription or purchase of certain convertible bonds or warrants being offered have not yet been publicly announced; and

(c)   where the stabilising manager has an option or other right to purchase relevant securities from the issuer, such as an over-allotment option, unless the existence and principal terms of the option or right have already been disclosed in the relevant offering document or in a public announcement.

9.5.4   *Pricing limits*

The Rules place an upper limit on the price at which securities may be stabilised. The Rules provide that no bid may be made by a stabilising manager at a price higher than any price indicated in the table included in the Rules and reproduced below:

	Column A	Column B	Column C
	Relevant securities (including *associated securities* which are in all respects uniform with them).	*Associated securities* (other than *associated call options*) excluding those in column A.	*Associated call options.*
Time of Action			
(1) Initial stabilising action.	The offer price.	The market bid price of the associated securities at the beginning of the stabilising period.	The market price of an option at the beginning of the stabilising period.
(2) Later, but where there has been a deal[1] at a price above the stabilising price on the relevant exchange.[2]	The offer price, or the price at which that deal was done, whichever is the lower.	The market bid price in B(1), or the price at which that deal in the associated securities was done, whichever is the lower.	The market price in C(1), or the price at which that deal in an option was done, whichever is the lower.

[1]   References to deals done in the second row of the table are to deals done by or on the instructions of persons other than the stabilising manager.

[2]   "Relevant exchange" means the investment exchange which the stabilising manager reasonably believes to be the principal investment exchange on which securities are dealt in at the time of the transaction.

	Column A	Column B	Column C
(3) Later, but where there has been no deal in (2).	The offer price, or the initial stabilising price, whichever is the lower.	The market bid price in B(1), or the initial stabilising price for the associated securities, whichever is the lower.	The market price in C(1), or the initial stabilising price of the option, whichever is the lower.

The price limits are broadly similar whether the stabilising action is concerned with relevant securities or associated securities (including call options). The pricing limits, however, do not apply to stabilising action relating to bonds (other than certain convertible bonds), Government securities and depository receipts. Pricing with respect to these is subject to the general purpose of the Rules that any stabilising action is taken to support the market price. The Rules also make it clear that the stabilising manager may buy or subscribe for relevant securities or associated securities in order to close out a short position established with a view to supporting the price of the relevant securities without regard to the pricing limits.

The pricing limits operate in the following manner. In the event of the stabilising manager seeking to stabilise relevant securities, the initial stabilising price may not exceed the offer price (or starting price, if there is no offer price). If there are no independent market sales or purchases above the initial stabilising price subsequent stabilising action by the stabilising manager may be at or below the initial stabilising price. If an independent buyer and seller complete a transaction on the principal exchange which is at a price higher than the initial stabilising price then the stabilising manager will have a new maximum price, being the lower of the price at which that transaction was completed and the offer price.

Where associated securities or associated call options are not in existence or capable or being traded at the beginning of the stabilising period the Rules are to be read as if references to the market bid price at such time were a reference to the first market bid price of such securities or options during the stabilising period of which the stabilising manager is or reasonably should be aware.

9.5.5 *Management of stabilisation*

The Rules provide that, where the stabilising manager is an authorised person, stabilising action must be properly managed and that a record must be kept of the stabilising action taken.

There may be no stabilising action unless the stabilising manager has established the register described below and complies with the registration requirements for all earlier stabilising transactions in the offer in question.

There may be no stabilising action except by the stabilising manager itself or its appointed agent. The agent is responsible to the stabilising manager. The stabilising manager is responsible to others for the acts or omissions of the agent.

In the draft form of the Rules contained in the FSA's Consultation Paper 40 ("CP40"), the FSA had proposed permitting multiple stabilising managers – broadly as a result of current market practice in the bond market. However, in the final form of the Rules the FSA has reverted to requiring a single stabilising manager with the ability to appoint agents responsible to the stabilising manager. This was the position under the price stabilising rules which were in effect prior to 1 December 2001. This change occurred partly as a result of the comments received in response to CP40, but also because the Committee of European Securities Regulators (formerly, the Forum of European Securities Commissions (FESCO)) (CESR) is considering whether multiple stabilising managers should be permitted. Pending resolution of the issue by CESR, the FSA has decided that it will maintain the approach of the price stabilising rules in effect prior to 1 December 2001.

If an agent outside the UK breaches the Rules the stabilising manager and any other agents will lose the "safe harbour" provided by the Rules. As a result, agents outside the UK should stabilise in accordance with the Rules as well as any local stabilisation rules.

The Rules provide that except where neither the stabilising manager nor its agent knew or could reasonably have been expected to know the identity of its counterparty, the stabilising manager may not during the stabilising period enter into a transaction as principal in relevant or associated securities with any of its appointed agents.

9.5.6   *Recording of stabilising action taken*

The stabilising manager must keep a register for each offer of securities containing either in real-time or updated overnight (from business day to business day):

(a)   the names and terms of the appointment of each agent;

(b)   the general parameters (including the initial stabilising price) laid down by the stabilising manager for its agents and the date and time of their communication, variation or revocation;

(c)   each transaction effected in the course of stabilising action, including the type of security, the unit price, the size, the date and time and details of the counterparty;

(d)   details of the allotment of relevant securities (allottee and amount allotted); and

(e)   details, so far as known to the stabilising manager, of any deal which constitutes a deal at an independent market price above the then stabilising price for the purposes of the pricing limits table set out in Section 9.5.4 above.

The register containing this information must be kept in the UK or, if it is not kept in the UK, it must be capable of being brought to the UK within 48 hours of a request for access from anyone entitled to inspect the register. Furthermore, if the register is not kept in the English language, it must be capable of being translated into the English language within this 48-hour period.

Where the offer relates to an issue of relevant securities, the stabilising manager must permit the issuer of the securities to inspect that part of the register which contains the information with respect to stabilising transactions referred to in paragraph (c) above (other than details of the counterparty) on any business day for the three months from the end of the stabilising period. The register must be retained for a period of at least three years from the end of the stabilising period.

9.5.7   *Overseas stabilisation*

The FSA may make rules which treat a person stabilising investments in conformity with certain foreign stabilising rules as acting in conformity with the Rules. The FSA may specify which stabilising rules made outside the UK it will recognise. If such rules are altered their recognition continues to apply, but only if before the alteration the FSA has notified the body concerned and has not withdrawn its notification that it is satisfied with its consultation procedures.

The FSA has provided in the Rules that a person who, outside the UK, stabilises investments in conformity with certain United States federal or Japanese laws in an offer governed by the law of such countries is to be treated as acting in conformity with the Rules.

In relation to United States federal law the specified provisions are Regulation M promulgated by the United States Securities and Exchange Commission (the "SEC") under the United States Securities Exchange Act of 1934, as amended. Regulation M was adopted by the SEC in December 1996 and became effective in March 1997. Regulation M was accompanied by an adopting release (Securities Exchange Act Release No. 34-38067 (December 20, 1996)).

The provisions of Japanese law referred to above are the Securities and Exchange Law of Japan (Law No. 25, April 13, 1948), Article 159, paragraphs 3 and 4; Cabinet Orders for the Enforcement of the Securities and Exchange Law of Japan (Cabinet Order 321, September 30, 1965), Articles 20 to 26; Ministerial Ordinance concerning the Registration of Stabilisation Trading (Ordinance of the Ministry of Finance, No. 43, June 14, 1971); and Ministerial Ordinance concerning rules and otherwise governing the soundness of securities companies (Ordinance of the Ministry of Finance, No. 60, November 5, 1965), Article 2.

The FSA has indicated that it is satisfied with the consultation procedures of the United States and Japanese securities regulatory bodies.

The mutual recognition of overseas stabilising rules is currently being discussed among CESR members. The consultation paper published by FESCO (now CESR) envisages that CESR member states will introduce common rules which may then be mutually recognised by all member states. As a result, the FSA has decided for the time being to recognise only the United States and Japanese stabilising rules, pending CESR consultation. Once other European jurisdictions introduce such rules, the FSA will be able to recognise them by expanding the list contained in the Rules.

There may be circumstances when the FSA will need to investigate whether a recognised overseas rule has been breached. In such case, the FSA has indicated that it would expect to discuss a stabilising manager's or agent's conduct in relation to the overseas rule with the relevant home authority. The scope of recognition of the overseas rules is such that these rules will only be applicable to the overseas part of an issue.

In addition to providing a defence under Section 397(5) to an action brought under Section 397(3) FSMA, the Rules also provide that acting in accordance with the specified United States federal and Japanese stabilising rules will confer a defence with respect to proceedings under Part VIII FSMA in cases of market abuse, disciplinary proceedings under Part XIV FSMA in cases of the breach of other price stabilising rules and proceedings under Part XXV FSMA (injunctions and restitution) in relation to market abuse or the breach of other price stabilising rules. However, while conformity with the recognised overseas stabilising rules may assist in proceedings brought under Section 397(3) FSMA, it will not assist in proceedings brought under Section 397(2), nor in proceedings brought under Part V Criminal Justice Act 1993 (insider dealing). In addition, absent compliance with the United States and Japanese stabilisation rules where these are applicable, the extra-territorial effect of the legal risks described in Sections 9.4.1, 9.4.2 and 9.4.3 could expose a stabilising manager to liability for stabilising action conducted outside the UK, unless such stabilising action is carried out in accordance with the Rules.

9.6   Conclusion

In the consultation which preceded the finalisation of the Rules, the FSA stressed that, in view of the tight timetable for the implementation of the new market abuse regime and the general absence of evidence of significant problems with the pre-existing rules, a limited review of the rules was all that was appropriate at that time. As a consequence of this policy the amendments made to the pre-existing rules are relatively limited in scope. The FSA has stated that it intends to conduct a more general review of the whole area no later than two years after the implementation of the new Rules. Of relevance to this review will be the results of initiatives on both stabilisation and market abuse currently underway in Europe. These include the paper entitled "Stabilisation and allotment – a European supervisory approach" published by FESCO (now CESR) and the proposed EC Directive on insider dealing and market manipulation.

Chapter 10

Equities

Lucy Fergusson
Partner
Linklaters

10.1   Introduction

The preceding Chapters have described different aspects of the regulatory regime as they apply to investment banking activities generally. This Chapter outlines the principal relevant areas of regulation, and highlights some of the practical issues that investment banks may confront, under the FSMA regime when carrying on equity capital markets activities.

10.2   Regulatory overview

10.2.1   Regulated activities

The equity capital markets activities of an investment bank typically include:

- advising a company or its shareholders on a proposed new issue or sale of equity securities;
- obtaining the mandate to manage a new issue or sale;
- sounding out investors on a new issue or sale;
- book building;
- acting as sponsor in connection with a new issue in accordance with the UK Listing Authority ("UKLA") Listing Rules;
- agreeing to underwrite a new issue or sale;
- selling the equity securities the subject of the new issue or sale, either as agent for the issuer (or existing shareholder) or as principal, having acquired or agreed to acquire the equity securities from the issuer or existing shareholder;
- stabilising activities;
- publishing research relating to the issuer;
- giving general corporate broking advice;

- buying and selling equity securities, as agent or as principal;
- making a market in equity securities.

Each of such activities falls within, or may involve, one or more of the following categories of regulated activity, requiring authorisation by the FSA pursuant to Section 19 Financial Services and Markets Act 2000 (the "FSMA"):

(a) dealing in investments as principal or agent, which for the purposes of the FSMA and the rules made thereunder includes the underwriting of securities;

(b) arranging deals in investments, including the making of arrangements for or with a view to another person buying, selling, subscribing for or underwriting a particular investment;

(c) advising on investments, where an investment bank is involved with its client base in discussing the merits of subscribing for or purchasing securities; and

(d) sending or causing to be sent de-materialised instructions on behalf of another person relating to a security where the issue is to be settled through CREST.

One definition relevant to this Chapter is that of "designated investment business". This includes those activities specified in paragraphs (a) to (d) above and also managing investments, safeguarding and administration of assets and arranging such safeguarding and administration.

10.2.2   *The FSA Handbook*

As an authorised person, an investment bank conducting equities business will need to consider a number of elements of the FSA Handbook including the following:

- Principles for Businesses;
- Principles and Code for Approved Persons;
- Conduct of Business Rules;
- Market Conduct, including the Code of Market Conduct, the Price Stabilising Rules and the rules relating to Inter-Professional Conduct; and
- the UKLA Listing Rules and Guidance Manual.

Key provisions of these rules are discussed in this Chapter.

10.2.3 *Part VI FSMA (Official Listing of Securities)*

Part VI FSMA provides the framework for the admission of securities to the Official List and the publication of listing particulars and prospectuses. The FSA, when acting through its division the UKLA, is designated as the competent authority for listing with the power to make Listing Rules. In addition, Part VI (Section 88 FSMA) provides that the Listing Rules may require an issuer to make arrangements with a sponsor for the provision of services by that sponsor as specified by the Listing Rules. The responsibilities and liabilities of sponsors are discussed in more detail in Section 10.3.2 below.

10.2.4 *Recognised investment exchanges ("RIEs")*

Where securities are admitted to trading on an RIE, including the London Stock Exchange, certain of the rules of that exchange will be relevant to investment banking activities. For example, the requirements imposed in respect of market making activities or trading, settlement and clearance will be relevant. Consideration of the rules of the various RIEs is outside the scope of this Chapter.

10.2.5 *Market abuse*

The behaviour of an investment bank, when dealing as principal or when advising clients, will be subject to the market abuse regime under Section 118 FSMA. The topic of market abuse is covered in more detail in Chapter 8 of this book. However, examples of the application of the market abuse provisions and the Code of Market Conduct in relation to equities activities are considered in Sections 10.3.1.3–5 and 10.4.1.2 below.

10.2.6 *Financial promotion*

The financial promotion regime under Section 21 FSMA is again covered in detail elsewhere in this book (Chapter 7). Investment banks in particular will need to consider the application of the financial promotion regime to the documents and other communications they publish, make or are involved with in the course of their equities business, including listing particulars, any prospectus or other document, and other communications with the market, such as announcements, roadshows and broker research. These are considered in more detail in Section 10.5 below.

10.2.7   Public Offers of Securities Regulations 1995 (the "POS Regulations")

The POS Regulations will continue to apply to offers of securities to the public for the first time where no application has been made for the securities to be admitted to the Official List. The POS Regulations impose obligations upon issuers of securities in respect of the form, content and publication of, and the persons responsible for, a prospectus.

10.2.8   Misleading statements and practices and insider dealing

Investment banks must continue to have regard to the offences of market manipulation and insider dealing. Section 397 FSMA, which replicates the offence previously contained in Section 47 Financial Services Act 1986 relating to misleading statements and practices, applies to a person who makes a statement knowing it to be, or reckless as to whether it is, misleading, false or deceptive in a material respect, or who dishonestly conceals a material fact, in each case, to induce another to enter into an agreement or exercise rights in respect of a relevant investment. A breach of this provision constitutes a criminal offence as does a breach of the insider dealing provisions of the Criminal Justice Act 1993. These provisions are considered in more detail in Chapter 8 of this book.

10.3   Primary market activities

In this Chapter, the term "primary market activities" is used to mean activities relating to the offering of equity securities not previously traded on a market, whether the securities are newly issued or are being sold by existing holders. The term includes initial public offerings ("IPOs") by companies whose shares are not already publicly traded, as well as further capital raisings by companies already admitted to listing and/or to trading on an RIE. It includes the sale of shares by existing shareholders where these are marketed in the same way as a new issue of shares, even though such share sales are often called "secondary" sales. The term "secondary market activities" is used in this Chapter to cover dealing, trading and market-making on an RIE.

This section examines primary market activities primarily from the point of view of an investment bank underwriting or lead managing a deal, who may also be acting as sponsor, if the securities are, or are to be listed, or providing corporate finance advisory services. Certain of the issues raised will also apply to investment banks who are merely acting as co-managers in an underwriting syndicate.

10.3.1 *Underwriting and lead managing issues*

10.3.1.1 *Nature of business*

Designated investment business relating to the offering, issue or underwriting of shares and carried out by a firm with or for any issuer or shareholder constitutes corporate finance business for the purposes of the FSA Rules.

The definition of "corporate finance business" is broad enough to cover not only the underwriting of securities (whether as lead underwriter or as one of the other underwriters in a syndicate) but also the ancillary activities carried on by an investment bank who is lead managing and underwriting an issue, such as advising the issuer on the markets and on the structuring of the issue, assisting it with the marketing of the issue and selling shares it has underwritten to investors.

10.3.1.2 *Application of Conduct of Business rules – customer classification*

Like other investment businesses, an investment bank conducting primary market activities is required to classify its customers. In the first place, it will be important for the bank to ascertain who exactly it is acting for, as there may be several parties involved. For example, one or more shareholders may be intending to sell shares in an IPO, in which the company is also issuing shares to raise capital. One of the selling shareholders may have initially instructed the bank, although its advice is being given principally to the company.

For the purposes of client classification, a listed company is automatically an intermediate customer, unless it is a large intermediate customer classified as a market counterparty in accordance with COB 4.1.12R. This ability to reclassify from intermediate customer to market counterparty is a new feature of the FSMA regime so that little practical experience of its application exists. However, one would imagine that most companies would prefer not to be reclassified as a market counterparty and thereby lose the protections afforded to them as customers (as summarised in COB 4.1.13G).

A company whose shares are not already listed or admitted to trading on an EEA exchange will not automatically be an intermediate customer, and will therefore be a private customer unless it satisfies the size criterion: that it, or another member of its group, has within the last two years had called up share capital or net assets of at least £5,000,000.

Other persons for whom an investment bank acts in relation to an equity issue, such as shareholders (who may be anything from private individuals to a government body), will need to be classified according to their status.

In the context of corporate finance business, the rules on customer agreements and terms of business set out in COB 4.2 do not apply and accordingly these do not affect the terms of bank engagement or mandate letters, or of underwriting agreements.

"Corporate finance contacts" are not required to be dealt with as clients. These are defined as persons with or for whom a bank carries on designated investment business in the course of, or as a result of, carrying on corporate finance business on their own behalf, or on behalf of a client, provided:

(a) the bank does not behave towards them in a way that would reasonably lead them to expect they were being treated as a client; and

(b) the bank indicates clearly that it is not acting for them and will not be responsible to them for providing protections afforded to clients of the bank, or be advising them on transactions.

In the context of primary market activities, corporate finance contacts are likely to include shareholders, employees, investors and potential investors. To make clear that these are not clients, any circulars, prospectuses and other documents issued in connection with the transaction will need to carry appropriate legends giving the indications referred to in sub-paragraph (b) above.

Designated investment business carried on by a firm as principal for its own account in the course of other corporate finance activities will not itself be corporate finance business if it involves transactions as principal with, or advice on an investment to, a private customer (*see* paragraph (b) of the definition of "corporate finance business"). An investment bank therefore needs to take care to ensure that nothing it does takes it outside the definition of "corporate finance business". For example: an investment bank is advising an issuer on, and underwriting, its IPO. The IPO is to include an offer to the issuer's employees. The bank should avoid entering into transactions with the employees, for example by selling the shares to them as principal, or giving advice to the employees. If its activities cease to be corporate finance business a large number of COB rules that are not otherwise applicable will apply.

10.3.1.3 *Market abuse and code of market conduct – scope*
The scope of market abuse, though wide, is confined to behaviour which occurs in relation to qualifying investments "traded on" prescribed markets. In the context of IPOs, therefore, the market abuse regime does not bite until the shares start trading (unless the issuer has other securities such as bonds, which are traded on, or are related to, securities traded on a prescribed market).

The Code of Market Conduct clarifies the meaning of "traded" so as to make clear that investments are only "traded" from (and including) the first trade on the relevant exchange. Securities for which application has been made to the Official List will therefore not be "traded on" a prescribed market until the first trade is made on the London Stock Exchange or other market to which the securities are admitted. In cases where the London Stock Exchange allows "when issued" trading prior to admission to trading under its Rule 2.3, trading will begin with the first "when issued" trade. All markets established under the rules of an RIE are "prescribed markets" and therefore, for example, securities traded on the Alternative Investment market ("AIM") are also subject to the regime.

In the period prior to the launch of an equity issue, the lead manager, and any other investment bank involved in the issue, is likely to be in possession of material information concerning the issuer and its securities which is "relevant information" for Code of Market Conduct purposes. The possession or use of such information in relation to a company proposing to do an IPO, and whose securities are not yet admitted to trading will not fall within the market abuse regime, as the securities are not traded on any prescribed market. However, an investment bank needs to be sure that it will not commit the misuse of information offence if either the issuer's securities are already traded on a prescribed market or, once the shares start trading, the bank continues to have "relevant information" which has not been disclosed in the offering document.

It should be borne in mind that "relevant information" potentially has a wider definition than the information which is relevant for the purposes of the general obligations of disclosure which apply to issuers under Chapter 9 of the Listing Rules or under Section 80 FSMA (general duty of disclosure in listing particulars). It is also wider than the definition of price-sensitive information under the Criminal Justice Act. Accordingly, there is at least a theoretical possibility that even when a prospectus or listing particulars meeting the statutory disclosure obligations have been published, the issuer and/or the investment bank may still be in posses-sion of information which is "relevant information" for the purposes of the Code of Market Conduct and which has not been disclosed. Were the bank subsequently to deal on the basis of such information, this could constitute misuse of information. It may be unlikely that there would be any information not disclosed (but which is discloseable or announce-able) which would materially influence a bank's decision to deal (rather than its dealing being on the basis of all the other information that has been disclosed, or under its underwriting obligations, or for other reasons). However, MAR 1.4.4(1)E provides that the information need not be the only reason for dealing, so long as it is one of the reasons. Therefore there must be some risk that companies and the investment bank involved in an issue will need to consider the "relevant infor-mation" test as being the test for required disclosure in addition to the other relevant tests. This will be the case, for example, where little infor-mation is required to be disclosed under other rules, such as where a company makes a further issue of securities of less than 10 per cent of a class already listed, where there is no requirement for listing particulars.

10.3.1.4 *Market abuse – potential offences and safe harbours*
MAR 1.4, which deals with misuse of information, provides that dealing or arranging deals in shares would be a misuse of information if based on relevant information which is not generally available and which a regular user would expect to be disclosed.

Thus, for example, where a company which already has its shares traded on a prescribed market is proposing to place new shares with insti-tutional investors to raise cash, the investment bank advising it will have knowledge which, on the basis that the regular user would expect it to be disclosed, is "relevant information", namely about the fact and details of the issue. Accordingly, in the absence of a safe harbour, a bank would not be able to proceed with the sale, and employees of the bank engaged in trading activities might not be able to deal, without committing market abuse, unless the details of the deal were previously disclosed.

Various safe harbours may be relevant, including those relating to Chinese walls and underwriting agreements:

(a) The bank will need to have its Chinese walls or equivalent arrangements operating in order to rely on the safe harbours from market abuse afforded under MAR 1.4.24C and COB 2.4.4R. These provide that relevant information is not regarded as influencing a decision to deal or arrange deals if the information is held on the other side of a Chinese wall from the individuals who dealt, or they did not have access to the relevant information because of arrangements equivalent to Chinese walls.

(b) MAR 1.4.26C provides a safe harbour with regard to "trading information". This states that dealing or arranging deals will not amount to a misuse of information solely because it is based on information as to that person's intention, or any other person's intention, to deal or arrange deals in any qualifying investment. However, this safe harbour does not include dealing or arranging deals "based on information relating to new offers, issues, placements or other primary market activity" (MAR 1.4.26(2)C). A safe harbour for the facilitation of bids and other market operations allows for dealings in connection with or for the purpose of an acquisition or disposal of an equity stake (MAR 1.4.28C). It is not entirely clear whether this safe harbour assists where equity securities are being acquired in the context of primary market activities as well as in respect of stakebuilding and takeovers.

(c) Another safe harbour is provided by MAR 1.4.31C, which states that "agreeing to underwrite an issue of securities will not of itself amount to a misuse of information". This allows banks to enter into an underwriting agreement, but they will still need to consider carefully whether any other activities they are carrying out in connection with the issue, or based on their knowledge of the issue, could constitute market abuse. It should also be noted that the safe harbour covers only "issues" and not sales of securities. However, it is unlikely that entry into an underwriting agreement for a sale of existing securities would, absent other complicating factors, be regarded by a regular user as market abuse.

(d) A safe harbour is provided in respect of compliance with Listing Rule 9.10, which relates to the obligation of a listed company to notify to the market without delay the results of any new issue of listed securities, or of a public offering of existing securities. This rule, however, permits the issuer, at its discretion, to delay making such an announcement where the securities are underwritten until the obligation by the underwriter to take or procure others to take securities is finally determined or lapses. Such a delay permits, for example, the placing of the "rump" of shares not taken up on a rights issue before the market is notified of the size of a rump. It is common for the underwriters to disclose the size of the rump privately to placees. To the extent that this information is likely to constitute relevant information for market abuse purposes, the placees will need to be made insiders and to refrain from dealing, unless they can show that the dealing was not based on the information or did not influence their decision to deal, until the information becomes public or ceases to be relevant.

10.3.1.5 Stabilisation and ancillary activities

Equity offerings are frequently accompanied by stabilisation activities in order to support the price of securities during the initial period after completion of the offering. Stabilisation activities are by their nature activities which could constitute market abuse, but if carried on in accordance with the Price Stabilising Rules they will benefit from the stabilisation safe harbour.

As an action ancillary to stabilisation activities the lead manager, in determining allocations, may over-allot securities, allocating to investors more securities than are to be issued or sold in the issue. It may satisfy the over-allotments either by purchasing securities in the market or by exercising an option, provided for in the underwriting agreement, to subscribe or purchase additional securities. Such an option is commonly known as an over-allotment or greenshoe option.

It is normal market practice not to disclose the extent to which the manager over-allots securities. In addition, an over-allotment option over shares may be structured, where it would otherwise give the manager a disclosable interest under Section 198 of the Companies Act 1985 (because it is an option over existing shares of a UK company), in such a way as to avoid the disclosure obligations that would arise each time the stabilisation manager bought or sold shares in the market. The stabilisation manager generally wishes (to the extent permissible, and taking into account other regulatory disclosure obligations including, for example, the trading disclosure obligations of the exchange on which it is trading) to avoid disclosure of its market activities.

Although ancillary to stabilisation, these activities are not expressly permitted by the Price Stabilising Rules and thus do not benefit from the stabilisation safe harbour. It is arguable that information regarding over-allotments and stabilisation purchases could be considered "relevant information", and its non-disclosure could constitute market abuse. Alternatively, over-allotments could be argued to give a misleading impression of the supply of securities and constitute market abuse for that reason. In order to continue with such practices it may be necessary to fall back on the argument that, since such non-disclosure is accepted market practice, it should be acceptable to a regular user, and hence not constitute market abuse.

Chapter 9 of this book deals more fully with the regulations relating to stabilisation.

10.3.2   *Sponsor activities*

Where an investment bank is involved as financial adviser or lead manager on an issue of shares which are to be admitted to the Official List, it may also be acting as sponsor to the issuer. This Section describes the regime that applies to sponsors.

10.3.2.1   *The role of sponsors*
Issuers of equity securities which are to be admitted to the Official List are required by the Listing Rules to appoint a sponsor in certain circumstances. A sponsor's main responsibilities, which it is required to discharge using due care and skill, are to help an issuer to prepare for listing, to provide advice on the application and interpretation of the Listing Rules, to ensure that the issuer complies with the Listing Rules and to provide any information known to the sponsor as required by the UKLA for the purpose of verifying that the Listing Rules are being complied with. In addition, the Listing Rules require a sponsor to carry out a number of specific services, many of which are pre-requisites to a successful application for listing. Examples include the sponsor's obligation to confirm to the UKLA that an issuer's working capital statement has been made after due and careful enquiry.

10.3.2.2   *The regulation of sponsors*
Prior to the introduction of the FSMA the regulation of sponsors was based upon contractual undertakings provided by the sponsor to the UKLA, by virtue of which sponsors were bound by the applicable provisions of the Listing Rules.

Sections 88 and 89 FSMA provide a statutory framework for the approval and discipline of sponsors. With effect from N2 the eligibility criteria and disciplinary regime for sponsors are included within the Listing Rules, although with few substantive changes from the pre-FSMA regime.

10.3.2.3   *The main changes*

The most significant changes under the FSMA relate to the procedures relevant to applications for approval as a sponsor, cancellation of such approval and disciplinary measures, where, in each case, a statutory procedure exists to regulate the UKLA's decision making processes. These procedures are amplified in Chapters 4 and 8 of the UKLA Guidance Manual.

10.3.2.4   *Approval criteria*

In order to be approved, a sponsor must be an authorised person under the FSMA (which includes passported institutions), be able to satisfy the UKLA that it is competent to discharge the services required of a sponsor and have at least four eligible employees. These are employees at a level of sufficient seniority who have advised on the application or interpretation of the Listing Rules or the rules of AIM at least three times in the last 36 months and at least once in the last 12 months.

10.3.2.5   *Discipline*

The power of the UKLA to discipline sponsors is limited to publishing a statement censuring the sponsor (to which the statutory procedures referred to above will apply) and the UKLA's ability to impose financial penalties does not extend to sponsors. It is thought likely that the UKLA will continue to deal with minor breaches by private warning and will not in every circumstance seek to publish a censuring statement.

10.3.2.6   *Sponsor responsibility*

(a)   Listing Rules

Previously, the Listing Rules expressly provided that the responsibilities of sponsors in the Listing Rules were owed solely to the UKLA. This provision no longer appears in the Listing Rules, which may marginally increase the risk of an investor being able to bring a successful negligence claim against a sponsor. Under Section 150 FSMA, however, third parties do not have a right to bring actions for breaches of statutory duty against sponsors in respect of breaches of the Listing Rules.

(b)   Prospectus/listing particulars

A sponsor should only be considered responsible for and, as a consequence, liable in respect of, a prospectus or listing particulars where it accepts responsibility for or authorises all or part of the document. Some doubt exists as to whether a sponsor, in providing general advice in connection with the issue, in effectively controlling the release of the document or because its name appears at the front of the document, could be said to have authorised the contents of the document and thus be fixed with liability in respect of it.

In addition, a sponsor may, where a prospectus or listing particulars turn out to be misleading, be fixed with liability to investors under common law in respect of misrepresentation or negligent misstatement if a duty of care could be shown to exist to such investors. Accordingly sponsors will continue to be concerned to protect themselves by means of an appropriate combination of due diligence, verification of key statements and seeking contractual protections from the issuing company or selling shareholders in respect of potential liabilities.

10.3.3 Publication of research

The publication of research reports by analysts connected with the managers of an issue is a common feature of IPOs and sometimes occurs in connection with other primary market offerings. Procedures are normally adopted to try to ensure that such research does not become associated with the offering document (listing particulars, prospectus or other information memorandum) which the issuer intends to be the sole disclosure document forming the contractual basis of the investor's decision to purchase shares. These procedures, which are not based directly on any statutory or regulatory requirement, include limiting the issuer's role in the drafting and production of the research report so as to ensure that the research is demonstrably an independent product of the analyst. In addition, a "blackout period" is usually imposed. This is a period, generally of up to four weeks before the publication of the offering document, during which the research may not be distributed. The regulatory regime under FSMA does not affect the need for such procedures to be adopted.

Where research is published in connection with an IPO, connected analysts (analysts from investment houses involved in the offering) will be briefed and their research published prior to trading of the issuer's shares commencing. On that basis such research should not give rise to market abuse concerns, unless the issuer has other securities traded on a prescribed market.

Where the issuer's securities are already traded, the analyst, and the issuer, will need to consider whether information included in the research report constitutes relevant information which is not generally available. If it does, even though the information will subsequently be included in an offering document, the analyst could be committing the offence of requiring or encouraging behaviour (misuse of information) which would amount to market abuse. Distribution of the research report to clients is not likely to be regarded as making the report's contents generally available, in light of the FSA's antagonism towards selective disclosure. Analysts should also be aware of the restrictions that exist under the Listing Rules, the PSI Guide (the UKLA's guidance on dissemination of price sensitive information), the Admission and Disclosure Standards and AIM Rules of the LSE and the insider dealing regime under the Criminal Justice Act 1993. *See* also the discussion of analysts at Sections 10.5.3.3 and 10.5.3.5 below.

10.4   Secondary market activities

This Section considers certain secondary market activities that an investment bank may undertake as part of their equities activities. Although matters such as trading and market-making activities will be covered by the rules of the relevant RIE, which rules fall outside the scope of this book, some over-arching rules are applicable under the FSMA regime. Since the main focus of this book is on corporate finance activities, this Section does not focus in detail on the rules applicable to such trading activities but gives a brief overview of some of the key issues since trading operations may be ancillary to primary market activities, for example, where trading is carried out for the purposes of price stabilisation.

10.4.1   *Trading and market-making*

10.4.1.1   *Conduct of business and inter-professional conduct*
An investment bank's trading and market-making activities will normally be conducted with market counterparties. Where the business is "inter-professional business" carried on from a permanent UK place of business and is conducted with a market counterparty, the FSA's Inter-Professional Conduct ("IPC") rules and guidance will apply, with only certain of the COB rules (principally relating to Chinese walls, client classification, personal account dealing and client assets) applying. Inter-professional business includes dealing, arranging deals or advising on inter-professional investments, which include equities, with or for a market counterparty. Excluded from this definition are certain activities, including approving financial promotions and corporate finance business.

The IPC contains relatively few rules but a considerable amount of guidance relevant to equity market activities, including guidance on the application of the Principles for Businesses. The IPC needs to be read alongside the provisions on market abuse and the Code of Market Conduct, both because of the subject matter of the rules and because, like other guidance, it helps to establish the expectations of a regular user for market abuse purposes.

Among the rules that are particularly relevant to equities trading is a prohibition on entering into non-market price transactions unless the bank has taken reasonable steps to ensure that the counterparty is not entering into the transaction for an improper purpose. Improper purposes include not only market abuse, but also, for example, the improper concealment of a profit or loss, window-dressing transactions to disguise the true financial position of a person, and vulnerable transactions under the Insolvency Act 1986.

Where the investment bank is acting as a broker for private and intermediate customers, the full conduct of business rules will apply to the firm's dealings with such customers.

10.4.1.2 *Market abuse*

As might be expected, the market abuse and the Code of Market Conduct provisions are especially pertinent to the activities of brokers, dealers and market-makers. It is not practicable here to give more than a few examples of their application to equities business. Chapter 8 of this book describes the market abuse regime in more detail.

"Relevant information" can include information about market activities such as impending significant trades. However, under the safe harbour at MAR 1.4.26C, dealing will not amount to a misuse of information solely because it is based on information as to an intention to deal or information concerning transactions that have taken place. Thus, a dealer who is about to execute a large purchase or sale order, which may by reason of its size have an effect on the market price, is able to do so. Whilst this may not constitute market abuse, it may breach COB 7.4.3R if the order is not executed fairly and in due turn with respect to other customer orders. Such activities must also comply with COB 7.13 in respect of personal account dealing. Also, MAR 1.4.26C expressly does not legitimise the front running of customer orders.

The false or misleading impression and market distortion elements of market abuse are of particular concern in relation to secondary market trading activities.

Transactions which will have the principal effect, or are likely to do so, of inflating, maintaining or depressing the apparent supply, demand or value of securities in a misleading way, may be market abuse, unless the regular user would regard them as having a legitimate commercial rationale and the transaction has been executed in a proper way.

A transaction such as taking a short position in shares is potentially misleading, since it might be thought that the seller owned the shares when in fact he did not, potentially creating a false picture of the supply of shares on the market. A transaction is not automatically regarded as having a legitimate commercial rationale simply because the purpose behind the transaction was to make a profit or a loss. Moreover, a transaction will not normally be considered to have a legitimate commercial rationale if there was a motive (albeit not necessarily the only motive) of inducing others to trade, or moving the price of shares or other qualifying investments. Factors relevant to whether behaviour amounts to market abuse in this context are set out in MAR 1.5.11E and 1.5.12E and include whether a transaction causes the supply or demand or price of an investment to increase where the person has an interest in that level or a transaction takes place at a time when those levels are relevant to the calculation of reference or settlement prices or valuations. Where a transaction opens a new position or closes out an existing position this will tend to suggest that the behaviour does not amount to market abuse.

Safe harbours are provided in relation to creating a false or misleading impression, for example, for arbitrage transactions taking advantage of a difference in price where shares are traded on two different markets (MAR 1.5.24C). However, these safe harbours are still subject to the requirements that there should be a legitimate commercial rationale and that the transaction be executed in a proper way.

For a transaction to be considered executed in a "proper way" it must "take into account the need for the market as a whole to operate fairly and efficiently" (MAR 1.5.10E). Execution in a manner which is designed to create a false or misleading impression would not be regarded as a "proper way". MAR 1.5.10E cites market rules on reporting and executing cross-transactions as examples of market rules concerned with ensuring that dealings occur in a proper way. However, compliance with an RIE's rules is not of itself a safe harbour. On the other hand, MAR

1.5.10E does helpfully make clear that transactions will not necessarily be considered to have been executed in an improper way simply because the way in which they were executed did not disclose the firm's intentions or positions to the market.

There is some overlap between the misleading impression and the market distortion elements of market abuse. Transactions that may constitute market distortion include price positioning: behaviour designed to position the price of investments at a distorted level, even if this is not the sole purpose, will not have a legitimate commercial rationale, and is likely to constitute market abuse (MAR 1.6.9E and 1.6.10E).

10.5 Communicating with investors and the market

Chapter 7 of this book describes the financial promotion regime in general. However, it may be helpful to begin with a brief overview of the rules that will apply in the context of an investment bank's equities practice, before looking at their application to specific types of communication.

10.5.1 FSA rules on communications and financial promotion

The definition of who makes a "communication" under the financial promotion regime is broad – it can include not only the author of a financial promotion but also anyone causing the financial promotion to be made, as well as any person passing it on. Thus, for example, the FSA's draft guidance on financial promotion explains that "sending a prospectus to a potential investor is making a communication, irrespective of whose prospectus it is and the identity of the potential investor" (AUTH App 1.6.2G). This interpretation would appear to create additional risk for investment banks by providing grounds for arguing that persons who are not the authors of documents are responsible for the contents of those documents if they pass them on, so making them their own communications. Banks may also have specific obligations as a result of the Conduct of Business rules in respect of communications which they pass on.

Principle 7 of the FSA's Principles for Business, on communications with clients, requires firms to pay due regard to the information needs of their clients and communicate information to them in a way which is clear, fair and not misleading.

COB 2.1.3R provides that firms must take reasonable steps to communicate with customers in a way which is clear, fair and not misleading – like Principle 7, this rule extends not only to financial promotions but to all communications, including client agreements, periodic statements, telephone calls and general correspondence.

An investment bank will need to ensure that it is in compliance with the rules applicable under Senior Management Arrangements, Systems and Controls and, in particular, SYSC 3. It will need to have appropriate systems and controls in place to provide for the approval of a financial promotion, including that the review of the communication is delegated to a suitable employee who is appropriately supervised.

The main Handbook requirements on financial promotion are set out in COB 3. While COB 3 applies to corporate finance business, it does not apply with respect to inter-professional business, although if a financial promotion is approved for the purposes of Section 21 FSMA in the course of inter-professional business, the COB rules will still apply. In addition COB 3 does not apply to communications which are exempt from the provisions of Section 21 FSMA or to communications to market counterparties or intermediate customers, although if a bank does approve such communications it must be able to show that it has taken reasonable steps to ensure that it is clear, fair and not misleading. Because of the scope of the exemptions under the Financial Services and Markets Act 2000 (Financial Promotion) Order 2001 (as amended) (the "Financial Promotion Order"), many documents and other communications that arise in the course of an investment bank's equities activities will be outside the scope of COB 3. Nevertheless, there will be circumstances where COB 3 does apply. The application of the exemptions to Section 21 FSMA to some of the documents produced in connection with an equity issue is considered in more detail in Section 10.5.3 below.

COB 3.6.1R requires that, before a firm either communicates or approves, for Section 21 purposes, a non-real time financial promotion (other than an exempt communication), it must confirm that the financial promotion complies with the rules in COB 3. In particular, a firm must be able to show that it has taken reasonable steps to ensure that the financial promotion is clear, fair and not misleading. If it becomes aware that the communication no longer complies it should cease to communicate it and notify any person it knows to be relying on its approval or confirmation (COB 3.6.3R). Where private customers who have responded to a financial promotion may have been misled the firm should consider whether they should be contacted, have the position explained and be offered redress if they have suffered loss. The record-keeping requirements of COB 3.7 must be complied with. COB 3.12.2R provides that a firm must not approve a real time communication.

If a bank is responsible for any misleading communication, it may, in addition to any breach of FSA rules, be guilty of market abuse, or of an offence under Section 397 FSMA, as well as having potential liabilities for misrepresentation or negligent misstatement under the common law.

10.5.2 Scope of financial promotion regime

Section 21 FSMA prohibits the communication by a person, in the course of business, of an invitation or inducement to engage in investment activity, unless that person is an authorised person or the content of the communication has been specifically approved by an authorised person. A number of exemptions are provided by the Financial Promotion Order. Of these exemptions, the most important, in the context of equities activities, are likely to be those relating to investment professionals (Article 19), persons in the business of disseminating information (Article 47) and high net worth entities (Article 49); documents required or permitted by an RIE (Article 67) or other required documents such as listing particulars and prospectuses (Articles 70 and 71) and annual reports and accounts (Article 59). While Section 21 FSMA does not restrict communications by authorised persons, they need to be aware of its provisions and the exemptions, both in order to advise and assist clients, and also because, as explained above, the exemptions affect the extent of their own obligations under COB. In particular, the rules on financial promotion contained in COB 3 do not apply to making communications which are exempt under the Financial Promotion Order.

10.5.3 Communications relating to equities activities

This Section considers the status under the FSMA regime of some of the key promotional materials that an investment bank is likely to come across as part of its equities business. It does not separately consider communications that a bank will make with market counterparties in the course of market making or dealing activities, or with co-managers, sub-underwriters or placees on an offering, for example, invitation and allotment telexes, sub-underwriting or placing letters. Such communications will usually fall outside the scope of COB 3, although they will be subject to the general clear, fair and not misleading obligations to which authorised persons are subject.

10.5.3.1 *Offering documents*

Equity offerings generally involve some kind of disclosure document. In the case of listed securities, this will generally be listing particulars or, where an offer to the public in the UK for the first time is involved, a prospectus, prepared under the Listing Rules pursuant to Part VI FSMA. Such an offering document is issued by, and is primarily the responsibility of, the company issuing the securities and its directors, or, on occasion, the selling shareholder(s). Investment banks acting as sponsor to an issue should be aware of the risk that they may also be held responsible for the document, as a person authorising its contents, under Section 79(3) FSMA and Regulation 6 FSMA (Official Listing of Securities) Regulations (*see* also Section 10.3.2 above). In the case of unlisted securities where an offer to the public in the UK is involved, a prospectus under the POS Regulations will be required.

Listing particulars and prospectuses under Part VI FSMA or the POS Regulations are exempt documents under Articles 71 and 72 of the Financial Promotion Order. COB 3 does not apply, but nevertheless, investment banks should note COB 2.1.3R, which imposes the general obligation that communications to customers be clear, fair and not misleading. Investment banks will wish not to be subject to this rule, if practicable, because of the responsibility for due diligence on the document it will give rise to. This, therefore, illustrates the importance of ensuring that such documents include the kind of legend referred to at Section 10.3.1.2 above, making clear that the bank does not have a customer relationship with potential investors and other corporate finance contacts to whom they may distribute the document.

Where an offering document is prepared in respect of an offering of existing listed securities, for example where a controlling shareholder is selling down a significant part of its holding, there is no legal requirement for listing particulars or a prospectus, since the shares are already listed. In this case, unless the distribution is kept within one or more of the other applicable exemptions under the Financial Promotion Order (such as the investment professionals exemption under Article 19), any document that is prepared for marketing purposes will require approval by an authorised person for the purposes of Section 21. COB 3 including the confirmation of compliance requirements described above will apply.

An offering document for unlisted securities which are to be traded on an RIE, for example shares which are to be admitted to AIM, may fall under an exemption such as that for promotions required by market rules under Article 67 of the Financial Promotion Order.

For equity offerings by entities which will not be listed or traded, for example, venture capital offerings to individual business "angels", the new exemption under Article 48 of the Financial Promotion Order for persons certified by an authorised person as high net worth individuals may apply. The financial promotion cannot, however, invite the recipient to engage in investment activity with the authorised person who signed the certificate.

In the absence of any other applicable exemption, the offering document will need to be approved by an authorised person.

10.5.3.2 *Preliminary offering documents*
Draft offering documents distributed to potential investors are normally only distributed to institutional investors, and the company will generally rely on the institutional investors exemption under Article 19 of the Financial Promotion Order, together with the exemption for high net worth entities under Article 49.

Investment banks should be aware of the conditions under these Articles for regarding a communication as being made or directed only to persons of the kinds described in these Articles, which make it necessary for documents to include legends, and appropriate procedures to be put in place, to ensure that only persons falling within the exemptions can participate in the offering.

10.5.3.3 *Road show materials and presentations to analysts*
Potential investors are frequently invited to roadshow presentations made by the management of a company to promote an equity offering. Typically, the lead manager works closely with the company in preparing the materials, but they are presented solely by the company. The invitees to the presentation will generally be representatives of institutional investors, and the company will rely on the investment professionals exemption (Article 19) or other exemptions such as Article 49 (high net worth entities) under the Financial Promotion Order. While it organises and attends the roadshow presentation, a bank will not normally be responsible for its content.

Analysts' presentations, of the kind where a large number of analysts are invited to attend and hear a presentation by management, accompanied by slides, handouts and visual aids, will be non-real time financial promotions to the extent that they are not interactive. However, according to the FSA's guidance, if a question is asked, the response will be a real time financial promotion, at least to the person who asked the question. Since, under COB 3.12.2R, authorised persons cannot approve real time financial promotions, it may be necessary for companies to ensure that they do not permit persons who fall outside any of the exemptions to attend such presentations, or that, if such persons do attend, the presentations are held on a non-interactive basis. Where an investment bank approves a presentation script to enable members of the public to attend presentations (including by electronic means such as teleconferencing and webcasts), company executives will need to be warned that they must stick to the script otherwise they may be making an unapproved financial promotion in contravention of Section 21. These issues are particularly important, since the PSI Guide encourages companies to make such presentations open to the general public as well as to the narrow analyst community.

10.5.3.4 *Announcements made by an issuer*

Where a bank is acting as lead manager and/or financial adviser to a company prior to an IPO or secondary offering, it may well be called upon to approve press announcements or other advertising materials made by that issuer, if these fall into the category of financial promotions, and if no applicable exemption applies. Companies which are already listed can frequently rely, in such circumstances, on the general exemptions under Articles 67 and 69 for promotions required under the Listing Rules or materials which do not contain express invitations to acquire shares and which comply with certain other content requirements. These exemptions do not apply to companies whose securities are not already admitted to listing or trading, and accordingly it will be more common for Section 21 approval to be required for announcements by companies that are new to the market, prior to flotation. As indicated above, approval will require the investment bank to confirm compliance with the requirements of COB 3.

Another situation in which investment banks may become involved in announcements made by issuers is in the course of general corporate advisory services, for example, where (acting as sponsor, or simply as a financial advisor) a bank advises a company on its disclosure obligations under the Listing Rules. Announcements pursuant to disclosure obligations will be exempt under Article 67 or 69 of the Financial Promotion Order, and so will not require approval by an authorised person. However, an investment bank acting as financial advisor to a company may physically send the company's announcements to the relevant information services on behalf of the company. In such a case the announcement may be regarded as the bank's "communication" (*see* Section 10.4.1 above). In addition a bank should consider the provisions of MAR

1.5.20E, which applies when information is disseminated through an "accepted channel for the dissemination of information". This means an approved channel of communication for formal dissemination of information, such as the Regulatory News Service of the London Stock Exchange. MAR 1.5.20E states that those who disseminate information through such accepted channels should take reasonable care to ensure the information is not inaccurate or misleading. Where they do not, and the information is likely to give rise to a false or misleading impression, they will be regarded as engaging in behaviour which amounts to market abuse. It will therefore be incumbent on all investment banks who submit announcements to information services on behalf of their clients to take reasonable care to ensure that such announcements are not false or misleading and so prevent market abuse from occurring or, at least, in order to be able to rely on the "reasonable belief" defence to market abuse under Section 123(2) FSMA.

10.5.3.5 Research reports
Section 10.3.3 considers some of the issues connected with the publication of research ahead of an IPO or other offering. This Section considers issues related to the activities of analysts in other contexts.

The production of research reports by brokers is an important method for them to maintain relationships with their investor clients. In addition, a respected analyst in a particular sector at an investment bank can be influential in attracting companies in that sector to use the corporate finance services offered by the investment bank.

Research reports are generally prepared by means of a combination of talking to the management of companies and independent financial, economic and sector research and analysis. Analysts publish the results of their research in the form of a report often containing the recommendation to "buy", "hold" or "sell". To the extent that such research reports are sent only to clients who are investment professionals under Article 19 of the Financial Promotion Order or fall within one of the other exemptions, COB 3 will not apply and the broker will simply be subject to the general obligations to ensure that communications are fair, clear and not misleading under principle 7 and COB 2.1.3R. If the distribution is wider, then COB 3 will apply.

The market in a particular company's shares frequently reacts, with resultant changes in the company's share price, to the publication of research by investment bank analysts. Given this level of influence there is potential scope for market abuse.

For example, consider the following scenarios:

(a) An investment bank analyst publishes a strong buy recommendation on an issuer shortly before the announcement of a capital raising issue by that company, which is underwritten by the investment bank. It would be market abuse if the investment bank had deliberately talked up the market in the company's shares in order to ensure the success of the issue. In order to establish a defence, the bank would have to show that the report represented the honest opinion of the analyst, since if it did not it might be guilty of creating a false or misleading impression. In addition, it would have to show that there was an effective Chinese wall, or equivalent arrangement, such that the analyst did not have any knowledge of the impending issue. If he had had such knowledge, he could also have been potentially guilty of giving a misleading impression by omitting to mention the issue in his research report.

The investment bank should also consider whether, if those who were involved with the impending issue knew that the analyst was likely to publish such a report, they should have taken steps to prevent him from doing so. Even if Chinese walls prevented the execution team from knowing of the research report, the bank's legal and compliance department might have knowledge of both the impending issue and the research report as a result of its internal review procedures. In that case, its failure to prevent the publication of the report could make the bank guilty of requiring or encouraging market abuse to the extent that the behaviour of the analyst was behaviour which, if those who knew about the issue had themselves engaged in, would have amounted to market abuse.

(b) An analyst is given information by a director of a listed company which is "relevant information" for the purposes of the market abuse regime. The analyst would be guilty of misuse of information if he dealt on the basis of that information himself. If he includes the information in his report and distributes it to clients he may be guilty of the requiring or encouraging offence by virtue of encouraging clients to deal on the basis of that information.

(c) An analyst goes on a site visit to a company, entering its factories or workshops or other non-public areas. The impression he gains, say from observing attitudes of workers, and their working practices, is that the company's management is ineffective and that productivity gains promised by management may not be achieved. The analyst returns to the City and publishes a "sell" recommendation (changed from "buy") based on what he has seen. Since his impressions were not gained in a public place he may not be able to rely on the argument that the information he has gained by observation is generally available (unlike the example given in the Code of Market Conduct of the man with a mobile phone on a train who observes a burning factory). The analyst in this example could be guilty, if he sold shares himself, of market abuse and may be guilty of the requiring or encouraging element of market abuse, through his "sell" recommendation. However, it is possible that the information on the basis of which his impressions were formed would not be regarded as announceable or disclosable, and hence that this element of the test for misuse of information under the Code of Market Conduct was missing. Alternatively the regular user might not regard the analyst's behaviour in this example as unacceptable, and so come to his defence.

Chapter 11

Mergers and Acquisitions

Stuart Evans
Partner
Simmons & Simmons

11.1 Introduction

The role and responsibilities of investment banks in relation to mergers and acquisitions will vary from transaction to transaction. The bank may be advising a buyer, a seller or a target. In addition it may be acting as sponsor and/or underwriter of new securities to be issued to fund an acquisition. The rules which regulate investment banks are primarily those of the market abuse regime introduced by Sections 118–131 FSMA and the financial promotion regime introduced by Section 21 FSMA.

The acquisition of UK public companies continues to be governed by the City Code on Takeovers and Mergers as administered by the Panel on Takeovers and Mergers. The Financial Services Authority endorses the Takeover Code pursuant to Section 143 FSMA. In addition to complying with the cold-shoulder and cooperation rules made under Section 138 FSMA, practitioners have to have regard to the interface between the Takeover Code and the market abuse regime.

The financial promotion regime will have only limited application in the public takeover arena as those communications made in the context of public offers which constitute an invitation or inducement to engage in investment activity are likely to be approved as to their content by an authorised person and, in many cases, to be made by an authorised person. However, this regime will come into focus in the private M&A arena, particularly where information is to be communicated relating to companies and businesses proposed to be sold.

11.2 The Panel and the Takeover Code

The public mergers and acquisitions regime in the UK has historically been a non-statutory regime. It is operated by the Panel on Takeovers and Mergers through a body of rules comprised in the Takeover Code. It aims for fair and equal treatment of all target shareholders in relation to takeovers and provides an orderly framework within which takeovers are conducted.

The Takeover Code is based upon a number of General Principles and a series of more detailed Rules. These are applied by the Panel in line with their spirit to achieve their underlying purpose and the Panel can modify or relax them where appropriate. For this reason, where there is any doubt as to whether any proposals will comply with the Takeover Code, the Panel should always be consulted in advance.

There are appeal procedures within the Panel's constitution. Ultimately its decisions can be reviewed in the UK courts.

The Takeover Code also contains a separate set of rules, the Rules Governing Substantial Acquisitions of Shares, ("SARs"), which apply outside the context of a formal offer.

The new regulatory regime interfaces with the Panel and the Takeover Code through the endorsement of the Takeover Code (*see* Section 11.4) and the provisions governing market abuse (*see* Section 11.5). The restrictions on share dealing contained in the Takeover Code and the SARs are referred to in Section 11.6. The provisions contained in the Takeover Code and the SARs relating to communications are dealt with in Section 11.7.

11.3 The endorsement of the Takeover Code (FSA Consultation Paper 87)

11.3.1 Background

The Securities Investment Board ("SIB") endorsed the Takeover Code for the purposes of Principle 3 of the Statements of Principle which required firms to observe high standards of market conduct and to comply with codes and standards in force. The effect of the endorsement was that the Takeover Code became legally part of the principles and compliance could be enforced by self-regulated organisations ("SROs"), Recognised Professional Bodies ("RPBs") and the SIB.

With implementation of the FSMA the FS Act has been repealed and the previous endorsement no longer has any effect. The relevant provision of the FSMA is Section 143 and the FSA has agreed to the Panel's request to continue to endorse the Takeover Code. The cold-shoulder and cooperation rules are made under Section 138 FSMA and these replicate as closely as possible the existing rules.

11.3.2 Endorsing rules

The effect of the endorsement is that if a firm fails to comply with the Takeover Code, the Panel can request the FSA to exercise its powers under the FSMA. Under Section 143(5) FSMA, a failure to comply with a Panel ruling has the same effect as a breach of the Takeover Code itself. The FSA can exercise its powers to take action for breaches of the Takeover Code or Panel rulings only at the Panel's request. Enforcement action by the FSA can take the form of:

(a)   variation or cancellation of permission to carry on regulated activities under Part IV FSMA;
(b)   disciplinary measures under Part IX FSMA (public censure and financial penalties); and
(c)   seeking an injunction or requiring restitution under Part XXV FSMA.

Breaches of the Takeover Code or a Panel ruling may also be taken into account by the FSA when considering other types of enforcement action including:

(i)   withdrawal of approval under Section 63 FSMA – on the basis that the approved person is not fit and proper; and
(ii)   making a prohibition order under Section 56 FSMA against an individual; and
(iii)   disciplinary action against an approved person under Section66(2)(a) FSMA for a breach of a Statement of Principle for approved persons.

The FSA believes that the endorsement will apply to similar number of firms as the current endorsement with the exception of professional firms. At present, about 15,000 firms are authorised DPBs ("Designated Professional Bodies") for investment business and only about 2,000 are carrying on activities requiring authorisation. Firms previously subject to the pre-N2 endorsement which fall outside endorsement because they are exempt under the FSMA may be required by their own professional guidance to comply with the Takeover Code.

11.3.3 Cold shoulder and cooperation rules

The cold-shoulder rule require firms not to act for any person on a Takeover Code transaction if the firm has reason to believe that the person was not complying with or was likely not to comply with the Takeover Code. The Panel publishes notices naming those who, in its opinion, have breached or are likely to breach the Takeover Code and the FSA expect firms to keep themselves informed of these notices.

The cooperation rule requires a firm whose permitted activities include any designated investment business to comply with a request by the Panel to provide it with information and documents to allow the Panel to perform its functions under the Takeover Code. In addition, at the Panel's request the firm must provide all such assistance as it reasonably can to allow the Panel to perform its functions under the Takeover Code.

A breach of either the cold-shoulder rule or the cooperation rule by a firm will allow the FSA to take enforcement action in the same way as it would for other rule breaches under the FSMA. The cold-shoulder rule is seen as an effective way of ensuring that both authorised persons to whom the rule applies and unregulated persons comply with the Takeover Code. It has been used only once since it was made, in 1992. The co-operation rule helps the Panel in investigating potential rule breaches and monitoring compliance with the Takeover Code.

11.4   Market abuse

11.4.1   Introduction

The introduction of provisions governing market abuse is designed to protect markets from abuse or malpractice in order to protect general investor confidence in those markets. The FSA and theTreasury have attempted to achieve a balance between a free and open market place and the prohibition of illegitimate activity.

Insider dealing is a criminal offence and is unaffected by the new regime; misleading statements and practices are illegal under Section 397 FSMA. Market abuse is a new civil regime introduced because of the perceived inability of the existing provisions properly to regulate market conduct due to the difficulty of successful criminal prosecution.

11.4.2 *Summary of market abuse regime*

This is examined more thoroughly in Chapter 8, but briefly market abuse consists of behaviour in relation to shares traded on any Regulated Investment Exchange ("RIE") where the behaviour:

(a) is based on information which is not generally available to those using the market but which, if available to a regular user of the market, would or would be likely to be regarded by him as relevant when deciding the terms on which transactions in investments of the kind in question should be effected ("Misuse of Information"); or

(b) is likely to give a regular user of the market a false or misleading impression as to the supply of, demand for, or as to the price or value of investments of the kind in question ("False or Misleading Impression"); or

(c) is likely to be regarded by a regular user of the market as behaviour which would, or would be likely to, distort the market in investments of the kind in question ("Market Distortion"); and

would be likely to be regarded by a regular user of the market as a failure on the part of the person concerned to observe the standard of behaviour reasonably to be expected of a person in the position of the person in question.

Market abuse is also committed by a person who requires or encourages another person to commit market abuse. It may be committed by anyone – not just by a firm regulated under the FSMA. There need not be an intent to abuse the market, it is the effect or likely effect which is relevant.

11.4.3 *Background to MAR*

Section 119 of FSMA requires the FSA to issue a code "containing such provisions as the Authority considers will give appropriate guidance to those determining whether or not behaviour amounts to market abuse". This is the Code of Market Conduct ("MAR").

MAR gives guidance on whether or not behaviour constitutes market abuse and includes descriptions of behaviour that, in the FSA's opinion do or do not amount to market abuse and factors that are to be taken into account in determining whether or not behaviour amounts to market abuse.

The "final" MAR was published in April 2001 (*Code of Market Conduct Feedback on CP 59 and CP 76*). MAR was amended on 19th July with some minor amendments. MAR now forms Chapter 1 of the FSA Market Conduct Sourcebook. It came into force on 1st December 2001.

In preparing MAR, the FSA has specifically stated that its objective is to provide a document which is not comprehensive or intended to give an answer for all circumstances but which will give an adequate level of detail and be more than merely "big picture" so that firms and advisers are able to form reasonable views on market abuse.

11.4.4   MAR safe harbours

MAR provides safe harbours for each of the three limbs of market abuse. Such a safe harbour is an absolute defence to a market abuse allegation, although it will be seen that the extent of available safe harbours is narrowly drawn.

The following provisions will be relevant in the context of takeover bids:

11.4.4.1   Misuse of Information

(A)   Dealing or arranging deals does not amount to Misuse of Information, if the possession of the relevant information that is not generally available did not influence the decision to deal or arrange a deal. This will be treated as being the case where the relevant information was held behind an effective Chinese wall and those who dealt were on the other side of it. This will, for example, protect firms acting as financial advisers to a prospective bidder where its dealing arm buys shares in the target in ignorance of the information within its corporate finance arm that a bid for the target might be launched.

(B)   Arranging deals consisting solely of the acquisition or disposal of an equity stake in a company by a person (or someone acting in concert with him) where the information concerned relates to the decision to purchase or sell that equity stake does not amount of Misuse of Information. This safe harbour will, for example, facilitate the following:

(1)   seeking from holders of securities irrevocable undertakings or expressions of support to accept or reject a takeover offer;

(2)   making arrangements for the issue of any consideration shares or other securities to be issued as consideration for a takeover offer or to fund it, for example, arranging a placing, rights issue or open offer;

(3)   making arrangements to offer cash as consideration for a takeover offer as an alternative to shares by means, for example, of a cash underpinning.

In addition, a person will not be prevented from acquiring a stake in a target company merely because he knows that he will be making a bid for it, nor will his advisers be prevented from acquiring interests on his behalf in such circumstances. This safe harbour will not cover situations where the adviser acquires interests on his own behalf or either party acquires merely economic exposure to the stock through, for example, the purchase of a derivative.

(C)   Agreeing to underwrite an issue of securities such as a rights issue or open offer to fund a takeover offer, will not of itself amount to misuse of information.

11.4.4.2   *False or Misleading Impression*

Making a disclosure will not of itself give rise to a False or Misleading Impression if the disclosure was made in the way specified by any applicable regulatory requirement and the disclosure was expressly required or permitted by the FSA's Conduct of Business Rules, the rules of a prescribed market or the rules of the Takeover Code or SARS or by any other applicable regulation. There is also a safe harbour which protects an organisation which releases false or misleading information where the person disseminating it does not realise it is false or misleading because he is unaware of some information held behind an effective Chinese Wall within the organisation.

11.4.5   *The Takeover Code and safe harbours*

The Panel has responsibilities to ensure fair and equal treatment of all shareholders in relation to takeovers. The Takeover Code provides a framework within which takeovers are conducted. In parallel the FSA must pursue its objectives of market confidence and integrity and, in doing so, aims to prevent, detect and deter market abuse. The FSA recognises that this will result in a common interest between the Panel and the FSA in any market abuse which may arise in the context of the takeover. Working together, the FSA and the Panel have adopted an approach which has resulted in the creation of safe harbours for provisions of the Takeover Code dealing with disclosure and publication, and the timing of both the standards of care for these types of announcements and rules where restrictions on dealing can be lifted with the Panel's consent.

However, for the purposes of the market abuse regime, it is the FSA not the Takeover Panel which decides whether provisions of the Takeover Code which benefit from the safe harbour have been complied with or whether there has been market abuse hence the need for the FSA to keep itself informed as to the way the Takeover Panel interprets the Takeover Code.

The FSA and the Panel will put in place operating arrangements enabling the FSA to do this within the takeover timetable.

If the relevant provisions of the Takeover Code have been complied with, then market abuse will not have occurred. However, it is important to note that if the provisions are not complied with, this does not necessarily mean that market abuse has occurred (although the Takeover Panel may take action against the individual or company for breach of its rules).

The safe harbours are not relevant to, and not available for the Misuse of Information element of market abuse. According to the FSA, this is because the criminal offence of insider dealing has been dealt with for a number of years by bodies such as the London Stock Exchange and the DTI without disrupting the takeover process. This suggests to both the Panel and the FSA that specific safe harbours for the Takeover Code are not required in this area.

Compliance with the Takeover Code may therefore give defence to a charge of market abuse in two ways:

(A)   Regular user test: A "regular user" would not regard behaviour in compliance with the restrictions on share acquisitions in the Takeover Code and SARs as giving false or misleading impressions and would take into consideration general compliance with the Takeover Code and SARs.

(B)   Safe harbours: as stated above certain provisions of the Takeover Code have been granted a safe harbour status. These provisions deal mainly with announcements, disclosures and other communications and releases of information, the timing, dissemination and contents thereof, and the standards of care that need to have been met. Under Section 120 FSMA, the FSMA is required to keep itself informed as to the way in which the Panel interprets and administers these provisions. As stated above these safe harbours are not relevant and are not available for the misuse of information element of market abuse.

11.4.6 Specific safe harbours under the Takeover Code and the SARs

The provisions of the Takeover Code and the SARs for which safe harbours are provided are set out below.

11.4.6.1 Takeover Code

Disclosure of information which is not generally available
Rule 1(a) – the offer must be put forward in the first instance to the board of the offeree company or its advisers.

Rule 2.1 plus notes – the maintenance of secrecy before an announcement.

Rule 2.5 – the announcement of a firm intention to make an offer.

Rule 2.6 – the obligation on the offeree company to circulate announcements.

Rule 2.9 plus notes – publication of an announcement about an offer or possible offer.

Rule 8 – disclosure of dealings during the offer period.

Rule 19.7 – distribution and availability of documents and announcements.

Rule 20.1 – equality of information to shareholders.

Rule 20.2 – equality of information to competing offerors.

Rule 20.3 – information to independent directors in management buy-outs.

Rule 28.4 – publication of reports and consent letters.

Rule 37.3(b) – public disclosure of redemption or purchase of securities by the offeree company.

Rule 37.4(a) – public disclosure of redemption or purchase of securities by the offeror company.

Standards of care
Rule 2.8 – statements of intention not to make an offer.

Rule 19.1 – standards of care relating to documents, advertisements and statements during the course of an offer.

Rule 19.5 second sentence and note 2 – use of previously published information *only* in telephone campaigns.

Rule 19.8 – information released following the ending of an offer period pursuant to Rule 12.2.

Rule 23 plus notes – the general obligation as to information.

Rule 28.1 – standards of care in relation to profit forecasts.

Timing of announcements, documentation and dealings
Rule 2.2 – when an announcement is required.

Rule 5.4 – disclosure of acquisitions from a single shareholder.

Rule 6.2(b) – announcing a revised offer following purchases after a Rule 2.5 announcement.

Rule 7.1 – immediate announcement required if the offer has to be amended.

Rule 11.1 note 6 only – announcement of a revised offer.

Rule 17.1 – timing and contents of announcements of acceptance levels.

Rule 21.2 – disclosure of inducement fees in Rule 2.5 announcement.

Rule 30 – posting the offer document and the offeree board circular.

Rule 31.6(c) – announcement on the 60th day.

Rule 31.9 – offeree company announcements after day 39.

Rule 33 (only in so far as it refers 31.6(c) and 31.9 only) – timing and revision in relation to alternative offers including cash alternatives.

Rule 38.5 – disclosure of dealings in relevant securities by an exempt market-maker.

Content of announcements
Rule 2.4 – the announcement of a possible offer.

Rule 19.3 – unacceptable statements.

11.4.6.2 SARs

Timing of disclosure
Rule 3 – disclosure.

Rule 4.1(a) and (e) – publishing tender offers and supplying copies of advertisements.

Rule 4.3 – circulation of tender offer and other documents.

Rule 4.4 – announcement of the results of a tender offer.

11.4.7 Guidance

The FSA recognises the novelty of the regime and will give guidance in relation to its operation. Guidance may take two forms:

(a) written guidance in relation to a particular circumstance. The FSA has stated that it will take no action against a person who has followed the FSA's written guidance provided that the guidance relates to specific circumstances. In other words, it will not provide a defence where it is relied on in analogous circumstances or where the FSA concludes that there has been non-disclosure of material facts. There will, of course, be the question as to whether the FSA could produce written guidance in time for any specific set of circumstances; and

(b) oral guidance will be provided on the basis of full disclosure of material issues. Firms will not be able to rely on this guidance to provide a defence to market abuse issues but the fact that guidance was sought will be a material issue.

11.5 Restrictions on sharedealing under the Takeover Code and the SARs

11.5.1 Introduction

The Takeover Code contains detailed rules which restrict share dealings in the context of a public offer. *Behaviour* in compliance with those provisions of the Takeover Code and the SARs which restrict the commercial freedom of a person by, for example, restricting the speed at which shares can be acquired (*see* Section 11.5.6 above), will not be regarded as giving a False or Misleading Impression, as such restrictions will be taken into account in assessing whether *behaviour* falls below the standard reasonably to be expected. The safe harbour is not available in any case where the *behaviour* which conforms with the particular rule of the Takeover Code is nonetheless in breach of any Takeover Code General Principle.

In cases where none of the safe harbours apply, the regular user may not necessarily consider that complying with applicable requirements of the Takeover Code or the SARs will be sufficient in and of itself to demonstrate that *behaviour* does not amount to market abuse. If, for example, a person were to comply with Rule 1 of the SARs in building a stake, but his decision to build the stake was based on *relevant information* and none of the safe harbours in MAR 1.4 then applied, that person's *behaviour* would be likely to amount to market abuse. Nevertheless, the question whether a person has complied with relevant provisions of the Takeover Code and the SARs which do not give a safe harbour may be relevant to a regular user's assessment of whether or not that person's *behaviour* has fallen below reasonably expected standards.

The principal restrictions on share dealing contained in the Takeover Code and the SARs are set out below.

11.5.2 Selling shares

The bidder can only sell shares in the target with the consent of the Panel and after a public announcement that it may sell (Takeover Code Rule 4.2). The bidder will not then be able to buy more shares or, except in exceptional circumstances, revise its offer.

11.5.3   *Dealing contrary to published advice*

Directors and advisers should not deal in shares in their company contrary to any advice they have given to their shareholders without giving sufficient notice of their intentions and an explanation (Takeover Code Rules 4.1 and 4.2, Note 5).

11.5.4   *Dealings by target advisers*

During the offer period, the target's financial advisers and brokers must not purchase target shares or deal in options or derivatives relating to them. Nor may they provide finance (other than in the ordinary course of business with established customers) or enter into any other arrangements to assist or induce others to do so (Takeover Code Rule 4.4).

11.5.5   *Acting in concert and associates*

Many parts of the Takeover Code (in particular those relating to shareholdings and dealings) apply not only to the bidder and the target, but also to those "acting in concert" with the bidder, to "associates" of the bidder or the target and to persons who have an indemnity or other arrangement with either side to induce that person to deal or not to deal.

"Acting in concert" is broadly defined under the Takeover Code. A person will be taken to be acting in concert with the bidder if, pursuant to an agreement or understanding (whether formal or informal), he actively cooperates, through the acquisition of shares, to obtain or consolidate control of the target. Certain categories of persons are presumed to be acting in concert with the bidder, for example its directors (together with their close relatives and related trusts), other group companies, financial advisers and stockbrokers.

"Associates" are defined by the Takeover Code as all persons (whether or not acting in concert) who directly or indirectly own or deal in the shares of the bidder or target and who have (in addition to their normal interests as shareholders) an interest or potential interest, whether commercial, financial or personal in the outcome of the offer. The Takeover Code gives examples of persons who will normally be associates. These include:

(a)   members of the target/bidder groups and their associated companies (shareholdings of 20 per cent or more);
(b)   target's/bidder's advisers and members of the advisers' groups;

(c) directors of members of target/bidder group (including associated companies);

(d) pension funds of members of target/bidder group (including associated companies); and

(e) funds under the discretionary management of other associates.

Anyone dealing under an indemnity or special arrangement is likely to be regarded as acting in concert or as an associate, as appropriate. Any such arrangement will usually have to be disclosed publicly.

11.5.6 *Timing of buying*

Some rules of the Takeover Code and the SARs affect the timing of any buying. The SARs slow down the rate at which a potential bidder can acquire shares or rights over shares (e.g. irrevocables) carrying voting rights between the levels of 15 per cent and 30 per cent. A potential bidder cannot buy shares or rights over shares carrying 10 per cent or more of the voting rights of the target during any seven day period if, as a result, it would hold between 15 per cent and 30 per cent of the target (SAR Rule 1). There are exceptions to this rule – in particular the SARs will not apply once the bidder has announced a firm intention to make an offer and a bidder will usually be able to secure irrevocables immediately before the announcement provided the offer is recommended by the board of the target (SAR Rule 2).

Where any person (together with those acting in concert with him) has shares or rights over shares representing less than 30per cent of the voting rights of the target he cannot buy through 30 per cent except in limited circumstances (Takeover Code Rule 5.1). Similarly where he holds over 30per cent, but less than 50per cent, he cannot buy any further shares. These rules apply even after an offer has been announced, but will not apply to a recommended offer. The restrictions fall away after the first closing date has passed provided there are no merger clearances outstanding (Takeover Code Rule 5.2).

11.5.7 *Disclosure of dealing*

In many cases, dealings by a bidder or potential bidder and by the target and their respective associates will have to be publicly disclosed.

Before the offer period (which starts with the announcement of an offer or possible offer):

(a)   if the bidder buys shares carrying 3 per cent or more of the voting rights of the target it must disclose its shareholding within two business days (Section 198 CA 1985). It must then make a further disclosure each time its shareholding exceeds a whole percentage point; and

(b)   if the bidder buys shares or acquires rights over shares it must if, as a result, it would hold shares or rights over them carrying 15 per cent or more of the voting rights of the target make an announcement by noon the following day (SAR Rule 3). Further announcements must be made each time the bidder increases such a stake beyond any whole percentage point.

There is a specific safe harbour limited to the timing of disclosures under SAR Rule 3.

During the offer period:

(a)   all dealings by the bidder or the target, and their respective associates; and

(b)   all dealings by anyone who has or buys 1 per cent or more of the target;

must be publicly announced by noon the following day (Takeover Code Rule 8).

There is a specific safe harbour limited to compliance with Takeover Code Rule 8 in relation to the disclosure of information which is not generally available.

Important points to note are:

(a)   "dealing" has a wide meaning and will include taking, granting or exercising an option;

(b)   the rule applies to all "relevant securities" which will include certain other classes of security in the company involved as well as options and derivatives; and

(c)   dealings in the bidder's shares only have to be disclosed where the bidder is offering its own securities as consideration.

11.5.8 *Where the bidder is listed*

If the bidder is listed on the official list of the UK Listing Authority, in addition to the above rules, some share purchases could have to be announced, or even be approved by shareholders in advance, if they fall within certain classes of transaction under the Listing Rules.

11.6 Communications in a public takeover

11.6.1 Introduction

The Takeover Code and the SARs contain detailed rules covering the supply of information and the making of statements during the course of an offer. *Behaviour* conforming with any of the rules of the Takeover Code or the SARs in relation to the timing, dissemination or availability, content and standard of care applicable to a disclosure, announcement, communication or release of information (*see* Section 11.5.6) does not of itself amount to market abuse in that the *behaviour* does not give rise to a False or Misleading Impression or Distortion in so far as the *behaviour* is expressly required or expressly permitted by the rule in question. This safe harbour is not available if the *behaviour* conforms with the particular rule but breaches any of the Takeover Code General Principles.

If the rule in question in the Takeover Code is about the timing of an announcement, then the safe harbour is conferred on the *behaviour* insofar as timing is relevant. However, the method of dissemination, the content and the standard of care will not be protected unless they are respectively in compliance with the relevant provisions of the Takeover Code or the SARs relating to dissemination, contents and standard of care.

It should be noted that many such communications will constitute invitations or inducements to engage in investment activity and so be subject to the financial promotion regime unless they are removed from the prohibition contained in Section 21 FSMA as a result of:

(a) the person making the communication being an authorised person; or

(b) the content of the communication being approved for the purposes of Section 21 FSMA by an authorised person.

The principal provisions relating to communications with shareholders, the press and the public are set out below.

11.6.2 *Sufficiency of information*

Shareholders must be given sufficient information and advice to enable them to reach a properly informed decision. They must have sufficient time to do so. No relevant information should be withheld from them (Takeover Code General Principle 4).

11.6.3 *Equality of information*

During the course of an offer, or when an offer is in contemplation, neither the bidder nor the target, nor any of their respective advisers may give information to some shareholders which is not made available to all shareholders (Takeover Code General Principle 2).

There is a specific safe harbour limited to compliance with Takeover Code Rule 20.1 in relation to making information about companies involved in an offer equally available to all shareholders as nearly as possible at the same time and in the same manner.

11.6.4 *Standards of information*

Any document or advertisement addressed to shareholders containing information or advice from a bidder or the board of the target or their respective advisers must, as is the case with a prospectus, be prepared with the highest standards of care and accuracy (Takeover Code General Principle 5).

There is a specific safe harbour limited to compliance with Takeover Code Rule 19.1 which sets standards of care in relation to the preparation and presentation of documents, advertisements and statements.

11.6.5 *Misleading statements*

All parties to an offer must use every endeavour to prevent the creation of a false market in the securities of the bidder or the target. They must take care that statements are not made which may mislead shareholders or the market (Takeover Code General Principle 6).

It is a criminal offence to make deliberately misleading statements to induce anyone to deal in shares (or not to deal) or to accept (or not accept), an offer (Section 47(1) FS Act).

11.6.6 Public statements

Those involved in an offer must take care not to issue statements which, while not factually inaccurate, may mislead shareholders or the market or create uncertainty (Takeover Code Rule 19.3). Examples are statements that:

(a) the bidder might increase or extend its offer (without actually committing itself to do so); or

(b) statements of a given level of support.

The Panel is likely to require that statements of this sort are clarified immediately. In some instances, misleading statements could even amount to criminal offences under the FS Act or the Theft Act 1986.

11.6.7 Statements to the press

The Directors of the bidder or the target should take great care when having any conversations with journalists. There is always the risk that remarks may be misunderstood or misattributed, which may lead to the Panel demanding that they are clarified or withdrawn. In particular, discussions relating to sensitive subjects, such as future profits, prospects and asset values should be avoided. For this reason, Directors should not speak to the press in person or by telephone unless they have been specially briefed by their financial advisers, or a representative of their financial advisers is present.

11.6.8 Profit forecasts, merger benefit and earnings enhancement statements

The Takeover Code contains detailed requirements to ensure that profit forecasts and asset valuations made by either side during an offer are properly verified (Takeover Code Rules 28 and 29). They may also cover any informal or unguarded statement, for example to the effect that "profits have grown this year". Similar rules apply to quantified statements about improved earnings or the perceived financial benefits of a merger if the offer is a share for share offer and is either hostile or a competing offer emerges (Takeover Code Rule 19.1 Note 8 and Rule 28.6(g)). If the statements cannot be properly verified, the Panel will usually insist that they are formally withdrawn. For this reason, great care must be taken not to make a statement which may, unintentionally, be treated as a profit forecast, asset, valuation, merger benefit or earnings enhancement statement.

There is a specific safe harbour limited to compliance with Takeover Code Rule 6.2(b) which sets standards of care in relation to the compilation of profit forecasts.

Usually, any profit forecast which has been made since the last financial results but before the commencement of an offer period must be examined, inspected and reported on in the document sent to shareholders.

11.6.9 Advertisements

The publication of advertisements in connection with an offer is prohibited unless the advertisement falls within the certain specified categories and (in some cases) has been cleared in advance by the Panel (Takeover Code Rule 19.4). In addition, most advertisements will need to be approved by financial advisers in order to comply with the FS Act.

11.6.10 Meetings

Meetings between the bidder or the target and shareholders are only allowed if shareholders are not given new information (Takeover Code Rules 20.1). The financial adviser to the bidder or the target must be at the meeting to see that the Takeover Code is complied with.

There is a specific safe harbour limited to compliance with Takeover Code Rule 20.1 in relation to making information about companies involved in an offer equally available to all shareholders as nearly as possible at the same time and in the same manner.

11.6.11 Telephone campaigns

The Takeover Code restricts the extent to which the bidder or the target may contact shareholders by telephone (Takeover Code Rules 4.3 and 19.5) as does Section 56 FS Act and the rules of other regulatory bodies. For this reason proposed meetings and telephone calls should be carefully discussed in advance with advisers.

11.7 Private M&A transactions

11.7.1 Use of information memorandum

Investment banks and sometimes other authorised financial advisers routinely prepare and distribute information memoranda in respect of companies or businesses proposed to be sold by vendors on behalf of whom they are acting. An information memorandum typically contains detailed financial and non-financial information concerning the target company or business which is intended to enable prospective purchasers to make an informed assessment of their interest or otherwise in entering into detailed negotiations for a purchase. Often the prospective purchaser will be required to give a non-binding indication of the price it expects to pay on the basis of the assessment it forms from the information memorandum.

In this Section the typical boilerplate disclaimers and other rubrics which should appear in such documents are explained or commented on.

11.7.2 Legal status of an information memorandum issued in contemplation of a sale

An information memorandum will in many cases be a financial promotion within Section 21 FSMA. This will be the case if (a) the property proposed to be sold includes "investments" within Schedule 2 FSMA, and (b) the information memorandum does not fall within one of the exemptions contained in the Financial Promotions Order.

If the proposed sale is of shares in a company, or of a business where the assets to be sold include shares (which may, e.g., be shares in subsidiaries of the vendor), then clearly these are "investments". But even where there is a business sale not including any shares, there may be other "investments" included, such as debentures, futures contracts, etc. The fact that any "investments" may be immaterial in the context of the proposed sale as a whole does not seem to permit the information memorandum to escape from being a financial promotion.

11.7.3 Financial Promotions Order exemptions

11.7.3.1 Article 19
There are various exemptions in the Financial Promotions Order which could be helpful, depending upon the circumstances. The one probably most frequently relied on in the past is the investment professional exemption which is now contained in Article 19 of the Financial Promotions Order and covers promotions made to persons authorised under the FSMA, persons whose ordinary activities involve investments, governments, local authorities and the directors, officers and employees of such organisations involved in investment activity.

11.7.3.2   Article 49

Another potentially useful exemption is in what is now Article 49 of the Financial Promotions Order, which covers high net worth body corporates, unincorporated associations and trustees and the directors, officers and employees of such organisations involved in investment activity. A high net worth body corporate is one having a called up share capital or net assets of:

(a)   in the case of a body corporate which has more than 20 members, or is a subsidiary undertaking, not less than £500,000; or

(b)   otherwise, of not less than £5 million.

Of considerably less use in most sales, are the new exemptions for certified high net worth individuals, and sophisticated investors, which are contained in Articles 48 and 50 of the Financial Promotions Order respectively. These are only likely to be of use in relation to very small transactions.

11.7.3.3   Article 62

There is also the exemption relating to sales of body corporates in what is now Article 62 of the Financial Promotions Order. The qualifying conditions are wide enough to cover most disposals of subsidiaries. The communication concerned must relate to a transaction comprising at least 50per cent (previously 75 per cent) of the voting shares of a body corporate (less any percentage already held by the acquirer) where the acquisition or disposal is, or is to be, between parties each of whom is a body corporate, a partnership a single individual or group of individuals.

11.7.3.4   *Combining exemptions*

There is a practical difficulty in combining the Article 19 exemption with the others. Although Article 11 of the Financial Promotions Order states that, in respect of a communication relating to controlled activities falling within any of paragraphs 3 to 11 of Schedule 1 (which covers all controlled activities other than insurance or accepting deposits), a "person" may rely on the application of one or more of the exemptions in Parts IV and V (which covers all the relevant exemptions). The investment professionals exemption applies to a communication made *only* to such persons and, although paragraph 19(6) states that a communication may be treated as made to investment professionals if it is also made to other persons to whom it may lawfully communicated, the wording of the specified rubric, limiting the availability of the investment to investment professionals and stating that others should not rely on the communication, effectively makes it impossible to combine this exemption with others. There is no difficulty in combining the high net worth corporates exemption in Article 49 with the sale of private company exemption in Article 62 (for this exemption no rubric is specified). For the Article 49 exemption the specified rubric limits the availability of the investment to persons within that exemption and any others to whom it may lawfully be directed.

The apparent difficulty of combining the Article 19 exemption with the others might be overcome by distributing copies of the information memorandum under different cover sheets, each with rubrics appropriate to the intended recipients, but it is uncertain whether they could really be regarded as separate communications for the purposes of the exemptions, and there might well be practical difficulties in ensuring that each version was sent only to the correct people.

In practice, it is likely to be found that the other exemptions will cover all the persons to whom it is desired to distribute the information memorandum without the need to make use of the investment professional exemption, although there may be difficulties where it is desired to distribute it to an FSA authorised person who is acting as agent for third parties as yet unknown. However, it would be normal only to distribute it to principals, who have already signed a confidentiality undertaking.

11.7.3.5 *Approval*
An alternative would be for the investment bank to approve the information memorandum under Section 21 FSMA, so that it can be distributed without having to worry whether the exemptions are satisfied. However, the investment bank may well be unwilling to do this, as it is unlikely to be satisfied that the information memorandum has been verified to a sufficiently high standard. An approver of a financial promotion communication will have the responsibilities set out in the Financial Promotions Order – *see* Chapter 3 of the FSA's Conduct of Business Sourcebook – including an obligation to take reasonable care to ensure that the communication is clear, fair and not misleading.

11.7.3.6 *Rubrics*
It should be mentioned that the specified rubrics are not compulsory. Both Articles contain safe harbour provisions under which if the rubrics are included, the communication is to be regarded as directed to the relevant persons. If they are not included the distributor of the communication takes his chance as to whether he can show that it was so directed. Best practice will therefore be to include the rubrics.

11.7.3.7 Disclaimers

Where an information memorandum is a financial promotion (i.e. as noted above, it relates to "investments" and it does not fall within an exemption), it was previously thought that it was not possible to avoid it being a financial promotion through the use of any disclaimer. The reality is that any such information memorandum issued to prospective purchasers in contemplation of a sale will contain information which is "calculated to lead directly or indirectly" to recipients entering into an investment agreement (Section 57(2) FS Act), whatever the strength of the disclaimers to the effect that the recipient should not rely on the document. This wording does not however appear in Section 21 FSMA, which refers only to a financial promotion being the communication of an "invitation or inducement" to engage in investment activity. It may be argued that disclaimer wording is effective to prevent the information memorandum being an invitation or inducement, but having regard to the purpose of the information memorandum which is to induce recipients to make offers for, or enter into discussions with a view to, the purchase of the target, this is probably not a sustainable view. It is probably an inducement, although not an invitation.

11.7.4 Danger of prospectus

Where the information memorandum relates in whole or part to shares or debentures of a company then, unless appropriate care is taken in drafting it, the document could constitute a prospectus within the definition in Section 744 CA 1985. As it will not be intended that the information memorandum should be a prospectus (since its content and distribution arrangements will not comply with the requirements applicable to prospectuses) it is normal to include language expressly directed at ensuring the document can not be treated as a prospectus.

11.7.5 Responsibility for content and responsibility for distribution

It is important that the roles and responsibilities of the investment bank or other financial adviser concerned and its vendor client should be clearly understood between themselves and be clear to prospective purchasers to whom the information memorandum is distributed, in relation to both (a) responsibility for the content of the document and (b) responsibility for the distribution of it.

Most often, the intention will be:

(a) that the bank's involvement should be such as to provide comfort (without legal recourse) to prospective purchasers that the information memorandum has been prepared to a reasonably high standard, with the benefit of its professional involvement; but

(b) the vendor and bank will want to ensure that the information memorandum does not give rise to any legal liability to prospective purchasers, even if it is substantially incorrect, on the basis that liability should be determined by the sale contract alone (to which the bank will not be a party).

These objectives are typically met by the bank issuing the information memorandum as its own document with the incorporation of an express statement that it has been prepared by the bank, but with its role clarified by express statements to the effect that:

(a) it has been prepared on the basis of information supplied by the vendor or the target which the bank has not verified or sought to verify;

(b) the bank has not approved it as a financial promotion pursuant to Section 21 FSMA;

(c) the vendor is the only party responsible for the information contained in the information memorandum;

(d) the document is issued by the bank as agent for the vendor (although this would doubtless be implied even without an express statement); and

(e) further disclaimers aiming to exclude liability in relation to the information memorandum.

11.7.6 Possible requirement for Section 240 CA 1985 statement

The information memorandum may contain information amounting to non-statutory accounts of the vendor or the target within the meaning of Section 240 CA 1985, in which case a statement complying with Section 240(3) CA 1985 should be included.

11.7.7 Contractual status of boilerplate/rubrics

In drafting or reviewing boilerplate, it is important to know whether or not it is intended to have contractual force between the bank as agent for the vendor on the one hand and the recipient of the information memorandum on the other. If the text is intended to impose *contractual* obligations (e.g. in relation to confidentiality, the use of the information memorandum or acceptance of the disclaimers) and these are not otherwise recorded, then for certainty, it will be necessary to provide for and obtain an express written acceptance of these. Information memoranda sometimes purport to provide for "deemed acceptance" if the document is not immediately returned, but on ordinary contract principles this would be inadequate.

Probably the best approach for the vendor and bank to take is as follows:

(a) require that a separate confidentiality undertaking is signed by prospective recipients of the information memorandum, which contains provisions excluding liability for the accuracy of the information supplied, including information comprised in the information memorandum, before the information memorandum is distributed; and

(b) do not incorporate further contractual obligations into the information memorandum, and so avoid the need for a further written acknowledgement or agreement at this stage.

11.7.8   Checklist of what the boilerplate should achieve

The boilerplate should be drafted so as to achieve the following (except where any is inappropriate for any reason):

(a) identify the authorised recipient to whom the copy is sent;

(b) specify or cross-refer to the confidentiality obligations of the recipient including restrictions on on-distribution;

(c) specify the purpose of the information memorandum and the context in which it is being distributed;

(d) guard against and disclaim any legal liability that might otherwise arise in respect of the information memorandum, to the extent this can be avoided;

(e) incorporate any necessary rubrics required by the bank in order to comply with its obligations under FSMA and any relevant FSA rules, or its own in-house compliance rules, or law in any jurisdiction in which the document will be distributed; and

(f) if appropriate, highlight any unusual features applicable to the provision of the information or any action the recipient is required to take upon or following receipt (e.g. if any of the boilerplate is to have contractual effect it may provide for written acceptance of this – but *see* Section 11.7.7(a).

11.7.9   Responsibility statements

In some (limited) circumstances it may be considered appropriate to include a positive responsibility statement, whereby the vendor or its directors or the bank, represent that, for example, they are satisfied that reasonable care has been taken in the preparation of the information memorandum (or perhaps in relation to a particular part – there may for example be a profit estimate for a past but unaudited period, or a profit forecast for the future). Alternatively, it might be appropriate to expressly accept some specified level of responsibility for the information in the document.

Such a responsibility statement may sometimes assist where there would otherwise be a questionmark in relation to the likely appeal to purchasers of what is being sold – there may, for example, have been a prior history of public problems in relation to the target, or the entities sold may be overseas where the vendor might in the absence of some acceptance of responsibility appear to be distancing itself from the information provided, or again the attractiveness of the target may be heavily dependent upon the reliability of estimated or projected financial information.

In any case where a positive responsibility statement is to be included it is essential that those accepting responsibility understand the effect of it, that appropriate verification or due diligence is in fact undertaken to support it, and that those involved in distributing the information memorandum obtain confirmations in writing of the acceptance of responsibility and otherwise take appropriate steps to protect themselves;

11.7.10   Protection of copyright

If the document is being distributed only in the UK, the inclusion of a copyright symbol is not necessary to protect the copyright of the originator of the document (but may nevertheless help inhibit copying in practice), but if it is being distributed in the US or in certain other jurisdictions it may be a necessary pre-condition to the availability of certain remedies.

11.7.11   Additional protections

The bank should protect itself in relation to the issue of any information memoranda by some or all of the following steps:

(a) ensuring that the extent of its responsibilities in relation to the preparation and issue of the information memorandum have been agreed in writing with its client and that the bank has been appropriately indemnified in relation to any liability that may arise by means of an indemnity contained in its engagement letter, or by means of a separate indemnity;

(b) taking appropriate steps to satisfy itself that the information memorandum is prepared to a suitably high standard to ensure compliance with the FSA requirements and the bank's in-house procedures, notwithstanding that there may be a disclaimer limiting the bank's responsibility;

(c) in particular, ensuring that the content, issue and distribution of the information memorandum is approved by the board or a duly authorised committee of the board of the vendor;

(d) possibly obtaining a representation letter from some or all of the directors of the vendor;

(e) taking appropriate legal advice in relation to any unusual features and any overseas aspects;

(f) if the bank is distributing the document and any reliance is being placed on an exemption under the Financial Promotions Order, ensuring that the bank takes appropriate steps (including possibly obtaining representation letters from potential recipients) to ensure copies are sent only to permitted recipients.

11.7.12   *Practical steps*

It should be borne in mind that:

(a) the information memorandum will have to be verified;

(b) the disclaimer wording clearly states that the information memorandum is a draft and that reliance should not be placed upon it;

(c) the bank will not in any case be prepared to distribute or allow the information memorandum to be distributed unless it is happy with its content; and

(d) the bank can ensure that it takes an appropriate indemnity and it is likely that the indemnity in the bank's engagement letter will be adequate to cover this.

Chapter 12

E-Commerce and Investment Banking

James Perry
Partner

David Toube
Barrister
Ashurst Morris Crisp

12.1   Introduction

The e-commerce frenzy has earned its place in the history books, alongside the South Sea Bubble and Dutch tulip mania. Nevertheless, although the initial excitement engendered by the "internet revolution" has abated, the use of the internet is firmly entrenched as an important part of the daily life of most players in the investment banking community. Accordingly, certain regulatory issues relevant to investment banking and e-commerce continue to arise. This Chapter explores some of these key issues.

However, two caveats need to be made. First, although the primary focus of this Chapter is the financial services regulatory law of the UK, it should be appreciated that, because the internet has a potentially global reach, it will not always be possible to take a parochial approach to e-commerce regulatory issues. It used to be said that the internet was unregulated and incapable of regulation. Although the second description is perhaps true, the first statement is not. The reality – at least as far as regulatory lawyers are concerned – is that the internet is the most regulated entity in history. Material carried on web pages and transactions carried out between parties which are in multiple jurisdictions may well be subject to the regulatory law of more than one state. Moreover, the provision of financial services tends to be particularly closely regulated in most countries. The regulatory approaches of different jurisdictions may well conflict with each other. Taken together, these factors make the global compliance an issue which is impossible to ignore. Of course, the compliance costs involved in carrying out an audit of every jurisdiction in the world mean that a pragmatic approach to global regulatory issues is usually necessary. Global compliance is often an aspiration, rather than an absolute. Accordingly, this Chapter does not seek to précis the regulatory law of every jurisdiction in the world. Instead, it touches upon some of the more influential international responses to e-commerce-related global compliance problems. From the UK perspective, this Chapter will chiefly consider the circumstances in which e-commerce related investment banking activities carried out from both within the UK and by overseas practitioners are likely to fall within the ambit of UK regulation.

Second, it should be remembered that the regulatory questions which emerge in the context of those activities which take place online are in essence no different from those which arise in the offline world. The internet is no more than another medium of communication. Therefore, in the majority of cases, the concerns raised by the use of the internet are similar to those which arise where any other medium of communication is employed. Many of the issues, as one might expect, will be familiar to traditional investment bankers who use telephones and letters rather than e-mails and webpages to communicate globally.

12.2   International compliance: themes and contexts

It is difficult to list all the circumstances in which regulatory issues involving the internet may arise. Indeed, during the passage of the Financial Services and Markets Act 2000 (the "FSMA"), the Government's approach was characterised by a recognition of the impossibility of adopting a "shopping list" approach to regulation, and by a set out, and desire to render the legislation "technologically neutral". A similar approach has been taken by the Financial Services Authority ("FSA").[1] Furthermore, the legislation itself has been drafted so that it is capable of adapting to innovations in financial services industry practice. Two of the most important parts of the FSMA – the Regulated Activities Order and the Financial Promotion Order – are to be found, not hard-wired into the body of the Act itself, but in statutory instruments; to the extent that new technologies require a different approach to be taken, the law may be amended in a relatively straightforward manner.

---

[1] The FSA's approach to the regulation of e-commerce, FSA Discussion Paper, June 2001.

12.2.1 *Verification of identity and system security*

The Financial Law Panel, in its Report on Jurisdiction and the Regulation of Financial Services on the Internet,[2] summarised the regulatory challenges presented by the internet as "validation: how do I know who you say you are?" and "encryption: how secure is the communication?". Validation of a person's identity is in many ways an easy problem to solve in theory: the financial services industry is used to carrying out identity checks from a money laundering and "know your client" perspective. The problem in practice may be that validation will involve a delay in access to material delivered via the internet while a person's identity is checked. It may also require the delivery of original documents which are only presently available in paper form. The delay caused by the verification process tends to destroy one of the significant advantages of communication by the internet: its immediacy. Encryption is a separate problem. Individuals, institutions and regulators alike have serious, and not always misplaced, concerns about the security of the internet. Security tends to be expensive, both in terms of the hardware and expertise which is necessary to ensure that security processes work. In the UK, the FSA takes the issue of security very seriously indeed: persons applying for a Part IV permission under the FSMA are required to fill in an Electronic Commerce Systems Form[3] which has ten sections, requires an enormous quantity of information and supporting documentation to be provided, and which must be reviewed and reported upon by the applicant's auditors. The nature of the information required is such that it will often need to be completed in-house by technical personnel who have little experience of dealing with a regulator.

12.2.2 *E-mail and websites*

It is worth making a distinction between material which is actively "pushed" to the reader and material which is "pulled" by them. For example, e-mail is now one of the traditional routes for communication between participants in any deal. In many ways, the use of e-mail is not qualitatively different from the use of surface mail or the international telephone network as a medium for communication and presents relatively few novel problems. By contrast, websites – and particularly websites which have not been password protected – are something of a different case, precisely because of the internet's versatility and

---

[2] October 1998, www.flpanel.demon.co.uk.
[3] Annex 1 to the FSA Application Pack.

accessibility. The information displayed on websites is open to everybody. Websites are easier to assemble, cheaper, have a broader territorial reach and are therefore more widely used than say, satellite television. Websites have been used for "webcasting": audio and visual presentations have been streamed online, where they can be viewed on demand by interested parties. Prospectuses and IPO documents and other similar publications can be displayed on webpages with minimal cost and effort. There can be few investment banks which do not have a website which may be used to communicate with their present and future customers: compliance officers will be well aware of the problems which such websites can present.

Material published on websites can be more "interactive" than newspapers and magazines; viewers can often immediately respond and interrelate with material on websites through the use of chat rooms and forums. The form and content of webpages can also be designed so that they may be tailored to the needs and preferences of each viewer. The use of search engines that index the content of the internet in a manner which makes the content of all webpages easy to search – mean that users frequently enter websites not from the front page, but at potentially any point within the website.[4] Therefore, to the extent that health warnings and disclaimers are encountered, any website design must take into account the possibility that a viewer may encounter sensitive issues without ever viewing those disclaimers.

12.2.3   A server does not know where your viewer is located

An issue is that it is difficult to block access to websites to persons from particular jurisdictions. Self-certification by website viewers – asking readers to click on buttons which identify the country in which they are located – are not regarded as effective in some jurisdictions. Unfortunately, IP logging[5] is not a failsafe way of identifying the location of the viewer: a person in France may have a "dot com" address rather than a "dot fr" address. Similarly, a person with a "dot uk" address might travel to Spain and log onto to a website in the USA remotely by telephoning

---

[4] Readers may care to connect to www.altavista.com and type in a common search term such as "IPO" or "mutual fund" to appreciate the nature of the problem.

[5] An IP address is the numeric version of an html://address: "DNS lookup" is employed in order to convert the "www.xxx.xxx" address into four groups of number which identify a computer on an internet. When a viewer accesses a webpage, their IP address is loggable by the server which receives the request for information.

a service provider in Germany. Neither are disclaimers and health warnings always the answer. To the extent that they do work in particular jurisdictions, global compliance can result in multi-jurisdictional disclaimers of dubious effectiveness and sometimes extreme length being drafted. Indeed, disclaimers are a recipe for conflict between compliance officers and aesthetically minded website designers.

12.3   The international perspective

It is not easy to generalise about international compliance. Although national regulators are increasingly awake to the problems presented by financial services e-commerce, some regulators are still adopting a "wait and see" approach. Many national regulatory regimes have been reformed in order to meet the challenges presented by e-commerce: the FSMA is a case in point. Many have not, and have typically employed guidance and other forms of quasi-legislation in order to perform the procrustean task of shoehorning the internet into the existing regulatory framework. The UK's experience in relation to the old "investment advertisement" regime under the Financial Services Act 1986 demonstrates some of the problems which manifest themselves when such an approach is adopted (*see* below).

Moreover, national regulators have yet to co-ordinate their approaches to financial services regulation at a global level. The International Organisation of Securities Commissions is a useful forum within which regulators may exchange information, provide mutual assistance, and cooperate with each other. It is not, however, a legislative body. In considering the nature of the problem, it is important to realise that national regulators are subject to the gravitational pull of conflicting policy approaches. At the highest level, they have an interest in maintaining the competitive position of their financial service industries which generally speaks in favour of deregulation and international co-operation. However, they will be concerned to protect market confidence and the interests of consumers (however they may be defined). At the most basic level they may – perhaps somewhat chauvinistically – simply think that their approach to regulatory problems is best or, like any bureaucracy, be reluctant to surrender their own authority. Put simply, regulatory regimes can and do differ significantly, and the approach to e-commerce regulation is no exception.

For the compliance officer of an investment bank the problem comes down to resources. Only the largest of financial institutions are in a position to conduct "global compliance exercises" and transactions are always subject to time constraints. In most circumstances, global compliance is ultimately an exercise in risk management, and is subject to budgetary constraints. When such issues arise in the context of transactions, advisors will need to consider in which jurisdictions there is a particular need for specific legal advice. Legal advice will typically be taken in relation to the jurisdictions whose regulatory systems are regarded as especially important, either because, for example, an offer is to be made to its nationals or because its regulators are particularly powerful or influential relation to the offering of securities and other investments.

12.3.1 High level consensus

Nevertheless, a high level consensus has developed between international regulators. Although this consensus cannot be relied upon in all circumstances, it is at least a sensible starting point. Regulators are more likely to assert their jurisdiction where the conduct affects, or potentially affects persons in their jurisdiction. IOSCO has published an Internet Report[6] which suggests that regulators should consider a series of factors when deciding to take action in relation to an offer of securities via the internet.

Factors which would justify a regulator taking enforcement action include:

(a)   the targeting of residents in the regulator's jurisdiction. For example, regulators in non-English speaking countries typically look to such indicia as whether the website is in the national language or whether the products offered are denominated in the local currency;

(b)   the acceptance of purchases from or provision of services to persons within the jurisdiction outside the scope of any applicable exception; and

(c)   the "pushing" of services to residents: for example, by sending e-mails to particular individuals in that jurisdiction.

---

[6] www.iosco.org.

Factors which tend not to lead to enforcement action being taken include:

(a) the use of health warnings or statements listing the jurisdictions in which the securities or services are authorised (or are not authorised) to be offered or provided;

(b) the clear identification of persons or classes of person to whom the offer is made, rather than "appearing to extend the offer into any jurisdiction"; and

(c) the maintaining of systems and controls which are designed to prevent the service or product being provided to person in the regulator's jurisdiction.

A good illustration of the "targeting" approach in practice is the position taken by the US SEC in relation to offshore internet offerings.[7] The SEC has interpreted the Securities Exchange Act of 1934 so as to require a non-US based broker or dealer to be registered under that Act. Likewise, an offshore investment or securities company may need to be registered under the Investment Company Act of 1940 or the Securities Act of 1933. Similarly, the Investment Advisers Act of 1940 may impose such a requirement upon an investment adviser. However, if a website is not targeted at persons in the US, then the obligation to register is not applied. The SEC has indicated that an offshore offer will be considered not to be so targeted if:

(a) the website includes a prominent disclaimer which makes it clear that the offer is directed only to countries other than the US; and

(b) the website offeror implements procedures that are "reasonably designed to guard against sales to U.S. persons".

In practice therefore it will be sensible to include a statement on a website to the effect that the securities are not available either to US persons or in the US. Similarly, it will be prudent to ensure that any purchaser of securities gives a valid non-US address (which can be checked against an electoral register or telephone directory, if appropriate). Likewise, effective systems and controls should be sensitive to attempts to circumvent these safeguards: if a prospective purchaser attempted to pay for products or services from a US bank account, at the very least, further enquiries should be made of that person.

---

[7] SEC Release No. 33-7516: Statement of the Commission regarding use of internet websites to offer securities, solicit securities transactions or advertise investment opportunities offshore, 23 March 2000: SEC Release No. 33-7856, "Use of electronic media", April 2000.

12.3.2 International co-operation between regulators

There is a degree of international co-operation between regulators in relation to enforcement. The practical problem which national regulators face is that of asserting jurisdiction in circumstances in which they would have problems in enforcing any order which they might choose to make. Accordingly, the most important national regulators have entered into memoranda of understanding ("MoU") which facilitate co-operation between the regulators. For example, on 27 October 1997, the FSA and the Bank of England entered into a MoU with the CFTC and the SEC in the USA governing exchanges of information between the institutions.

The FSMA also contains mechanisms which enable the FSA to exercise its powers in support of any overseas regulator which is recognised as a competent regulator. First, the FSA may deploy its broad investigatory power in support of an overseas regulator.[8] Secondly, the FSA may exercise various powers of intervention in relation to an EEA firm or a Treaty firm at the request of or for the purpose of assisting an overseas regulator.[9]

12.3.3 The European Union (the "EU")

In the longer term, it is to be hoped the Committee of Wise Men's Report on the Regulation of European Securities Markets (the "Lamfalussy Report") will ultimately result in more rapid and extensive integration between the integrating measures taken by member states in implementing the framework principles of directives, and that the roles of the European Securities Committee ("ESC") and the Committee of European Securities Regulators ("CESR") envisaged by the Lamfalussy Report will result in increased co-operation between EU securities regulators. The real challenge from a European perspective is to achieve harmonisation of conduct of business rules: although resistance to reform has been strong. Nevertheless, it is the disparity at this level of regulation that presents the real impediment to internet based investment banking activities including marketing, offering and dealing in securities. The only sensible solution is to move towards home state regulation of not only prudential but also conduct of business regulation.

Account will need to be taken, where appropriate of the Electronic Commerce Directive, (Directive 2000/31/EC of the European Parliament

---

[8] Section 169 FSMA.
[9] Section 195 FSMA.

and of the Council of 8 June 2000 on certain legal aspects of information society services, in particular electronic commerce, in the Internal Market: OJ L178 of 17 July 2000) which imposes a limited "country of origin" regulatory approach. The Directive must be implemented by member states by 16 January 2002. In particular, implementing states will be under an obligation to ensure that financial services provided by firms comply with those requirements which fall within the Directive's "co-ordinated field", and will not be in a position to restrict the freedom to provide services falling within the co-ordinated field. There are however important derogations from the Directive within the field of financial services: the Directive is not a panacea, and firms are likely to continue to require compliance advice in each jurisdiction.

12.4   UK compliance issues

The FSA has taken the challenge presented by e-commerce seriously, and in 2000 embarked upon a review of its approach to e-commerce. The FSA has also identified 17 "priority risks" arising from e-commerce, in terms of both business risks (i.e., risks which regulated firms face, such as exposure to financial fraud) and regulatory risks arising within FSA itself (such as failures which arise from the application of regulatory require-ments which are inappropriate in the context of e-commerce) that the FSA is determined to tackle. The FSA's provisional conclusions[10] were that work would need to focus on the following three areas:

(a)   ensuring that the IT systems and controls of firms and markets appropriately address the risks in their businesses. The FSA does not propose to set detailed standards for the systems and controls which a regulated firm should employ; judgment on that issue is reserved to the senior management of the firm;

(b)   ensuring that consumers have access to relevant and comprehens-ible information and guidance relating to obtaining financial services, and that they understand that they "have a responsibility to protect themselves from the risks they can best manage"; and

(c)   ensuring that the FSA adapts regulation to developments in e-commerce. For example, the FSA is considering creating a *.fin (or a *.fin.uk) domain name which would be both compulsory for, and only open to, regulated firms.

---

[10] The FSA's approach to the regulation of e-commerce, FSA Discussion Paper, June 2001.

The third of these concerns will be of marginal relevance to investment banking: the first two will be of fundamental importance.

Investment banking regulatory concerns in the UK fall into two broad categories. First, certain activities when carried out online may result in the participants requiring a license. Although it will generally be easy to predict cases where those activities will fall within the scope of regulation, fine judgements may need to be taken in borderline cases. Secondly, merely the publication of investment-related material may require the preparation and filing of a prospectus and/or the intervention of a licensed/authorised investment professional. In the UK, a distinction between these two issues is enshrined in the FSMA; the distinction being between the carrying on of "regulated activities"[11] in the UK by way of business (on the one hand) and engaging in "financial promotion"[12] (on the other). Furthermore, where securities are being offered to the public for the first time, it may be necessary to consider the application of the Public Offers of Securities Regulations 1995 (the "POS Regulations") or Official Listing prospectus requirements in the FSMA to that offer.[13] The interplay between these three parallel regimes and traditional investment banking activities will only be considered here to the extent necessary for the purposes of discussing the interplay between the UK securities law and e-commerce.

12.4.1 UK regulation: regulated activities and overseas persons

Investment banking services which constitute the regulated activities of dealing in investments, arranging deals in investments or advising on investments will frequently be provided by persons who are outside the UK, to UK persons.

Under the FSMA, a person who breaches the "general prohibition"[14] may be guilty of a criminal offence, and if convicted may be imprisoned for two years or be liable to be fined.[15] Significantly, breach of the general prohibition can also result in agreements being unenforceable against the counterparty. The general prohibition provides that no person may carry

---

[11] Section 22 FSMA; The Financial Services and Markets Act 2000 (Regulated Activities) Order 2001 (SI 2001/544).

[12] Section 21 FSMA; The Financial Services and Markets Act 2000 (Financial Promotion) Order 2001 (SI 2001/1335).

[13] (SI 1995/1537).

[14] Section 19 FSMA.

[15] Section 23(1) FSMA.

on a regulated activity in the UK, or purport to do so, unless he is an authorised person or an exempt person.[16] An "authorised person"[17] is a person who has a "permission"[18] to carry on one or more regulated activities or an "EEA firm" or "Treaty firm".[19] Are investment bankers who provide their services remotely from New York in danger of imprisonment when they step of the plane at Heathrow. The answer, in most cases, is that they are not.

12.4.1.1 *The general prohibition and the territorial scope of the FSMA*

The territorial reach of the FSMA is not clearly set out in the Act. Readers familiar with the Financial Services Act 1986 (the "1986 Act") will recall that a person fell within the scope of regulation if (broadly) he carried on investment business either from a permanent place of business maintained by him in the UK, or in a way which constituted the carrying on of a business in the UK. There is no similar explicit statement of territorial scope in the FSMA. However, the overseas person exemptions, which are discussed below, will usually have the effect of taking certain services outside the definition of regulated activities in the FSMA.

In any event, a regulated service provided by an investment banker in New York to a person in London will not, in most cases, fall within the territorial scope of UK regulation, as a matter of English law. In many cases, it can be said that the activity is carried on overseas and not in the UK at all. Accordingly, the general prohibition will not be breached.

In very brief summary, the best view in relation to various regulated activities is as follows:

(a) A deposit is accepted at the physical location at which the liability to repay it has been assumed, which ordinarily will be taken to be the office at which the deposit is held.[20]

(b) Purchases and sales of investments are, under English common law, generally concluded at the physical location where the acceptance of an offer has been received by the offeror if the method of communication of the acceptance is in real-time,[21] although the question may still be open in relation to e-commerce.

---

[16] *See* Section 38 FSMA: for example, International Monetary Fund.

[17] Section 31 FSMA.

[18] Part IV FSMA.

[19] *See* Schedules 3 or 4 FSMA.

[20] *Joachimson* v *Swiss Bank Corp* (1921) 3 KB 110.

[21] *Entores Ltd* v *Miles Far East Corp* [1955] 2QB327.

(c)   The FSA is of the view that investments are managed at the physical location at which the investment manager is present when it is taking investment decisions.[22]

(d)   The FSA generally considers that arranging deals in investments takes place at the physical location where the arranger is located. For example, "book building" or syndication arrangements carried out, at least in part, through e-mail correspondence, is probably carried on where the arranger is to be found, rather than in jurisdiction in which the recipient is located.

(e)   Conversely, it is not clear whether investment advice is given at the physical location where it is provided or at the physical location where it is received, although the FSA has previously indicated that it treats investment advice as being given at the place where it is received.

It should also be noted that the European Commission has argued that where "cross-border" services are provided under the Banking Consolidation Directive[23] the service is provided at its place of "characteristic performance", and that the service will frequently be performed at the location where the provider of the service, rather than the customer, is located. Accordingly, the Commission has stated:

> "the provision of distance banking services, for example through the Internet, should not, in the Commission's view require prior notification, since the supplier cannot be deemed to be pursuing its activities in the customer's territory."[24]

This position is likely to be correct in relation to the Investment Services Directive ("ISD"). Unfortunately, this is not a view which is shared by many European regulators.

12.4.1.2   *The overseas persons exemptions*

Nevertheless, in most cases, the issues discussed in the previous section are theoretical, and will not require a definitive answer. Rather, the remote provider of the investment banking services in question may be

---

[22] "Carrying on Investment Business in the United Kingdom": Securities and Investments Board, Consultative Paper No. 19 (March 1989).

[23] (2000/12/EC).

[24] Commission of the European Communities, Interpretative Communication: "Freedom to provide services and the interest of the general good in the Second Banking Directive" (SEC (97) 1193), June 1997.

in a position to take advantage of the "overseas persons" exemptions contained in the Regulated Activities Order.[25]

An overseas person is a person who neither carries on nor offers to carry on regulated activities, from a permanent place of business maintained by him in the UK.[26] In most cases, this description will cover investment professionals employed by overseas firms. The exemption will assist an overseas person who carries out various regulated activities including dealing in investments as a principal or as an agent, managing investments, or providing investment advice. It should be noted that the overseas person exemption does not cover either deposit-taking and insurance activities.

In order to fall within the scope of the overseas person exemptions, an overseas person must, broadly speaking either:

(a) deal or arrange deals in investments with or through an authorised person or exempt person; or
(b) deal or arrange deals in investments, manage investments or give investment advice resulting from a "legitimate approach".

A legitimate approach is defined as either an approach made to the overseas person which is either unsolicited, or which has been solicited in a manner which does not breach the financial promotion regime[27] or alternatively an, approach made by the overseas person in a manner which does not breach the financial promotion regime (*see* below). Though these exemptions need to be considered carefully in each case, they will often apply to inter-professional business in the M&A and capital markets where overseas firms market or provide services to UK companies or investors.

For the sake of completeness, it should be noted that although EEA "investment firms" may be in a position to passport their services into the UK under the ISD when they propose to do business with a person in the UK remotely via the internet (*see* below), it will often be possible for them to use the overseas person exemptions rather than relying upon their passports.

---

25 Articles 65 and 72 The Financial Services and Markets Act 2000 (Regulated Activities) Order 2001 (SI 2001/544).
26 Article 3, The Financial Services and Markets Act 2000 (Regulated Activities) Order 2001 (SI 2001/544).
27 Section 21 FSMA.

12.4.1.3 *Passporting and the ISD*

A firm which qualifies under the Banking Consolidation Directive 2000 or the ISD can receive a single market "passport" to provide cross-border services in different EEA states which obviates the need to obtain a regulatory licence for each relevant EEA state in which it does business. Accordingly, qualifying firms are licensed by their "home state" and are supervised on the basis of harmonised prudential standards. Once they have passported their services into the "host state", they are subject to conduct of business rules imposed by that state.

As has been observed above, qualifying EEA firms which might carry out occasional investment banking activities remotely through the medium of the internet with persons in the UK will rarely need to passport their services cross border, on the basis that the overseas person "carve-outs" should apply in most cases. However, this is an option which is theoretically open to such firms: the process by which passporting rights may be exercised are set out in schedule 3 to the FSMA.

In addition, schedule 4 to the FSMA creates the new concept of a "Treaty firm" which is a firm that is authorised to carry on a regulated activity in an EEA state in which it also has its head office, but which has no right to use a "passport" for services in the manner in which it seeks to provide them. Such firms may qualify for authorisation, and thereafter provide services cross border into the UK. However, such a step is of course unlikely to be taken merely to facilitate low level e-commerce based cross border activities which will often be covered by the overseas person exemptions.

12.4.2 *Financial Promotion, the POS Regulations and Offers of Listed Securities*

Even though a provider of investment banking services who is located overseas may not need to be authorised under the FSMA, it may nevertheless need to comply with the financial promotion regime and (where relevant) the POS Regulations. Therefore, an investment banker in New York who sends an e-mail to a person in the UK, or who puts up a password protected website containing, for example, an offering circular for Euro-denominated notes may well not breach the general prohibition. However, depending upon the person to whom the e-mail is sent or the password is provided, he may well fall foul of the Financial Promotion regime or may breach the POS Regulations. The potential consequences of such a breach are just as serious as breach of the general prohibition.

Financial promotion is extensively dealt with in Chapter 7 of this Guide. Accordingly, this Chapter does no more than touch upon the issues as they apply to communications through the internet and the two should therefore be read together.

12.4.3 Financial Promotion

The financial promotion regime[28] governs communications that are made in the course of business and which amount to invitations or inducements to engage in investment activity. Engaging in investment activity is defined as:

(a) entering into an agreement the making or performance of which by either party constitutes a controlled activity; or

(b) exercising any rights conferred by a controlled investment to acquire, dispose of, underwrite or convert a controlled investment.

The financial promotion regime prohibits the communication of such an invitation or inducement unless made by an authorised person, or unless its content is "approved" by an authorised person. The "approval" process may be time-consuming and expensive to conduct, in part because approver may well need to conduct or arrange a verification exercise in relation to the communication which is to be issued. Under Section 25(1) FSMA a person who contravenes the prohibition is liable to a term of imprisonment of up to two years or a fine or both. Furthermore, agreements resulting from unlawful communications may be unenforceable, and may also result in a claim for compensation or restitution.

It goes without saying that the global webpages of firms with a regulated UK establishment will as a matter of course be approved. Even when the webpages in question are issued by a non-regulated third party, but a UK authorised firm is involved in a transaction, the prudent course will often be for the pages to be approved. The flexibility of hypertext markup language may sometimes make it difficult to know how to apply rules to webpages; however, specific guidance on the application of the financial promotion rules to the internet and to other electronic media is set out at 3.14 of the Conduct of Business Rules. When a webpage is to be approved, it will be necessary to bear in mind the differences between electronic and conventional material. For example, the content of

---

[28] Section 21 FSMA.

webpages can be relatively easily altered, and so it often will be altered. It is important to put procedures in place to make sure that a webpage is not re-written without being re-approved, where necessary.

12.4.4   Real time and non real time communications

The financial promotion regime encompasses not only those communications that were investment advertisements under the previous regime; it also includes methods of communication which previously were described as "unsolicited calls". The FSMA itself does not distinguish between the two classes of communication. However a distinction between the two is maintained in the Financial Promotion Order,[29] which employs the terms "real time" and "non-real time" communication to distinguish between the two species of communication. Real time communications are "any communication made in the course of a personal visit, telephone conversation or other interactive dialogue". By contrast, a non-real time communication is defined as any other species of communication. The primary significance of the distinction is that certain exemptions from the financial promotion regime are not made available to real time communications.

From the perspective of persons communicating financial promotions during the course of investment banking business carried out through the internet – with the exception of live company or analyst presentations streamed from a website – the distinction will not be particularly significant. Article 7(3) fortunately makes it clear that e-mail communications are non-real time communications. It is also clear that a web page will ordinarily qualify as a non-real time communication.[30] The position of communications made, for example, through the medium of an internet chat room is moot, and will depend upon the presence of the following factors, set out in Article 7(5):

(a)   the communication is made to or directed at more than one recipient in identical terms (save for details of the recipient's identity);

(b)   the communication is made or directed by way of a system which in the normal course constitutes or creates a record of the communication which is available to the recipient to refer to at a later time;

---

[29] The Financial Services and Markets Act 2000 (Financial Promotion) Order 2001 (SI 2001/1335).

[30] FSA Handbook, Conduct of Business Rules 3.14.3.

(c)   the communication is made or directed by way of a system which in the normal course does not enable or require the recipient to respond immediately to it.

However, it is difficult to think of circumstances in the ordinary course where an investment banker will be well advised to do business through an internet chat room, and accordingly factors are unlikely to be relevant.

12.4.5   The key exemptions

The FSMA provides a series of exemptions which will, in many cases, allow overseas providers of investment banking services to use e-mail and (within certain limits) websites for financial promotion. If a communication falls within the scope of an exemption, it falls outside the scope of the financial promotion regime. The key exemptions are as follows:

12.4.5.1   Investment professionals
One of the most frequently used exemptions is the "investment professionals" exemption, which applies to communications which are either made only to recipients whom the person making the communication believes on reasonable grounds to be investment professionals or may reasonably be regarded as directed only at such persons.

The definition of "investment professional" includes authorised persons and any other person:

(a)   whose ordinary activities involve him in carrying on the controlled activity to which the communication relates for the purpose of a business carried on by him; or

(b)   who it is reasonable to expect will carry on such activity for the purposes of a business carried on by him.

Again, the "directed at" variation of the exemption might assist a person who wished to put up a non-password-protected website aimed at investment professionals. However, it will normally be prudent to password protect a website and not to rely upon the "directed at" test. If password protection is not feasible, all is not lost. The investment professionals exemption sets out three conditions which play a role in establishing whether a non-password protected website is directed at persons falling within the exemption. If all three conditions are met, then the exemption applies. If one or more condition is met, this must be taken into account in deciding whether the communication is directed to investment professionals; however even if no condition is met, it may still be regarded as directed at investment professionals. The conditions are as follows:

(a)   the communication is accompanied by an indication that it is directed at persons having professional experience in matters relating to investments and that any investment activity[31] to which it relates will be engaged in only with such persons;

(b)   the communication is accompanied by an indication that persons who do not have professional experience in matters relating to investments should not rely on it; and

(c)   there are in place proper systems to prevent recipients other than investment professionals engaging in the investment activity to which the communication relates.

The first two conditions can be satisfied by the use of a "health warning". The third condition will require off-line procedures to be implemented for "professionals-only" offerings and may prove more difficult in practice to satisfy.

12.4.5.2   *High net worth entities, etc.*

An equally helpful exemption permits communications to be made either to recipients whom the person making the communication believes on reasonable grounds to be qualifying high net worth entities or which may reasonably be regarded as directed only at such persons. The exemption has its origin in the former Article 11 Financial Services Act 1986 (Investment Advertisements) (Exemptions) Order 1996. Again, the "directed at" test relies upon three conditions, which perform a similar role to the conditions contained in the investment professionals' exemption. The high net worth exemption permits unapproved e-mails to be sent to bodies corporate with more than 20 members (or which is a subsidiary undertaking of a parent undertaking which has more than 20 members), called-up share capital or net assets of not less than £500,000, and trustees of trusts with assets of at least £10 million.

12.4.5.3   *Individuals*

As one would expect, considerable care needs to be taken in relation to electronic communications to or directed at individuals who are not investment professionals. In many circumstances, such communications will fall within the scope of another exemption – for example, because

---

[31] As defined in Section 21(8) FSMA: *see* above.

they are required or permitted by the rules of a relevant market[32] (e.g. prospectuses or other "permitted documents" advertising an IPO or secondary offering), or because the individual is a member or creditor of the company making the communication or a group company[33] or because the individual is an employee of the company making the communication.[34]

However, what if no such exemption applies? Under the previous regime, UK and overseas investment professionals were sometimes surprised to discover that communications to sophisticated or high net worth individuals needed to be issued or approved as investment advertisements (because some regulatory regimes permit such communications, including that in the US, provided certain conditions are satisfied. The Financial Services Act 1986 did not. The position is now different. The Financial Promotions Order contains two particularly helpful new exemptions for sophisticated investors and high net worth individuals. Unfortunately both exemptions are somewhat cumbersome, and particular care must be taken that the person to whom the communication is addressed actually does fall within the scope of the exemption. The sophisticated investors exemption requires that the recipient must have a current certificate signed by an authorised person to the effect that that person is sufficiently knowledgeable to understand the risks associated with that description of investment, signed and dated not more than three years before the date on which the communication is made.[35] Therefore, a copy of the certificate will need to be obtained before any communication is sent out. Additionally, the recipient must have signed, within the period of 12 months ending with the day on which the communication is made, a statement declaring that he is a sophisticated investor. As one might imagine, these steps will not always be easy to take, particularly if the issue is only recognised at a late stage before a transaction is due to be signed or announced. Finally, a "health warning" statement needs to be included with the communication.

The exemption for certified high net worth individuals[36] works in a similar manner, except that the recipient must have a current certificate of high net worth in legible form signed by the recipient's accountant or by the recipient's employer, which has been signed and dated within the

---

[32] Article 67 Financial Promotion Order.
[33] Article 43 Financial Promotion Order.
[34] Article 60 Financial Promotion Order.
[35] Article 50(4) Financial Promotion Order.
[36] Article 48 Financial Promotion Order.

period of 12 months ending with the day on which the communication is made,[37] stating that the person had an annual income of not less than £100,000 during the preceding year, or had net assets of not less than £250,000,[38] excluding the value of the recipient's house, pensions and various other property. Again, the certificate may not always be particularly easy to obtain at short notice.

The importance of taking these steps must be stressed. The exemption requires that communications be made to persons who have been appropriately certified: it is not sufficient that they be directed to such persons. Accordingly, it will often be the case that a communication by an overseas person to individuals falling within either of these two classes will need to be approved either on a prudential basis, or because it is simply the easiest step to take.

12.4.6   Territorial scope: "inward" communications

This Chapter deals primarily with persons who wish to communicate a financial promotion to persons in the UK. However, it is worth considering the position of a person who is outside the UK and who wishes to make a communication through the internet in a manner that results in its inadvertently being received by a person in the UK, even though this is not the primary intent of the communicator (e.g. an issuer which places its prospectus on a French website for solely domestic consumption). For example, such a person might put material on a website which constitutes a regulated communication and which is accessible from within the UK. The FSMA provides for an exemption for what one might term inadvertent "inward" communications. The exemption covers communications originating outside the UK (including, inter alia, overseas websites) which are *directed* only at persons outside the UK, notwithstanding that they may also be received within the UK.[39] The exemption operates by reference to certain "conditions". If:

(a)   the communication is not referred to in, or directly accessible from, any other communication which is made to a person or directed at persons in the UK by the same person; and

(b)   there are in place proper procedures to prevent recipients in the UK (other than those to whom the communication might otherwise lawfully have been made) engaging in that investment activity,

---

[37]   Article 48(3)(b) Financial Promotion Order.
[38]   Article 48(3)(c) Financial Promotion Order.
[39]   Article 12 Financial Promotion Order.

then the exemption will apply. The exemption may still apply if only one of the conditions, or if the other conditions are fulfilled. Indeed, it may still apply if none of the conditions is met but it can be established that it is not directed at persons in the UK.

Nevertheless, it will be prudent to include a "health warning" which fulfils two of the other article 12(4) conditions by making it clear that the communication is directed only at persons outside the UK and must not be acted upon by persons in the UK. Moreover, if the website is to be aimed at persons in the UK who fall within the scope of another exemption it will always be sensible to password protect a website and to issue the passwords only to persons who have been identified as falling within the scope of that exemption, if such a course of action is practicable.

12.4.7 The POS Regulations, Offers of Listed Securities

The FSMA's financial promotion regime is only one of the hurdles that need to be surmounted when a communication is sent electronically by a person outside the UK to a recipient in the UK. Under the POS Regulations, when securities are offered to the public for the first time, the offeror must publish a prospectus. Fortunately, the financial promotion regime is disapplied if the POS Regulations apply to an offer.[40] If an exemption applies, the financial promotion regime may still need to be considered.

If a prospectus needs to be published, the Regulations provide that such an offer of securities must:

(a)   comply with certain burdensome form and content requirements; and
(b)   be presented in a form which is as easily analysable and comprehensible as possible; and
(c)   contain all such information as investors would reasonably require and reasonably expect to find there, for the purpose of making an informed assessment of:
    (i)   the assets and liabilities, financial position, profits and losses and prospects of the issuer of the securities; and
    (ii)   the rights attaching to those securities.

---

[40] Article 72 Financial Promotion Order.

The POS Regulations provide that if information which is required to be included in the Prospectus by virtue of the form and content requirements is omitted, or if the prospectus contains an untrue or misleading statement, and as a result of either default, an investor has suffered loss in respect of the securities which he or she has purchased, the persons responsible for the Prospectus will be liable to compensate that investor. Likewise, under Section 84 FSMA and the Listing Rules, a compliant prospectus must be approved by the FSA, and published. If a prospectus is to be published, care must be taken to ensure that any internet version of such a document meets the contents and form requirements of the appropriate rules. Normally, such documents are electronically published in the Adobe Portable Document Format ("PDF") which ensures that the document which is delivered to the readers' screen looks very much like the printed version of the document.

Over the last few years, an increasing number of IPOs have been conducted online. In addition a number of specialist web portals have been established which serve the needs of persons who intend to make offers to the public. Such offerings have not been wholly unproblematic, but they are now sufficiently common that a reasonably consistent market practice has developed in relation to such offerings. It is, broadly speaking, possible to conduct a public offering online, intentionally (as opposed to fortuitously) directed to the UK in compliance with UK securities laws.

12.4.8   *Exemptions from the POS Regulations*

However, the more difficult problem arises when an overseas person wishes to use a website to broadcast material which, prima facie, might constitute a public offer of securities. If that person is not practically able to comply with the requirements governing the issue of a prospectus, but wishes to make an offer to at least some persons in the UK, it will be necessary to bring the offer within the scope of one of the exemptions established by Article 7 POS Regulations. Offers which fall within the scope of an exemption are deemed not to be an offer to the public in the UK. Certain, but not all, of the exemptions are cumulative, and if more than one exemption is to be employed, it is important to check that the exemptions may effectively be used together.

Most investment professionals will be reluctant to password protect a website through which a public offer of securities takes place. Password protection will not always be necessary if, for example, the exemption requires that the minimum consideration which may be paid by any person for securities acquired by him pursuant to the offer is at least €40,000 (or an equivalent amount).[41] However, in certain circumstances, password protection may well be necessary. For example, the exemption which requires that the securities are offered to no more than 50 persons[42] can only safely be operated if the website is password protected.

If an exemption which is premised upon access to the offer by a restricted number of class of persons is to be relied upon, and a password protection system is to be used as the method by which access to the website is restricted, it will be sensible to retain a list of the persons to whom the password is issued (and to whom the offer is therefore made). The ordinary precautions which one normally takes in issuing conventional publications should also be taken; for example, those persons who receive passwords should as a matter of good practice undertake not to pass them on to third parties, and so on, just as they would with a paper-based publication. In addition, it will be vital that the system relies not only upon password protection, but also rests upon effective systems and controls to ensure that persons who have improperly gained access to the website are not able to participate in the public offering.

---

[41] Article 7(i) POS Regulations.
[42] Article 7(b) POS Regulations.

Chapter 13

Corporate Finance Regulation: The US Perspective

Adrian Knight

Partner
Shearman & Sterling

13.1 Introduction

This Chapter provides an overview of how US federal securities laws regulate certain corporate finance activities and how the Financial Services and Markets Act 2000 and the related statutory instruments (the "FSMA") regulate certain of these activities when they are also carried out in the UK.

This Chapter considers the inter-relationship of US-UK securities regulation from the perspective a "foreign private issuer",[1] which generally includes any UK plc in the process of registering or which has already registered its securities with the US Securities and Exchange Commission (the "SEC") for trading on, for example, the New York Stock Exchange (the "NYSE") or the Nasdaq National Market System ("Nasdaq").

The regulatory regime relating to the distribution and trading of securities in the US comprises two principal statutes, the US Securities Act of 1933 (the "1933 Act") and the US Securities Exchange Act of 1934 (the "1934 Act"). The 1933 Act regulates offerings and sales of securities including disclosure items, registration of distributions of securities and exemptions while the 1934 Act regulates, the activities of broker-dealers,

---

[1] "Foreign Private Issuer" is defined by Rule 230.405 (Regulation C) under the 1933 Act. For the purposes of this Chapter it comprises a corporation that is incorporated or organised under the laws of a country other than the US but excluding any corporation which has more than 50 per cent of its voting stock directly or indirectly owned by residents in the US and which meets any one of the following conditions: (i) the majority of the executive officers or directors are US citizens or residents; (ii) more than 50 per cent of the assets of the issuer are located in the US; or (iii) the business of the issuer is administered principally in the US.

trading and sale practices and periodic reporting requirements imposed on issuers of registered securities. In addition, in the US, the National Association of Securities Dealers Inc. (the "NASD"), which is a self-regulating body of the US securities industry, regulates broker-dealers.

The US and the UK have arguably, in the SEC and the Financial Services Authority (the "FSA"), two of the most experienced regulators of global corporate finance activity; however, the manner in which the SEC and the FSA regulate quite similar corporate finance activities has varied quite considerably.

One of the reasons for this variation is due to the different approaches adopted in particular in relation to the regulation of the offering and sales of securities, avoidance of market abuse and manipulation and disclosure of material information to investors. However, following the collapse of Enron, Inc. and the changes that the SEC proposes to introduce to US securities laws, in particular with regard to disclosure of material information to investors, some of these differences may lessen.

This Chapter also considers the practical consequences of extending a US style offering of securities into the UK and suggests that the FSMA should not result in unduly cumbersome restrictions being imposed in the UK when making a US style global offering of securities. This Chapter considers these issues from a UK perspective and therefore UK terminology has been adopted.

13.2 Securities offerings: US federal securities laws applicable to a foreign private issuer and registration under the 1933 Act and the 1934 Act

13.2.1 Introduction – US federal securities laws relevant to a foreign private issuer

The 1933 Act and the 1934 Act rely on a framework of "full and fair" disclosure to facilitate informed investment decisions by investors before purchasing securities from the issuer, its affiliates or the underwriter of the offering. The 1934 Act implemented a system of periodic reporting to the SEC to ensure that the issuer made the necessary disclosures to the market.

Any company offering securities to the public in the US must register the securities with the SEC under the 1933 Act. The operative provisions of the 1933 Act are the registration and prospectus delivery requirements of Section 5 (*see* Section 13.2.2); the exemptions from registration in Sections 3 and 4 (*see* Sections 13.2.3 and 13.2.4); the liability provisions of Sections 11, 12 and 15 relating to material misstatements contained in registration statements and prospectuses (*see* sub-Section 13.2.5); and the anti-fraud prohibitions of Section 17 (*see* Section 13.2.6).

Before the securities can be listed on the NYSE or traded on Nasdaq, the issuer and class of securities to be traded must be registered under the 1934 Act. Registration under the 1933 Act and the 1934 Act will subject the company to periodic public reporting obligations under the 1934 Act (*see* Section 13.11).

Each of the individual states within the US has its own securities laws ("blue sky" laws) that require registration with state agencies of securities offered within that state's borders. Under 1996 federal legislation, securities listed on the NYSE or traded on Nasdaq are exempt from registration under state law.

The NYSE and Nasdaq also impose their own rules which address a broad range of matters relating to disclosure, the issue of securities and the rights of security holders. Substantial accommodations have been made, however, in relation to the governance policies and practices of foreign private issuers that are in accordance with their home market laws and practices (*see* Section 13.11).

Foreign private issuer's entering the US market will also need to consider whether they will be subject to the US Investment Company Act of 1940[2]

---

[2] This act primarily governs the offer and sale of securities by, and the regulation of, mutual funds, unit trusts and similar types of issuers. Because of the broad scope of the definition of the term "investment company", the 1940 Act can often be a difficult area for non-US companies, especially those that maintain large investment portfolios or hold a significant minority position in other companies. Since compliance with the 1940 Act is not an option for non-US companies and in any event is not practical for most US companies, it is important to identify possible issues arising under the 1940 Act at an early stage in the offer process.

or whether they will be classed as a passive foreign investment company under US tax law.[3]

13.2.2 *The registration and prospectus delivery requirements of the 1933 Act*

US federal securities laws are intended to protect investors by requiring information to be disclosed to investors so that they can make an informed investment decision. The 1933 Act requires detailed information to be provided to purchasers concerning the issuer and the securities offered for sale, and that all offers and sales of securities be registered with the SEC, unless an exemption from registration is available. The 1933 Act provides exemptions from registration for certain specified types of securities (*see* Section 13.2.3 below). Certain transactions are also exempt from registration under the 1933 Act. These include: transactions by persons other than an issuer, underwriter or broker-dealer; non-public offers or private placements (discussed in Section 13.3); exchanges of securities of the same issuer where no special solicitation compensation is paid; certain specified offers by issuers, not exceeding $1 million annually; and limited small offers of up to $5 million. Generally, sales of securities by affiliates of an issuer are treated as sales by the issuer for the purposes of determining the need to register the transaction under the 1933 Act.

Under the 1933 Act, a registered offer may be divided into three stages. First, before filing the registration statement with the SEC (the "pre-filing period"). Second, after filing the registration statement with the SEC but before it is declared effective (the "waiting period"). Finally, the period after the registration statement becomes effective (the "post-effective period").

Section 5 1933 Act regulates each stage of the offering process. It provides that:

> "(a) Unless a registration statement is in effect as to a security, it shall be unlawful for any person, directly or indirectly – (1) to

---

[3] A non-US body corporate may be classified as a passive foreign investment company (a "PFIC") if it meets either of two tests; one based on the extent of passive income, the other on the extent of gross assets producing passive income. If classified as a PFIC, holders of shares in the US would be subject to an onerous tax regime although the NYSE has recently modified its policy against listing the US securities of a PFIC by requiring disclosure of the adverse tax treatment of holders of shares in a PFIC.

make use of any means or instruments of transportation or communication in interstate commerce or of the mails to sell such security through the use or medium of any prospectus or otherwise; or (2) to carry or cause to be carried through the mails or in interstate commerce, by any means or instruments of transportation, any such security for the purpose of sale or for delivery after sale.

(b) It shall be unlawful for any person, directly or indirectly – (1) to make use of any means or instruments of transportation or communication in interstate commerce or of the mails to carry or transmit any prospectus relating to any security with respect to which a registration statement has been filed under this [Act], unless such prospectus meets the requirements of Section 10; or (2) to carry or cause to be carried through the mails or in interstate commerce any such security for the purpose of sale or for delivery after sale, unless accompanied or preceded by a prospectus that meets the requirements of sub-Section (a) of Section 10.

(c) It shall be unlawful for any person, directly or indirectly, to make use of any means or instruments of transportation or communication in interstate commerce or of the mails to offer to sell or offer to buy through the use or medium of any prospectus or otherwise any security, unless a registration statement has been filed as to such security, or while the registration statement is the subject of a refusal order or stop order or (prior to the effective date of the registration statement) any public proceedings or examination under Section 8."

Therefore, generally, no offers, oral or written, to sell securities may be commenced until a 1933 Act registration statement containing the prescribed disclosures is filed with the SEC. A sale can only be made after this registration statement has become effective and either before, or at the time of the written confirmation of the sale, the purchaser must have received a copy of the prospectus which complies with Section 10(a) 1933 Act. Failure to comply with the registration and prospectus delivery requirements gives the purchaser of the security the right to rescind the purchase[4] or to damages if the securities have been sold. Violation of the

---

[4] Section 13a 1993 Act provides that no action shall be maintained to enforce any liability under Section 12(a)(i) (dealing with liability for breach of Section 5 1933 Act), unless the action is brought within one year after the violation on which it is based. However, in no event shall any action be brought to enforce a liability under Section 12(a)(1) more than three years after the security was bona fide offered to the public.

registration and prospectus delivery requirements may trigger an enforcement action by the SEC.

13.2.3 Exempted securities

Section 3 1933 Act exempts certain securities from the registration and prospectus delivery requirements of Section 5 1933 Act.[5]

A foreign private issuer can rely upon Section 3(a)(9) to issue securities exchangeable for its existing registered securities without being obliged to register the exchangeable securities.

In connection with an exchange offer of a company incorporated in the UK implemented by means of a scheme of arrangement pursuant to Section 425 UK Companies Act 1985, the bidder can rely upon Section 3(a)(10) to avoid any obligation to register securities issued by the bidder, notwithstanding that the securities may be acquired by persons in the US. For example, Glaxo Wellcome plc and SmithKline Beecham plc relied upon Section 3(a)(10) to exempt from registration the securities issued by the merged group's new holding company, Glaxo SmithKline plc, created by way of a scheme of arrangement of Glaxo and SmithKline Beecham.

13.2.4 Exempted transactions

Section 4 1933 Act exempts certain transactions from the registration and prospectus delivery requirements of Section 5 1933 Act, the principal one of interest to a foreign private issuer being Section 4(2) which exempts "transactions by an issuer not involving any public offering" that is, a private placement; this exemption and its use in conjunction with Rule

---

[5] Generally, Section 3 1933 Act will be of little interest to a foreign private issuer, save for Sections 3(a)(9) and 3(a)(10) described in the main text. Otherwise, Section 3 exempts, inter alia, securities issued or guaranteed by: the US government or any territory thereof 3(a)(2); religious and charitable organisations 3(a)(4); savings and loan associations and certain tax-exempt farmers co-operatives 3(a)(5); in connection with railroad equipment 3(a)(6); in connection with bankruptcy proceedings 3(a)(7); in connection with certain US insurance contracts 3(a)(8); in single state transactions 3(a)(11); and US national or state banks 3(a)(12). Section 3(a)(3) also exempts commercial paper and notes with maturities of less than nine months which arise out of or where the proceeds are used for current transactions; notes can be renewed but again for no more than nine months.

144A to effect an on-sale of such securities in the US to institutional investors are discussed in further detail in Section 13.3.[6]

13.2.5 Liability under Sections 11, 12 and 15 1933 Act and under Rule 10b-5 1934 Act

Section 11(a) provides that any person acquiring securities subject to a registration statement that has become effective may claim compensation where the registration statement "contained an untrue statement of a material fact or omits to state a material fact required to be stated therein or necessary to make the statements therein not misleading". The persons liable to pay compensation include (1) every person who signed the registration statement, including the issuer; (2) every person who was a director in the issuer at the time of filing; (3) every person, who with his consent is named in the registration statement as being or about to become a director or performing a function similar to a director; (4) certain professional advisers who made a statement in the registration statement and who consented to being named in the registration statement, or in a report or valuation used in connection with the regis-tration statement; and (5) every underwriter of the issue.

---

[6] Generally Section 4 1933 Act will be of little interest to a foreign private issuer, save for Section 4(2), otherwise Section 4(1) exempts inter alia "transactions by any person other than an issuer, underwriter, or dealer"; this permits an ordinary investor to sell securities whether on an exchange, or on the over-the-counter market or privately. Section 4(3), the so-called "dealer exemption" exempts "trans-actions by a dealer (including an underwriter no longer acting as an underwriter in respect of a security involved in such transaction), except for transactions: (i) which take place before the end of the 40 day period following the first date on which the security was first bona fide offered to the public* by the issuer or by or through an underwriter; (ii) which take place before the end of the 40 day period after the effective date of the registration statement or before the 40 day period after the first date on which the securities were bona fide first offered to the public by the issuer or by or through an underwriter after such effective date, whichever is later; and (iii) in securities constituting the whole or part of a dealer's unsold allotment or subscription as a participant in the distribution of the securities by the issuer or by or through an underwriter; and Section 4(4) exempts from registration brokers transactions executed upon customers' orders on any exchange or in the over-the counter market but not the solicitation of such orders.

* The term "bona fide first offered to the market" is not a term of art but is designed to ensure that an issuer does not attempt to get round the time period by claiming that the securities were offered at a different date to the one on which they were first offered 'bona fide' to the market.

Consistent with the position in the UK, persons purchasing securities covered by the registration statement in the market after the closing of the offering are also entitled to rely upon the registration statement and claim under Section 11 should the registration statement contain such an untrue or misleading statement.[7]

Section 11(b) sets out various defences that the persons referred to in Section 11(a) (except the issuer which has absolute liability) can rely upon to defend a Section 11(a) claim. These defences are similar to the defences available in the UK. There are two procedural defences. Where a person no longer has a relationship or connection with the issuer or the offering which would otherwise confer liability under Section 11(a) and that person has advised the SEC to this effect (Section 11(b)(1)). Where part of the registration statement has become effective without the knowledge of a person and that person complied with Section 11(b)(1) and gave reasonable public notice to that effect (Section 11(b)(2)). The substantive defence – the so-called "due diligence" defence – is set out in Section 11(b)(3); it is similar to the defence set out in Schedule 10 of FSMA in relation to listing particulars.

The "due diligence" defence permits each of the persons referred to in Section 11(a), other than the issuer, to avoid liability if he can prove that, "he had, after reasonable investigation, reasonable grounds to believe and did believe, at the time such part of the registration statement became effective, that the statements therein were true and that there was no omission to state a material fact required to be stated therein or necessary to make the statements therein not misleading". To the extent that parts of the registration statement are purported to be made on the authority of an expert (other than such person) or purporting to be a copy of or an extract from a report or valuation of an expert (other than such person) then it will be a defence for a person, other than an issuer, to show that "he had no reasonable ground to believe and did not believe, at the time such part of the registration statement became effective, that the statements therein were untrue or that there was an omission to state a material fact required to be stated therein or necessary to make the statements therein not misleading".

---

[7] However, Section 11(a) also provides that where the issuer has made generally available an earnings statement covering a period of at least twelve months beginning after the effective date of the registration statement the claimant must demonstrate to the court that it did rely upon the untrue statement (or omission) in the registration statement.

Section 11(c) provides that the test for "reasonable investigation" and "reasonable ground for belief" shall be satisfied by that standard of reasonableness required "of a prudent man in the management of his own property".

The principal difference from the defences in Section 11(b) is that, for those parts of the registration statement based on an expert's report the defendant (but not the issuer) must have reasonable grounds for believing that the contents of the expert's report were true, but he is not required to base his belief on "reasonable investigation". For those sections of the registration statement not based on an expert's report the defendant (but not the issuer) can only bring the defence that he had reasonable grounds to believe that the registration statement was true, if these grounds are based on reasonable investigation.

Section 11(e) provides that the liability of an underwriter for damages generally shall not be in excess of the "total price at which the securities underwritten by him and distributed to the public were offered to the public" (accordingly an underwriter in the US will usually have only a several obligation to purchase its proportion of the underwriting commitment). Section 13 1933 Act provides that no claim shall be brought under Section 11 after a period of one year after the discovery of the untrue statement or omission or after the discovery should have been made by the exercise of reasonable diligence. Section 12 provides a cut-off date to any action brought under Section 11 – being three years after the security was bona fide offered to the public. However, any defendant (including the issuer) can avoid liability if it can prove to the court that the purchaser knew of the untruth or omission at the time of purchase.

Section 12 1933 Act imposes civil liability in connection with a prospec-tus and communications and provides that any person who offers or sells a security in violation of Section 5 1933 Act (Section 12(a)(1)) or who offers or sells a security by any means of interstate commerce or by means of a prospectus or oral communication which includes an untrue statement or omits to state a material fact required in order to make the statements in the light of the circumstances under which they were made not misleading (Section 12(a)(2)) shall be liable to the purchaser of the security.

The defendant in an action under Section 12(a)(2) can use a due diligence defence similar to that available under Section 11(b)(3) if he can demon-strate that he did not know, and could not have known of the untruth of the statement complained of or of the omission.

The Supreme Court of the US has held[8] that liability under Section 12(a)(2) applies only in the case of a public offer by an issuer or a controlling security holder and therefore an investment bank will not be liable under Section 12 when making a private placement or certain other secondary market transactions, although it could still be liable under Rule 10b-5 (*see* below). However, market practice continues to operate as if the 1933 Act applied to private placements.

Section 15 1933 Act makes any person who controls any person liable under Sections 11 or 12 1933 Act jointly and severally liable with that person for breaches of those sections. "Control" can be through means of share ownership, agency or pursuant to an agreement or understanding with one or more other persons. However, it is a defence for the alleged "controlling person" to show that they had no knowledge of, or had no reasonable grounds to believe in, the existence of facts by reason of which the liability of the "controlled person" is alleged to exist.

In addition to Sections 11 and 12 1933 Act the courts have imputed a private remedy to purchasers of securities under Section 10(b) 1934 Act which is applicable to all transactions in securities. This is available notwithstanding that Section 12 does not apply to securities exempt under Section 3(2) 1933 Act or, after the *Gustafson* case, to private placements.

Rule 10b-5 made under Section 10(b) 1934 Act provides that it:

> "shall be unlawful for any person, directly or indirectly, by the use of any means or instrumentality of interstate commerce, or of the mails, or of any facility of any national securities exchange, to employ any device, scheme or artifice to defraud, to make any untrue statement of a material fact or omit to state a material fact necessary to make the statements made, in the light of the circumstances under which they were made, not misleading, or to engage in any act, practice, or course of business which operates as a fraud or deceit on any person in connection with the purchase or sale of any security."

However, a claim under Rule 10b-5 requires proof of "scienter" knowledge of the statement's misleading nature on the part of the person making it, or at the least, a reckless disregard for its accuracy or completeness. Therefore, an underwriter or an issuer who has performed

---

[8] *Gustafson* v *Alloyd Co.*, 115 S.Ct. 1061 (1995).

adequate due diligence is unlikely to have the requisite intention to be in breach of Rule 10b-5. Liability under Rule 10b-5 is not limited to the registration statement, liability can attach to any other document published or any oral statement made in the context of the offering. A plaintiff must bring an action under Rule 10b-5 within "one year of the discovery of the facts constituting the violation and within three years after such violation".

Section 20(a) 1934 Act contains a similar provision to Section 15 1933 Act in that it can make a controlling person liable for the defendant in an action under Rule 10b-5 unless the controller acted in good faith and did not directly or indirectly induce the act constituting the violation or cause of action.

13.2.6 Liability under Section 17 1933 Act

Section 17 1933 Act makes it unlawful for any person offering or selling securities by use of any means or instruments of transportation or communication or by the use of the mails, to employ any device or scheme to defraud, or to obtain money or property by means of making an untrue statement of a material fact or any omission to state a material fact necessary in order to make the statements made not misleading or to engage in any transaction, practice, or course of business which operates as a fraud or deceit on a purchaser of securities. In addition it is unlawful for any person to publish or give publicity to, or circulate via an advertisement, newspaper, article or letter or other communication which though not purporting to offer a security for sale, describes such security for a consideration received, directly or indirectly, from an issuer, underwriter or dealer without fully disclosing the receipt, whether past or prospective, of such consideration or amount thereof. This section applies to all securities, including those which are exempt from the registration requirements of Section 5 by virtue of Section 3.

13.3 Securities offerings: Exemptions and unregistered offerings: Regulation S and Rule 144A

13.3.1 Introduction

A foreign private issuer can avoid the registration requirements of Section 5 1933 Act by relying on the private placement exemption under

Section 4(2) 1933 Act and Regulation D safe harbour or, where offers and sales of securities are conducted outside the US, by relying on the Regulation S safe harbour under the 1933 Act. Since securities sold under Section 4(2) and/or Regulation D or Regulation S are not registered there are restrictions on a general on-sale of such securities in or into the US. Rule 144A provides a safe harbour exemption from the registration requirements of the 1933 Act when such restricted securities are resold to certain sophisticated institutional investors in the US.[9]

13.3.2 Private placements

US securities laws recognise that the registration process and the protections afforded to investors under Section 5 1933 Act are not necessary when securities are sold to sophisticated investors. Section 4(2) 1933 Act provides an exemption from the registration requirements of Section 5, and Regulation D is a safe harbor made under Section 4(2). Section 4(2) applies to offers not involving a "public offering" of securities and Regulation D provides a safe harbour for offers to certain sophisticated investors known as "accredited investors". Issuers can rely on Section 4(2) or Regulation D, or a combination of both to avoid registration of the securities under Section 5 1933 Act.

13.3.3 Section 4(2) – not a "public offering"

Section 4(2) provides that Section 5 1933 Act does not apply to transactions not involving any public offering. As it does not define "public offering", case law and practice has developed in order to determine whether an offering falls within Section 4(2). The onus of proving compliance falls on the person relying on the section. Issuers therefore need to consider whether the issue of securities involves a public offer of securities. In summary the following factors are considered determinative of whether an offer is to the public:

---

[9] Although out of the scope of this Chapter Rule 144(a)(3) includes within the definition of "restricted securities" shares acquired from an issuer that are subject to the resale limitations of Rule 502(d) under Regulation D; equity securities of a US issuers acquired in a transaction subject to the conditions of Rules 901 or 903 under Regulation S; and securities acquired in a transaction meeting the requirements of Rule 144A.

(a)   are offerees sufficiently sophisticated to evaluate the financial risk of the proposed investment, in other words, are they able to "fend for themselves"[10] or do they need the protection of the 1933 Act?;

(b)   the number of persons to whom securities are offered; generally a private placement should be offered to a limited number of people; however, there is no rule on what figure will be small enough to satisfy the test;

(c)   the nature and form of the securities offered; do the offerees understand that the securities are being sold subject to re-sale restrictions (because of legends on the share certificates and such like) or that stock underlying convertible debt securities is subject to the restrictions applying to the debt securities?;

(d)   the method for making the offer; clearly the offer should not be published to the general public but should be limited to a select number of offerees; and

(e)   the securities cannot be re-sold to the public; however, they may be re-sold in accordance with Rule 144A (if available) or in another private transaction or outside the US in accordance with Regulation S.

Although issuers and financial intermediaries can rely on the Section 4(2) exemption the more common practice is to rely on a combination of Regulation D and Section 4(2).

13.3.4   Regulation D

13.3.4.1   Introduction
Regulation D offers a safe harbour to an issuer from the registration and prospectus delivery requirements of the 1933 Act for offers and sales of securities made in a private placement in compliance with Rules 501 to 506 of Regulation D. However, the anti-fraud, civil liability, and other provisions of US federal securities laws will continue to apply to an offering made under Regulation D.

Rule 502 contains the general conditions of the exemption, including advertising (discussed in Section 13.4.9), furnishing of information, the exercise by the issuer of reasonable care that the purchasers of the

---

10 The term "fend for themselves" comes from the Ralston Purina Case, (346 US 119 (1953) in which the Judge held that the applicability of the private offering exemption should depend on whether the particular class of persons affected needed the protection of the 1933 Act, which depended on whether such persons could "fend for themselves".

securities are not underwriters and integration of the issue with other transactions. Rule 503 provides that there must be a public notification of sales in reliance on Regulation D. Rule 506 is the most relied upon since it enables private placements to be made to an indefinite number of accredited investors. Rule 501 contains the definition section.

13.3.4.2   *Sales to accredited investors*
Rule 506(b)(2)(i) limits the safe harbour to offers of securities to less than 35 persons. However, Rule 501 provides that accredited investors are excluded from the calculation of the number of purchasers for the purposes of Rule 506(b). The exclusion of accredited investors and the wide variety of persons included in the definition of accredited investor means that a private placement that complies with Regulation D can be made to a large number of persons. However, whenever securities are offered to persons other than accredited investors the issuer must believe that they, either alone or with their purchaser representatives, have sufficient knowledge and experience in financial and business matters to enable them to evaluate the merits and risks of the prospective investment.

13.3.4.3   *Information requirements*
Rule 502(b) provides that where sales are made to persons who are not accredited investors they must be given certain information prior to the sale. The information given depends on whether the issuer is registered under the 1934 Act and on the size of the offering.

If the issuer is registered then it will be obliged to make available to purchasers information contained in its most recent annual and quarterly reports. If the issuer is not registered it will be obliged to provide certain non-financial information comparable to the information required to be filed in a public offer and certain financial information, depending on the size of the offer. (Different requirements apply for offers up to $7.5 million and for offers above this figure.) Purchasers who are not accredited investors must have the opportunity to ask questions regarding the offering and to obtain additional information.

The SEC recommends that where there is a sale to one non-accredited investor then all the purchasers should receive the same information as provided to the non-accredited investor. However, if all of the purchasers are accredited investors then the issuer is not required to provide any specific information.

13.3.4.4 Restriction on re-sales under Regulation D and interaction with Rule 144A

Shares placed under a Regulation D private placement cannot be re-sold unless they are registered under the 1933 Act or pursuant to an exemption.

The issuer must therefore guard against re-sale in breach of Regulation D by:

(a) exercising reasonable care[11] to ensure that the purchasers are not underwriters (Rule 502(d));

(b) requiring that all purchasers sign letters of investment intent (i.e. that they intend to hold the securities for investment purposes and not for re-sale); and

(c) taking all precautions against re-sales including issuing appropriate transfer instructions to the transfer agent and placing a legend on the share certificate indicating the transfer restriction.

Re-sales of securities received in a private placement may be sold under an exemption from registration and, therefore, private placements under Regulation D are often coupled with a sale to a non-US person in reliance on the Re-sale Safe Harbour under Regulation S (*see* Section 13.3.5.4) or to a qualified institutional buyer under Rule 144A (*see* Section 13.6).

However, an issuer having a class of securities registered under the 1934 Act cannot rely upon Rule 144A subsequently to make a private placing of securities of the same class; securities cannot be sold under Rule 144A if at their date of issue they are fungible with, that is, are of the same class of, securities traded on a national securities exchange or quoted in a US automated inter-dealer quotation system.

13.3.4.5 No integration with other exempt offerings

Rule 502(a) provides that all sales which are part of the same Regulation D offering must meet all of the terms and conditions of Regulation D and that offers and sales that are made before or more than six months after the completion of a Regulation D offering will not be considered part of that offering, provided that, during the six month period there were no

---

[11] Reasonable care can be demonstrated if (i) the issuer makes inquiries as to whether the purchaser is acquiring the securities for itself or on behalf of other persons and (ii) if the issuer provides a written disclosure that the securities have not been registered under the 1933 Act and cannot be re-sold unless they are registered or an exemption from registration is available.

offers or sales of securities by the issuer that are the same or of a similar class as those sold under Regulation D other than offers or sales of securities under employee benefits plans. The question of whether separate offers of securities will be regarded as part of the same offering will depend on all the facts and circumstances of each case. However, violation of this rule could result in the Regulation D safe harbour being lost. For example, a private offering followed by a public offering, in which the private offering loses the benefit of the Regulation D exemption, could be considered as "gun jumping" in breach of Section 5 1933 Act.

13.3.4.6   Filing requirements

Under Rule 503 an issuer who is selling securities in reliance on Regulation D is required to file five copies of a notice on a prescribed form (Form D) within 15 days of the first sale of the securities. An amendment to the regulation removed the filing of the Form D as a condition to obtaining the exemption under Regulation D. However, the form should nevertheless be filed because the SEC has the power under Rule 507 to seek an injunction against an issuer who has violated the filing requirements of Rule 503.

13.3.4.7   Insignificant deviations from Regulation D

Finally, by an amendment to Regulation D, Rule 508 provides that an insignificant failure to comply with a provision of Regulation D, which is not directly intended to protect the investor, does not undermine the availability of the exemption, provided that the issuer has made a good faith and reasonable effort to comply with Regulation D in any event.

13.3.5   Regulation S

Regulation S under the 1933 Act governs offers and sales of securities outside the US. Regulation S comprises one general exemption from registration (contained in Rule 901 and known as the "General Statement") and two safe harbours (contained in Rules 903 and 904). The defined terms are set out in Rule 902.

13.3.5.1   The General Statement – Rule 901

The General Statement provides that for the purposes only of Section 5 1933 Act the terms "offer", "offer to sell", "sell", "sale" and "offer to buy" . . . shall be deemed not to include offers and sales that occur outside the US". The Issuing Release for Regulation S provided that the determination as to whether an issue is inside or outside of the US would depend on the facts and circumstances of each case. If an issuer can demonstrate that an offer or sale of securities occurred outside the US the registration provisions of the 1933 Act will not apply, even if the conditions of the safe harbours in Rules 903 and 904 do not apply. In practice, however, issuers prefer to rely on the safe harbours contained in Rule 903 (the "Issuer Safe Harbour") and Rule 904 (the "Re-sale Safe Harbour") because there can be uncertainty as to what constitutes an "offer" or "sale" outside of the US for the purposes of Rule 901.

13.3.5.2 The two General Conditions for use of the Safe Harbours

Before an issuer, distributor[12] or any of their affiliates[13] can rely on the Issuer Safe Harbour or any person (other than the issuer, distributor or any of their affiliates) can rely upon the Re-sale Safe Harbour, two general conditions must be satisfied.

General Condition One. First, the transaction must be an "offshore transaction" which is defined in Rule 902(h) as a transaction where (1) the offer is not made to a person in the US and (2) either (a) at the time the buy order is made the buyer is outside the US, or the seller and any person acting on its behalf reasonably believes that the buyer is outside the US, or (b) (i) for the purposes of the Issuer Safe Harbour, the transaction is executed in, on or through, a physical trading floor of an established foreign securities exchange[14] that is located outside the US or (ii) for the purposes of the Re-sale Safe Harbour, the transaction is executed in, on or through the facilities of a designated offshore securities market[15] and neither the seller nor any person acting on behalf of the seller knows that the transaction has been pre-arranged with a buyer in the US. However, offers and sales of securities targeted at identifiable groups of

---

[12] "Distributor" means any underwriter, dealer, or other person who participates, pursuant to a contractual arrangement, in the distribution of the securities offered or sold in reliance of Regulation S.

[13] Regulation S also extends to persons acting on behalf of such an issuer, distributor or any of their affiliates.

[14] The term "established foreign securities exchange" is not defined and will therefore, be a question of fact in èach case.

[15] Under Rule 902(b), the SEC has designated the following to be "designated offshore securities markets": the Eurobond market, as regulated by the International Securities Market Association; the European Association of Securities Dealers Automated Quotation; and the stock exchanges of Alberta, Amsterdam, Australia, Bermuda, Brussels, Copenhagen, Frankfurt, Helsinki, Hong Kong, Ireland, Istanbul, Johannesburg, London, Luxembourg, Mexico, Milan, Montreal, Oslo, Paris, Singapore, Stockholm, Tokyo, Toronto, Vancouver, Warsaw and Zurich. The SEC is empowered under rule 902 to designate other foreign securities exchanges or non-exchange markets as designated offshore securities markets.

US citizens abroad (e.g. US armed forces serving overseas) are not deemed to be made in "offshore transactions".

General Condition Two. Second, there must be no "directed selling efforts" in the US by an issuer, distributor or any of their affiliates. Directed selling efforts are defined as "any activity undertaken for the purpose of, or that could reasonably be expected to have the effect of, conditioning the market in the US for any of the securities being offered in reliance on" Regulation S, which would include placing an advertisement in a publication "with a general circulation in the US".[16] The following activities are not, however, "directed selling efforts":

(a)   Advertisements in the US, which are required to be published under US or foreign law, or under the rules or regulations of a US or foreign regulatory or self-regulatory authority, provided the advertisement contains no more information than legally required and includes a statement to the effect that the securities will not be registered and will not be offered or sold in the US without registration or an exemption from registration.

(b)   The distribution of a tombstone advertisement in the US provided it complies with the detailed requirements set out in the definition of "directed selling efforts".

(c)   The distribution in the US of foreign broker-dealer quotations by a third-party system that distributes quotations mainly in foreign countries if:

   (i)   the system does not permit transactions between foreign broker-dealers and persons located in the US; and

   (ii)   contacts must not be initiated within the US or with US persons beyond those allowed under the SEC's safe harbour rule for foreign broker–dealers contained in Rule 15a-6 under the 1934 Act.[17]

---

[16] "General circulation in the US" means that a publication is either (i) printed primarily for distribution in the US or (ii) has, in the previous 12 months, had an average circulation in the US of 15,000 or more copies per issue. In the case of a foreign publication which produces separate editions generally circulated in the US, only the US edition will be counted if the affiliated non-US editions alone do not meet the requirements of paragraph (ii) of the definition.

[17] Rule 15a-6 exempts foreign broker-dealers from the registration requirements of Section 15 1934 Act. Under Section 15 it is unlawful for any broker or dealer to use interstate commerce to effect transactions in, or attempt to induce the purchase or sale of any security unless such broker-dealer is registered with the SEC under Section 15(b). However, to come within the exemption foreign broker-dealers must

(d) The distribution, or publication in the US of information, opinions or recommendations concerning the issuer or any class of its securities could constitute directed selling efforts depending on circumstances, however, for reporting issuers the publication of information, opinions and recommendations in an analyst's research report that meets the requirements of Rule 139(b) under the 1933 Act will not be "directed selling efforts". (*See* Section 13.5.7.3.)

(e) The dissemination of routine information of the character and content normally published by a company and unrelated to a securities offering. (*See* Section 13.4.3.2.)

(f) The conduct of bona-fide journalistic activities or the flow of normal corporate news. (*See* Section 13.4.3.2.)

13.3.5.3 The Issuer Safe Harbour – Rule 903
If the two General Conditions and the conditions described below are also satisfied, an offer or sale of securities shall be deemed to occur outside the US within the meaning of Rule 901. There are three categories of additional conditions:

---

satisfy certain conditions. In summary a foreign broker-dealer will only be exempt from registration to the extent that:

(i) the foreign broker-dealer effects transactions in securities with persons that have not been solicited by the foreign broker-dealer;

(ii) the foreign broker-dealer furnishes reports to major US institutional investors, and effects transactions in securities subject to research reports if (i) the reports do not recommend the use of the foreign broker-dealer to effect trades (ii) the foreign broker-dealer does not initiate follow up contact with US institutional investors after issuing the report (iii) transactions in securities the subject of a report are made through a registered broker-dealer (where the foreign broker-dealer has a relationship with such registered broker-dealer);

(iii) the foreign broker-dealer induces a US institutional investor to deal in a security (i) he does so though a registered broker-dealer, and provides the SEC with information (ii) he does so from outside the US (unless accompanied on visits in the US with a registered broker-dealer or associate thereof who accepts responsibility for the foreign associated person's communications with the US institutional investor).

In addition, the registered broker-dealer through whom the foreign broker deals, is subject to certain other requirements under Rule 15a-6, such as maintaining books and records relating to the transaction effected on behalf of the foreign broker-dealer, and ensuring that the foreign broker-dealer is not subject to any statutory disqualification from membership of a Self Regulatory Organisation.

Category 1 transactions. Under Rule 903(b)(1) the following offers and sales may be made without registration under the 1933 Act:

(a)   offers and sales of equity or debt securities of a foreign issuer, defined as any issuer other than a domestic issuer (i.e. a foreign government or a foreign private issuer) where the issuer reasonably believes at the beginning of the offer that there is no "substantial US market interest" in the class of securities being offered or sold.[18] A substantial US market interest exists in a class of equity securities if US exchanges and inter-dealer quotation systems constituted the single largest market for such securities in the last fiscal year or 20 per cent or more of all trading in such securities took place during such period on US exchanges and inter-dealer quotation systems and less than 55 per cent of such trading took place in or through the market facilities of a single foreign country;[19]

(b)   securities offered and sold into a single country which is not the US (a so called "overseas directed offering"), to residents of that country and the offer is made in accordance with local laws, customary practices and documentation of that country;

(c)   securities which are backed by the full faith and credit of a foreign government; or

(d)   securities which are offered and sold to employees of the issuer or its affiliates under an employee benefit plan set up and administered in accordance with the law of a country other than the US and the customary practices and documentation of such country.[20]

Category 2 transactions. If an offering is not eligible to be classified as a Category 1 transaction and if the securities are equity securities of a reporting foreign issuer or debt securities of a reporting issuer or of a

---

[18] For an offer of warrants there must be no substantial US market interest in the securities to be purchased on the exercise of the warrant. For an offer of convertible securities there must be no substantial US market interest in either the convertible securities or the underlying securities.

[19] A substantial US market interest exists in a class of debt securities if all of the following conditions are satisfied (i) the issuer's debt, preferred and asset backed securities are held of record by 300 or more US persons; (ii) $1 billion or more of such securities is held by US persons; and (iii) 20 per cent or more of the outstanding amount of such securities is held by US persons.

[20] To be eligible for the Issuer Safe Harbour securities offered and sold under an offshore employee benefit plan must satisfy a number of additional conditions, including that the issuer must take reasonable steps to preclude an offer and sale to US residents other than employees on temporary assignment to the US.

non-reporting foreign issuer, Rule 903(b)(2) permits an issuer to offer and sell securities without registration under the 1933 Act if:

(a) the offer or sale is not made to or for the account of a US person if such offer is made before the end of a 40 day "distribution compliance period",[21] all sales by distributors of their unsold allotment are deemed to be made during the distribution compliance period;

(b) offering restrictions are implemented, being restrictions defined in Rule 902(g) and which in summary require that (i) all distributors enter into a written contract that all offers and sales of securities before the end of the distribution compliance[22] period be made only in accordance with Regulation S or pursuant to registration under the 1933 Act or an available exemption from registration, and (ii) that all offering materials and documents (other than press releases) used prior to the expiration of the distribution compliance period state that the securities have not been registered under the 1933 Act and are not permitted to be sold in the US or to a US person other than in a registered or exempt transaction under the 1933 Act;[23]

(c) every distributor selling securities to a distributor, dealer or person receiving a selling concession, fee or other remuneration before the end of the applicable distribution compliance period must notify the purchaser that the purchaser will be subject to the same restrictions on offers and sales that apply to a distributor.

Category 3 transactions. Rule 903(b)(3) includes all transactions not eligible to be classified as a Category 1 or a Category 2 transaction, including those most at risk of "flow back" into the US; accordingly such transactions are subject to more stringent offering restrictions than Category 2 transactions. Examples of Category 3 transactions are debt or equity offerings by non-reporting US issuers (including issuers who were

---

[21] The "distribution compliance period" is defined by Rule 902(j) as the period that begins on the later of the date on which the securities are first offered to persons other than distributors in reliance on Regulation S or the closing date of the offer. However, the distribution compliance period for the issue of equity securities by a US issuer under Regulation S will be one year. In the case of a continuous offering the restricted period begins on "completion of the distribution of such tranche, as determined and certified by the managing underwriter". All offers and sales by a distributor of an unsold allotment are deemed to be made during the restricted period. After the expiration of the restricted period the securities (other than unsold allotments) are no longer subject to restrictions.

[22] *See* footnote 21 above.

[23] Where equity securities of domestic issuers being offered are sold no hedging transaction can be covered during the distribution compliance period.

formerly reporting issuers but who are no longer required to report under the 1934 Act because they have less than 300 holders of the securities in question), or equity offerings by reporting US issuers or by a non-reporting foreign issuer where there is a substantial US market interest. Under Category 3, although an issuer need not register the securities being offered and sold under the 1933 Act, in addition to the offering restrictions described for a Category 2 transaction, it will be necessary for the issuer to impose the following restrictions:

(a) for debt securities: the securities must not be sold to or for the account of a US person during a 40 day distribution compliance period.[24] In addition the debt securities must be represented upon issue by a non-exchangeable temporary global security only exchangeable into the underlying security at the end of the 40 day distribution compliance period. In addition the global security is only exchangeable if the person to whom it is issued certifies that it is a non-US person;

(b) for equity securities: the securities must not be sold to or for the account of a US person during a one year restricted period and the purchaser (if not a distributor) (i) must certify that it is not a US person and is not acquiring the securities for the account or benefit of a US person or it must certify that it acquired the securities under an exemption from registration and; (ii) must agree to re-sell the securities only in accordance with Regulation S, or pursuant to registration under the 1933 Act or in reliance on an exemption from registration; (iii) if a US issuer, the securities must contain a legend that transfer is not permitted except in accordance with Regulation S; and (iv) the issuer must enter into an agreement (or include provision in its constitutional documents) to refuse to register any transfer of securities not made in accordance with Regulation S (except if they are in bearer form or overseas law prohibits such refusal).

13.3.5.4   *The Re-sale Safe Harbour – Rule 904*

This states that an offer or sale of securities by a person other than the issuer, distributor or any of their affiliates[25] shall be deemed to occur outside the US within the meaning of Rule 901 if the offer and sale is made in compliance with the two General Conditions described above (i.e. that the offer and sale is made in an offshore transaction and that no

---

[24] *See* footnote 21 above.

[25] Rule 904 extends to a person acting on behalf of the issuer, distributor or any of their affiliates.

directed selling efforts are made into the US) and the offer and sale is made in compliance with the following additional conditions:

(a) a dealer or person receiving a selling concession, fee or other remuneration in respect of the securities being sold may rely on Rule 904 and sell the securities prior to the end of the applicable distribution compliance period[26] only if neither the seller nor any person acting on its behalf knows that the offeree or buyer of the securities is a US person; and

(b) where the seller knows that the purchaser is a dealer or person receiving a selling concession, fee or other remuneration in respect of the securities being sold, then the purchaser of the securities must be notified that the securities may be offered and sold during the applicable distribution compliance period only in accordance with Regulation S or in a transaction that is registered or exempt from registration under the 1933 Act.[27]

13.3.5.5 *1988 amendments*
In 1998 the SEC adopted various amendments to Regulation S principally to address certain abuses of Regulation S by US issuers. Since this Chapter is concerned with foreign private issuers those amendments have not been described in detail.

13.3.6 *Rule 144A*

Rule 144A provides a non-exclusive safe harbour from the registration and prospectus delivery requirements of the 1933 Act for re-sales of restricted securities to certain sophisticated institutional investors described in Rule 144A(a)(1) and defined as qualified institutional buyers ("QIBs") (*see* Section 13.3.6.2 below). Before Rule 144A was adopted in 1990 restricted securities could only be sold on a very limited basis under Rule 144. (*See* Section 13.3.1.)

Rule 144A provides that any person, other than the issuer or a dealer, who offers or sells securities in compliance with Rule 144A shall be

---

[26] *See* footnote 21 above.

[27] In the case of an offer and sale of the securities of an issuer by an officer or director of the issuer or a distributor, who is an affiliate of the issuer or distributor solely by virtue of holding that position, he may not be paid a selling concession, fee or other remuneration in connection with the offer or sale of a security other than the customary broker's commission that would be received by a person executing the transaction as agent.

deemed not to be engaged in a distribution of such securities and therefore, shall not be an underwriter for the purposes of Sections 2(2) and Section 4(1) 1933 Act. Given that Section 4(1) provides that the registration requirements of Section 5 will not apply to an issuer, underwriter or dealer, the effect of Rule 144A is that the seller can rely on the exemption from registration set out in Section 4(1). If the seller is a dealer it can rely on the exemption from registration set out in 4(3) 1933 Act.

However, the person relying on Rule 144A can only come within these exemptions and sell the securities without registering them under Section 5 the 1933 Act if they satisfy the conditions of Rule 144A described in Section 13.3.6.1 below.

13.3.6.1   Permitted resales of securities under Rule 144A
Under Rule 144A securities may be re-sold if:

(a)   the securities are offered or sold only to QIBs or to a person that the seller reasonably believes is a QIB and in determining whether or not a purchaser is a QIB the seller is entitled to rely upon the non-exclusive methods described in Rule 144A;[28]

(b)   the seller takes reasonable steps to ensure that the purchaser is aware that the seller is relying on the Rule 144A exemption from registration in connection with the re-sale;

(c)   at the date of their issue, the securities are not of the same class of securities listed on a national securities exchange or quoted in a US automated inter-dealer quotation system; and

(d)   in the case of an issuer that is not obliged to disclose information in the US,[29] the holders of the securities and potential purchasers have the right to obtain from the issuer certain specified minimum "reasonably current" information regarding the issuer. This information will include for example, a brief description of the issuer's business, products and services, the most recent balance sheet and

---

[28] To establish whether a person qualifies for QIB status and thereby establish a "reasonable belief" that a person so qualifies, sellers can rely on the most recent available financial statements or other information in documents filed with SEC, in each case subject to certain time limits, or on a certificate signed by an executive officer of the potential purchaser.

[29] Rule 144A obliges disclosure where the issuer is neither subject to Sections 13 or 15(d) 1934 Act, nor exempt from reporting pursuant to Rule 12g3-2(6) under the 1934 Act nor a foreign government as defined in Rule 405 eligible to register securities under Schedule B 1933 Act.

profit and loss and retained earnings statement for the two preceding fiscal years.

13.3.6.2 *Qualified Institutional Buyers*
QIBs include:

(a) insurance companies, registered investment companies, registered investment advisers, registered business development companies, and certain employee benefit plans (as listed in Section 501(c)(3) US Internal Revenue Code), generally, any trust fund having a bank or trust company as trustee; to qualify as a QIB each entity must in aggregate own or invest on a discretionary basis at least $100 million in securities of non-affiliated issuers;

(b) dealers registered under the 1934 Act which, either for their own account or the accounts of other QIBs, in aggregate own and invest on a discretionary basis at least $10 million in securities of non-affiliated issuers or act in a "riskless principal transaction"[30] on behalf of a QIB;

(c) registered investment companies, acting for their own account or the accounts of other QIBs, being part of a family of investment companies which own in aggregate at least $100 million in securities of non-affiliated issuers; (4) banks, savings and loan associations whether US or foreign, acting for their own account or the accounts of other QIBs that in aggregate own and invest on a discretionary basis at least $100 million of non-affiliated securities and each entity has an audited net worth of at least $25 million.

13.3.6.3 *Interaction of Regulation S and Rule 144A*
Foreign private issuers often rely on a combination of Regulation S and Rule 144A in respect of international offerings, so that securities offered outside of the US will be exempt from registration under the 1933 Act under Regulation S and securities offered into the US will be exempt from registration under the 1933 Act where they are offered and sold in reliance of Section 4(2) and/or Regulation D and resold to QIBs in reliance on Rule 144A.

This combined use of Rule 144A and Regulation S will also enable a purchaser of securities acquired under Rule 144A to rely on the Re-sale Safe Harbour of Regulation S to resell restricted Rule 144A securities into

---

[30] One in which a dealer buys a security from any person and makes a simultaneous offsetting sale of such security to a QIB, including another dealer acting as a riskless principal for a QIB.

the local non-US market and will also allow a purchaser of securities during the Regulation S distribution compliance period[31] to resell them to QIBs under Rule 144A.[32]

13.4 Securities offerings: publicity restrictions

13.4.1 *FSMA and publicity restrictions*

Section 13.4 of this Chapter describes how the 1933 Act imposes significant restrictions on publicity that "conditions the market" for any proposed securities offering and how the SEC permits certain communications, in particular, "ordinary course communications" and communications which satisfy the terms of the "safe harbour" against liability under Section 5 1933 Act pursuant to Rules 135 and 135e.

Unlike the position in the US, UK securities law does not draw a distinction between the timing of the publicity at the various stages of the proposed securities offering (*see* Section 13.2.2 above).

Depending upon the facts and circumstances of each case, Article 67 Financial Services and Markets (Financial Promotion) (Amendment) Order 2001 is likely to be the exemption relied upon when information relating to securities being registered under the 1933 Act, is communicated to persons in the UK.

Article 67 provides that the financial promotion restriction contained in Section 21(1) FSMA will not apply to any communication which:

(a) is a non-real time communication or a solicited real time communication;

(b) relates to an investment which falls within paragraphs 14 to 18 of Schedule 1 to the Financial Promotion Order (which include, shares or stock of any body corporate wherever incorporated, but

---

[31] *See* sub-Sections 13.3.5.3 on Category 2 and Category 3 transactions and 13.3.5.4.

[32] However, equity securities of US issuers are defined as "restricted securities" under Rule 144 which means that equity securities of a US issuer sold in a Regulation S Issuer Safe Harbour transaction cannot be freely resold into the US.

excluding an open-ended investment company;[33] instruments creating or acknowledging indebtedness; government and public securities; instruments giving entitlements to investments and certificates representing certain securities, such as Global Depositary Receipts conferring contractual or property rights to any such investment);

(c)   relates to an investment which is "permitted to be traded or dealt in on a relevant market"; a relevant market will include the NYSE and Nasdaq; and

(d)   is "required or permitted to be communicated" by:

    (i)   the rules of the relevant market;

    (ii)   a body which regulates the relevant market, which will include the boards that regulate the NYSE and Nasdaq respectively; or

    (iii)   a body which regulates offers or issues of investments to be traded on such a market, such as the SEC in relation to its regulation of the NYSE and Nasdaq.

To come within the Article 67 "safe harbour" an issuer seeking to register its securities under the 1933 Act must satisfy the principal conditions; that the relevant investment is "permitted to be traded or dealt in" on the NYSE or Nasdaq and that the communication made into the UK in respect of such investment is "required or permitted to be communicated" by one of the entities referred to in sub-paragraphs (i) – (iii) above, such as the SEC.

---

[33] Paragraph 14 also includes (in sub-paragraph 1) the shares or stock of any unincorporated body constituted under the law of a country or territory outside the UK and (in sub-paragraph (2) the following are deemed included in sub-paragraph (1); any shares of a class defined as deferred shares for the purposes of Section 119 Building Societies Act 1986; any transferable shares in a body corporate under the law of, or any part of, the UK relating to industrial and provident societies or credit unions or in a body constituted under the law of another European Economic Area ("EEA") state for the purposes equivalent to those of such body. Paragraph 14(1) excludes, in addition to the shares or stock of an open-ended investment company (unless included by sub-paragraph (2)); (b) the shares and stock of a building society incorporated under the law of, or any part of, the UK; (c) any body incorporated under the law of, or any part of, the UK relating to industrial and provident societies or credit unions; and (d) any body constituted under the law of an EEA state for purposes equivalent to those of a body falling within paragraph (b) or (c).

Communications in respect of which the SEC has either provided guidance or a "safe harbour" to issuers during registration will therefore be "permitted to be communicated" for the purposes of Article 67. Whether this part of Article 67 can be satisfied by an issuer is a question of US federal securities law and whether, in particular by the time the marketing of the securities commences in the "waiting period", the relevant securities can be said to be "permitted to be traded or dealt in" for the purposes of the relevant market.

The marketing of a securities offering will only commence after the lead underwriter is satisfied that the SEC has completed its review of the issuer's 1933 Act registration statement; the issuer has filed its 1934 Act registration statement; and the issuer has satisfied the eligibility requirements for listing and trading the securities on the relevant market, for these purposes, the NYSE or Nasdaq. At that stage, the only hurdles to prevent the securities actually being "traded or dealt in" on the relevant market will be: that the shares are not priced and sold; that the underwriters are still entitled to terminate their obligations under the underwriting agreement; and, that theoretically, the SEC imposes a stop order on the offering process (this would be unusual if the 1933 Act registration statement has been reviewed by the SEC) which would prevent the registration statement becoming effective.

Considering these steps in greater detail, where the initial registered offering is made by a foreign private issuer, it is permitted to make a confidential filing with the SEC. By the time the issuer publicly files its registration statement, the SEC will have completed its review of the document. Theoretically, the registration statement could then be declared effective – however, it would still be necessary for the lead underwriter to market, price and sell the securities.[34]

When an existing registrant makes a "follow-on offering" it will file its registration statement with the SEC and will be informed by the SEC within five days of filing whether or not the SEC will review the document. If the SEC decides not to review the document, marketing the securities will commence since the SEC has, in effect, agreed in principle

---

[34] The practical position regarding a US issuer registering its securities for the first time is similar to a foreign private issuer. A US issuer will make a so-called "quiet-filing", the registration statement being publicly available from the SEC but the lead underwriter not marketing the securities until after the SEC has completed its review of the registration statement.

that the registration statement can be declared effective at the appropriate time.

The practice is for the 1934 Act registration statement (a two page document which incorporates by reference the 1933 Act registration statement) to be filed during the waiting period shortly after the 1933 Act registration statement is filed with the SEC.

Before filing the 1933 Act registration statement with the SEC, the lead underwriter will have cleared with the NYSE or Nasdaq the eligibility criteria of the issuer to have its securities listed on the relevant market. During the waiting period the issuer will complete the necessary documentation to apply formally for securities to be listed on the relevant market.

The lead underwriter will market the securities and commence the "book building" in reliance upon the preliminary prospectus (as permitted by Rule 430 to the 1934 Act) filed with the SEC as part of the registration statement.

At any stage during the waiting period the NYSE or Nasdaq will write to the issuer to confirm that its application for listing has been accepted. Conventionally, this happens after the printing of the preliminary prospectus since the "red herring" language on the document often states that the issuer has applied to the relevant market for listing – this language is occasionally omitted when the listing application has already been confirmed.

Depending upon the timing of the confirmation from the NYSE or Nasdaq, it is possible by the time the preliminary prospectus is printed and the marketing "road show" commences for the 1933 Act registration statement to have been filed and reviewed, the 1934 Act registration statement to have been filed and the NYSE or Nasdaq to have accepted the issuer's application for listing. At this stage, for the purposes of US securities laws, the securities will be "permitted to be traded or dealt in".

Where it is proposed that the "road show" be extended into the UK and the issuer's web-site includes documents that the SEC permits[35] the issuer to communicate during its "road show", the issuer and lead underwriter

---

[35] It is necessary to consider which "ordinary course" communication documents are and are not "permitted" to be communicated by the SEC for the purposes of Article 67. *See* sub-Section 13.4.8.

may wish to bring forward the date of receipt of the written confirmation of the relevant market that the issuer's securities have been accepted for listing which will enable the issuer and lead underwriter to navigate more effectively the restrictions imposed by the FSMA in relation to communication of financial promotions in the UK, since the issuer and lead underwriter will be entitled to rely upon Article 67, where any communication comprises either a non-real time communication or a solicited real time communication, to avoid the obligation that the contents of the documents must first be approved by an authorised person for the purposes of Section 21(1) FSMA.

However, when considering the potential liability issuer and the lead underwriter under UK securities law it is more likely that the marketing documents (in particular the materials that the issuer is entitled to distribute at a "road-show" in the UK pursuant to and in accordance with the safe harbour under Rule 135e (*see* Section 13.4.3.2 below)) will be communicated only to professional investors who satisfy the conditions in Article 19 Financial Promotion Order.[36]

A registered issuer making a follow on offer will be entitled to rely upon Article 67 for each of the three periods of the proposed offering of securities, assuming that the securities to be offered are of the same class traded or dealt in on the NYSE or Nasdaq. A new issuer can only rely upon Article 67 from that time in the "waiting period" (but only after the SEC has completed its review of the registration statement) the relevant market has confirmed that the securities will be listed and during the "post-effective" period of its IPO.

If communications which are permitted to be published by the SEC in the "pre-filing" period of an IPO are also communicated into the UK, the issuer should consider alternative exemptions from the financial promotion restriction in Section 21(1) FSMA such as Article 19 (*investment professionals*) or Article 49 (*high net worth companies*) of the Financial Promotion Order in the event that an investment bank is unable or unwilling to approve the contents of the document for the purposes of Section 21(1) FSMA.

---

[36] Where offers made in the UK during the "waiting period" on the basis of the information included in the preliminary prospectus are restricted to professional investors, the issuer and the lead underwriters can rely upon paragraph (2)(a) of Regulation 7 POS Regs to deem any such offer not to be an offer to the public for the purposes of the POS Regs.

13.4.2   Registered offerings

13.4.2.1   Background
During any securities offering, the prospectus should be the only document on which investors rely in deciding whether or not to purchase the securities on offer. Therefore, so as not to dilute the value of the prospectus or confuse potential investors, the 1933 Act restricts publicity that may be released while an offering is taking place.

13.4.2.2   Publicity restrictions on registered offerings.
The 1933 Act imposes significant restrictions on publicity that "conditions the market" for a securities offering. In registered offerings, different publicity restrictions apply during the pre-filing, waiting and post-effective periods.

13.4.3   Pre-filing period

13.4.3.1   Legal principles
Before filing the registration statement, generally no offers to sell a security, written or oral, can be made. Offers made in the pre-filing period, often referred to as "gun jumping", are precluded by Section 5(c) 1933 Act. Section 5(c) makes it unlawful for any person to make use of interstate commerce or of the mails in the US "to offer to sell" a security unless a registration statement has been filed with the SEC.

The SEC interprets "offer to sell" broadly to include any communication that conditions the market or arouses public interest in the offering. Press reports or oral comments attributable to an issuer whether or not they specifically refer to the offering, can constitute gun-jumping, as can interviews, speeches or participation at a conference.

Sanctions for offers made in the pre-filing period can be disruptive to the offer process. Where the SEC believes that a disclosure has had the effect of conditioning or arousing interest in the market, the SEC may require a "cooling-off" period (usually several weeks although it can be several months) so that the effect of the disclosure can dissipate. More typically, the SEC may request that an issuer include in its prospectus information disclosed and in violation of Section 5, and in a number of cases the SEC has required inclusion of a risk factor discussing the potential rescission rights available to investors arising out of the violation.

This type of sanction is rarely seen in the UK. Where an issuer's listing particulars or prospectus has been submitted for approval in accordance with the UK Listing Authority ("UKLA") Listing Rules ("Listing Rules"), it is unusual for the UKLA to require additional disclosures in the disclosure document based on publicity attributable to the issuer. The UKLA can however, rely upon paragraphs 12.21 to 12.27, in conjunction with paragraph 3.1 (under which the UKLA may make the application for listing subject to "special conditions" and the UKLA has an absolute discretion as to what they may be) of the Listing Rules, to require any profit forecast or estimate included in any publicity in the disclosure document to be reported upon.

Whatever the position adopted by the UKLA, the advisers to the issuer must be satisfied that the publicity does not oblige the issuer to make additional disclosures in the disclosure document to comply with the general duty of disclosure in listing particulars required by Section 80 FSMA.

Publication of information in the US on the website of an issuer is subject to the same publicity restrictions as for any other written communication.

13.4.3.2   *Permitted communications*

Every communication by an issuer should be considered with a view to whether it might be seen by the SEC as an attempt to "condition the market". However, the SEC has recognised the difficulties facing an issuer and its advisers and has agreed to permit three types of communications which would otherwise be prohibited by Section 5 1933 Act:

(a)   "ordinary course" communications;

(b)   communications in accordance with the Rule 135 "safe harbour"; and

(c)   communications in accordance with the Rule 135e "safe harbour".

Communications meeting the objective criteria set out in the two "safe harbour" rules will not be deemed to be an "offering" of securities in the US for the purposes of Section 5(c) 1933 Act, although the anti-fraud and other provisions of US securities law, particularly those relating to material misstatements, apply to such communications. Ordinary course communications will be permitted, although since they are permitted pursuant to SEC guidance and not under a safe harbour rule care needs to be taken to avoid "gun jumping" even where an "ordinary course" communication is ostensibly within the SEC's guidelines.

"Ordinary course" communications

In SEC Release 33-5180, the SEC cautioned issuers not to *initiate* publicity during registration, but encouraged issuers to *continue* to advertise products and services, and issue press releases regarding factual business and financial developments (e.g. receipt of a contract, settlement of a strike, opening of a plant, or similar events of interest to the community in which the business operates), and in the case of an existing registered issuer or a foreign private issuer having securities already traded on a UK or overseas exchange, the SEC guidance provides that companies can continue to send out customary financial information to shareholders, publish policy statements and other circulars to shareholders, send out dividend notices and hold regular shareholder meetings at which the issuer may answer enquiries as to factual matters and answer unsolicited factual enquiries from securities analysts, shareholders and the press. In addition, these communications should reflect the issuer's previous communication methods in terms of the level of information, the media used, and the regularity of announcements.

However, in Release 33-5180, the SEC specifically cautioned *against* issuing forecasts, projections or predictions relating to (but not limited to) revenues, income or earnings per share, and publishing opinions concerning values.

In the context of an issuer registering securities, the SEC's line between prohibited and permitted communications is not always clear. The judgment as to whether a particular communication, or product or image advert, is permitted is fact-specific. The SEC considers each situation in light of the relevant facts and circumstances, including the nature and content of the communication, the scope of its distribution, the timing in relation to the offering and the relationship between the issuer and the party responsible for the communication.

Rule 135 safe harbour

To alleviate the concern that issuers are not able to communicate information relating to any contemplated securities offerings to their shareholders, issuers are allowed to provide limited information about an offering prior to the filing of a registration statement.

Rule 135 under the 1933 Act allows an issuer to make a limited announcement of a proposed public offering of securities prior to the filing of a registration statement. Rule 135 allows an announcement to contain no more than certain specified basic information, including: the name of the issuer; the title, amount and basic terms of the securities offered; the amount of the offering; the anticipated time of the offering; whether the issuer is directing its offering only to a particular class of purchasers; and any legends required by the laws of any state or foreign country.

The announcement may also include a brief statement of the manner and purpose of the offering without naming the underwriters. The announcement *must* state that it is not an offer of any securities for sale. Where an offering is a rights offering or exchange offer (in UK parlance, a takeover bid), certain additional information can be included in the Rule 135 announcement. Because of these strict content limitations, the SEC does not consider such a press release to be an "offer" for the purpose of Section 5 1933 Act, thereby avoiding any "gun-jumping" concerns.

Rule 135e safe harbour for non-US companies

The second safe harbour is contained in Rule 135e under the 1933 Act. This rule is only available to a foreign private issuer and permits the issuer (or its selling security holders or their respective representatives) to distribute written press related materials relating to the offering at press conferences and meetings held *outside* the US, even if US journalists attend. The press conference/meeting must meet four objective conditions:

(a) The offering must be a global offering of the securities of a foreign private issuer, requiring the securities to be offered outside the US.

(b) The press conference or meeting, including all offshore written press-related materials, printed and otherwise, as well as all follow up contacts, must take place outside the US. Telecommunication links to the US are not permitted.

(c) Both US and non-US journalists must be permitted to attend and to receive the offshore written press-related materials. However, the issuer is not required to verify whether non-US journalists actually attend the conference or receive the related materials.

(d) All offshore written press-related materials must:
  (i) contain a warning label to the effect that securities may not be sold in the US unless they are registered or exempt from registration;
  (ii) if the issuer (or selling security holder) intends to register any part of the offering under the 1933 Act, include a statement regarding this intention; and
  (iii) *not* contain any purchase order form, coupon or other means by which a person may express an interest in the offering.

The 135e safe harbour covers:

(a) contacts with both print and broadcast journalists;
(b) one-on-one interviews;
(c) press releases; and
(d) press conferences. However, paid advertisements are not eligible for the 135e safe harbour.

Materials or press conferences that are disseminated through the internet would not otherwise comply with Rule 135e because they may be accessed by individuals in the US. However, a foreign private issuer may still take advantage of the Rule 135e safe harbour and disseminate materials and press conferences on its website provided that "procedures are implemented to assure that only permitted recipients under the rules are able to access the information".[37] The limitations on web-side access are described below in Section 13.4.6.

Although the SEC has not provided details about what procedures would qualify under Rule 135e, in other similar circumstances, issuers have installed "postal code blockers" on their websites to deny access to individuals in the US based on their postcodes.

13.4.4 *Waiting period*

13.4.4.1 *Legal principles*
During the "waiting period" after the SEC has completed its review of the registration statement the preliminary prospectus contained in the registration statement filed with the SEC will be used to market the securities. Only the preliminary prospectus can be used as a marketing document since Section 5(b)(1) 1933 Act provides that no "prospectus" other than one conforming to the requirements of Section 10 1933 Act may be used in connection with the offering.

The term "prospectus" is defined broadly to include all written or broadcast communications, including "any prospectus, notice, circular, advertisement, letter or communication, written or by radio or television, which offers any security for sale". Therefore, no written offering materials other than the prospectus on file with the SEC may be used, and save for these "ordinary communications" permitted by SEC Release 33–5180, broadcast communications and communications on the internet and on the issuer's website offering the securities are also prohibited. A

---

[37] Use of Electronic Media, Securities Act Release No. 33-7856, n. 68 (28 April, 2000) ("2000 Interpretive Release").

foreign private issuer can continue to rely upon Rule 135e to provide a safe harbour in relation to marketing presentations outside the US provided the presentation complies with the conditions in Rule 135e. Oral solicitations are subject to the anti-fraud and other provisions of the US securities laws, particularly those relating to material misstatements, and should be consistent in tone with the prospectus.

13.4.4.2   *Rule 134 announcement*

Rule 134 provides that a press release may be issued after the filing of the registration statement with the SEC without violating US federal securities laws. Typically, a press release complying with Rule 134 will be issued immediately after the initial public filing (but not the initial confidential submission available upon request and at the discretion of the SEC to a foreign private issuer for its first registration) of the registration statement. The press release is restricted to certain specified information, including: the name of the issuer; the title of the securities and the amount being offered; the timing of the proposed sale to the public; the price of the securities, or if the price is not known, the method of its determination or the probable range as specified by the issuer or the managing underwriter; a brief description of the issuer's business; the names of the managing underwriters; the name of the sender of the communication and whether or not it will participate in the distribution of securities; and any legends required by the laws of any state or foreign country.

In addition, the press release must include: (a) a specific legend stating that the registration statement has been filed with the SEC but has not yet become effective; (b) a statement as to whether the offering is a primary or a secondary offering, or both, and whether it represents new financing or refunding; and (c) the name and address of the persons from whom a written prospectus complying with Section 10 is available. The Rule 134 announcement is filed with the SEC.

13.4.5   *Post-effective period*

13.4.5.1   *Legal principles*

Once the registration statement is effective, sales may be made under Section 5(a) 1933 Act. However, Section 5(b)(2) requires that a final prospectus meeting the requirements of Section 10(a) 1933 Act must be delivered to an investor either before or accompanying a confirmation of the sale or delivery of the securities.

Section 2(a)(10) defines the term "prospectus" for the purposes of the 1933 Act to include any communication which confirms the sale of a security except that a communication sent or given after the effective date of the registration statement shall not be deemed a prospectus if prior to, or at the same time of, the communication a prospectus complying with Section 10(a) was sent or given to the person to whom the communication was made.

13.4.5.2 Permitted communications

After the effective date of the registration statement, the distribution of written materials in relation to the issuer is technically permitted (known in the US as "free writing"), so long as they are accompanied or preceded by the final prospectus. However, the practice is for no offering materials other than the final prospectus to be distributed after the effective date and all communications continue to be reviewed and cleared for at least one month after the final pricing of the offering, in light of the existence of an over-allotment option, which will generally extend beyond the closing date, the market's sensitivity to public disclosures immediately after an offering, and related anti-fraud issues.[38]

13.4.6 Communicating through a website during a registered offering

Publication of information on the internet or on the issuer's website, if found to "condition the market" for the offering of securities covered by the registration statement, could constitute either an offer or a non-conforming prospectus. Information on websites is viewed by the SEC as a written communication and thus subject to the same restrictions as any other written communication during a registered offering.

---

[38] If the offering written materials were also distributed in the UK in the post-effective period it will be necessary to consider whether or not they constitute a financial promotion for the purposes of Section 21(1) FSMA and if so whether such communication is either a non-real time communication or a solicited real time communication for the purposes of the Financial Promotion Order. Where the other materials comprise a broker-dealer's research note, the entity communicating the report into the UK will need to be an authorised person or have the contents of the research approved by an authorised person. The latter would be expected to be a member of the same group as the broker-dealer. Where the other materials constitute "ordinary course" communications for the purposes of SEC Release 33-5180 the communication can continue to rely upon Article 67 Financial Promotion Order, otherwise it will be necessary for the contents of those materials to be approved by an authorised person or their distribution in the UK to be limited to persons such as professional investors.

13.4.6.1 Permitted communications

The SEC has set out guidance on website communications in "Use of Electronic Media" No. 33-7856 ("the 2000 Interpretive Release"). Electronic communications published on an issuer's website are subject to the SEC's publicity restrictions (and their exceptions) for non-electronic communications during the pre-filing, waiting and post-effective periods of a registered offering.

The issuer can make "ordinary course" communications on its website. However, if an issuer is preparing for its first registered public offering and contemporaneously establishes a website, the issuer may need to apply the "ordinary-course" communications safe harbour more strictly than an issuer with an established website. If the issuer does not have a history of "ordinary-course" communication through a website, the SEC may deem the website content to "condition the market" in violation of its publicity restrictions.

During the three periods of registration outlined above, the relevant safe harbours outlined above also apply to information communicated electronically. However, for a foreign private issuer to take advantage of the Rule 135e safe harbour, an issuer must implement procedures on its website to exclude individuals in the US receiving information disseminated under Rule 135e.

13.4.6.2 The "envelope theory" and hyperlinking

Issuer websites often include "hyperlinks" which send internet users to non-company websites. Although, the SEC has not adopted a specific rule that hyperlinked information is imputed to an issuer, it issued guidance that if an issuer embeds a hyperlink in a website-posted document that is required to be filed or delivered to the SEC under US federal securities laws, the issuer will be deemed to have adopted the hyperlinked information. Further, an issuer is in registration, hyperlinks to information that meet the definition of "offer to sell", "offer for sale" or "offer" under Section 2(a) 3 1933 Act will raise a strong inference that the issuer has adopted that information for the purposes of Section 10(b) 1933 Act and Rule 10b-5. However, if the issuer establishes an intermediate screen between its website and the hyperlinked website which clearly states that the internet user is leaving the issuer's website or if the issuer disclaims responsibility for the hyperlinked information, the SEC is less likely to impute the hyperlinked information to the issuer.

The SEC has noted that concerns had been expressed that the posting of a Section 10 prospectus on a website during a registered offering may cause everything on the website to become part of the prospectus and that information on a website outside the strict interpretation of the Section 10 prospectus, but in close proximity to it, would be considered "free writing" and not all of this material may constitute permitted "ordinary course" communications.

In response, the SEC stated that information on a website would be part of a Section 10 prospectus only if an "issuer . . . acts to make it part of the prospectus". Such action could include an embedded hyperlink in a Section 10 prospectus whereby the hyperlinked information would be considered to be part of the prospectus. With respect to the free writing concern, the SEC cautioned issuers that irrespective of where the Section 10 prospectus is posted, the website as a whole must be reviewed "in its entirety" to determine whether it contains impermissible "free writing". The SEC warned that it will continue to raise questions about information on an issuer's website that is inconsistent with the issuer's Section 10 prospectus or information that would constitute an "offer to sell", "offer for sale" or "offer".

13.4.7 Risks and sanctions

If publicity is viewed as "conditioning the market" by arousing investor interest, investors have a right of rescission and to damages if the securities have been sold. Another risk arises from the US legal principle that any writing which could be construed as an offering document may be deemed to be a prospectus. The 1933 Act makes it unlawful to transmit a prospectus unless the contents comply with the detailed requirements of Rule 430 to the 1933 Act. If an issuer is in breach, a purchaser of securities could theoretically seek to rescind the purchase on the grounds that the publicity did not comply with the statutory requirements as the contents of a prospectus. A purchaser also may be able to claim under the anti-fraud provisions of the securities laws on the grounds that the publicity was materially misleading or omitted material facts. More typically, the consequences of a breach of US publicity restrictions is that the SEC imposes a "cooling-off" period which will disrupt the timetable for the US public offering.

13.4.8 FSMA and communication for registered offerings

Potential issues will arise under Section 21(1) FSMA and the Financial Promotion Order after the lead underwriter starts to market the offering of the securities and the "road show" is extended to persons in the UK.

The issuer and lead underwriter should be able to rely upon Article 67 Financial Promotion Order in respect of any non-real time communication (which will include the preliminary prospectus, the written materials to be made available under the Rule 135e safe harbour, the Rule 134 Notice and those materials that are "ordinary course" communications (*see* Section 13.4.3.2) and any solicited real time communication (which will include a press conference or presentation held in the UK where the investor has responded to an invitation to attend), so it will not be necessary for an investment bank to approve the contents of the financial promotion for the purposes of Section 21(1) FSMA; although it may be more practicable in the context of managing the potential liability of the issuer and the lead underwriter that the financial promotion be communicated only to investment professionals and high net worth companies.

In the unlikely event that the Rule 135 notice is communicated into the UK, the exemption contained in Article 67 will not be available and, unless its communication is limited to investment professionals and high net worth companies, it will be necessary for the contents of the Rule 135 notice to be approved by an investment bank for the purposes of Section 21(1) FSMA.

UK persons can be expected to access the issuer's website and carry out research into the issuer via the internet. The issuer's website will be a non-real time communication under Section 21(1) FSMA, save to the extent that it includes any web-cast which features interactive dialogue which cannot be construed as a solicited real time communication under Section 21(1) FSMA.

Issuer-related information which is only included on the issuer's website after the "road show" has commenced on the basis described in Section 13.4.1, can be communicated electronically to persons in the UK. However, if the issuer and lead underwriter decide to limit the communication of offering materials in the UK to professional investors the issuer may prefer to rely upon Article 12 Financial Promotion Order and limit all internet access in the UK only to professional investors and the internet communication is deemed to be a communication to persons outside the UK.

Where the issuer's website publishes the preliminary prospectus, but makes it clear that outside the US the offering of securities will be restricted to investment professionals, it is difficult to see how that communication will constitute an offer of securities for the purposes of paragraph (a) of Regulation S (*see* Section 13.3.2.2) or an invitation to treat for the purposes of paragraph (b) of Regulation 5 Public Offers of Securities Regulations 1995 ("POS Regs"). However, the standard procedure in the UK is to seek to limit access to the website in the UK only to those persons who satisfy the professional investors exemption set out in paragraph 2(a) of Regulation 7 POS Regs.

13.4.9 Unregistered offerings publicity restrictions on private placements

13.4.9.1 Legal principles
Because private placements restrict the offer and sale of securities to particular classes of investors (i.e. accredited investors or to 35 or fewer non-accredited investors (*see* Section 13.3.4.1)) the SEC imposes a corresponding restriction on publicity relating to these offerings. In order to qualify for a private placement safe harbour, there can be no general solicitation in connection with the offer and sale of securities. Rule 502 of Regulation D places a restriction on general solicitation or general advertising including any advertisement, article, notice or other communication published in any newspaper, magazine or similar media or broadcast by television or radio and any seminar or meeting whose attendees have been invited by any general solicitation or general advertising.

13.4.9.2 Permitted communications
As in registered offerings, "ordinary course" communications and communications that fall within the Rule 135e safe harbour are permissible in relation to private placements. However, the Rule 135 safe harbour for registered offerings is not available for a non-registered offering. Instead, issuers proposing to issue or sell securities in a private placement are permitted to announce the proposed placement pursuant to Rule 135c, which permits an issuer reporting under the 1934 Act (and certain foreign private issuers exempt from 1934 Act reporting under Rule 12g3-2(b) 1934 Act) to publish a notice that it proposes to make, is making or has made an unregistered offering of securities. This is *provided* that such notice: is not used for the purpose of conditioning the market in the US for the securities offered; contains no more than the following additional information: "the name of the issuer, the title, amount and basic terms of the securities offered, the amount of the offering, if any, to be made by selling security holders, the time of the offering and a brief statement of the manner and purpose of the offering without naming the underwriters"; includes a legend stating that the securities will not be and have not been registered and may not be offered

or sold in the US absent registration or an applicable exemption from registration; and is filed with or furnished to the SEC under cover of Form 8-K or 6-K,[39] or pursuant to Rule 12g3-2(b).

Rule 135c provides that such a notice will not be deemed to be an "offer" of securities for purposes of Section 5 1933 Act, and Rule 502(c) of Regulation D provides that such a notice will not be deemed to constitute a general solicitation or general advertising under Regulation D.

13.4.10   Regulation S

13.4.10.1   Background
Regulation S is often relied upon where a company with shares listed on the London Stock Exchange wishes to offer further shares of the same class and offer these both to QIBs[40] in the US and to investors outside the US. In making the latter offer, the issuer will need to comply with Regulation S, otherwise it may breach Section 5 1933 Act.

13.4.10.2   Publicity restrictions on Regulation S offerings
The principal publicity restriction with respect to the Regulation S safe harbour is a ban on "directed selling efforts" into the US. The phrase "directed selling efforts" is broadly defined to be "any activity undertaken for the purpose of, or that could reasonably be expected to have the effect of, conditioning the market in the US for any of the securities being offered in reliance on . . . Regulation S". Offers and selling efforts in connection with a registered offering or exempt offering in the US are not deemed to be directed selling efforts.[41] Generally, directed selling efforts may not be made during the period in which the issuer, underwriters or their affiliates are offering and selling the securities.

---

[39] Form 8-K is required to be filed by every issuer (except a foreign private issuer) registered under Section 12g 1934 Act, upon the occurrence of certain events such as changes in control of the registrant; bankruptcy or receivership, changes in a registrant's certifying accountant, change in director, financial statements, other events and Regulation FD disclosures. A registered foreign private will be required to file Form 6-K on the occurrence of a disclosure obligation arising under the laws of the issuer's home jurisdiction or other exchange on which the issuer's shares are listed and on the occurrence of other events which the issuer thinks is likely to be of interest to its investors.

[40] *See* Section 13.3.6.2 for a description of "QIBs".

[41] Offshore Offers and Sales, Securities Act Release No. 33-6863 (24 April, 1990) (the "Regulation S Adopting Release").

Permitted communications

The SEC specified in the Regulation S Adopting Release that the rule is not intended to inhibit routine activities conducted in the US for purposes other than inducing the purchase or sale of securities being distributed abroad. The SEC noted that "the dissemination of routine information of the character and content normally published by a company, and unrelated to a securities selling effort, generally would not be directed selling efforts". For example, press releases regarding the financial results of the issuer or the occurrence of material events with respect to the issuer generally will not be deemed to be directed selling efforts.[42] On the other hand, the SEC warned that the dissemination of "routine corporate communications or product advertising shortly before or during an offshore offering" by a company which does not have a history of disseminating such information might well constitute directed selling efforts.[43]

The SEC also noted that "legitimate" selling efforts carried out in the US in connection with an offering registered under the 1933 Act or exempt from registration will not constitute directed selling efforts with respect to offers and sales made under Regulation S. For example, "legitimate US selling activities made in connection with the sale of securities in compliance with Rule 144A, or in a private placement exempt under

---

[42] Regulation S Adopting Release.

[43] The Commission has specifically carved out of the definition of directed selling efforts the following:

(1) Advertisements carried in publications with a general circulation in the US if the advertisements are legally required and contain a legend to the effect that the securities have not been registered under the 1933 Act.

(2) "Tombstone" advertisements if in a publication with less than 20 per cent of its circulation (calculated by aggregating its comparable US and non-US editions) in the US, such advertisement contains the legend required by Rule 902(b)(2) of Regulation S, and the advertisement contains no more information than:

The issuer's name; the amount and title of the securities being sold; a brief indication of the issuer's general type of business; the price of the securities; the yield of the securities, if debt securities with a fixed non-contingent interest provision; the name and address of the person placing the advertisement and whether such person is participating in the distribution; the names of the managing underwriters; the dates, if any, upon which the sale commenced and concluded; whether the securities are offered or were offered by rights issued to security holders and, if so, the class of securities that is entitled or were entitled to subscribe, the subscription ratio, the record date, the dates (if any) upon which the rights were issued and expired, and the subscription price; and any legend required by law or any foreign or US regulatory or self-regulatory authority.

Section 4(2) or Rule 506 of Regulation D generally will not result in directed selling efforts". Thus, the distribution of offering circulars, roadshows or research that is limited to qualifying purchasers should not raise directed selling efforts issues in the context of an exempt offering.

Directed selling efforts do not include "providing any journalist with access to press conferences held outside the US, to meetings with the issuer or selling security holder representatives conducted outside the US, or to written press-related materials released outside the US, at or in which the offering of securities is discussed, if the requirements of Rule 135e are met".

13.4.11 *Communicating through a website during a private placement or Regulation S offering*

13.4.11.1 *Communicating through a website during a private placement*
Without implementing procedures to restrict access to a class of permitted purchasers, the SEC views the placing of private offering materials on a company's website as violating the prohibition against general solicitation advertising. The SEC has taken the position in a no-action letter that the qualification of accredited investors or QIBs, and the posting of a notice of a private offering in a password-protected page on a website accessible only to such qualified individuals would not involve a "general solicitation".[44]

Private offering materials may be transmitted electronically to prospective purchasers who have been identified without a general solicitation and who have given proper consent to their electronic delivery.

13.4.11.2 *Communicating through a website during a Regulation S offering*
To maintain the exemption provided by Regulation S, electronic communications undertaken during an offshore offering must not be targeted at the US. The SEC has established different restrictions for non-US issuers and US issuers conducting Regulation S offerings.

Non-US issuer
The SEC maintain that an offshore internet offer made by a non-US issuer would not be viewed by the SEC as targeted at persons in the US if:

---

[44] IPOnet, 1996 SEC No-Act. LEXIS 642 (26 July, 1996).

(a)   the website includes a prominent disclaimer making it clear that the offer is directed only to countries other than the US;[45] and

(b)   the issuer and underwriters implement procedures that are reasonably designed to guard against sales to US persons in the offshore offer. For example, such procedures may include the use of a blocker requiring that a postal code or phone number be given and/or requiring a social or national identity number be given before the user has access to the offer.[46]

These procedures are not exclusive. Other procedures that suffice to guard against sales to US persons also can be used to demonstrate that the offer is not targeted at the US.

If, despite the issuer's implementation of reasonable procedures, a US person circumvents such procedures and buys the securities, this would not, of itself, cause the SEC to consider the offer to be targeted at US persons so long as the issuer did not have reason to believe the buyer was a US person. However, frequent circumventions may cause the reasonableness of the procedures to be questioned.

In addition, precautions of the nature described above will not safeguard solicitations that appear by their content to be targeted at US persons. For example, if the solicitation includes a discussion of the US tax advantages of the investment, it is likely to be viewed as being targeted at the US.

US issuers
The SEC requires additional precautions with respect to electronic communications for US issuers undertaking unregistered offshore offerings because of such issuers' increased contact with US investors, the likelihood of "flowback" of the securities into the US and the SEC's belief of investor expectations that securities offerings by US issuers will be subject to US securities laws. Accordingly, in addition to the precautions outlined above, a US issuer must also implement a limited-access system using password-type procedures that are reasonably designed to ensure that only non-US persons can obtain access to the offer.

---

[45] An example of such a disclaimer would be, "This offering is intended only to be available to residents of countries within the European Union".

[46] Use of internet websites to Offer Securities, Solicit Securities Transactions, or Advertise Investment Services Offshore, Securities Act Release No. 33-7516 (23 March, 1998).

Concurrent Regulation S/Private Placement

It is possible for the issuer to offer and sell the same class of securities to QIBs in the US under Rule 144A and to persons outside the US under Regulation S. Each offer has a separate set of re-sale restrictions. Accordingly, an issuer must prevent electronic communications publicising its offshore Regulation S offer from being used to solicit participants for its US based exempt offering. Issuers should use reasonable precautions to prevent persons using the internet to respond to an offshore Regulation S offer and seek to participate in its exempt US offering, even if qualified to do so. Accordingly, in addition to the use of postal code/residence blockers, the Regulation S offering materials should relate only to the offshore offering. Materials should contain only that information (if any) concerning the US private placement that is required by foreign law to be provided to investors participating in the offshore Regulation S offering.

13.4.11.3   Risks and sanctions

If publicity were issued which was viewed to be a general solicitation or directed selling efforts in the US, the offering of securities – whether a private placing or a Regulation S offering – would violate the registration requirements of Section 5 1933 Act, which would give US investors the right of rescission of the contract under which the securities were purchased and to damages where the securities have been sold.

13.4.11.4   Position under FSMA

The FSMA and the Financial Promotion Order may be less relevant in the context of a private placement or Regulation S offering by a foreign private issuer.

Although it is difficult to generalise, a private placement into the US by a foreign private issuer incorporated in the UK or elsewhere in Europe is likely to include offering and selling documentation and possibly a disclosure document such as listing particulars that has been approved by the relevant competent authority so that the relevant securities can be traded or dealt on a UK or other European exchange. If the securities are "permitted to be traded or dealt" on a European relevant market other than London the Article 67 exemption may be available should the documentation be distributed in the UK. Unless the relevant securities are also to be admitted to the Official List in London to avoid the making of a public offer in the UK it is likely that the offer and selling documentation and any disclosure document will be distributed only to those persons described in Regulation 7(2)(c)(i) POS Regs.

A similar analysis is likely to apply to a Regulation S offering of securities by a foreign private issuer.

Since securities offered and sold by way of a private placement or Regulation S are unlikely to be traded or dealt on the NYSE or Nasdaq, the Article 67 exemption by reason of compliance with US federal securities laws will not be available, notwithstanding that the issuer will have to comply with the various SEC safe harbours to avoid a breach of Section 5 1933 Act.

If Article 67 cannot be relied upon it will be necessary to limit non-electronic communication of any non-real time communication or solicited real time communication to professional investors and high net worth companies, pursuant to and in accordance with Articles 19 and 49 Financial Promotion Order, unless the investment bank is able and willing to approve the contents of the relevant documents for the purposes of Section 21(1) FSMA.

Where a foreign private issuer makes a private placement to QIBs and/or accredited investors in the US and/or, assuming the issuer is not a UK corporate making a Regulation S offering of securities outside the US and that the foreign private issuer makes an electronic communication of offering materials on its website (and assuming that the issuer cannot rely upon Article 67) the foreign private issuer will likely rely upon Article 12 Financial Promotion Order. This provides that the financial promotion restriction will not apply to a non-real time communication or solicited real time communication published on the issuer's website on the basis that the materials are communicated to persons deemed to be outside the UK; provided that the issuer complies with certain conditions. If the issuer wishes to offer securities in the UK, it can still rely upon Article 12 provided that offers are made only to such professional investors and high net worth companies as such persons are deemed to be persons outside the UK for the purposes of Article 12.

13.5   Securities offerings: analysts' research reports

13.5.1   *Background*

These are usually prepared by analysts to provide information and research material, and often an investment opinion, with respect to an issuer, industry or country.

The SEC is concerned that in many global equity offerings for private foreign issuers, the market practice has been for the underwriters to sell the securities on the basis of disclosures contained in research reports prepared by underwriters in the syndicate, rather than the registration statement. As a result the SEC has imposed a number of restrictions on the use of research reports in connection with offerings of securities. The SEC consider a research report to constitute an "offer" during the pre-filing period and a "prospectus" during the waiting and post-effective periods[47] with the result that the SEC strictly regulates distribution of research reports throughout the offering.

13.5.2   1933 Act violations in registered deals

Section 5 1933 Act provides that unless a registration statement is in effect as to a security it shall be unlawful to sell the "security through the use or medium of any prospectus or otherwise" or "offer to sell or offer to buy" the security "through the use or medium of any prospectus or otherwise". Since a research report is capable of being the basis upon which an offer for securities can be made, the publication and distribution of research reports containing information, opinions or recommendations with respect to a proposed offering could, under certain circumstances, violate Sections 5(c) or 5(b)(1) or (2) 1933 Act.

13.5.2.1   Publication during the Pre-filing period

Generally, no offers, written or oral, can be made prior to the filing of a registration statement (as is explained in more detail in Section 13.2). The term "offer" is broadly defined to "include every attempt or offer to dispose of, or solicitation of an offer to buy, a security or interest in a security, for value".

The SEC has long cautioned that the publication of research reports may violate the "gun-jumping" prohibition of Section 5(c) because the research report might be considered an "offer", under the broad definition of Section 2(a)(3).

Sanctions for "gun-jumping" violations can disrupt the proposed timetable for a transaction. The SEC may impose a "cooling-off" period until the effect of the publication of the research report has dissipated.

---

[47] For an explanation of the pre-filing period, the waiting period and the post effective period *see* sub-Section 13.2.2.

13.5.2.2 *Publication during the waiting period*

Section 5(b)(1) 1933 Act prohibits the publication or issue of a prospectus during the waiting period in respect of which a registration statement has been filed, unless such prospectus meets the requirements of Section 10 1933 Act.

Publication of a research report after filing the registration statement, therefore, creates a different risk to publication in the pre-filing period. The report will no longer be deemed an "offer" for the purposes of Section 2(a)(3) but may be considered a "prospectus" for the purposes of Section 2(a)(10). During the waiting period, securities may be orally offered for sale, but an actual sale or a contract to sell securities is prohibited, and only a preliminary prospectus whose contents comply with Rule 430[48] 1933 Act may be distributed. Therefore, when the underwriters market the deal by means of a "road show" to "build a book" on the basis of the preliminary prospectus, they are prohibited from distributing any other written materials together with the preliminary prospectus. Even a cover note accompanying the prospectus would technically violate the provisions of Section 5(b)(1).

Therefore, during the waiting period the only publications permitted by the SEC in addition to the preliminary prospectus are the Rule 134 notice, the offering materials permitted to be published outside the US by a foreign private issuer under Rule 135e and research that satisfies the specific safe harbours referred to in Sections 13.5.7.1 to 13.5.7.3 below.

13.5.2.3 *Publication during the post-effective period*

During this period, sales may be made. However, Section 5(b)(2) 1933 Act requires that a final prospectus meeting the requirements of Section 10 be delivered to an investor prior to or with their sales confirmation. Therefore, an underwriter publishing or distributing a research report prior to the delivery of the Section 11 prospectus will violate Section 5(b)(2).

---

[48] Rule 430 under the 1933 Act provides that a form of prospectus filed as part of a registration statement shall be deemed to meet the requirements of Section 10 1933 Act prior to the effective date of the registration statement provided such prospectus contains the information required by the 1933 Act. However, Rule 430 allows the omission of the offering price, underwriting discounts or commissions, discounts or commissions to dealers, amount of proceeds, conversion rates, call prices, or other matters dependent on the offering price.

Sanctions for using a non-conforming prospectus during the waiting period and post-effective periods may vary from administrative penalties by the SEC to the underwriting syndicate excluding the rogue underwriter from the syndicate.

13.5.3   *1933 Act violations in unregistered deals*

13.5.3.1   *Private placements and Rule 144A offerings*
Section 4(2) exempts all "transactions by an issuer not involving a public offering" from the registration and prospectus delivery requirements of Section 5 1933 Act. The SEC has adopted a framework to govern reliance on this exemption now contained in Regulation D which was promulgated as a safe harbour under Section 4(2) 1933 Act.

In addition, the SEC adopted Rule 144A which enables securities to be sold to "qualified institutional buyers" ("QIBs").[49]

In order to rely on the Section 4(2) exemption and/or the Regulation D safe harbour and the re-sale safe harbour under Rule 144A, the private placement must comply, among other things, with limitations on the scope of the solicitation. There can be no "general solicitation" or "general advertising" in connection with the offering of securities. Similarly, Rule 144A restricts offers and sales to QIBs.

The publication of a research report may violate the private placement or the Rule 144A framework, and due to the broad content of a research report it is unlikely that it would fall under either the Rule 135c or 135e safe harbours (discussed in Sections 13.4.3.2 and 13.4.8.3). Since research reports may be widely distributed, they may be deemed to be a violation of the "general advertising" or "general solicitation" requirements of Section 4(2) or Regulation D and may be considered an "offer" to someone other than a QIB for the purposes of Rule 144A.

13.5.3.2   *Regulation S*
In order for an issuer to rely on the safe harbour provisions of Regulation S, it must meet two general conditions. First, the offer and sale must be made in an "offshore transaction" and second, there must be no "directed selling efforts" in the US.

---

[49] Private placements under Section 4(2) and Rule 144A offerings are discussed in more detail in Section 13.3.

The SEC have indicated that the publication of research reports in the US could constitute an "offer" in the US, which would violate the "offshore transaction" and "directed selling efforts" requirement of Regulation S.[50] A research report may violate the "offshore transaction" requirement of Regulation S if it is considered an "offer" made to "US persons" and it may constitute "directed selling efforts" if it is seen as an "activity undertaken for the purpose of, or that could reasonably be expected to have the effect of conditioning the market in the US . . .".

The SEC also indicated that where an issuer is not a reporting issuer, "the effect on the market of publication or distribution of [research reports] about the issuer or its securities can be expected to be more significant due to the possible absence of other publicly available information about the issuer. Distributors and their affiliates should exercise greater caution in publication or distribution of [research reports] concerning nonreporting issuers or their securities".[51]

13.5.4 *1933 Act violations*

13.5.4.1 Regulation M
Regulation M outlines the SEC's regime for the anti-manipulation regulation of securities offerings which are described in more detail in Sections 13.6 to 13.9 of this Chapter.

The publication of a research report may violate the anti-manipulation prohibitions of Regulation M as a prohibited "inducement to purchase" during the restricted period specified under Regulation M. However, Rule 101 of Regulation M expressly permits the "publication or dissemination of any information, opinion or recommendation" in a research report during the restricted period if done in compliance with either Rules 138 139 1933 Act.

13.5.4.2 Proxy rules
The proxy rules do not apply to a foreign private issuer. However, very briefly, with the passage of the 1934 Act, the US Congress wanted to address the issue of corporate fraud that had been perpetrated by directors and officers of US corporates soliciting shareholders for their proxy at general meetings without appropriate disclosure to shareholders of the matters to be voted upon. Accordingly, Section 14 1934 Act

---

[50] SEC Securities Act Release No. 33-6863 (2 May, 1990).
[51] Ibid.

was enacted to regulate shareholder voting of corporations. In order to monitor the proxy solicitation disclosure, issuers other than foreign private issuers are required to file their proxy solicitation materials with the SEC. "Solicitation" is broadly defined to include any "communication to security holders under circumstances reasonably calculated to result in the procurement, withholding or revocation of a proxy".

13.5.5   *Distribution restrictions during an offering*

The distribution of research reports during an offering may pose various legal risks including violations of Section 5 1933 Act, Regulation D (for private placements), Rule 144A, Regulation S, Regulation M, and the proxy rules.

Accordingly, lead underwriters often impose various conditions and restrictions on the distribution of research reports. In a global offering the distribution of research is prohibited within the US, unless one of the safe harbour rules described in Section 13.5.7 is available, but research generally is permitted outside the US. To avoid further the characterisation of a research report as an offer of securities or a prospectus, the lead underwriters will require certain legends to be used and generally restrict the use of "buy" or "sell" recommendations.

13.5.5.1 *Restricted period*
In a global offering, a "restricted period" is established during which each prospective syndicate member must ensure that no research report relating to the company is distributed into the US unless it falls within one of the safe harbour provisions described in sub-Section 13.5.7. This is achieved by legending the research report and by restricting its distribution only to those institutional customers who have addresses outside the US. The restricted period, decreases the risk that the report will violate Section 5 1933 Act. To further decrease this risk, research reports should only be prepared and delivered in physical form, as opposed to electronic form unless adequate measures can be taken to ensure that the report is not viewed in the US, and research reports should not be distributed to the media. Typically, although not always, such restrictions are also extended to "US persons" outside the US because of the concern that a US person is more likely to send a research report back into the US than a non-US person.

In a follow-on offering, research that complies with Rule 139 (as described in Section 13.5.7) may be distributed during the restricted period. In a Rule 144A offering, although the underwriters may distribute research to QIBs during the restricted period without affecting their Rule 144A exemption, this may increase their potential liability since no issuer will indemnify a bank for its research reports and research reports do not go through the same diligence process as a prospectus.

The restricted period typically begins on the date that the prospective syndicate member submits a proposal to become a syndicate member or is invited to join one of the syndicates and lasts until the end of the "black-out period", which generally conforms to the length of time that a dealer is required to deliver a prospectus to a purchaser when selling the relevant securities.

13.5.5.2   Blackout period

During a global offering and after the commencement of the "restricted period", a "black-out period" is imposed during which no research reports may be sent out anywhere in the world. There is no US securities laws basis for the blackout period. The idea behind the blackout period, which started in the early UK privatisations, was to separate the research report from the prospectus so that the research report could be insulated from the offering liability attaching to the prospectus as a result of the law of the relevant jurisdiction in which the offering is being made. Although the relevant English provision, which provided that a statement incorporated in a report "issued with a prospectus" would be deemed to be included in that prospectus for the purposes of the liability provisions of Sections 56 to 70 of the Companies Act 1985, has been repealed, the concept of the blackout period continues. The blackout period will include the offering period and will commence with the distribution of the preliminary prospectus and usually from an earlier date where a period in advance of the distribution date is selected to provide an additional window of safety.

In the early UK privatisations, the blackout period usually commenced 60 days prior to the distribution date of the pathfinder prospectus but that period was subsequently reduced to 30 days. Generally, the practice today is to begin the blackout period two weeks prior to the distribution date of the preliminary prospectus. This two week time period can be eliminated, in which case the blackout period will commence on the distribution date of the preliminary prospectus if the lead underwriters agree.

The coming into force of the FSMA has not affected the analysis of a blackout period under English law.

The termination of the blackout period, and subsequently the restricted period, coincide with the following prospectus delivery requirements under US securities laws:

(a) *Registered initial public offering:* if the issuer's securities are listed on a national securities exchange or quoted on Nasdaq, the black-out period ends 25 days after the later of the effective date of the registration statement or the first date on which the security was bona fide offered to the public. This coincides with the prospectus delivery requirements of Section 4(3)(B) 1933 Act and Rule 174(d) 1933 Act;

(b) *Registered follow-on-offering:* if the issuer is subject, immediately prior to filing the registration statement with the SEC, to the reporting requirements of Sections 13 or 15(d) 1934 Act, the blackout period ends upon the closing of the offering, assuming the distribution of the preliminary prospectus was completed. There is no prospectus delivery requirement for an issuer satisfying the requirements of Rule 174(b);

(c) *Rule 144/Regulation S:* the blackout period is generally 40 days after pricing the offering in order to conform to the period in Section 4(3) 1933 Act during which broker-dealers must deliver a prospectus when selling securities.

The blackout period can also be extended to equate to local permissible stabilisation periods (*see* Section 13.9).

13.5.5.3 Other restrictions

The timing restrictions are one way in which the underwriters in the syndicate can reduce the risk that the distribution of research reports will violate the provisions of the 1933 and 1934 Acts. To avoid further the characterisation of a research report as an offer of securities or as a prospectus, the lead underwriters will require that:

(a) the research report contains legends stating that the report may not be distributed in the US, does not constitute an offer for sale and should not be relied upon for any investment decision;

(b) the research report makes clear that it does not, and does not attempt to, contain everything material about the issuer; and

(c) the research report is written by someone independent of the issuer.

Explicit "buy" or "sell" recommendations, or implicit recommendations (such as "undervalued"), are usually excluded from the research report.

13.5.6 *Content restrictions during an offering*

Each underwriter in the syndicate, as well as the issuer, will also want to limit the reputational and liability risks for the content of research published by other syndicate members during an offering. To minimise these risks, the lead underwriter and the issuer may choose to review research reports before they are distributed. Any review, however, is on the understanding that no liabilities will be accepted by the issuer or lead underwriter for any reliance on any comments provided and that each report is presented as the independent work of its author. In addition, the lead underwriter may also want to restrict the use of projections and valuations, which are more susceptible to liability.

13.5.6.1 *Independence of research reports*
To reduce the risk of Rule 10b-5 or other disclosure based liability, it is important to establish that each report is independently produced by the report's authors and not the responsibility of the issuer, the lead underwriter or any other underwriting syndicate member. As such, the research guidelines distributed by the lead underwriter usually require that:

(a)   the source of the information in the report must be made clear. To the extent that there are any statements that cannot be substantiated, this must be made clear, in particular, statements that are matters of opinion or conjecture of the authors must be highlighted;

(b)   various legends are placed within each research report that state that the document has been independently prepared by the author and is not to be relied upon as a representation of the issuer, the lead underwriter or any other underwriting syndicate member;

(c)   any impression that the research report is definitive or authoritative, that it contains or is based on information provided by the issuer or any other underwriting syndicate member, or that it represents the views of persons other than the authors should be clearly negated.

13.5.6.2 *Projections and valuations*
The inclusion of projections or valuations, may lead to a greater potential liability. In addition, some local securities regulators, such as the French *Commission des Opérations* may in certain cases require information included in research reports (including projections or valuations) to be disclosed in the issuer's disclosure documents. The UKLA's principal sanction in this regard is paragraphs 12.21 to 12.27 Listing Rules (*see*

Section 13.4.3.1). As a result, some lead underwriters do not allow projections and valuations to be included in research reports but if they are there should be a disclaimer.

13.5.7   1933 Act safe harbour rules for registered deals

The issues and concerns relating to the dissemination of broker-dealer research reports during a distribution were examined in 1969 in the Wheat Report.[52] Rules 137, 138 and 139 were promulgated pursuant to the Wheat Report recommendations to provide guidance and safe harbour protection regarding the dissemination of broker-dealer research reports which discuss an issuer in registration.

In the 1998 Aircraft Carrier Release,[53] the SEC proposed a new regulatory regime allowing for free and open offering communications. Due to severe criticism, the Aircraft Carrier Release was never adopted. However, in 1999, the SEC announced that it intended to move forward separately with individual aspects of the release, including the initiatives on research reports.

That the SEC's Aircraft Carrier Release initiatives on research reports would have substantially expanded the existing safe harbours is an acknowledgement of the benefits provided to investors by research. However, one consequence would have been that research reports would have made the broker-dealers subject to potential Section 12(a)(2) 1933 Act liability. Section 12(a)(2) imposes liability on any person who offers or sells a security by means of a prospectus or oral communication "which includes an untrue statement of a material fact or omits to state a material fact necessary in order to make the statements in the light of the circumstances under which they were made, not misleading". Breach of Section 12(a)(2) would entitle an investor to rescind the purchase contract, or if the security is no longer owned, a right to damages. This liability would extend to any person who sold the securities by means of the research report, whether or not that person was an underwriter. Therefore, the threat for heightened liability to the underwriters for research published during the offering period outweighed the advantages of the liberalisation of the rules. Potential liability under Section

---

[52] Disclosure to Investors – A Reappraisal of Administrative Policies Under the '33 and '34 Acts (27 March, 1969). The report was prepared for submission to the Commission at the director of Commissioner Francis M. Wheat.
[53] Securities Act Release No. 33-7606A (November 14, 1998) ("Aircraft Carrier Release").

12(a)(2) continues to discourage continued updating of research during the offering period, at least in the US.

13.5.7.1 Rule 137

Rule 137 permits persons not having any arrangements with participants in the distribution to publish research reports with respect to securities of a *reporting company* that has filed or proposes to file a registration statement. The rule states that such publication will not constitute an "offer" of securities if the reports are published in the *regular course of its business* as a broker-dealer that:

(a) is not, and does not propose to be, a participant in the distribution of the relevant securities, and

(b) receives no consideration, directly or indirectly, from the reporting company or any other participant in the distribution.

Rule 137 therefore confirms that a person not participating in a distribution is not restricted by Section 5 1933 Act and thus has no limit as to what it can publish concerning a company in registration. There would be no violation of the Section 5(b) 1933 Act since the report is not be deemed to be a prospectus either in the waiting period or post-effective period, nor would it violate the Section 5(c) "gun-jumping" provisions in the pre-filing period since no offer is being made.

However, Rule 137 has several limitations. First, it applies only to reporting companies (i.e. companies registered or otherwise already reporting under the 1934 Act) and therefore cannot be relied upon in the case of an IPO. Second, underwriters who are distribution participants cannot rely on this safe harbour. Third, since Rule 137 is not applicable to non-reporting companies, it does not give non-distribution participants an advantage in IPOs.

13.5.7.2 Rule 138

Under Rule 138, broker-dealers *participating in a distribution* may, in the *regular course of business*, publish research reports which contain information, opinions or recommendations:

(a) solely relating to a non-convertible debt security or non-convertible, non-participating preferred shares, if the issuer proposes to file or has filed a registration statement solely relating to the issuer's ordinary shares or debt or preferred shares convertible into the issuer's ordinary shares; or

(b)   solely relating to ordinary shares or debt or preferred ordinary shares convertible into the issuer's ordinary shares, if the issuer proposes to file or has filed a registration statement solely relating to non-convertible debt or non-convertible, non-participating preferred ordinary shares.

Rule 138 regards a research report that satisfies the conditions of that Rule as neither constituting an "offer" or a "prospectus". The SEC's reasoning is that since the markets for non-convertible senior securities and ordinary shares differ significantly, Rule 138 provides a safe harbour in circumstances where the opportunity to condition the market is lessened.

In an instruction to the rule, the SEC noted that if the offering is a shelf registration, then the distribution participant may rely on either exemption depending on the type of security being offered.

Rule 138 does, however, have several limitations. First, the rule is limited to reporting companies that qualify to report to the SEC using Form S-2/ F-2 or Form S-3/F-3,[54] or to specified foreign private

---

[54] The registrant must meet all the conditions for the use of Form S-2 or F-2 or it must meet the registrant requirements of Form S-3 or F-3. Forms S-2 and S-3 apply to US companies and Forms F-2 and F-3 apply to foreign private issuers. Forms S-2 or F-2 and S-3 or F-3 apply to the registration of securities of issuers meeting minimum eligibility requirements as to the availability of current public information and satisfactory financial conditions and Form S-3 or F-3 apply only to registration of securities in specified types of transactions. A foreign private issuer may use Form F-2 to register securities under the 1933 Act if; (a) the registrant is registered under the 1934 Act and has filed annual reports on Form 20-F, on Form 10-K or, in the case of registrants who come within the exception in (c) below, on Form 40-F, on Form 40-F under the 1934 Act and: (b) the registrant: (i) has been subject to the requirements of Section 12 or 15(d) 1934 Act and has filed all the information required to be filed pursuant to Section 13,14 or 15(d) for a period of at least 36 calendar months immediately preceding the filing of the Form F-2(b) has filed all reports required to be filed during the 12 calendar months immediately preceding the filing of the Form F-2 and, if the issuer has used (during that time) Rule 12b-25(b) under the 1934 Act with respect to a report, that report has actually been filed within the time period prescribed by the rule; except that (c) the provisions of this paragraph (b)(i) do not apply to any registrant if: (•) the aggregate market value worldwide of the voting and non-voting common equity of the registrant held by non-affiliates is the equivalent of $75 million or more, or if non-convertible debt securities that are "investment grade debt securities," are being registered; and (•) the registrant has filed at least one Form 20-F, Form 40-F or Form 10-K that is the latest required to have been filed.

issuers.[55] The reasoning expounded by the SEC is that limiting the rule to reporting companies eligible to use Form S-2 or F-2 prevents the possibility that the market for a non-reporting issuer's ordinary shares could be conditioned because research reports on a non-reporting registrant's nonconvertible senior securities prevent such a possibility.[56] Second, the securities being offered cannot be covered in the research report.

13.5.7.3   *Rule 139*

Rule 139 provides safe harbour protection to participating broker-dealers distributing information or recommendations concerning reporting companies with securities in registration. The rule allows publication and distribution of reports by a broker-dealer even if such reports relate to the securities being offered and even if the broker-dealer is a participant in the distribution of the securities to be registered, provided that the registrant meets one of two sets of requirements relating to its reporting history and public profile and the report meets certain criteria.

A foreign private issuer may use Form F-3 to register securities under the 1933 Act if it satisfies the same requirements described above for Form F-2 (except that the requirement that the foreign private issuer be subject to the requirements of Section 12 or 15 (d) 1934 Act for a period of 36 calendar months does not apply). Form F-3 only applies to registration of securities in connection with certain transactions such as; primary offerings for cash (provided the market value worldwide of the issuer's stock is $75 million or more); primary offerings of non-convertible investment grade securities; secondary offerings and; rights offerings; dividend or interest reinvestment plans, and conversions or warrants. In addition, to be eligible to use a Form F-3 neither the registrant nor any of its consolidated or unconsolidated subsidiaries must have, since the end of their last fiscal year for which certified financial statements of the registrant and its consolidated subsidiaries were included in a report filed pursuant to Section 13(a) or 15(d) 1933 Act: (a) failed to pay any dividend or sinking fund instalment on preferred stock; or (b) defaulted: (i) on any instalment on indebtedness for borrowed money, or (ii) on any rental on one or more long-term leases, which defaults in the aggregate are material to the financial position of the registrant and its consolidated and unconsolidated subsidiaries, taken as a whole.

[55] A foreign private issuer that meets all the registrant requirements of Form F-3 except for the 12 month reporting history requirement, may still meet the requirements if it meets the alternative offshore trading history test. Under the alternative test, such foreign private issuer's securities must have been traded on a designated offshore securities market (as defined in Regulation S) for a period of at least 12 months. This elimination of the reporting history requirement, eliminates the requirement that a foreign private issuer be previously reporting pursuant to the Securities Exchange Act of 1934 and have filed at least one annual report (SEC Release 22-7120 (12 December, 1994).

[56] SEC Securities Act Release No. 33-6492 (Oct. 6, 1983).

Issuer requirements (Rule 139(a))

Rule 139(a) relates to broker-dealers participating in a distribution of securities by a registered issuer which meet the registrant requirements of Form S-3 or F-3,[57] or are specified foreign private issuers (*see* Section 13.5.7.3 above), and the minimum float or investment grade criteria of the respective forms. Pursuant to the rule, the publication of the report must be in the normal course of business and must occur with reasonable regularity. There is no explicit guidance on the definition of "reasonable regularity". The rule will not cover research concerning a company with respect to which a broker-dealer is not publishing research and will not apply to IPOs. The phrase "reasonable regularity" is included with the intention of ensuring "that the purposes of Section 5 are met" and of giving "the rule adequate flexibility to accommodate changes in research practices".

The registrant and transaction requirements of Form S-3 or F-3 are included so that the safe-harbour will be available for discussions of seasoned reporting companies which meet a minimum float test or are issuing non-convertible investment grade debt or preferred securities. According to the SEC, in the case of equity securities, the float requirement "assures that the registrant discussed will be one with a widespread following in the marketplace".[58] The SEC believes that widespread market following greatly lessens the potential for the abuses Section 5 was intended to prevent.[59] The investment grade security criteria were based on the belief that "investment grade debt or preferred securities are purchased primarily on the basis of interest rates and security ratings and thus are to a large degree fungible".[60] The SEC stated that investors generally evaluate new offerings of such securities by looking at comparably rated securities of other registrants. This fungibility makes price manipulation very difficult, and, thus the opportunity to condition the market is lessened.[61]

---

[57] *See* note above for the registrant requirements of Form S-3 or F-3. The SEC decided not to extend the rule to registrants that qualify under Form S-2 or F-2 because "the marketplace following of [such] registrants .... is not sufficiently wide to insure adequate dissemination of information with respect to such registrants" (SEC Release Securities Act 33-6550 (Sept. 19, 1984)).

[58] SEC Securities Act Release No. 33-6492 (6 October, 1983).

[59] Ibid.

[60] Ibid.

[61] Ibid.

Rule 139(a) specifically states that the publication and distribution of a research report is not an "offer" for purposes of Section 2(10) or Section 5(c) 1933 Act, even if made by a distribution participant.

Research Report Requirements (Rule 139(b))
Rule 139(b) provides that research reports concerning reporting companies which do not meet the Form S-3 or F-3 registrant and transaction criteria must:

(a)   be contained in a publication that is distributed in the normal course of business;
(b)   include similar research with respect to a substantial number of companies in the issuer's industry or sub-industry or contain a comprehensive list of securities currently recommended by such broker-dealer;
(c)   be given no *materially*[62] greater space or prominence in such publication than that given to other securities of the issuer; and
(d)   be no more favourable (i.e. contain no upgrade) as to the issuer or any class of its securities than that published by the broker-dealer in its last publication addressing the issuer or its securities prior to the commencement of its participation in the distribution.

The SEC stated that "where a publication covers a broad range of companies in an industry and is issued not on a sporadic but on a regular schedule, the possibility that such a publication could condition the market is lessened".[63]

With respect to projections in the research report, Rule 139(b) conditions the safe harbour on three requirements:

(a)   projections must have been published previously on a regular basis;
(b)   the report must either include projections for all companies covered, not just the issuer, or the report must include projections for a substantial number of companies in the registrant's sub-industry and the projections must cover the same period for all companies covered; and
(c)   since projections constitute opinions within the meaning of Rule 139, they must meet the "no upgrade" requirements.

---

[62] The SEC amended the rule to add the word "materially" to provide greater flexibility to the interpretation of the rule. Ibid.
[63] Ibid.

13.5.8   1933 Act safe harbour rules for unregistered deals

Rules 138 and 139 apply only to reporting companies. The SEC provided interpretive guidance that currently allows reliance on Rule 138 or Rule 139 in the context of a Regulation S offering. The Aircraft Carrier release states that the SEC's interpretive position is that "brokers and dealers may publish and distribute research reports as described in current Rule 138 or Rule 139 without such reports being deemed directed selling efforts".

13.5.9   1934 Act "safe harbours"

13.5.9.1   Regulation M

The SEC adopted exception 1 to Rule 101 of Regulation M, which explicitly permits the "publication or dissemination of any information, opinion or recommendation" by a distribution participant relating to a covered security (as defined in Regulation M) if the conditions of Rule 138 or Rule 139 are satisfied. This exception more closely aligns Rule 101 with the 1933 Act rules governing permissible research activities by broker-dealers participating in offerings of securities. This exception also covers electronically disseminated research.[64]

The SEC also stated that although Rules 138 and 139 apply by their terms to registered offerings, the exception from Rule 101 would be available during distributions that are not registered under the 1933 Act so long as the other conditions of either rule are met, other than those pertaining to the filing of a registration statement.

Despite requests that research distributed outside the US during a global offering be exempted from Rule 101's coverage, the SEC determined that the conditions of Rules 138 and 139 "define the appropriate parameters" even for research disseminated outside the US during a global offering, whether or not in conformity with local rule or custom, if securities are to be distributed in the US. The SEC's reasoning is that "research activities outside the US in connection with a distribution subject to the rule could be used to facilitate the distribution in the US".[65] The SEC noted, however, that "many of the securities distributed in global offerings will be subject to the Rule 101 actively-traded securities exception and, therefore, will not be subject to Rule 101's provisions".[66] The SEC noted

---

[64] Exchange Act Release No. 34-38067 (3 January 1997).

[65] Ibid.

[66] Ibid.

that it will provide guidance on a case-by-case basis for when dissemination of research need not meet the conditions of Rules 138 or 139 in global offerings.

The SEC also stated that research directed to particular customers may in certain circumstances be deemed to be a solicitation of an order to buy a security and thereby preclude the ability of a distribution participant from relying on the exception to Rule 101's prohibition against unsolicited brokerage transactions.

13.5.9.2 *Proxy solicitation*
The publication of research reports by a financial adviser must be evaluated in light of the proxy rules applicable to domestic issuers. In a no-action letter, the SEC took the position that the dissemination of reports during a distribution does not raise proxy solicitation issues so long as such reports are eligible for the Rules 138 or 139 safe harbour and include all disclosures required by all applicable rules and regulations governing disclosure of the relationship between the financial advisor and any party to the transaction. The SEC's no-action position does not affect the application of the anti-fraud provisions; nor does it address research commenting on an issuer engaged in a transaction exempt under the 1933 Act, which, remains subject to a fact-specific analysis.

The SEC has proposed to codify the Merrill Lynch No-Action Letter in proposed 1934 Act Rule 14a-1(1)(2)(v). This new rule would provide that the distribution of research complying with Rules 138 or 139 in connection with a registered offering of securities subject to the proxy rules would be an exempt solicitation for purposes of the proxy rules.

13.5.9.3 *Research reports and FSMA*
The FSMA does not legislate specifically for research reports. However, the FSA has taken the opportunity to update the UKLA's guidance on price sensitive information which at Sections 11 – 13 provides guidance with regard to analysts, corrections of analysts' forecasts and draft reports from analysts.

13.6 Introduction to Regulation M

Sections 9(a) and 10(b) 1934 Act and Section 17(a) 1933 Act make it unlawful to carry our certain manipulative transactions.

Section 9(a) makes unlawful, inter alia, creating a false or misleading appearance of active trading in securities; the creation of actual or apparent active trading in securities to raise or depress the price of a security for the purpose of inducing a third party to trade; making false or misleading statements to induce a third party to trade; and stabilising the price of securities. In connection with the sale and purchase of securities, Section 10(b) makes unlawful any manipulative or deceptive device. Section 17(a) makes unlawful, inter alia, employing any device or scheme to defraud, obtaining money by means of making an untrue statement of material fact or any omission to state a material fact necessary to make a statement not misleading; and engaging in any transaction which operates or would operate as a fraud on any purchaser of securities.

In Regulation M the SEC determined that securities offerings present special opportunities for manipulation that require special regulatory attention.

Regulation M is therefore not a safe harbour – instead the SEC "continues to believe that a prophylactic approach to anti-manipulation regulation is the most effective means to protect the integrity of the offering process by precluding activities that could influence artificially the market for the offered security".

Regulation M therefore proscribes certain market activities that participants in securities offerings can use to manipulate the market price. The general anti-fraud and anti-manipulative provisions of US federal securities laws including Sections 9(a), 10(b) and 15(c) and Rules 10b-5 and 15cl-2 1934 Act and Section 17(a) 1933 Act continue to apply to participants.

However, the SEC recognised that it was appropriate in Regulation M to relax certain restrictions on market manipulation "to allow greater flexibility for market participants to engage in activities that enhance competition in the market place".

Sections 13.6–13.9 describe the market activities proscribed by Regulation M in relation to securities offerings. Regulation M contains six rules (contained in Rules 100–105) covering the following activities during a securities offering:

(a)   activities by underwriters or other persons who are participating in a distribution (so called "distribution participants") and their affiliated purchasers (Rule 101);

(b)   activities by the issuer or selling security holder and their affiliated purchasers (Rule 102);
(c)   Nasdaq passive market making (Rule 103); and
(d)   stabilising, transactions to cover syndicate short positions and penalty bids (Rule 104); and short selling in advance of a public offering (Rule 105). Rule 100 contains the definitions used in Rules 101 to 105.

Some of the guiding principles behind Regulation M in seeking to prohibit the manipulation of securities markets and the price of securities being offered are similar to the principles the FSA has in having the power to impose penalties for market abuse pursuant to Section 118 FSMA.

A more detailed study shows that in the US, market participants have potential criminal liability and breach of Rules 101–105 of Regulation M will be an offence.[67]

In the UK where behaviour is deemed to be market abuse for the purposes of The Code of Market Conduct ("COMC", the first part of the Market Conduct sourcebook ("MAR")) and Section 118 FSMA, even if an offence has not been committed the FSA has the power to impose a civil law penalty under Section 123(1) FSMA, subject to the defences available to the market participant under Section 123(2). This civil law remedy is in addition to any criminal liability that a market participant may incur in the UK in violation of Sections 397(2) or 397(3) FSMA, subject to the defences set out in Sections 397(4) and 397(5) respectively.

There are a number of differences between the US and UK regulations. In the US, Rules 101–103 do not apply to securities of the major global corporates where there is a high worldwide average daily trading volume in their securities and the market capitalisation of these corporates represents a high public float value. These thresholds and their calculation are described in Section 13.7. In addition Rules 101, 102 and 105[68] apply only during a relatively short period, (the "restricted period") discussed in Section 13.7.

---

[67] Strictly speaking a breach of Rule 103 (Nasdaq passive market making) itself is not unlawful, but it will be unlawful for the purposes of Rule 101.

[68] Since this Chapter is considering Regulation M primarily from the position a foreign private issuer, the discussion of Rule 102 in Section 13.7 will exclude a number of the transactions in securities which may be more relevant to a US issuer.

It seems that under Rules 101–103 the SEC is seeking to regulate a different kind of market behaviour – that in relation to a distribution of securities rather than a more general concept of market abuse that the FSA is seeking to regulate. It is possible that the much greater liquidity of the US capital markets when compared to the UK markets permits the SEC to take a more commercial approach to potential manipulation in the securities of the global corporates so that the FSA's Code of Market Conduct is possibly an acknowledgment that UK capital markets are less liquid and therefore more susceptible to market manipulation.

The differences between the SEC and FSA appear to lessen when regulating the stabilisation of transactions in securities. (Section 13.8 below compares Rule 104 of Regulation M and the FSA's Price Stabilising Rules.) Although each regulator recognises the other's rules, (respectively establishing a "safe harbour" under the FSA's rules and under proceedings brought under Section 397(3) (but not Section 397(2)) FSMA and being deemed not to be a violation of Rule 104), on closer inspection the US and UK stabilisation regulations are quite different.

13.7 Market manipulation

13.7.1 Rule 101 – activities by distribution participants

13.7.1.1 Introduction
Rule 101 governs the activities of persons participating in distributions[69] of securities, other than issuers or selling security holders[70] and their affiliated purchasers.[71] In practice, this restriction will apply to investment banks distributing the securities in their capacity as broker-dealers in the US.

In general, Rule 101 prohibits distribution participants[72] and their affiliated purchasers from bidding for, purchasing, or attempting to induce

---

[69] "Distribution" is defined as any offer of securities, whether or not subject to registration under the 1933 Act, which is distinguishable from ordinary trading transactions by the magnitude of the offering and the presence of special selling methods.

[70] "Selling security holders" is defined as any person on whose behalf a distribution is made, other than an issuer.

[71] *See* Section 13.7.1.4.

[72] *See* Section 13.7.1.2.

any person to bid for or purchase a so called "covered security"[73] during the restricted period.[74] The distribution participants subject to Rule 101 will typically be broker-dealers who in their capacity as financial intermediaries routinely engage in market transactions for their own account or for customers as part of their businesses.

A distribution of securities under Regulation M is distinguished from ordinary trading transactions by the "magnitude of the offering" and the presence of "special selling efforts and selling methods". Where the average daily trading value and public float value of a security are not sufficiently material to take the relevant securities outside the ambit of Rules 101–103, the restricted periods for a particular distribution will be relatively short, commencing either one or five business days[75] before the day of the pricing of the securities being offered and continuing until the distribution is completed.

Even during the restricted period, Rule 101 permits distribution participants and their affiliated purchasers to engage in a variety of market activities, such as: the routine dissemination of research reports and the exercise of options and other securities. Rule 101 also permits certain *de minimis*[76] transactions that would otherwise violate the rule.

---

[73] *See* Section 13.7.1.6.

[74] "Restricted period" is defined in Rule 100 of Regulation M as (a) for any security with an average daily trading volume of $100,000 or more of an issuer whose common equity securities have a public float value of $25 million or more, the period beginning on the later of one business day prior to the determination of the offering price or such time that a person becomes a distribution participant, and ending upon such person's completion of participation in the distribution, (b) for all other securities, the "restricted period" is the period beginning on the later of five business days prior to the determination of the offering price or such time that a person becomes a distribution participant, and ending upon such person's completion of their participation in the distribution, and (c) in the case of a distribution involving a merger, acquisition, or exchange offer, the "restricted period" is the period beginning on the day proxy solicitation or offering materials are first disseminated to security holders, and ending upon the completion of the distribution.

[75] "Business days" is as the 24 hour period determined by reference to the principal market for the securities to be distributed and which includes a complete trading session for that market.

[76] "De minimis" is defined as a purchase during the restricted period, other than by a passive market maker, that totals less than two per cent of the average daily trading value of the security being purchased provided, however, that the person making such bid or purchase has maintained and enforces written policies and procedures designed to achieve compliance with the provisions of Regulation M.

13.7.1.2   *Persons subject to Rule 101*

Rule 101 applies to broker-dealers (and other distribution participants) involved in the distribution of the securities being offered.

Rule 101 applies to distribution participants who are defined in Rule 100 as an underwriter, prospective underwriter, broker, dealer or other person who has agreed to participate or is participating in a distribution. Rule 101 also specifies that any affiliated purchaser of an issuer or selling security holder that is also acting as a distribution participant may comply with the provisions of Rule 101 rather than Rule 102, provided that such affiliated purchaser is not itself the issuer or selling security holder. Therefore, during a distribution an underwriter affiliated with the issuer will be able to choose to comply with the provisions of Rule 101 rather than the more restrictive Rule 102.

A prospective underwriter is defined as a person who has submitted a bid to an issuer or selling security holder and knows or is reasonably certain that such bid will be accepted, whether or not the terms and conditions of the underwriting commitment have been agreed upon; or who has reached or is reasonably certain to reach an understanding with an issuer, selling security holder or managing underwriter that such person would become an underwriter, whether the terms and conditions of the underwriting have been agreed upon. This definition reflects the SEC's view that there is frequently some point in the offering process prior to when a bid actually has been accepted or a broker-dealer has been told that it will be an underwriter, when it is reasonably certain that such person will be an underwriter, and that the incentive to facilitate the distribution is present at that point.

13.7.1.3   *Completion of participation in distribution*

Under Regulation M the distribution participant determines when it has completed its participation in the distribution.[77] An underwriter is

---

[77] "Completion of participation in the distribution" is defined by Rule 100 of Regulation M which provides that (a) an issuer or selling security holder shall be deemed to have completed its participation in a distribution, when the distribution is completed; (b) an underwriter, shall be deemed to have completed its participation when their participation has been distributed, including all other securities of the same class that are acquired in connection with the distribution, and any stabilisation arrangements and trading restrictions in connection with the distribution have been terminated; Provided, however, that an underwriter's participation will not be deemed to have been completed if a syndicate over allotment

deemed to have completed its participation when its participation has been distributed, including all other securities of the same class that are acquired in connection with the distribution, and after any stabilisation arrangements and trading restrictions in connection with the distribution have been terminated.

However, an underwriter's participation is not deemed to be completed if a syndicate over-allotment option (the so-called "green shoe") is exercised in an amount that exceeds the net syndicate short position at the time of such exercise. This is intended to ensure that the underwriter's selling efforts in connection with the distribution have in fact ceased before trading prohibitions in Rule 101 are lifted. Any other distribution participant will have completed its participation when its allotment has been distributed.

13.7.1.4 *Affiliated purchasers*
The Rule 101 restriction on investment banks participating in the distribution will extend to other entities within that investment bank's group.

The restrictions in Rules 101 and 102 (*see* Section 13.7.2) extend to an affiliated purchaser of an underwriter, prospective underwriter, broker, dealer (under Rule 101) and an issuer or selling security holder (under Rule 102). "Affiliated purchaser" is defined as:

(a) a person acting in concert with a distribution participant, issuer or selling security holder in connection with the acquisition or distribution of a covered security;

(b) an affiliate who controls the purchase of such securities by a distribution participant, issuer or selling security holder or whose purchases are controlled by such persons, or whose purchases are made under common control with those of such persons; or

(c) an affiliate of a distribution participant, issuer or selling security holder (a "financial services affiliate") who regularly purchases securities for its own account or for the account of others or who recommends or exercises investment discretion with respect to the purchase or sale of securities.

---

option is exercised in an amount that exceeds the net syndicate short position at the time of such exercise; and (c) any other person participating in the distribution shall be deemed to have complied their participation when their participation has been distributed.

A financial services affiliate of a distributor will be excluded from the affiliate purchaser restriction and will be free to deal during the restricted period if:

(a)   the affiliate maintains and enforces written policies and procedures reasonably designed to prevent the flow of information to or from the affiliate that otherwise would result in a violation of Rules 101, 102 or 104 and contains an annual, independent assessment of the operation of such policies and procedures;

(b)   the affiliate has no officers (or persons performing similar functions) or employees (other than clerical, managerial or support personnel) in common with the distribution participant, issuer, or selling security holder that direct, effect, or recommend transactions in securities; and

(c)   the affiliate does not, during the applicable restricted period, act as a market maker (other than a specialist in compliance with the rules of, e.g., the NYSE), or engage as a broker-dealer in selected transactions or proprietary trading in covered securities. Therefore an "affiliate" can be a separately identifiable department or division of a distribution participant, issuer or selling security holder.

13.7.1.5   *Financial services affiliates*

The SEC believes that information barriers between financial services affiliates restrict the flow of non-public information which otherwise might inappropriately influence an affiliate to enter into a transaction in a security subject to Regulation M. For example, the SEC requires information barriers to prevent the communication within the investment bank of the details of pricing discussions with the issuer and potential purchasers or their knowledge as to the demand for the offering. The SEC believes that affiliates should be restricted from engaging in certain types of activities that present the greatest potential for manipulation during the course of a distribution. Therefore, any affiliate that, during the applicable restricted period, acts as a market maker (other than as a specialist in compliance with the rules of a national securities exchange and subject to Rule 103 and the ability of the market maker to carry on passive market making), or engages as a broker or a dealer in solicited transactions or proprietary trading activities in covered securities, is an affiliated purchaser. An affiliate (whether an internal unit or a separate legal entity) engaging in these activities cannot be excluded from the affiliated purchaser definition and is therefore prohibited by Rule 101 from engaging in market activities in relation to the relevant securities. In contrast, by relying on the proviso to the definition of "affiliated purchaser" an affiliate acting as an investment company or investment adviser or in some other "non-broker-dealer" capacity would be eligible for the exclusion.

13.7.1.6   Securities subject to Rule 101

The trading restrictions of Rule 101 apply to "covered securities", which include the security that is the subject of a distribution ("subject security") and any reference security. A "reference security" is defined as a security into which a subject security may be converted, exchanged or exercised or which, under the terms of the subject security, may in whole or in significant part determine the value of the subject security. In practice, where an underwriter is distributing convertible securities, the underwriter will be restricted from trading in the convertible or the underlying securities. However, when the underwriter is distributing the underlying securities the trading restrictions apply only to the underlying securities and not to the convertible securities.

The SEC believes that transactions in reference securities can have a direct and substantial effect on the pricing and terms of the security being distributed. The definition of a reference security also encompasses an underlying security such as an "equity-linked security" that does not give the holder the right to acquire the security, but whose value is or may be derived from such security. A security will be a reference security only when it, or any index of which it is a component, is referred to in the terms of a subject security. A security of the same or similar issuer will not be deemed to be a reference security merely because its price is used as a factor in determining the offering price of a security being distributed.

Derivative securities (i.e. those that derive all or part of their value from a security being distributed) are also not subject to the trading prohibition in Rule 101. Therefore, bids for or purchases of options, warrants, rights, convertible securities or equity-linked securities are not restricted during a distribution of the related underlying securities because, while they derive their value from the security being distributed, they do not by their terms affect the value of the security being distributed. Although the SEC recognised that derivative securities could be used to manipulate the price of an underlying security through inducing arbitrage and other transactions involving the underlying security, the SEC preferred to focus its trading restrictions on those securities that present the greatest manipulative potential on the securities being distributed. However, any attempt to manipulate a security in a distribution by transactions involving derivative securities will be subject to the general anti-manipulation provisions, including Sections 9(a)(2) and 10(b) of, and Rule 10b-5 1934 Act.

Therefore, a transaction in derivative securities during the distribution of an underlying security, including put options, is not subject to Rule 101 during the offering of the underlying securities. In addition maintaining a short put position is not deemed to be a continuing bid for the underlying security for the purposes of Regulation M.

Bids for and purchases of outstanding nonconvertible debt securities are not restricted by Rule 101 unless the security being purchased is identical in all its terms to the security being distributed. For example Rule 101 does not apply to a security if there is a single basis point difference in coupon rates or a single day's difference in maturity dates, when compared with the security subject to the distribution.

13.7.1.7   Actively traded securities

Excluded from Rule 101 are actively-traded securities: those with an "average daily trading volume" ("ADTV", *see* Section 13.7.1.8) of at least $1 million and where the issuer's common equities securities have a public float value of at least $150 million. The SEC takes the view that exclusion of actively-traded securities under Rule 101 is appropriate since the costs of manipulating such securities generally are high, thus disincentivising abusive behaviour. In addition, because actively-traded securities are widely followed by the investment community, aberrations in price are more likely to be discovered and quickly corrected. Moreover, actively-traded securities are generally traded on exchanges or other organised markets which tend to be markets with high levels of transparency and surveillance.

For securities with an ADTV and/or public float value below these thresholds, Rule 101 restricts transactions by distribution participants in covered securities for the relevant restricted period, again calculated on the basis of the ADTV and/or public float value of the relevant securities.

In a distribution of a security with an ADTV of at least $100,000, and where the issuer has in issue equity securities having a public float value of at least $25 million, the restrictive period begins on the later of one business day prior to the date on which the subject security's price is determined or the date on which the person becomes the distribution participant, and ends upon that person's completion of its participation in the distribution.

In a distribution of any other security the restricted period begins on the later of five business days prior to the date on which the subject security's price is determined or the date on which the person becomes a distribution participant, and ends upon that person's completion of its participation of the distribution.

13.7.1.8 *Calculation of ADTV and public float value*

The ADTV of a covered security is defined on the basis of reported worldwide average daily trading volume during a specified period prior to filing of the registration statement or prior to the pricing of the offering. The rule permits distribution participants to use a two calendar-month or sixty day rolling period. The sixty day rolling period for calculating ADTV must end within ten calendar days of the filing of a registration statement or, if there is no registration statement or if distribution is a shelf distribution, within ten calendar days of the pricing of the offering.

The SEC does not prescribe acceptable information sources for determining ADTV, rather distribution participants should have flexibility in determining ADTV of a security from information that is publicly available, if the participant has a reasonable basis for believing that the information is reliable. In calculating the US dollar value of ADTV any reasonable and verifiable method may be used; for example it may be derived from multiplying the number of shares by the price in each trade or from multiplying each day's total volume of shares traded by the closing price on that day.

With regard to the public float value the SEC adapted the definition used in the Form 10-K (i.e. the aggregate amount of common equity securities held by non-affiliates), which can be calculated on the basis of the issuer's most recent Form 10-K or based upon more recent information available to the issuer.

13.7.1.9 *Offerings subject to Rule 101*

Rule 101 applies in connection with the distribution of securities. These include public offerings, private placements, shelf offerings, mergers and other acquisitions, exchange offers, forced conversions of securities, warrant solicitations and "at-the-market offerings". With regard to shelf offerings, each take down off a shelf is to be individually examined to determine whether such offering constitutes a distribution, that is, whether it satisfies the "magnitude" of the offering and "special selling efforts and selling methods" criteria of a distribution. Therefore, where a broker-dealer sells shares on behalf of an issuer or selling security holder in ordinary trading transactions into an independent market (i.e. without any "special selling efforts") the offering will not be considered a distribution and the broker-dealer will not be subject to Rule 101.

However, the broker-dealer is likely to be subject to Rule 101 if it enters into a sales agency agreement that provides for unusual transaction-based compensation for the sales even if the securities are sold in what would otherwise constitute ordinary trading transactions.

Rule 101 also applies to mergers and acquisitions and exchange offers involving distributions of securities with effect from and including the day when proxy solicitation or offering materials first are disseminated to security holders and ends with the completion of the distribution (i.e. the time of the shareholder vote or the expiration of the exchange offer).

A restricted period will also apply during any period where the market price of the offered security will be a factor in determining the consideration to be paid pursuant to a merger, acquisition or exchange offer. Thus activity prescribed by Rules 101 and 102 must cease one or five business days before the commencement of any valuation period and for the duration of such periods. In "at-the-market-offerings", sales prices are established during the course of the offering based upon market conditions at the time of the individual sale. The restricted period for such an offering will commence one or five business days before the price of each sale and continues until the person's participation in the distribution is completed.

13.7.1.10 Securities excepted from Rule 101
In addition to actively traded securities (*see* Section 13.7.1.7), non-convertible debt securities, non-convertible preferred securities and asset-backed securities (provided that the security being distributed is rated investment grade by at least one nationally recognised statistical rating organisation) are also excepted from Rule 101 on the basis that their yields and credit ratings are largely fungible and therefore less likely to be subject to manipulation.[78]

13.7.1.11 Activities excepted from Rule 101
Rule 101 contains eleven exceptions, described below.

Research reports. Rule 101 exempts certain research. Underwriters are permitted to continue to circulate research reports during a distribution so long as the research satisfies the conditions applicable for the

---

[78] Certain government securities and municipal securities referred to in Section 3(a)(12) 1934 Act are also excepted from Rule 101.

distribution of research during the registration process for any registered offering are satisfied (set out in Rule 138).

Although Rules 138 and 139 relate to the dissemination of research during registered offerings, the SEC interprets this exemption to be available during distributions that are not registered under the 1933 Act, as long as the conditions of either Rule 138 and 139 are satisfied, other than those relating to the filing of a 1933 Act registration statement. The SEC also takes the view that the conditions of Rules 138 and 139 (other than registration) define appropriate parameters for research activities involving securities distributed in the US and these conditions would also apply to research disseminated outside the US during a global offering because these research activities could be used to facilitate a distribution in the US.

However, as a practical matter, most underwriters will impose a "quiet period" on the dissemination of research in the period prior to pricing the deal in order, from a liability perspective, to distance the contents of the research from the decision to purchase the securities.

Passive market making and stabilisation. Rule 101 exempts passive market making transactions conducted on Nasdaq and stabilising transactions that comply with Rules 103 and 104 respectively.

Odd lots. A distribution participant bidding for or purchasing odd lots of securities during the restricted period or transactions by an underwriter to effect any purchases necessary to permit odd-lot holders to round up their holdings to 100 shares will also be exempt from Rule 101.

Exercises and conversions of securities. Rule 101 exempts certain exercises of rights in respect of securities. Rule 101 permits distribution participants to exercise any option, warrant, right or other conversion privileges set forth in the instrument governing the securities. The exemption does not make a distinction between call options acquired before a person became a distribution participant from those acquired afterwards on the basis that the exercise of the option does not involve significant manipulative potential because of the unpredictability of the timing and the extent of purchases by persons writing call options.

Unsolicited transactions. Rule 101 also exempts unsolicited principal transactions and unsolicited purchases that are not effected from or through a broker-dealer on a securities exchange or through an inter-dealer quotation system or electronic communications network.

Basket transactions. Rule 101 also exempts purchases of covered securities made in connection with basket transactions, where the aggregate dollar value of any bids for a covered security constitutes five per cent or less of the total dollar value of the basket being purchased and the basket contains at least 20 stocks. The exception is available with respect to both index-related baskets and customised baskets. To qualify for this exception, the basket transaction must be a bona fide transaction effected in the ordinary course of business (i.e. the decision to include the security being distributed in the basket must be independent of the distribution). The exception also permits bids and purchases for the purpose of adjusting an existing basket position related to a standardised index made in the ordinary course of business to the extent necessary to reflect a change in the composition of the index.

De minimis transaction. Unaccepted bids and purchases during the restricted period that in the aggregate do not exceed two per cent of the ADTV of the security being purchased are exempted from Rule 101 if the person has maintained and enforced written procedures reasonably designed to achieve compliance with the rules. Once inadvertent transactions are discovered subsequent transactions would not be covered by this exception. The *de minimis* exception does not apply to Nasdaq passive market making transactions pursuant to Rule 103 (*see* Section 13.8).

Securities being distributed. Rule 101 exempts offers to sell or the solicitation of the offers to buy the securities being distributed (including securities acquired in stabilising) or securities offered as principal by the person making such offer of solicitation. This allows distribution participants to sell the securities being distributed.

Transactions between distribution participants. Rule 101 permits transactions among distribution participants in connection with the distribution and purchases from an issuer or connected selling security holder in connection with the distribution that are not effected on a securities exchange or through an inter dealer quotation system or through an electronics communications network.

Rule 144A Transactions. Rule 101 exempts transactions in securities eligible for re-sale under Rule 144A, provided that sales within the US are made solely to QIBs or persons reasonably believed to be QIBs, in transactions exempt from registration under the 1933 Act; or to persons not deemed to be "US Persons" for the purposes of Rule 902(k)(2) of Regulation S under the 1933 Act, during a concurrent Rule 144A distribution to QIBs. The exception covers both the securities being distributed under Rule 144A and any reference security.

Case by case basis. Finally, Rule 101 permits the SEC to exempt any transaction or transactions from Rule 101 on a case-by-case basis. An exemption may be granted either unconditionally or on specified terms and conditions.

13.7.2   *Rule 102 – activities by issuers and selling security holders*

13.7.2.1   *Prohibition under Rule 102*
Generally, Rule 102 imposes the same restrictions on issuers, selling security holders and their affiliated purchasers during a distribution of securities as are imposed on underwriters under Rule 101.

Rule 102 provides that issuers and selling security holders and their affiliated purchasers must refrain from bidding for, purchasing or attempting to induce any person to bid for or purchase a covered security during the applicable restricted period, unless an exception permits the activity.

Rule 102 contains fewer exceptions than Rule 101. Rule 102 exempts the following transactions (that are also excepted from Rule 101):

(a)   transactions in non-convertible investment grade securities;
(b)   transactions during Rule 144A distributions;
(c)   exercises of options and other securities, including rights; and
(d)   odd-lot transactions and associated round up transactions during an issuer odd-lot tender offer.

In contrast to Rule 101, Rule 102 has no general exception for actively traded securities (although there is a limited exception for certain actively traded reference securities that are not issued by the issuer or any affiliate of the issuer of the security in distribution) or for *de minimis* transactions.

Rule 102 also has special exceptions which do not apply to Rule 101. These are for: close-end investment companies that engage in self-tenders; commodity pool redemptions; and transactions involving employee stock plans. Most transactions connected with dividend reinvestment and stock purchase plans are also excluded from Rule 102. Only employee plan distributions involving securities obtained directly from the issuer are subject to Rule 102.

13.7.2.2 Persons subject to Rule 102

Rule 102 applies to issuers, selling security holders and their affiliated purchasers until such persons have completed their participation in a distribution. For these purposes, an issuer will be deemed to have completed its participation in a distribution when the entire distribution is completed.

Rule 102 provides also that where an affiliated purchaser of an issuer or selling security holder is also a distribution participant then they can choose to comply with Rule 101 (which is less restrictive than Rule 102) but only if they are not the issuer or selling security holder. This will accommodate the ordinary market activities of broker-dealers and other financial institutions participating in a distribution because they are subject to SRO[79] surveillance.

13.7.2.3 Securities subject to Rule 102

The restrictions of Rule 102 apply to covered securities in the same manner as Rule 101. Therefore, persons subject to Rule 102 are precluded during the restricted period from bidding for or purchasing the "subject security" or any "reference security" (*see* 13.7.1.6 above).

13.7.2.4 Offerings subject to Rule 102

Rule 102 applies only when there is a distribution of securities. In the case of an offering of securities pursuant to a shelf registration statement, an issuer and its affiliated purchasers are subject to the applicable restricted period of Rule 102 when sales off-a-shelf by an issuer or by an affiliated purchaser constitute a distribution of securities under Regulation M. Similarly, when a selling security holder sells off-a-shelf, such sales also constitute a distribution and all other shelf security holders who are affiliated purchasers of the selling security holder will be subject to the applicable restricted period of Rule 102.

13.7.2.5 Securities exempted from Rule 102

Rule 102 provides that issuers and selling security holders and their affiliates should not be able to trade in their securities whether or not the securities are actively traded securities for the purposes of Rule 101.

---

[79] "SRO's" are the self regulatory organisations which under US federal securities laws are the principal means of enforcement of fair, ethical and efficient practices in the securities and commodities futures industries. They have their own rules by which members must abide. The SRO's include all the national securities and commodities exchanges in the US as well as NASD and the Municipal Securities Rule making Board (created under the Securities Acts Amendments of 1975).

However, Rule 102 permits hedging activity for actively traded reference securities that are not issued by the issuer of the security in the distribution or by any affiliate of the issuer. Therefore, the issuer of an equity-linked security or a security holder selling an equity-linked security can purchase in a hedging transaction an actively traded reference security issued by an unaffiliated entity. However, the general anti-fraud and anti-manipulation provisions will still apply to any transaction associated with distributions for equity-linked securities.[80]

13.7.3   Rules 101, 102 and the Code of Market Conduct

A number of global corporates have their securities traded both in London and either the NYSE or Nasdaq. Although trading volume will generally be greater in one market, usually that of the primary listing, a Regulation M distribution participant for Rule 101 purposes may wish to carry out certain market transactions between the NYSE/Nasdaq, (assuming that the US is the primary market and the global offer is made pursuant to US securities laws), and the London Stock Exchange, since to constitute market abuse for the purposes of Section 118(1) FSMA behaviour must take place on a prescribed market.

Assuming that market transactions carried out in the US by a distribution participant neither violate Regulation M nor other US federal securities laws, it is necessary to consider the consequences of carrying out similar market transactions in London.

Where market transactions are carried out both in the US and the UK and are not in violation of Rule 101 the distribution participant should be able to satisfy the "regular user" set out in Section 118(1) FSMA.

COMC 1.2.3.E(2) provides that in determining whether the distribution participant's behaviour falls below the standards expected, the regular user is likely to consider the rules and regulations of the market in question and any applicable laws and "the extent to which the behaviour is in compliance with the standards prevailing in that overseas jurisdiction". However, COMC 1.2.5.E states that the fact that the behaviour of

---

[80] Rule 102 also exempts government and municipal securities (together with other securities listed in Section 3(a)(12) 1934 Act), investment grade non-convertible debt, non-convertible securities and asset backed securities and so-called face amount certificates or securities issued by an open-ended management investment company or unit investment trust.

a distribution participant conforms with US practice, will not itself be determinative as to whether market abuse has taken place.

COMC 1.2.4E will oblige a distribution participant to consider the detailed guidance given at COMC 1.4–COMC 1.6 as to which different types of behaviour are unacceptable since COMC 1.2.9G also provides that compliance with US federal securities laws is not determinative as to whether behaviour will be abusive for the purposes of Section 118 FSMA.

The activities that are likely to require consideration by a distribution participant are described in COMC 1.5 and MAR1.6.

Regarding False or Misleading Impressions, the behaviour will amount to market abuse if the behaviour engaged in is likely to give rise to a price or value or volume of trading which is materially misleading and in circumstances where there might be a real likelihood that the behaviour will have this effect (COMC 1.5.4E); however, a distribution participant can take comfort from COMC 1.5.5 that the "regular user" in the US market is not likely to obtain a False or Misleading Impression as to the price or value of the securities on account of the "structure of the market, including its reporting, notification and transparency requirements". This is consistent with the SEC statement in the Regulation M Adopting Release explaining why the SEC was comfortable with replacing the old Trading Practice Rules with Regulation M. In addition the forms of market abuse referred to in COMC 1.5.4E would be an offence for the purposes of Section 9(a) 1934 Act and compliance with Rule 101 is unlikely to violate Section 9(a).

COMC 1.5.7 provides that certain types of behaviour will be market abuse if that behaviour gives rise to give rise to a False or Misleading Impression. However, in both COMC 1.5.8 and 1.5.21 (which concern behaviour relating to artificial transactions and course of conduct), it will not be market abuse where there is a "legitimate commercial rationale" for the transaction and where "the way in which the transaction is to be executed is proper".

Where the activities of a distribution participant in both the US and the UK are consistent with US practice (and do not breach US federal securities laws) then these activities will have a legitimate commercial rationale and, provided the transaction is executed and disclosed in compliance with SEC and NASD rules (and in the UK in accordance with UK disclosure rules), the transaction will be properly executed.

The distribution participant's behaviour must not distort the market in the relevant securities by interfering with the proper operation of market forces with the purpose of positioning the price of the security to a distorted level in circumstances where there is a real likelihood that the behaviour will have that effect (COMC 1.6.4E).

COMC 1.6.3E refers to a person engaging in behaviour that "interferes with the proper operation of market forces and so with the interplay of proper supply and demand and so has a distorting effect". However, as COMC 1.6.5 recognises, when a distribution participant trades in sizes beneficial to it and seeking to make maximum profit from its dealings it is unlikely that this will constitute distortion.

Again, consistent with the SEC's analysis in the adopting release for Regulation M such behaviour, generally speaking, improves the liquidity and efficiency of markets and non-violation of Rule 101 is unlikely to constitute a violation of Section 9(a) 1934 Act.

13.8 Passive market making (Rule 103 of Regulation M)

Rule 103 permits broker-dealers to engage in market-making transactions in covered securities that are Nasdaq securities without violating the provisions of Rule 101, except that Rule 103 shall not apply to any security for which a "stabilising" bid subject to Rule 104 is in effect or during any "at the market offering" or "best efforts" marketing.

The purpose of Rule 103 is to alleviate special liquidity problems that could exist for a Nasdaq security in a distribution, if distribution participants or their affiliates who are Nasdaq market makers were required under Rule 101 to withdraw as market makers during the restricted period. Exchange traded securities, on exchanges such as the NYSE, usually do not experience this problem because exchange specialists who can regulate the amount of liquidity in any particular security in most cases are not affiliated with distribution participants.

Rule 103 generally limits a passive market maker's bids and purchases to the highest current independent bid[81] (i.e. a bid of a Nasdaq market

---

[81] "Independent bid" means a bid by a person who is not a distribution participant, issuer, selling security holder or affiliated purchaser.

maker who is not participating in the distribution).[82] Additionally, Rule 103 limits the amount of net purchases that a passive market maker can make on any day to 30 per cent of its ADTV limitation, although an initial ADTV limit of 200 shares is available for less active market makers. The 30 per cent ADTV limitation[83] is designed to keep the level of the market maker's permitted purchasing activity below a level where the price effects of such purchases could constitute stabilisation of the securities, while generally permitting a level of activity associated with normal market making in those securities to continue during the restricted period. The rule also contains a provision limiting the bid size the passive market maker may display and requirements relating to notification, identification and disclosure of passive market making.

All Nasdaq securities qualify for passive market-making including Nasdaq referenced securities. However, "best efforts" and "at the market offerings" remain ineligible for passive market-making under Rule 103 and so will be subject to the restrictions of Rule 101 (unless exempted by Rule 101).

Rule 103 permits passive market making throughout the entire restricted period.

Rule 103 contains a prospectus disclosure requirement such that a prospectus for any registered offering in which a passive market maker intends to effect transactions in any covered security must contain certain prescribed information.[84]

---

[82] If a passive market maker is involved in a contemporaneous purchase and sale of a security the passive market maker can net transactions for the purpose of its ADTV calculation as long as the two transactions are reported within 30 seconds of each other. Also Rule 103 allows passive market makers to make bids or purchases at a price above the highest independent bid when necessary to comply with any SEC or NASD rule relating to the execution of customer orders.

[83] "30 per cent ADTV limitation" is defined in Rule 100 of Regulation M as 30 per cent of the market maker's ADTV in a covered security during the reference period, as obtained from NASD.

[84] The prescribed information is set out in Sections 229.502 and 229.508 of Regulation S-K (amended by Regulation M). Sections 229.502 provides that the inside front cover and outside back cover packaging a prospectus shall include the following statement (amended as appropriate) "certain persons participating in this offering may engage in transactions that stabilise, maintain or otherwise affect the price of (identify securities, including (list types of transactions))". For a description of these activities, *see* "Plan of Distribution". Section 229.508 provides that if the underwriter or any selling group member intends to engage in stabilising,

13.9 Comparison of stabilising and stabilisation (Rule 104 of Regulation M and FSA's Price Stabilising Rules)

13.9.1 Introduction

Regulation M governs activities in connection with the offering or distribution of securities including activities designed to support the price of securities during an offering, known as price stabilisation.

Under Rule 104 it is unlawful for any person, directly or indirectly, to stabilise or to effect any syndicate covering transaction[85] or to impose a penalty bid[86] in connection with an offering of any security, in contravention of Rule 104. Broadly, these activities can only be carried out in accordance with the provisions of Rule 104.

The SEC believes that although "stabilisation" is price influencing activity intended to induce others to purchase the offered security, when appropriately regulated it is an effective medium for fostering an orderly distribution of securities and promotes the interest of shareholders, underwriters and issuers.

The principles adopted by the SEC in Rule 104 are quite different to the FSA's Price Stabilising Rules. This probably reflects the fact that stabilisation in the US and UK are quite different corporate finance activities.

13.9.2 What is stabilisation for the purposes of Rule 104?

The purpose of Rule 104 is to permit underwriters and syndicate members to conduct stabilising transactions in compliance with Rule 104's pricing and other terms for the purpose of preventing a decline in

---

syndicate short covering transactions, penalty bids, or any other transaction in connection with the offering that may stabilise, maintain or otherwise affect the security's price, then such person must indicate their intention to do so, and briefly describe the transactions in the plan of distribution in the prospectus.

[85] "Short covering transaction" means the placing of any bid or the effecting of any purchase on behalf of the distributor or underwriting syndicate to reduce a short position created in connection with an offering.

[86] "Penalty bid" means an arrangement that permits the managing underwriter to reclaim a selling concession from a syndicate member in connection with an offering, when the securities originally sold by the syndicate member are purchased in a syndicate covering transaction.

the market price of a security designed to facilitate an offering. Notwithstanding that Rule 104 includes a number of provisions that are market driven, it is understood that as a matter of market practice, unless a follow-on-issue is subject to adverse market conditions, underwriters and syndicate members in the US rarely stabilise during the offering.

Stabilisation is defined in Rule 100 of Regulation M as the "placing of any bid or the effecting of any purchase, for the purpose of pegging, fixing or otherwise maintaining the price of a security". In contrast to the FSA's Price Stabilising Rules, Rule 104 does not expressly provide that stabilisation is limited only to those US securities equivalent to those securities referred to in paragraphs 76–80 Financial Services and Markets Act 2000 (Regulated Activities) Order 2001 or to where the total cost of the securities subject to the offer at the price is at least £15 million or its equivalent.

Rule 104 and the Price Stabilising Rules show greater consistency in that Rule 104 cannot be relied upon by the underwriter of a Rule 144A offering and the Price Stabilising Rules can only be relied upon to stabilise public offers or offers that require a public announcement. The Price Stabilising Rules cannot be relied upon to stabilise a bought deal.

13.9.3 When can stabilisation take place under Rule 104?

Rule 104 does not expressly regulate when stabilisation is permitted to commence and when it is obliged to cease; Rule 104 has no concept of an "introductory period" or a stabilising period. Under the Price Stabilising Rules the stabilising manager may undertake stabilising activities during the stabilisation period being the period starting on the date on which the earliest public announcement of the offer, which includes the offer price is made, and ending on the 30th day after the closing date or, if earlier, the 60th day after allotment. Under Rule 104 stabilisation can be carried on for so long as the relevant securities are being offered.

In the US, the normal timetable for an offering will be as follows: the SEC declare the registration statement effective around midday, after closing of the market at 4 pm (Eastern Time); the offer is then be priced and the securities allocated; the underwriting syndicate (which may only have been formalised two business days before pricing) is no longer subject to any restrictions (both contractual and pursuant to Rule 101) not to deal in the market; and underwriters and syndicate members call clients to inform them of their allocation. On the following business day brokerdealers start to make a market. Within two business days of the securities being allocated, a prospectus, to include the offer price, is filed with the SEC and copies are delivered to persons to whom securities have been allocated. The securities are usually paid for three or four business days after the securities have been allocated, which will be the closing date for the issue.

Stabilisation is obliged to stop upon allocation of the securities. Where an offering is successfully marketed, priced and sold it is unlikely that the lead underwriter in the US will have been obliged to stabilise securities during the offering period. If any stabilisation takes place it is likely to be restricted to the date the registration statement is declared effective and the offering priced.

Any market activities akin to stabilisation that the lead underwriter may carry out in the market after allocation will not be subject either to Rule 104 or Rule 101.

Where an offering takes place in the UK it is now usual for the offering to adopt a similar timetable as that in the US.

However, there is now one principal difference between the US and the UK. Although in the US Rules 101 and 104 will no longer apply to the underwriting syndicate, in the UK these activities (e.g. to close out the five per cent short position when the offering is over allocated by 20 per cent) will still take place during the stabilisation period and will therefore be subject to the Price Stabilising Rules.

In the UK the stabilisation period commences on the date on which the earliest public announcement of the offer states the offer price – which on the timing of the UK offering is consistent with that of the US offering and will be the date the securities are allotted and priced (which for Rule 104 purposes will constitute the end of the offering period) and ending on the 30th day after the closing date of the offering (the closing date generally being three or four days after allocation) or, if earlier, 60 days after the securities have been allocated.

In the US, in the context of a follow-on offering in respect of further securities of a class already registered, stabilisation can commence upon filing the registration statement for the follow-on offer and will terminate upon completion of the offering of the securities (i.e. upon allocation).

13.9.4   *Cross-border recognition of stabilisation rules*

Both Rule 104 and the Price Stabilising Rules recognise and permit stabilisation carried out in accordance with the stabilisation rules of certain other jurisdictions.

Rule 104 provides that stabilisation to facilitate an offering of a security in the US shall not be a violation if the following conditions are satisfied:

(a)   there is no stabilising in the US;
(b)   stabilising outside the US is made in a jurisdiction with statutory or regulatory provisions governing stabilising that are comparable to the provisions of Rule 104; and
(c)   no stabilising is made at a price above the offering price in the US (except where permitted by Rule 104, which permits a bid in a currency other than the principal market for the security to be initiated, maintained or adjusted to reflect the current exchange rate).

The SEC has given recognition to the stabilisation rules contained in the Securities and Investment Board Rule Book, the predecessor to the Price Stabilising Rules.

Part 2.8 of the Price Stabilising Rules provides that a person outside the UK who stabilises in accordance with all of Regulation M is to be treated for the purposes of Section 397(5) FSMA as acting or engaging in conduct for that purpose and in conformity with the Price Stabilising Rules.

Since the distribution of the securities is also complete, any market activities by the underwriters and syndicate members after allocation will not be subject to Rule 104. When the securities are allocated it is usual for the syndicate to over-allocate, allocating, for example, 120 per cent of the shares being offered. The stabilising manager would usually expect to rely upon its "over-allotment" option to cover its short position in respect of, for example, 15 per cent of the allocation and would expect to rely upon "usual market activities" to close out the short position on the balance of five per cent. In the US none of these activities will be regulated by Regulation M and so would not need to be conducted in accordance with Rule 104.

13.9.5 *Securities traded in US and UK – whether to stabilise an offering of new securities under Rule 104 or the Price Stabilising Rules*

When a dual listed corporate makes a follow-on offering of additional securities and these are to be registered and marketed and sold on the basis of a US style timetable it is likely that the lead underwriter and the underwriting syndicate will want to carry out market activities to support the price after allocation of the new securities.

The lead underwriter must decide whether to carry out these activities in the US, the UK or both the US and UK.

Where the volume of trading is principally in the US it probably makes sense to carry out market activities in the US. Rules 101 and 104 will not apply because the distribution will have been completed. Theoretically the activities of the lead underwriter and the syndicate will be subject to the anti-manipulation and anti-fraud provisions of US federal securities laws. However, the market activities carried out by the leading investment banks are unlikely to result in a breach of the US criminal law. These activities will also have the benefit of the limits of the UK safe-harbour set out in Part 2.8 of the Price Stabilising Rules.

However, where the lead underwriter decides that market activities should also be carried out in London it will be necessary to comply with the Price Stabilising Rules (Part 2.8 safe-harbour is not available if stabilising is done in the UK, and after allocation Regulation M will cease to regulate stabilisation); as a consequence it will be necessary during the introductory period for the offering materials to include the disclosure rubric required by MAR 2.3.2R. Full compliance with the Price Stabilising Rules will also enable the lead underwriter to achieve a non-exclusive safe-harbour under US securities law; the safe-harbour will extend to provide that the underwriter acted in conformity with the Price Stabilising Rules for the purposes of UK insider dealing legislation – both Section 397(4) and 397(5)(6) FSMA – and the underwriters behaviour will not constitute market abuse for the purposes of Section 118 FSMA.

Stabilisation in accordance with the Price Stabilising Rules will give the underwriter a safe-harbour under Section 118 FSMA. Should stabilisation be carried out only in the US, with the result that the underwriter's market activities in the US affect the corporate's share price on the London market, the underwriter would need to consider whether or not its US market activities was behaviour constituting market abuse for the purposes of the FSMA's Code of Market Conduct. It will be necessary to carry out an analysis similar to that described in Section 13.7.3.

13.9.6   Limitations on stabilisation

Rule 104 prohibits bids or purchases not necessary to prevent a decline in the security's price, and bids stabilising for manipulative purposes, at a price resulting from unlawful activity, or in an at the market offering.[87] This is consistent with MAR 2.2.4.R(3) and 2.3.8.

Rule 104 requires that priority must be given to independent bids, regardless of its size, when the market where the stabilising takes place permits or requires such priority.

Rule 104 prohibits the placing of more than one stabilising bid in any one market at the same price and at the same time.

13.9.7   Stabilisation and private placings

Rule 104 excludes from its provisions offerings of securities eligible for resale under Rule 144A for foreign or domestic issuers made solely to QIBs in transactions exempt from registration under the 1933 Act and to non-US persons under Regulation S that are made concurrently with a Rule 144A offering. Stabilisation during Rule 144A placements remains subject to the general anti-fraud and anti-manipulation provisions of US federal securities laws. Because of the re-sale restrictions under categories 2 and 3 of the Re-sale Safe Harbour under Regulation S it would be relatively unusual for a US registered issuer to offer securities (other than debt) under Regulation S, so that it is likely that where there is a Rule 144A private placement and/or Regulation S offering, the principal market for the securities will be outside the US. If the principal market is in the UK, stabilisation of those securities under the Price Stabilising Rules can be carried out. Where no stabilisation takes place in the US, Rule 104 will permit UK stabilisation to be carried out in accordance with the Price Stabilising Rules.

13.9.8   Stabilisation across different markets and the concept of the "principal market"

Although the majority of offerings in the US do not need to be stabilised, Rule 104 adopts an international approach to stabilisation since this may

---

[87] At the market offering means an offering of securities other than at a fixed price.

be made by reference to a principal market for the security wherever that principal market is located; a stabilising bid may be raised to match independent bids in the market and a stabilising bid that has not been discontinued can be carried over into another market.

Rule 104 also accommodates multi-national offerings by permitting stabilising bids to be made in the currency of the market where the bid is placed and by allowing adjustment to such stabilisation bids to account for fluctuations in the exchange rate between the two currencies.

Persons stabilising the price of a security can initiate a stabilised bid in any market with reference to the independent prices in the principal market for the security, wherever located, and then maintain, reduce or raise that bid to follow the independent market as long as the bid does not exceed either the stabilising bid in the principal market (including a stabilising bid in effect at the previous close of that market) or the offering price of the security. The Price Stabilising Rules operates on a similar basis.

Rule 104 provides that the appropriate price level for initiating stabilising is based on the security's principal market on the basis of two different scenarios: initiating stabilisation in any market when the principal market is open or closed.

Where the principal market is open, the permissible stabilising price level in any market is always established with reference to the last independent transaction price of the security in its principal market if two conditions are met: the security must have been traded in the principal market on the day stabilising is initiated or on the preceding business day; and the current asked price in the principal market must be equal to or greater than the last independent transaction price. If both conditions are *not* satisfied, stabilising may be initiated in any market at a price no higher than the highest current independent bid in the principal market.

When the principal market is closed, but quotations have opened in the market where stabilising will be initiated, Rule 104 provides that stabilisation may be initiated with the reference to the lower of: the price of which stabilising could have been initiated in the principal market at its previous close; or the last independent transaction price in the market where stabilising is being initiated. The independent transaction must have occurred that day or on the preceding business day and the current asked price in the market must be equal to or greater than the independent transaction price. If these conditions are *not* met, stabilising may only begin at a price no higher than the highest current independent bid for the security in the market where the stabilising is being initiated.

Rule 104 permits a stabilising bid to be initiated immediately before the opening of quotations in any market. Stabilising may be initiated with reference to the lower offer: the price at which stabilising could have been initiated in the principal market at its previous close; or the most recent price which an independent transaction in the offered security has been effected in any market after the close of the principal market, if the person stabilising knows of such transaction.

13.9.9 *Maximum caps on stabilisation price*

Rule 104 provides maximum caps on a stabilising price level: no stabilising bid may be initiated, maintained or otherwise adjusted in any market at a price higher than the stabilising bid in the principal market or the security's offering price.

Once a stabilising bid has been initiated in a market, that bid may be maintained in that market, subject only to the maximum caps. It also may be carried over into another market, irrespective of intervening changes in the independent bids or the transaction prices for the security. A stabilising bid in effect at the market's close may be maintained between trading sessions and used to establish a stabilising bid just prior to the market's opening of quotations on the next day. The stabilising bid may be maintained without reduction unless it would exceed the maximum cap. An underwriter may otherwise reduce a stabilising bid at its discretion. If the stabilising bid is discontinued (i.e. did not maintain the bid continuously during the trading session or is not in effect as of the market's close) stabilising may be resumed only at a level at which it then could be initiated in a particular market, without reference to the early stabilising bid. Rule 104 allows the stabilising bid to be increased to the level of the highest independent bid in the principal market, or, if the principal market is closed, the highest independent bid in that market at the previous close, provided such bid price does not exceed the maximum caps.

Where an independent market for an offered security does not exist, the maximum stabilising level is limited only by the offering price. Stabilisation may be conducted before an offering is priced, consistent with the conditions of Rule 104. After the offering price is determined, stabilisation may be resumed at a price at which stabilising then could be initiated.

Rule 104 provides for adjustments to a stabilising bid when the price of the security being stabilised is adjusted for the payment of dividends, rights, or distributions, or is expressed in the currency other than the currency of the principal market and there are changes in exchange rate between the two currencies. When securities are being offered as a unit, the component securities shall not be stabilised at prices that, in the aggregate, are higher than the permissible stabilising price of the unit.

13.9.10 Disclosure obligations

Rule 104 also requires any person effecting a syndicate covering transaction or placing or transmitting a penalty bid, to disclose that fact to the regulator. The disclosure to the regulator is not made public.

Item 508 of Regulations S-B and S-K requires a stabilising legend included in the prospectus. This will include a brief description of any prospective stabilising and other market activities, including syndicate covering transactions and penalty bids and their potential effect on the market price.

When a person, subject to Rule 104, conducts transactions in securities and the price of these securities may be or has been stabilised, that person is required at or before the completion of the transaction to send to a purchaser, a document containing a statement that the underwriter may effect stabilising transactions in connection with an offering of securities.

Rule 17a-2 under the 1934 Act requires the lead underwriter to keep records of syndicate covering transactions and penalty bids, in addition to stabilising information. The information is required to be monitored in a separate file or in a separately retrievable format, for a period of three years.

13.10 Securities offerings: short selling (Rule 105 of Regulation M)

Rule 105 provides that in connection with an offering of securities for cash, it shall be unlawful for a person to cover a short sale with offered securities purchased from an underwriter or broker or dealer participating in the offering if the short sale occurred during the shorter of:

(a) the period five business days before the pricing of the offered securities and ending with such pricing; or

(b) the period beginning with the initial filing of such registration statement. Rule 105 does not apply to short sales of derivative securities or shelf registered offerings. Such short sales could result in a lower offering price and reduce an issuer's proceeds.

When the securities of a global corporate are dual listed and the short selling in advance of an offering takes place in London rather than on the NYSE or Nasdaq, it will be necessary to consider whether or not the short selling constitutes market abuse under Section 118 FSMA.

Although the FSA has stated that in certain circumstances short selling raises some policy issues in that it could be used as part of an abusive strategy where it can distort the price or position of a stock at an artificial level (*see* Section 13.7.3). The FSA also appears to take the view that short selling in normal circumstances plays an important part in the efficient working of the securities markets, for example, improving liquidity and price discovery. The FSA has recently concluded that they would not make a formal review of the issues raised by short selling for the time being.

Instead of considering short selling separately on a US and a UK market, it is possible that a US broker-dealer sells short American Depository Receipts ("ADRs") of a UK issuer prior to that company pricing an offering of ordinary shares in reliance upon Regulation S (which offer is not extended to ADR holders) and the broker-dealer covers its short position by purchasing securities in the Regulation S offering, which will require consideration of both Rule 105 and The Code of Market Conduct.

13.11   Foreign private issuers: Disclosure obligations under the 1934 Act and future offerings by foreign private issuers

13.11.1   *An overview of the disclosure obligations in the US and the UK*

In the US, a foreign private issuer whose securities are registered under the 1934 Act is required to make periodic disclosures (*see* Section 13.11.3.1 below). To date, the SEC has required disclosure to the market on a mandated periodic basis, whereas UK securities laws (paragraphs 9.1–9.9

of Chapter 9 UKLA's Listing Rules and Sections 397(1) and (2) FSMA) require disclosure to be on a real-time basis.

What the SEC's historic position of mandated periodic disclosure has meant in practice for a foreign private issuer, is that disclosure is made in the issuer's registration statement (should it be in the process of registering securities), Form 20-F (the issuer's annual report and accounts restated or adjusted for US GAAP purposes including the management's discussion and analysis of the issuer's operating and financial review and prospects) and any disclosures required to be filed with the SEC on Form 6-K. Form 6-K provides that an issuer is required to furnish on whatever information such issuer makes or is required to make public pursuant to the law of the jurisdiction of its domicile or in which it is incorporated or organised. Therefore a foreign private issuer with securities listed with the UKLA will be obliged to furnish a Form 6-K with the SEC whenever it is obliged to disclose material information under the continuing obligations of Chapter 9 Listing Rules. Therefore for a foreign private issuer with securities listed in its home market, the distinction between the two regulatory approaches to the timing of disclosure may not be of great practical significance because of the obligation to file information which the foreign private issuer is required to disclose in its home market.

US case law is not clear in requiring an issuer to update any disclosure that it has made. Although the law is not entirely consistent, generally, where a disclosure to the market was not untrue or misleading on the date that the disclosure was made, there is no obligation under the 1934 Act imposed upon the issuer to correct the disclosure immediately upon discovery that the disclosure has become untrue or misleading even if such discovery is made prior to the issuer being obliged to make a mandated periodic disclosure. If, however, the issuer subsequently discovers that the disclosure was incorrect or misleading at the time the disclosure was made, there would be an obligation to immediately remedy that disclosure. In any event, whether or not there is a strict obligation to disclose, it is considered good practice in the US to remedy an incorrect disclosure, and moreover, as a result of the Enron affair the US may move to a regime of continuing disclosure (*see* Section 13.11.2 below).

13.11.2 *Changes to SEC disclosure obligations as a result of Enron*

The historic stance of the SEC to mandatory periodic disclosure has been challenged by the Enron affair. Early in 2002, the SEC Chairman suggested to US Congress the following initiatives for improving and modernising the current disclosure and regulatory system.

(a) A system of "current" disclosure.
(b) Public company disclosure of significant current "trend" and "evaluative" data.
(c) An updated and improved system of periodic disclosure.
(d) Financial statements that are clear and informative.
(e) Conscientious identification and assessment by public companies and their auditors of critical accounting principles.
(f) Accounting standard setting that responds expeditiously, concisely, and clearly, to current and immediate needs and reflects business realities.
(g) An effective and transparent system of private regulation of the accounting profession, subject to our rigorous oversight.
(h) A system that ensures that those entrusted with the important public responsibility of performing audits of public companies, are single-minded in their devotion to the public interest, and are not subject to conflicts that might confuse or divert them from their efforts.
(i) More meaningful investor protection by audit committees.
(j) Analyst recommendations predicated on financial data they have deciphered and interpreted.

Since the UK market has the benefit of "current" disclosure, and following the earlier "Guinness" and "Maxwell" scandals, both the UK City Code and the UKLA's Listing Rules have imposed on UK companies arguably greater disclosure obligations and more rigorous principles of corporate governance, the latter set out in the Combined Code included in the Listing Rules.

13.11.3   1934 Act periodic reporting requirements

Where a foreign private issuer's securities are listed on the NYSE, AMEX or other US exchange, or are traded on Nasdaq, then that issuer and its publicly traded securities must also be registered under the 1934 Act. A foreign private issuer whose securities are registered under the 1934 Act is required by the 1934 Act also to make periodic disclosures as set out below.

13.11.3.1   Annual reports on Form 20-F
Foreign private issuers who are registered under the 1934 Act are required by Sections 13a-1 and 15d-1 1934 Act to file their Annual Reports

on Form 20-F. The Form 20-F contains financial and non-financial information similar to an F-1 registration statement/prospectus. The Form 20-F must be filed not later than six months after the end of each fiscal year.

UK companies often coordinate the preparation and publication/filing of their Form 20-F with that of their Annual Report to shareholders. This process ensures that the information contained in each document is coordinated and avoids adding information to update the Form 20-F after the publication of the Annual Report.

13.11.3.2 *Periodic reports on Form 6-K*

Registered foreign private issuers are obliged by Section 13a – 16 1934 Act to furnish to the SEC under cover of Form 6-K material information:

(a) required to be made public pursuant to the law of the jurisdiction of its domicile or in which it is incorporated or organised. This means in practice that all disclosures required by the continuing obligations imposed by Chapter 9 UKLA Listing Rules will also be required to be disclosed in the US on Form 6-K;

(b) filed with and made public by any stock exchange on which the issuer's securities may be traded; or

(c) distributed by the issuer to its security holders (either directly or by means of a press release).

Not all information made public by a foreign private issuer must be provided to the SEC under Form 6-K. The SEC requires the furnishing of information that the foreign private issuer deems of material importance to its security holders, such as:

(i)   interim financial results;
(ii)   changes in business;
(iii)   hanges in management or control;
(iv)   material acquisitions or dispositions of assets;
(v)   bankruptcy or receivership;
(vi)   changes in the foreign private issuer's certifying accountants;
(vii)   changes in the foreign private issuer's financial condition and results of operations;
(viii) material legal proceedings;
(ix)   defaults on senior securities;
(x)   material increases or decreases in the amount outstanding of securities or indebtedness;
(xi)   the results of the submission of matters to a vote of security holders;

(xii) transactions with directors, officers, or principal security holders; and

(xiii) the granting of options or payment of other compensation to directors or officers.

Information in the foregoing categories must be furnished to the SEC "promptly" after being made public. If the issuer establishes a policy of furnishing to the SEC all information it makes public, it may adopt a system of furnishing Form 6-Ks on a monthly basis. Under this procedure, it would collect the material to be furnished to the SEC under cover of Form 6-K and file it together. This system would not apply, however, to press releases of special significance, such as interim financial results and other information that is likely to have an immediate impact on the market price of the issuer's securities. Such press releases should be furnished to the SEC as soon as possible after they are made public.

13.11.3.3 *Liability and incorporation by reference into prospectuses of Forms 20-F and 6-K*

Information filed in the Form 20-F and, to a lesser degree, material furnished to the SEC under Form 6-K may give rise to liability for inadequate or misleading disclosure. After an issuer has been subject to the SEC reporting requirements for a period of 12 calendar months it will be eligible to use the short-form F-3 registration statement/prospectus for issues of securities in the US public market, such form incorporates by reference the Form 20-F and specified Form 6-Ks. However, the risk of liability is greater with these Form 6-Ks as they are deemed part of the relevant prospectus.

13.11.3.4 *NYSE reporting requirements*

The NYSE requires issuers to disclose to the public any material information which would reasonably be expected to affect the value of their securities or influence investors' decisions. Typically, such information involves events of an unusual or non-recurring nature. Companies are also generally required to dispel unfounded rumours which affect the price of a security. The NYSE expects to be notified of any such disclosure immediately prior to the release to the public. In certain circumstances, the NYSE may call a trading halt to permit the information to be disseminated to the public; typically such a halt lasts one-half hour after the appearance of the news on the wire services.

Issuers must also file with the NYSE three copies of all reports and other documents required to be filed with the SEC. This applies to documents such as the Form 20-F and any Form 6-K. One originally signed and two conformed copies of all reports filed with the SEC should be filed with the NYSE on the same date they are required to be filed with the SEC.

Issuers will also be required to give prompt written notice to the NYSE regarding certain actions and events, including changes in the nature of the business, changes in accounting methods, charter amendments, change of auditors, fixing of shareholders' record dates or closing of transfer books, disposition of assets and changes of directors or officers. These events are set out in a company's Listing Agreement and any related side letter. The fixing of shareholder record dates or a date for the closing of transfer books must be notified to the NYSE at least 10 days in advance.

Electronic Data Gathering, Analysis and Retrieval ("EDGAR") refers to the computer system used to receive, accept, review and disseminate documents submitted by issuers in electronic format to the SEC. In September 2001, the SEC proposed a rule that would require all foreign private issuers to file using EDGAR.

Index